Right-Wing Women

Right-Wing Women

From Conservatives to Extremists Around the World

Edited by

Paola Bacchetta
and Margaret Power

Routledge
New York and London

Published in 2002 by
Routledge
29 West 35th Street
New York, NY 10001
www.routledge-ny.com

Published in Great Britain by
Routledge
11 New Fetter Lane
London EC4P 4EE
www.routledge.co.uk

Routledge is an imprint of the Taylor & Francis Group.
Printed in the United States of America on acid-free paper.

10 9 8 7 6 5 4 3 2 1

Library of Congress Cataloging-in-Publication Data

Right-wing women: from conservatives to extremists around the world /
edited by Paola Bacchetta and Margaret Power.
       p. cm.
  Includes bibliographical references and index.
   ISBN 0-415-92777-3 (hc.) — ISBN 0-415-92778-1 (pbk.)
    1. Conservatism. 2. Right-wing extremists—History. 3. Women in public life—
History. I. Bacchetta, P. (Paola) II. Power, Margaret.

  JC573 .R55 2002
  320.52'082—dc21

                      2002016571

Contents

part III. Interrogations: Right-Thinking, Feminisms, and the Left

part IV. Righted Bodies: Discipline, Excess, Pleasure

Acknowledgments

One of the most rewarding aspects of working on this book was the opportunity it gave us to work together with an outstanding group of scholars. We gratefully acknowledge the expertise, enthusiasm, and dedication that all of the authors contributed to their individual chapters and to the book as a whole. Putting this book together was a very demanding process. We thank the authors for their complete cooperation, support of the overall project, and for so many interesting dialogues along the way.

Paola would like to thank first and foremost Margaret Power. Combining our efforts and strengths to create this book together has again reinforced my faith in feminist collective efforts. We have been able to rely on each other, together in political and personal solidarity, every inch of the way. Working with Margaret, getting to know her and developing our friendship, learning from her especially about critical theory in history and critical feminist debates in Latin American studies, have made this project both a joyful and very meaningful experience.

For Margaret, working together with Paola to produce this book has been intense, exciting, productive, and fun. Although I barely knew Paola when we began this project in 1998, I now think of her as a dear friend and a highly trusted and respected colleague. I have learned a tremendous amount from her about many things, ranging from right-wing women in India to postcolonial and queer theory. I look forward to our next project together!

Paola would also like to thank Dr. Karl Raitz, Chair of the Department of Geography, Joan Callahan, Director of the Women's Studies Program, and Pat Cooper, former Director of the Women's Studies Program, all at the University of Kentucky (Lexington), for their constant, outstanding support. She is grateful to all members of the Women's Studies Steering Committee, the Department of Geography, the Social Theory Program, and the Gender Globals group at the University of Kentucky for fruitful dialogue. Thanks are due to Paola's many graduate students whose questions and comments keep her on her toes.

Paola would like to recognize the contributions through stimulating dialogues made by friends and colleagues who are members of the American Sociological Association's Caucus on Research on Gender and Sexuality in International Contexts, especially Frances Hasso, Jyoti Puri, Hyun Sook Kim, Seungsook Moon, and Natalie Bennett; participants in the Rethinking South Asia/New South Asia group at the University of California at Santa Cruz organized by Anjali Arondekar; and the Gender and Sexuality group organized by Janet Jakobson and Lauren Berlant. For their support, and for sharing all sorts of insights at various points, I would also like to thank Leila Ahmed, Ritu Menon, Veena Das, Geeta Patel, Ingrid Steinmeister, Rina Nissim, Laurence Cohen, Martine Van Woerkens, Sheba Chhachhi, Kathleen Blee, Winddance Twine, Sandhya Luther, Ashwini Sukthankar, and Heidi Nast.

We would both like to thank Amrita Basu for suggesting that we meet in the first place.

Margaret would like to thank Margaret Strobel, a pioneer in the study of women and global history. She suggested that I organize a panel for the 1997 American Historical Association conference that examines the right's construction of maternalism in different regions of the world. This book developed out of that panel. Margaret would also like to thank Temma Kaplan for her ongoing support, fantastic insights, and the generous advice she gave me just when I needed it most. I also appreciate Melinda Power's upbeat personality, positive outlook, and unwavering confidence in me. She is both a good sister and a true friend. Issam El Naqa has cheerfully helped me in countless ways, ranging from generously sharing his prodigious computer skills to discussing his thoughts on gender relations in the Middle East. I also thank the Organization of American States, the Harry Frank Guggenheim Foundation, and the Lewis Department of Humanities at the Illinois Institute of Technology for their generous support of my work.

We would like to thank Heather Brady for her initial work on the translation of Claudie Lesselier's chapter.

We are grateful to Ilene Kalish, our editor at Routledge, for her faith in us and for her commitment to this project, and to Kimberly Guinta for her efficient and competent work on this book.

Introduction

Paola Bacchetta and Margaret Power

Right-Wing Women comes out of our desire to engage with other scholars who work on this understudied subject, across national and regional contexts, and across disciplines. We hope this book contributes to increased understandings of and debates on the scope and importance of right-wing women and furthers anti–right-wing practice.

It is something of an understatement to remark that historically and currently studies of the right overwhelmingly focus on men. However, over the past twenty years feminist scholars have produced some provocative nation-specific or region-specific articles, books, and edited volumes on right-wing women located variously in Africa, Europe, the Middle East, North and South America, and South Asia (the bulk of this work is referenced within related individual chapters herein). *Right-Wing Women* builds upon this prior work and energetically extends it, to constitute the first globally comparative, interdisciplinary volume on right-wing women ever. The contributors write on right-wing women in Africa, Australia, Europe, the Middle East, North America, South America, and South Asia. Notwithstanding our efforts, the volume remains uneven in terms of the countries represented. That is, we contacted authors whom we knew and didn't know, and solicited articles through announcements in feminist journals and on the Internet. We also sought to balance the volume by searching for contributors through area studies channels, and writing to universities around the globe. We received many submissions on North American and western European right wings, very few on right-wing women in postcolonial societies across the globe, and none on areas such as Eastern Europe, Southeast Asia, China, Japan, and sub–Saharan Africa with the exception of South Africa. We feel this dearth of submissions reflects current power imbalances in "international" scholarly debates more widely. It also attests to the politics of the English language as an "international" Internet medium of "exchange." We note transnational imbalances in both the differential perceived relevance of this topic across borders and the possibilities and resources for such research. In addition, within borders, in many sites where resources exist, feminist scholars have preferred, understandably, to prioritize research on women whose perspectives they share because these have been silenced. However, we feel that feminist projects will benefit from understanding right-wing women precisely because in many cases they constitute major obstacles to feminism.

The chapters that are included in this volume come from disciplines across the social sciences and humanities: women's studies; history; sociology; area studies; French, Italian, and English literature; geography; political science; and cultural studies. Given the heterogeneity of the contributors' contexts, disciplines, and mother tongues, the chapters are necessarily positioned within some different, same, and intersecting sets of debates, and make use of some different, same, and overlapping theoretical tools. Many contributors provide brief literature reviews to place their scholarship in wider debates within and beyond their context, or explicate the context generously, to enable the unfamiliar reader to more easily situate the text and its arguments. In some cases, chapters herein constitute the first text on right-wing women's groups, organizations, or social actors in their context to ever appear in print. In other cases, scholars revisit prior scholarship in their area to push it further theoretically and empirically. In many cases, authors examine previously unexplored dimensions of right-wing women altogether. The reader will remark that some contributors' stances conflict with stances taken by other contributors. Indeed, we did not produce this book to present a homogenous feminist perspective on right-wing women; instead we desire to render accessible a heterogeneity of feminist debates and positions within this growing field of inquiry. As such, just as authors may disagree among themselves, so we as editors do not concur with every argument and point in every chapter presented herein. However, we do feel that every chapter, without exception, is extremely important to feminist transnational, interdisciplinary debates on right-wing women. We have learned immensely from the contributions of each author and hope the readers will, too.

Notwithstanding the breadth and depth of this book, a number of problematics and some common thematics emerge. Given our limitations of space here, we will point to a few of the more central ones.

Interrogating Notions of the Right through Gender, Geopolitics, and Power

By centering on right-wing women in diverse temporal and geographical settings, this book challenges dominant notions of the right: those that efface or downplay the place of women and gender; that limit the right wing to its manifestations in social movements, political parties, or states; that globalize particularistic Eurocentric defining criteria by applying it to all rights; or that recognize the far-right's anti-Other discourses and practices (fascisms) while too often deemphasizing similar attitudes and activities on the center-right.

In her insightful study of women and/in nationalism, Yuval-Davis (1997) discerns that women participate in nationalism in four ways: as biological, cultural, and national producers; as cultural embodiments of collectivities and their boundaries; as carriers of collective "honor"; and as participants in national and ethnic struggles. This volume confirms and extends these insights: women are found in all those categories within both national and transnational right wings, and they are often contradictorily positioned therein. Further, centering women and gender opens up the right to new interrogations across right-wing forms and across scale: the body, the city, streets, nation, region, and transnation. It enables us to more fully understand the scope of right-wing political projects: the ideologies that right wings produce and diffuse, their recruitment strategies, the modes of adherence and participation they include, the identities they produce, how they reproduce themselves across generations, and their actions.

Right-wing ideologies, whether forged by male or female ideologues, are always gendered and elicit gendered responses; gender is central to what makes them tick. For example, men and women may be drawn to the right because it produces and affirms masculinities and feminities with which they identify. Different types of male right-wing appeals that include, exclude, exalt, or denigrate women affect in gendered ways overall recruitment, participation, the right's reproduction of itself, and its ultimate goals. In some instances where they find their male right discourses and practices unacceptable, right-wing women creatively construct women-friendly ideologies and practices that place them conflict with their male counterparts. And the right uses unconscious and conscious desire and sexuality to market itself, recruit, and incite action. Women activists are highly implicated in practices of recruitment: they bring in other women and men, also transmit right-wing values to their children, thereby encouraging a next generation of rightists. From the individual, through the family, to the community, the nation, and the transnation, women's participation enables the right to organize a totalizing project that moves through different spheres and encompasses a variety of spaces. These chapters clearly illustrate that women in the right are neither dupes of right-wing men nor less powerful replicas of them. As a body, they demonstrate that rightist women consciously choose to support and help build the projects of which they are a part. In so doing, right-wing women carve out a space and identity for themselves and enhance the ability of their right wings to implement their agendas. In many cases, right-wing women and right-wing men interpret women's place and role in the right quite differently: it is not uncommon for men to understand women as just tea makers, while women act and see themselves as essential (see Gottlieb, this volume, chap. 2).

Women and gender are essential to the right throughout its many manifestations across the globe, across scale, within and across axes of power, within and across wider political settings. Beyond its presence as rightist states, or social movements and parties within states, the right operates trans nationally, in the forms of oppositional social movements, submerged social movement networks (Mellucci), and other collectivities across states. The right can emerge with and within, and merge with or oppose, modernity, postmodernity, colonialism, postcolonialism. Most important, the right has not only an ideological presence as doctrine and a material presence in institutions, social actors, practices, and rituals across its various forms. It is also an "elusive network of 'quasi-spontaneous' presuppositions and attitudes" (Zizec 1999).

The most widely diffused definitions of the right in scholarship are problematically derived from studies of European right wings, new and old, from conservative to fascist projects. They tend to posit the right oppositionally in relation to national left states, parties, and social movements, and in relation to "tradition" which right wings purport to "preserve." We find these definitions highly debatable. First, where these criteria are universalized and imposed beyond Europe, they inadvertently or even openly rest upon the assumption that politics itself within societies beyond Europe are European-derived. (This point was first made analogously by Chatterjee [1994] in his critique of Anderson's [1983] notion that "Third World" nationalisms are "modular," that is, merely mimicked upon official, original European nationalisms.) This problematically positions Europe at the center of the world, as the originator of all complicated social organization and thought. Second, the notion that every society actually has a left is disputable, a point illustrated for example by the Boer period in South Africa (see du Toit, chap. 4). And, in some cases where a left does exist, the right does not necessarily identify it as the main enemy, as evidenced by Karam's study of Egyptian Islamist women (see Karam, chap. 16). Third, in some postcolonial nations that do have a clearly defined left, the right may share anticapitalist and anti-imperialist positions with it, as is the case with some Islamist movements.

Some Eurocentric definitions of the right presuppose tradition as an essentialist, ahistorical entity and imagine the right preserving or reviving it. With many contemporary feminist and nonfeminist scholars of the right we understand "tradition" in Hobsbawmian (1993) terms, as something invented, dynamic, fluid, constantly being reformulated, but that is made to crystallize periodically in one site or another, in one form or another, and as always contestable. "Tradition" is produced by and crystallizes within internal and transnational relations of power. And "tradition" is gendered differently: women or men are supposed to embody, and women are most often called upon to symbolize, preserve, and transmit it. While many male and female rights do claim to be preserving or resurrecting "tradition," several chapters herein demonstrate that some right-wing women subjects frame their relationship to "tradition" in terms of purposefully redefining it to forge "new women."

For us, if there is anything that actually distinguishes (both the center and far) right from other political tendencies, it is the right's reliance on some form of internal or external Other. Right wings differentially draw on, produce, and mobilize naturalized or culturalized self/Other criteria to reify or forge hierarchical differences. These are based in gender, sexuality, class, ethnicity, religion, race, caste, or at their various intersections. Right wings may also work to aggravate some of these hierarchies (within the self/Other dichotomy but also within the self community), while actually proposing to reduce other hierarchies (within the self-community). Right-wing doctrines, diffused notions, and practices regarding Others may take many forms, from coexistence to annihilation, and may be subject to a range of justifications, from differentialist complementarity, to incompatibility, to total antagonism.

Subject-Positions, Subjectivities, and Practices

The women studied in this volume are situated across the right-wing forms enumerated above. They espouse a range of ideologies: conservativism, neoconservativism, secular extremist nationalism, religious nationalism, fascism. As subjects, they are positioned across the socioeconomic spectrum, from elite to poor. They are heterosexual, married, single, mothers, childless, and in one case (see Scheck, chap. 10) an out lesbian who is openly partnered. In many right wings, women activists are not under obligation to marry men as long as they frame their primary commitment as to the right-wing cause (ultimately dominated by men) (see Bacchetta, chap. 3) or to the higher power (God) that animates the cause (see Karam, chap. 16).

Across this volume, right-wing women are most often segregated into separate women's organizations. These are connected to male counterparts to varying degrees. All the right-wing women's organizations included here are structured in clearly hierarchic ways (not as collectives). Some mobilize primarily vertically, with vast gaps between the leadership and rank and file based in wider axes of class, "race," ethnicity, or castes. Others organize primarily horizontally, within classes, "races," ethnicities, religions, or castes. In some cases, a range of different but related right-wing women's organizations, connected to the same project, exist to mobilize different sectors of the same society, or to organize around specific issues or professions. Right-wing sex segregation has two main consequences. On the one hand it fosters women's exclusion from the realms of the overall (gender-combined) organizational power. But on the other hand, it can enable women to forge their own discourse, practice, and modes of solidarity in ways that sometimes have the potential to threaten the overall male-dominated right itself by contesting male power.

In general, right-wing women (like other female social actors) are less publicly visible than their male counterparts. When they are indeed highly visible they often exhibit exaggerated femininity while defending masculine right-wing values, or appear as transgressive, even bigendered, figures. For example, Pauline Hanson of Australia shifts from performing femme fatale, to everybody's daughter, to (antilesbian) lesbian chic while defending the same masculinist, racist, and capitalist stances (see Winter, chap. 14). In a different type of example, the mainstream media and tabloid press alike construct the women of the British Union of Fascists (BUF) not as newsworthy political activists but rather as female figures around whom crystallize highly publicized money and sex scandals (see Gottlieb, chap. 2). Finally, in another exception to the rule of lowered visibility, Hindu nationalist spokeswoman Sadhavi Rithambara provokes Hindu nationalist men to anti-Muslim violence through speech-performances that travel via cassette recordings into homes, courtyards, and the streets (see Ghosh, chap. 18). In these, Rithambara positions herself in a bigendered manner: she appropriates the privilege of male speech (curse words, sexual imagery), but also posits herself and other women as victims of Muslim male sexual aggression. Where right-wing women are less visible, their effacement is as often a function of their overwhelming positioning within the rather silenced mixed-gendered rank and file (see Blee, chap. 7) as in their society's preference for the authority of male speech and actions. In that sense, some right-wing women political actors are received and projected in ways not so unlike their left-wing female and feminist counterparts within their own societies.

One striking feature of a great many right-wing women leaders and full-time activists is their system of double standards. There is a huge gap between how right-wing women leaders and full-time activists live out their lives as individuals on the one hand, and the subjectivities they propose for other women on the other. Many behave in feisty ways that run against the grain of their discourses on ideal feminine domesticity (see Vervenioti, chap. 8; Scheck, chap. 10). Among them we find a divorced woman who opposes divorce (Winter, chap. 14), childless women who propagate the centrality of motherhood for women (Karam, chap. 16), and car-racing, plane-flying, dancing northern European supporters of Franco's solemn and highly sexist fascist regime in Spain, a country whose population they view with distanced contempt (Keene, chap. 13). In some cases, the right-wing women subjects' feistiness is primarily a product of their upper-class position, from which they draw confidence and a sense of superiority. Regardless of the reasons for these gaps between leaders' and activists' lives and the identities they propose for other women, it is a fact that in many cases right-wing women, leaders and activists, alike, fight for societies that would totally eliminate women who behave as they do.

We find that a number of right-wing women's trajectories into the right are through male family members who belong to the right (see especially Lesselier, chap. 9). Accordingly, many right wings conceptualize women's and men's participation along normative heterofamilial lines (see Saktanber, chap. 5, and Lesselier's analysis of the party as party-family). But, there are also cases wherein the typical familial gender circuit (but not the gender hierarchy) is reversed as women recruit their male or female family members (Gottlieb, chap. 2). In yet other cases, women circumvent the heterofamilial altogether as they recruit non-kin women (Schreiber, chap. 15; Power, chap. 19). In these latter cases, particularly where the right is a micro-oppositional and socially disrespected movement, joining can be a difficult choice pitting women *against* their families (Gottlieb).

The chapters indicate that women join and remain in the right for a wide range of reasons. First, many authors argue that women recruits feel the right, unlike accessible alternatives to it, provides them with a familiar, nonthreatening discursive and practice framework centering on problems they identify as vital, such as social disorder, immorality, crime, the "threatened" family, and degraded schools (see Blee; Deutsch, chap. 11; and Power). Second, the chapters demonstrate unequivocally that women feel their activism empowers them as women. It does so differently in each context, such as by positioning them variously as respectable, selfless agents of change deemed necessary, or as independent rebels. Whatever the case, their activism almost invariably permits them to inscribe themselves into the social in ways otherwise forbidden to women in their milieu.

Right-wing women's political activities are as wide-ranging as elsewhere within the political spectrum, encompassing both illegal and legal dimensions. Women's activities tend to depend upon how the right imagines women, how women activists imagine themselves, whether the particular right in question is a micro-oppositional movement or in power, and the degree of extremism of its ideology. Thus, women are more likely to engage in illegal acts where the right in question is more oppositional, more extremist ideologically, and wherein gender separatism operates to guarantee gender equilibrium (not egalitarianism [Bacchetta]) in the overall organizational structure. Some of their illegal activities are violent or violence-related, such as when they constitute women's militias or use explosives and arms. Others involve civil disobedience, such as defying curfews and bans on demonstrations, illegally supporting clergy and nuns and their social projects (Boylan), or hiding right-wing male criminals wanted by the law (Scheck). At the threshold of the law they organize boycotts (Blee), do daily paramilitary training (Bacchetta), incite male counterparts to violence against their Others (Ghosh), or replace male counterparts in leadership roles when the men are under repression or in prison (Gottlieb; Karam). Right-wing women can be "vicious perpetrators of terrorism against their Others" (Blee). For some of their activities they lose their jobs (see Keskin, chap. 17), and get arrested, detained, tried, and imprisoned (Karam; Gottlieb).

Right-wing women occupy all sorts of positions in and in relation to electoral politics. They stand as candidates in elections either on their own (Gottlieb; Ghosh; Winter) or to replace their temporarily ineligible men (Lesselier). They represent their country to the United Nations (Vervenioti). They influence their powerful male counterparts' political decisions (see Gallucci, chap. 1), sometimes inducing the latter to present their views as the men's own (Scheck). They lobby their governments (Schreiber). They draft legislation such as for censorship (Scheck). They canvass for votes, hand out leaflets, and hang up posters (Lesselier).

Right-wing women's daily activism takes on a variety of forms in the civil public space. They work across scales, at various local, national, and transnational levels. They aim to impose themselves and their projects for a right-wing society in the material, symbolic, and cultural dimensions of life. They are major protagonists in grass-roots organizing (Boylan; Saktanber; Enders, chap. 6). They infiltrate left groups, parents' groups at schools, cooperative societies, unions, and other organizations (Gottlieb). They organize protests against sex education in schools (Boylan). They write letters to the press or appear on radio shows to express their views to mass audiences (Gottlieb; Schreiber). They set up and run women's organizations (Karam), including women's charity unions (Vervenioti), and mixed-gender organizations (Lesselier). They compete with the state to provide community services (Boylan) by founding right-wing charities (Vervenioti), schools for the poor (du Toit, chap. 4) and for youth (Gottlieb), or structures providing hygiene, health services, clothing, and food (Boylan; Power). They publicly display their productions in art exhibitions and literary and musical events (Deutsch). Some set up public fashion shows (Saktanber) while others protest against them. They sell right-wing newspapers on the streets (Gottlieb). They spread rumors to discredit their Others (Blee). They organize activities such as sports events to produce healthy female bodies for bearing children and sublimating sex (Deutsch). In times of war, they knit garments for soldiers, serve in medical units (Keene), and fight. They reach transnational audiences, using the Internet to diffuse their ideas (Keskin). And they work across borders by supporting foreign right movements and regimes (Keene).

We find it troubling, albeit unavoidable, that many of the above right-wing women's activities are in form identical or similar to feminist ones. In addition, in a surprising number of cases, right-wing women are engaged in politically pluralist projects for women's rights, from suffragist movements (Vervenioti; Gottlieb) to movements for equal pay for equal work. Let us now turn to examine constants and variations in the systems of thought that right-wing women produce and mobilize to inform, provoke, and legitimize their activities, before turning to the very complex relations between right-wing women and feminism.

Right-Wing Women's Discourses and Discursive Strategies

Across the chapters, there are many more common and divergent thematics than we can reasonably discuss here. So, we focus on a few that very often recur and intersect: self/Other constructions, motherhood and the family, the right's male and female Others, sexuality, and space.

First, across the chapters, right-wing women define themselves and their positions in terms of selves/Others, by relying variously on criteria that are essentialist, political-choice based, culturalist, civilizational, or at the intersections of these. However, across the board they conceptualize relations between women and men in their own communities in terms of *essentialist-differentialist-complementarity*. That is, they posit that men and women are *essentially*, naturally, biologically different from each other, and that these naturalized *differences* should be the basis for distinct gender roles that are *complementary*. Yet several definitions of complementarity abound. In the most recurring definition, complementarity signifies that men and women are different but equal. A second notion of complementarity propounds divinely ordained subordination of women to men. And a third maintains that differentialist complementarity based on female subordination to their men actually translates into equality.

In contrast, the right-wing women in this volume differentiate themselves in relation to women of their communities who are not right-wing not through essentialist criteria but rather by political choice. For example, Egyptian Islamist women define themselves against the negative backdrop of Western women and "Westernized" or feminist women in their context (Karam). For Greek and Chilean right-wing women, leftist women serve that purpose. A whole range of right-wing women operationalize feminists as enemies to distinguish their own identities and positions (Keskin; Schreiber; Lesselier).

Finally, right-wing women rely on the widest range of arguments to erect boundaries between themselves and their female and male Others (those they claim do not belong to their racial, national, ethnic, or religious communities). In the United States, for example, women members of the Ku Klux Klan deploy biological notions to reduce African Americans, Catholics, Jews, and others, to animals (Blee), while Hindu nationalist Sadhavi Rithambara accuses Indian Muslims of being uncivilized (Ghosh).

Second, the right-wing women in this volume all exalt the motherhood of the women of their own community, even when they themselves are childless (such as Zaynab Al-Ghazali, an Egyptian Islamist woman discussed in chapt. 16). They may conceptualize motherhood in primarily material terms (as the KKK's "racial mothers" in Blee) or symbolic terms (as the mother goddesses in Ghosh; Bacchetta), or equally accentuate both dimensions (Saktanber; Power).

Nearly all right-wing women idealize the heteronormative family. (There are exceptions to this rule herein and beyond.) Those who exalt the family generally see it as the privileged site of women's power and self-realization, threatened by a host of internal and external Others. Beyond individual attachment to the family, right-wing women who glorify it extend it across spatial scales: it is the pillar of society, the bastion of society's security, order, and naturalized hierarchy (Lesselier), and a microcosm of society (Power; Lesselier) or of all humanity (Deutsch). Further, right-wing women and men often deploy the heteronormative family as a model for right-wing women's and men's relational subjectivities, for the structures of right-wing organizations, and for the relationship between women's and men's wings within the same overall right-wing project. Thus, the Turkish Islamist women Saktanber studied participate politically along a familial mode. Spanish fascist women idealize the fascist Primo de Rivera family as exemplary for the nation (Enders). And Hindu nationalists conceptualize the hierarchic relations between their respective leaders of men's and women's organizations as an elder brother–younger sister relation (Bacchetta).

A third constant in this volume (and without) is anti-Other discourse and practice. The Other is a site for the production and mobilization of fear that sustains many right-wing projects. But the Other is also gendered: for some, it is Othered women who are primary targets, while for others it is Othered men.

Nearly all right-wing women in this volume imagine Othered women in terms of a normative femininity and sexuality, as aggressors or victims. Some construct Othered women as sexually overactive, predatory, and duplicitous, but also as asexual, passive victims of their men, or baby breeders for the enemy camp (Blee). As aggressors, Othered women threaten the integrity of right-wing women's heteronormative family, "race," society, religious community, or nation. As victims of their male Othered counterparts, they can be used to illustrate the inherent inferiority of the Othered community, and the aggression of its men. Many right-wing men and women alike who will not critique the sexism within their own right-wing projects may strongly condemn women's conditions in Othered communities. For example, the French National Front, which consistently opposes feminist demands in France, maintains that African, Maghrebian, Caribbean, and Jewish men treat their own women badly (Lesselier). Beyond this volume, Laura and George W. Bush, who oppose most U.S. feminist demands and did not note any sexism in Taliban-ruled Afghanistan before September 11, 2001, now strategically position themselves as worldwide champions of Afghan women's liberation to soften the machoism of the "hunt 'em down" discourse and to attract U.S. women's complicity with the war. In some situations, individual Othered women are deployed to speak against their own communities, such as by publicly opposing affirmative action (Schreiber). Right wings also use Othered women to project an image of inclusion while maintaining policies of exclusion. Thus, the French National Front puts forward women members of color while opposing immigrant rights (Lesselier). And Integralists in Brazil appeal to women of native and African ancestry but oppose black demands for civil rights (Deutsch). In still other cases, what appears as an anti-Othered woman discourse can be at least partially based in an anticolonial stance, as is the case for Islamist women who condemn what they interpret as Western women's promiscuity (Karam, Keskin).

Othered men are major foci of right-wing disgust, hatred, violence, exclusion, and annihilation. But right-wing women and men target Othered males differently. In many cases right-wing women come out even more against the male Other than do right-wing men (see especially Scheck), though ultimately violence against the male Other remains the monopoly of right-wing men. We feel there are several explanations for this gendered targeting. First, male and mixed-gender right wings conceptualize men as the ultimate (but not exclusive) agents of their communities, and they support, directly or indirectly, men's more extensive power. Many right-wing women, like their male counterparts, project this preferential male agency onto Othered communities, such that Othered men are made to epitomize the Othered community. Second, while some right-wing women imagine male and female Others in vaguer, less targeted terms than do their own male counterparts (Lesselier), most right-wing women see Othered men in personal terms, often as sexualized threats to their and other women's physical purity and integrity (Blee; du Toit). Third, right-wing women's extremist stance against Othered males can be based in misguided antisexist stances. Some right-wing women recognize and contest sexism within their own communities; others do not. Across the board, right-wing women direct much of the rage they feel against mysogyny primarily against Othered men (see Scheck, Blee, Lesselier, Ghosh). The Other male must be made to epitomize misogyny, so that right-wing women can keep the peace with their own men. Right-wing men approve of this gendered Other targeting; it ensures that women remain within the bounds of the right-wing project, directs women's anger away from them, and eliminates the Othered male as potential heterosexual competition (Bacchetta).

Fourth, sexuality (heteronormative and homosexual) is yet another charged site for right-wing women. As the reader might expect, in this volume many right wings favor containing sexuality within the heteronormative married couple solely for reproductive purposes (Deutsch; Enders). They propose to control women's sexuality within and beyond the bedroom, through censorship of women's bodily expressions and of the media (Boylan). However, some right-wing women actually mobilize for recognition of their sexual claims (within heteronormative familial confines). For example, many Chilean Catholic right-wing women believed they had the right to sexual pleasure within heteronormative marriage, and some urged others to use "natural birth control" as one way to achieve it (Power).

On homosexuality we find similar complexities: on the one hand, the overwhelming majority of right-wing women abhor homosexuality. They consider it a threat to the heteronormative family or as a nasty habit that needs to be kept in the closet (Karam). Most often right-wing discourse produces and attempts to justify violence against lesbians, gays, transsexuals, and transgendered people. Notwithstanding this, at least one primarily heteronormative right wing, the Weimar Republic's DNVP, had an out lesbian leader, Käthe Shirmacher, who openly lived with her partner into old age (Scheck). And in one case, a heterosexual identified right-wing leader, Pauline Hanson of Australia, supports some forms of gay rights (Winter). Beyond this volume, in other, albeit rare cases, there are right-wing groups organized around homosexual subjectivities, such as the Log Cabin Republicans in the United States and gay Nazis in France.

Sexuality operates in right wings at unconscious to conscious levels to evoke pleasures, adherence, and other emotions that help sustain right-wing actions. For example, Ghosh argues that when Hindu nationalist Sadhavi Rithambara gives a public speech there is a radical disjuncture between the pedagogic intent of the speech-performance and its effect. Rithambara purports to be commenting on Hindus, Muslims, mosques, and temples, but in so doing sparks unconscious sexual desire. In other right wings, such as the BUF, performances of sexuality may take the form of sex-evocative salutes, drum corps, or the openly recognized "sexually charged image of young women in uniform, trained in physical fitness and self-defense" (Gottlieb). Still elsewhere in many rights, women experience male leaders in terms of their heterosexual, supposedly charismatic appeal (Lesselier; Enders). Some articulate this openly; for example BUF women have described Mosley, the movement's chief, as "the Rudolph Valentino of fascism" (Gottlieb).

Fifth, space is evoked in a myriad of modes throughout this volume: in women's ideologies and practices, in women's identities and subjectivities, as sites the right produces and intervenes within, and as actors that intervene in producing the right itself. Many right-wing women are directly involved in the right's construction and reconfiguration of space. Rights require and grow through territories in the form of communities, regions, nations, or transnations. Right-wing women create and/or reproduce discourses of self/Othered communities within and across nations (Blee). They produce new spatialities or reframe existing spatialities for their own purposes (Bacchetta). Right-wing women also take advantage of certain flows across space, such as in Turkey where rural migration to urban centers is key to the rise of Islamist movements and of women members therein (Keskin). But right-wing women are also used by their male counterparts to extend the right across space, such as when Hindu nationalist Sadhavi Rithambara's speeches at demonstrations are marketed to diffuse Hindu nationalism across scales (into the home, courtyard, neighborhood, nation, diaspora), or when right-wing women are made to be go-betweens in diasporic and cross national financing that extend right wings (Ghosh). Right-wing women also work to block flows constituted by their Others across space. These blockages may be bodily such in cases of anti-immigrant practices (Lesselier) and racial segregation (du Toit). They may also be discursive, such as when right-wing Catholics try to prevent Spanish atheism's entrance into Brazil (Deutsch). But furthermore, space also acts, variously, in women's subjectivities. For example, Egyptian Islamist Safinaz Qazim's international travels, including one trip to the U.S. that brought her into contact with the thought of Malcolm X, inspired her ideological productions, while in Ahmedabad a city park plays a key role in producing Hindu nationalist women as fierce (Bacchetta). Symbolic space mediates identities, such as when Hindu nationalist women construct and mobilize the Hindu nation's all-powerful territorial goddess as a model for their own militarism (Bacchetta). And combined material and symbolic space produces effects such as when railroads set in the South African landscape signify mobility and imperialist triumph in which right-wing women participate (du Toit).

The types of processes and mechanisms that right-wing women mobilize to produce their own separate discourses vary a great deal. In many cases, women ideologues selectively instrumentalize diffuse notions of popular culture to produce legitimate, unconventional models for women's identity. They choose from a pantheon of preexisting symbolic referents for women's identities and reframe them in right-wing terms. Some examples are: Islamist women saints (Saktanber), historical female heroes (Deutsch), the Virgin Mary (Power), powerful Hindu goddesses (Ghosh), St. Teresa of Avila (Enders), or Queen Isabella of Spain (Enders). The chapters demonstrate a whole array of discursive interventions, from right-wing women ideologues formulating and inserting women's identities and issues into the wider gender-mixed right, to women ideologues producing a totalizing female right-wing project that may have points of antagonism with their male counterparts' projects.

Right-Wing Women and Feminism

Among right-wing women, there are those who assert that they are antifeminist, and those, much less numerous, who actually claim to be feminist. The reasons for these stances, and how they translate into practice, merit discussion.

First, the overwhelming majority of right-wing women, like their male counterparts, position themselves as virulently antifeminist. Some right-wing women's organizations identify combating feminism as their sole raison d'être (Schreiber). In many cases, however, antifeminist rightist women spend their lives working for some form of women's empowerment (not liberation) within the context of the right (Karam; Keskin).

A range of right-wing antifeminist stances can be usefully distinguished in terms of geopolitical contexts, the type of right in question, and contextual definitions of the term feminism itself. Thus, colonizing right wings (such as British, French, Australian) and postcolonial ones (such as in the Middle East and South Asia) have different relationships to struggles for women's rights and to the term "feminism." Colonialism was a gendered and sexed project. It deployed heterosexual male projections of colonized women's bodies, status, and conditions to denigrate colonized subjects of both genders and to justify colonialism as a civilizing mission. The colonizers set themselves up, as Spivak (1994) aptly puts it, as white-men-saving-brown-women-from-brown-men. This savior narrative and the repressive colonial practices that accompany it variously bear upon postcolonial women, right or left, who critique their internal patriarchies, filiarchies, or fraternarchies. Postcolonial antiwoman forces may simply accuse postcolonial woman's liberation forces of collaboration with (neo)colonialism to undermine their own societies. In this light, some postcolonial women's antifeminist claims, whether on the right or the left, may be intended primarily to be anticolonial positions rather than antiwoman (Karam). Further, the notion that women's liberation struggles are not indigenous to the "Third World" is not only false but ultimately is complicit with the colonial savior narrative itself. As Jayawardena (1986) and others demonstrate, internal "Third World" struggles for women's liberation precede colonialism, continue parallel and integral to nationalist movements for liberation from colonialism, and abound in the postcolonial present.

At issue in many postcolonial contexts, for right-wing and left-wing women alike, is the politics of the term "feminism" itself, its definitions and its translatability. Many "Third World" women engaged in women's liberation have long used the term " feminist" to describe their struggles and to inscribe their solidarities with women across borders. But many others, who are not less committed to women's liberation and transnational solidarities with women's liberation elsewhere, reject the term. The reasons for this are many. Some feel the term is too widely associated with colonial and neocolonial cultural imperialism. Often the term "feminism" is untranslatable into local languages, thus standing out as foreign in the flow of discourse. Under these circumstances, some women feel that using the term would position them in an obligatory public combat to deconstruct feminism's colonial associations, thereby diverting their energies and undermining the public appeal of their struggles. Others who struggle for women's liberation projects do not self-designate as feminist because they feel that some of the projects globally that self-identify as feminist actually *are* imperialist. This position is clear in stances against certain "international" women's-rights-as-human-rights projects based in the West; they are critiqued for imposing Western notions of the self, of the human, and of rights, on postcolonial societies, in modes that collude with Western governments or operationalize the colonial savior narrative gender-substitutively (as white-women-save-brown-women-from-brown-men). In still other contexts, the political semantic and definitional problems of the term "feminism" are compounded by the difficulty of speaking of women's issues contextually. Thus, Karam points out that in the Egyptian Islamic context, where issues of justice and injustice are central, these issues are framed in terms not of women and men but rather *bani Adam* (human race). However, Karam categorizes the women she interviews as feminist even though they self-identify as antifeminist because they dedicate their lives to contesting many forms of sexism in their societies, braving their male counterparts' strong opposition.

The pro-feminist right-wing stances in this volume are located in the West or among West-origin sectors of postcolonial societies. They are specifically historical cases confined to the late nineteenth to early twentieth centuries. In that period, feminist movements in Western Europe, the United States, parts of Latin America, and South Africa organized for women's suffrage. (In contrast, in many postcolonial sites, suffrage was achieved as an integral part of national liberation from colonialism.) Suffragette activists did not necessarily seek to challenge heteronormative gender roles. Many believed they should be able to vote in order to protect their families and clean up politics. Most were positioned in dominant social sectors, such as Chilean conservatives (see Lavrin 1995; and in this volume Power), South African Boers (Du Toit), or Ku Klux Klan women (Blee), and argued they should obtain the vote to safeguard the elite position of their class or "race." In one case, a whole movement, the BUF, called for women's equality, a demand they attributed to the British character and one which they used to demonstrate their differences from and superiority to other (sexist) European fascist regimes (Gottlieb). Ultimately, self-declared feminist right-wing women saw no contradiction between their enfranchisement struggles and fascist or white supremacist projects. In their minds, both movements worked toward the same goal: their own political and social rights. This of course poses a serious problem for feminism, its definitions and projects, which we deal with below.

By the end of the twentieth century, definitions of feminism and some right-wing women's friendly relations with it had changed considerably. Feminisms began to challenge the "naturalness" of gender, to reject the conflation of womanhood with motherhood and the heteronormative family, to support diverse expressions of sexuality, and, as Pateman (1989) notes, to contest the notion of separate gendered spheres. Today, many right-wing women in the same earlier pro-feminist sites target feminism as their primary enemy because, in their eyes, feminism denies women's biological nature and thus their potential for fulfillment and happiness. For example, women of the National Front in France propose to "liberate women from feminism"; they see it as worsening women's position by dissolving the heteropatriarchal family (Lesselier). Islamist women in Egypt feel feminism's "sexual liberation" turns women into commodities for men (Karam). Further, many right-wing women oppose feminism because it now proposes cross-positional alliances that defy right-wing anti-Other tenets. Even though many right-wing women continue to favor some forms of women's rights (political representation, employment, etc.), they proactively oppose extending them to Othered women (and men).

Further, across the different rights examined in this volume, antifeminist and self-declared feminist women alike espouse views on gender and society that differ from their male counterparts (Blee; Karam). Some women critique the sexism of the men of their own and related right organizations (du Toit; Keene). Thus, Ku Klux Klan women flatly denounce their men's "hostility, condescension, and hypocrisy" toward women (Blee). DNVP women in Germany strategically framed sexism as a threat to the right and the race it defended: they warned that Nazi male preference for submissive women would lead to the downfall of the Nordic race because true Nordic women are self-assertive and bold (Scheck).

It is useful to distinguish between *women's liberation* and *women's empowerment,* and between different types of empowerment. Feisty right-wing women who fight for societies that would abolish women like themselves can be said to be engaged in *individual empowerment practices*. Those who work to improve conditions for all women in their self-defined communities can be considered *collective empowerment actors*. Both right-wing individual and collective empowerment are specifically anti-Other. Right-wing women create or preserve borders (between self and selves, or between self and Other) and they refuse to extend women's empowerment beyond their self-designated community.

Resisting the Right

The understanding gained about the right in this book leads us to some preliminary thoughts about resisting the right. One of the best ways to confront the right is to build or rebuild a women's *liberation* movement that not only confronts patriarchal, filiarchal, and fraternarchal attitudes and power and the right's multiple constructions of Otherness, but also offers women tangible, symbolic, and attractive alternatives. A feminism that can do more than empower certain sectors of women (who are often already relatively privileged in their society) must recognize intersecting oppressions (based in gender, "race," sexuality, religion, ethnicity, nation, colonialism etc.) and how they operate through and across scales transnationally, and must forge strategies with all women's liberation in mind. This means constructing transversal alliances within and across borders, and mutually and simultaneously opposing racism, homophobia, religious and ethnic oppressions, class oppression, neocolonialism, and war. In fact, intersections between the right and certain forms of feminism have been possible because some feminisms have been narrowly defined (Yuval-Davis 1998: 184–85). Second, in some instances right-wing assaults on feminisms have pushed feminists into defensive positions and effectively silenced feminists. We need to find ways to develop and diffuse feminist debates and actions in the public discursive space across scale, from the local to the transnational. Due to intersecting oppressions, it has been difficult for feminists to have an impact in the media. This is an area that we need to work on. Third, this volume provides a glimpse at reasons why women join the right; some of these could be countered to reduce recruitment. For example, the right produces, confirms, or protects identities and issues to which its women recruits relate (the heteronormative family, social order, crime, etc.). Feminists need to more extensively address these issues, providing alternative analyses and framing them in understandable ways. Like other political formations, the right mobilizes women's desires to be useful and to have an impact on events. In some sites feminists could extend invitations to a wider range of women to participate in corresponding feminist actions. Fourth, several authors have identified points of tension between the right-wing projects of men and their female counterparts. They often center on gender itself. The bulk of these tensions arise from wider societal gains by feminists, of which nearly all women, regardless of positionality or political choice, might benefit. While we do not see the right imploding because of its gender tensions (there are too many mechanisms in place within the right to prevent this), we hope that knowledge of the location of these tensions will encourage feminist possibilities for aggravating them through interventions in the public discursive space. If effectively and massively accomplished, this might induce some borderline right-wing women into eventually abandoning the right, thereby weakening it. And it might potentially curb the right's further recruitment of women.

Some Directions for Future Research

Briefly we would like to suggest some immediate future directions for research on right-wing women. It is important to find ways to support scholarship on right-wing women in sites where such scholarship is desired and yet has been inhibited. Also, many insights could be gained through future in-depth comparisons of rights within and across geopolitical contexts, colonizing, colonized, and post-colonial ideologies (fascisms, religious nationalisms, and transnationalisms, conservative rights, populist rights, colonial rights, postcolonial rights), forms (states, parties, movements, and less organized manifestations, within and across nations), generations, and contextual social positionings of rights (as majorities or oppositional formations). It would be useful to come to a better understanding of transnational connections between and among the rights, their exchanges of ideas and resources across borders and scales, the conditions that facilitate or block their collective alignments, and how they support and influence each other. Further work on right-wing women actors (leaders to rank and file [Blee]), their actions, organizational structures, finances and economic programs, ideologies, and modalities of ideological diffusion and their roles in reproducing the right across generations is necessary, as is more inquiry into right wings and sexuality. And finally, a local to transnationally comparative examination of forms of women's liberationist resistance to the right and how they fare would contribute to configuring future successful strategies against the right.

part I.

Agency/
Subjectivity/
Subject Positions

1

She Loved Mussolini:
Margherita Sarfatti and Italian Fascism

Carole C. Gallucci

Margherita Grassini Sarfatti (1880–1961) is famous for founding the *Novecento* art group in Italy in 1925, and infamous for being Benito Mussolini's mistress for nineteen years. An important and influential intellectual in her day, Sarfatti published thousands of articles on topics ranging from art and politics to literature and culture, hosted a literary and artistic salon that drew major cultural figures of the day, and enjoyed access to powerful people and institutions. Her biography of Mussolini, *Dux*, was an international best-seller translated into eighteen languages. So well known was Sarfatti that she was invited by President Franklin Delano Roosevelt and Eleanor Roosevelt to tea at the White House on April 15, 1934. In the 1930s she lost favor in Mussolini's Fascist regime and went into exile in Paris and Argentina, where she attempted to reclaim her earlier identities and recast her life. Sarfatti occupies seemingly multiple and contradictory subject positions, as Jewish and Catholic, politically left and right, feminist and Fascist. When studying Sarfatti, scholars typically speak of categories such as pre-Fascist, post-Fascist, feminist, antifeminist, postwar, and post-Mussolini. While these qualifiers rightly reflect the complexity of Sarfatti's life and works, they suggest an uncomplicated relationship of self to ideology that may prove to be too limiting. Is she, as Victoria de Grazia has argued, an "an organizer of culture," or is she, as Philip Cannistraro and Brian Sullivan have suggested, a Fascist ideologue?[1] If we take Barbara Spackman's theory of Fascist discourse (1996) as combining oppositional positions and apply it to Sarfatti, we are left with a perplexing question: is it possible to be both a feminist and a fascist?

A complex and contradictory figure, Sarfatti has been clearly viewed as a Fascist. While critics overwhelmingly agree that Sarfatti was a member of the Fascist Party, a proclamation she herself made in 1919, there is no critical consensus on whether she was, or can even be considered, a feminist. Scholars such as Franca Pieroni Bortolotti and Giovanna Bosi Maramotti have argued that even her so-called early period is nothing short of antifeminism in the service of self-interest.[2] More recent studies find a definite ideological break with feminism by Sarfatti in the mid to late 1920s, in part a result of the consolidation of the Fascist regime (de Grazia 1982, 152; Cannistraro and Sullivan 1993, 307; Harrowitz 1996, 145). Yet Sarfatti considered herself a feminist from her earliest writings beginning in 1901 and, to the best of my knowledge, never disavowed this position in her own writings. Rather, it seems, she simply changed, under

Fascism, what it meant to be a feminist. Indeed, Sarfatti's complicated (re)positionings over time raise important issues for subsequent critical studies on women and Italian Fascism, such as the relationship of feminism to fascism, the definition of feminism itself, and the factors that may condition producers of culture.

Sarfatti is an important figure to study for several reasons. First, an analysis of women intellectuals who supported Fascism in Italy will open up new areas of inquiry and alter feminist discourses. While Sarfatti herself may not be able to cross the lines between feminism and fascism or even occupy a liminal space between them, she severely complicates the notion that all Fascists were anti-women or that all women were anti-Fascist. Much work still needs to be done, for example, on the "Fasci Femminili," or women's auxiliaries of the Fascist Party, and their attempt to formulate a "Fascist feminism." By studying women's production, consumption, and attitudes of support toward fascism, future research will lead to the construction of a more accurate picture of women's writing in twentieth-century Italy and Europe. In this way, we can connect the work of Italian women Fascists with the history of other women intellectuals in Europe, particularly Germany, who openly sympathized with Nazism and fascism.[3] Furthermore, the previously unknown story of Fascist women supporters can be linked to a more established historiography of anti-Fascist activists, providing a better context for their actions.[4] The kind of research I propose may create alternative paradigms on women and fascism.[5]

In this essay, I propose a new study of Sarfatti's texts written between 1913 and 1955. I will explore how Sarfatti attempted to reconcile feminism with Fascism. I have organized Sarfatti's life and works into three phases: her early years of socialist feminism; her middle years at the height of Mussolini's power, when she is more clearly in line with Fascist thinking about women; and her later years, when she attempts to reposition herself in history and absolve herself from her own responsibility in the development of Fascism. This helps explain her silence about Mussolini in her final memoirs. Yet I would like to suggest even in her writings of the middle years, which are antiwomen, that Sarfatti is still concerned with women's issues and may even subtly contest some elements of Fascist ideology.

To this end, it will be useful to begin with an overview of Sarfatti's life. Sarfatti was an art critic, novelist, poet, literary critic, and journalist. She was internationally recognized as an art critic, both for her support of the arts and for her literary and artistic salon, which drew major figures of Italian and European intellectual life, such as Luigi Pirandello and F. T. Marinetti. Sarfatti began writing and publishing as early as 1901. Her writings appeared in major feminist and socialist publications, such as the socialist daily *Avanti!* in Milan, the feminist review *La Rassegna femminile* in Florence, and the socialist literary review *Avanti della domenica* published first in Florence and later in Rome. Many of her early writings addressed women's issues. In these early years from 1901 to 1925, Sarfatti positioned herself as a feminist and a supporter of women's rights. In 1901, Sarfatti joined the Milan Feminist League and wrote articles for that organization's journal, *Unione Femminile*, supporting voting rights for women. Socialist men and women were divided over whether female emancipation would take place under the revolution or whether women were immediately entitled to equal rights, including the right to vote. After years of debate, the Socialist Party officially endorsed universal suffrage for women only by 1910. In 1912, the year after

Sarfatti met Mussolini, she was writing for *La Difesa delle Lavoratrici* (*The Defense of Women Workers*), the official voice of socialist feminism. Sarfatti wrote articles for *La Difesa* on voting, work conditions, equal pay, family law, and divorce. For instance, in her 1913 article "Perchè le donne han bisogno del voto" ["Why women need the vote"], Sarfatti argued that, contrary to pervasive antiwomen rhetoric which said that granting women the vote would destroy the home, voting women had a higher intellectual and moral program then men: "[Women] have saved houses, families and innumerable hearths, for the present and the future" (2).

Sarfatti also supported legal rights for women. Sarfatti's 1914 article "Le nuove leggi sull'ordinamento della famiglia" ["New family laws"], listed the proposed bills for new family laws: "Bill for civil marriage over religious, bill for divorce, bill for paternity laws, who therefore would dare to say that politics is 'men's business,' that politics is 'something that doesn't concern women'?" (1). Sarfatti insisted that society, now that women were a significant presence in political life, correct the injustices affecting women (1). Sarfatti understood that society as a whole, and specifically the working class and the bourgeoisie, would have to band together in order to obtain equal rights for women.

Sarfatti often invoked the first-person plural in her early writings, insisting that "we women" take matters into our own hands. Using this rhetorical strategy, Sarfatti created a common bond and sense of community with her female readers. She attempted to universalize women's experiences by addressing the reader directly: "Italian women, you socialists and working women, be on the alert!" (1). Sarfatti reiterated the rhetoric first proposed by early feminists who encouraged female empowerment through increased economic and political participation. Sarfatti's subsumption of the category of women under the category of mothers in this early phase, sometimes construed as anticipating Fascist rhetoric, was rather a common rhetorical strategy of the natural rights philosophy of the Enlightenment.[6]

In her middle phase, roughly 1926 to 1936, Sarfatti recast her earlier positions on women's role and function in Fascist society. In this group of writings, Sarfatti was more in line with Fascist thinking about the proper place of Woman. For the Fascists, women's rights now meant prolific motherhood in service to the new Italy. Scholars have argued that as mistress to the duce, Sarfatti abandoned feminism and chose to concentrate instead on modern art, not modern women.[7] A more Fascist and less feminist Sarfatti appears in two of her major publications during this period: the 1926 biography, *Dux*, and the 1929 novel, *Il palazzone*.

Sarfatti considered her biography of Mussolini, *Dux*, her greatest literary achievement. Giuseppe Prezzolini had suggested the idea to Sarfatti in 1924 after being approached by an English publisher interested in a biography of Mussolini (Cannistraro and Sullivan 1993, 299). Sarfatti's biography was published first in English in 1925 with the title *The Life of Benito Mussolini*, and in Italian in 1926 as *Dux*. Mussolini, who had earlier provided Sarfatti with personal diaries and letters, wrote the preface to the Italian edition, and there he insisted: "In thus presenting myself I am giving the highest proof of human endurance for the moral edification of my fellow-mortals" (*The Life*, 9; *Dux*, 7). *Dux* quickly became a best-seller. It was translated into eighteen languages and went through seventeen editions from 1926 to 1938. Its status as a best-seller in Italy may have been determined by censorship laws and Fascist control of printing. The Fascist ideologue Arturo Marpicati went so far as to insist that it was the duty of everyone to read it: "It is one's duty to know it. It is necessary to those who live today, as it will be indispensable to the historical future."[8]

Fascist propagandists called Sarfatti the "artefice del Duce" or image maker of the duce (de Grazia 1992, 230). Historians, including Philip Cannistraro, have credited Sarfatti with creating a myth of Mussolini by helping to shape his cult of the personality (Cannistraro and Sullivan 1993, 302–305). Sarfatti created a myth for the masses of a man destined to remake Italy: "Benito Mussolini is an archetype of the Italian—he is a Roman from top to toe and to the marrow of his bones. . . . Roman in spirit and appearance, Benito Mussolini is the resurrection of the pure Italic type, which after many centuries flourishes once again" (*The Life*, 20; *Dux*, 10). As an officially sanctioned biography, Sarfatti rewrote the past and largely omitted Fascist violence, including the murder of Socialist leader Giacomo Matteotti in 1924 (*The Life*, 138, 149; *Dux*, 98). We can only speculate as to her knowledge or ignorance of Fascist violence and repression. Given her intimate relationship with Mussolini, it would appear that Sarfatti was well aware of such acts. She excused the murder of Matteotti as an expression of manly rivalries: "With a party of energetic young men, some of them inclined to violence, the more that is accomplished the more likely is friction to arise, and it is impossible that mistakes will not be made."[9] In his review of 1926, Luigi Tonelli saw *Dux* as the embodiment of an epoch: "Besides being a great and acute biography, *Dux* seems to be the story of thirty years of Italian political and spiritual life" (251; see also Cecchi 1926, 245). *Dux* reflects the height of Sarfatti's power in Fascist Italy.

Crucially, Sarfatti does not present an ideal ruler, but rather a very real man. She included his accounts of violence, opportunism, and antifeminism. Sarfatti presented Mussolini as a virile leader surrounded by adoring women. In the conclusion, Sarfatti defined the biography as "a woman's book." Reviewers agreed.[10] By doing so, while seemingly demeaning it, Sarfatti actually valorized microhistory and oral history by focusing on the relations between history and story. According to Sarfatti, History may be made up of, in this case, a great man and great deeds, but it is also made up of important women and quotidian stories. Although Sarfatti concluded that "[t]he scene, *Signor Presidente*, is dominated by your figure" (*The Life*, 346), she made quite sure that he was nonetheless surrounded by influential women, including Sarfatti herself.

When Sarfatti's only novel, *Il palazzone*, was published in the spring of 1929, she defined it a "love story."[11] In 1929, Goffredo Bellonci aligned *Dux* with *Il palazzone*, arguing that *Dux* recounted the story of a man representing "masculine virtues," while *Il palazzone* narrated "the feminine essence, woman" (8). The main themes of the novel include the obedient, subservient woman ["Woman, woman, woman: unremittingly woman!" (238)], male virility and domination, and the necessity of Fascism because Italy "needs a leader" (198). The representation of the main female character, Fiorella Maggi, conforms perfectly with Fascist thinking about women as lovers, sexual objects for the new man, and as "exemplary wife and mother" (*sposa e madre esemplare*; Meldini 1975). Fiorella is all of these, wife, mother, and lover, who exists insofar as men confer a social role on her: "to feel his, protected by him, led and scolded, possessed by him completely and totally!" (236). In the novel, Sarfatti set up a "war of the sexes" in which men are dominant, violent, and active, and women are tender, obedient, and passive (116, 121, 123–125).

According to Giovanna Bosi Maramotti, *Il palazzone* is clearly a Fascist novel:

"*Il palazzone* is a Fascist historical novel for its able introduction of myths which provide the basis of an education largely affirmed in the thirties" (1982, 106). While women are represented as sexual objects, men are violent Fascist leaders, aligned with unruly, violent, aggressive forces. For instance, the character Manlio Valdeschi, after attacking nearby workers, "impersonated [the] ideal of high and industrious virility" (240). Whereas femininity is presented as passive submission, masculinity is presented as positive aggression. Furthermore, in this book, Sarfatti presented striking workers as potential enemies of the state: "You must be joking! They are a hundred thousand chatterboxes, greedy to overpower, little tyrants by cowardice" (198). When not focusing on the specifics of a so-called female writing, critics seemed to applaud "the ideal story of a generation, our generation from war to Fascism" (Panzini 1929, 3).

Sarfatti herself seems to admit that the fictional novel is actually autobiographical in nature.[12] She saw herself in the role of Fiorella and Mussolini in the role of Manlio: "We will keep our secret [love] quiet, jealously, if you want it, but you must be mine and no one can stop it" (225). If we read *Il palazzone* as a romanticized version of Sarfatti's relationship with Mussolini, then we are immediately struck by her self-portrait, in which the real powerful working woman is reduced to the fictional passive sexual object. One must recall that this was Sarfatti's only foray into fiction writing. Besides her waning power, one possible explanation for this novel may be that her female representations and concomitant ideas seem to be based on prevalent literary trends, most notably the work of the Futurists and D'Annunzio (Bosi Maramotti 1982, 110–111). In these models, women are sexual objects to be conquered and dominated in a lyrical prose of hyperbolic proportions.

Sarfatti and her family converted to Catholicism in 1928. Scholars explain Sarfatti's conversion as a way to align herself with and protect herself from the increasingly intolerant Fascist regime, where Fascist ideologues began publicly voicing anti-Semitic sentiments.[13] Nancy Harrowitz, among others, points out that Sarfatti never abandoned her aesthetic principles on art (1996, 144), since she was dubbed the "Fascist dictator of culture" in the 1920s. Rather, Sarfatti continually argued for modernism in art, devoid of any so-called Fascist content, a highly controversial and increasingly unpopular position. This stance, together with her Jewish origins, were at least partly responsible for her waning influence on Mussolini and her decreasing position of power in the regime. Her increasingly difficult position may in part explain her other pro-Fascist articles published in the 1930s, which focus on the regime's demographic campaign and the cult of domesticity. One notable example is her speech "Women of Fascism," published in the *New York Herald Tribune Sunday Magazine* on November 12, 1933. Even so, it will be useful to recall that in the 1930s Sarfatti tried desperately to persuade Mussolini not to form an alliance with Hitler. Nonetheless, the regime passed and enforced the Racial Laws of 1938, which denied many rights to Italian Jews, including forbidding intermarriage between Italians and Jews, removing Jews from positions in government, banking, and education, and restricting their property.

One must consider that even in works in which Sarfatti is more closely aligned with Fascist ideology, these writings may also contain feminist impulses. For example, in *Dux*, besides offering readers a pervasive and positive self-portrait, Sarfatti also drew other positive portraits of women. Sarfatti presented Mussolini as a virile leader surrounded by worshiping women, as would be expected with myth making. Yet Mussolini's lovers are not the only women we encounter. Women are present in a variety of roles as lovers, intellectuals, advisors, socialists and Fascists. In *Dux*, Sarfatti attempted to reconcile feminism to Fascism by presenting women not only as lovers and mothers, but also as influential, intellectual women. Sarfatti included many lively portraits of important figures in Italian cultural life before Fascism, particularly socialist women leaders, such as Anna Kuliscioff and Angelica Balabanoff. Sarfatti showed how Fascist gender ideology disempowered women in many of her writings of this middle period. For example, she painted a portrait of Kuliscioff as a brilliant political woman whose power had to be channeled through men by convention: "Anna Kuliscioff ... was a great woman, with the hard brilliance and many-sidedness of a diamond. . . . She was destined to see the ambitions of her whole life thwarted by the mediocrity of the men through whom she worked" (*The Life*, 170–171; *Dux*, 129–130). Sarfatti reworked a much similar portrait in her 1955 final memoir, *Acqua passata*. In her female portraits, Sarfatti appears to be struggling with two pervasive Fascist female models: the lover and the "masculinized" intellectual woman. While Sarfatti presented Kuliscioff as brilliant but circumscribed, she reiterated cultural stereotypes of sexual difference and deviant femininity with her portrayal of Balabanoff. The rhetorical device of "we women" found in her earlier writings disappears because Sarfatti has set up (or admitted to) a conflictual relationship with her rivals.[14]

In 1937, Sarfatti published a memoir of her travels in the United States called *L'America, ricerca della felicità* (*America: The Pursuit of Happiness*). During her tour of the United States, the press called her the "most influential woman in Italy,"[15] a Fascist and a feminist. In an interview with Hope Ridings Miller of the *Washington Post* on April 17, 1934, two days after her meeting with the Roosevelts, a glowing photograph of Sarfatti identified her as "Italian feminist, Fascist editor, and official biographer of Mussolini." Here feminism and Fascism are juxtaposed without comment, suggesting that Sarfatti's dedication to women's issues, however defined, entitled her to be considered a feminist. What appears to be mutually exclusive is presented as paradoxically harmonious: Sarfatti can present Mussolini's demographic campaign as somehow pro-women because "all this domesticity doesn't prevent interest in things intellectual" (13). The hearth does not negate the mind. Sarfatti insisted that American and Italian women were simply "different in their ideas and aims" (13). Nearly half of the interview is dedicated to Sarfatti's great admiration for American women, including Eleanor Roosevelt, and American women writers, themes that will later run through *L'America*.

Sarfatti's book contains two representative chapters on women that demonstrate her continuing concern for women's issues. Sarfatti showed herself to be capable of writing an important study of comparative feminism, as she addressed the condition of women in America compared to Fascist Italy.[16] In a chapter titled "Eve in America," Sarfatti used the United States Constitution as a point of departure to talk about "the right to life, liberty and the pursuit of happiness" which American women fought for and obtained "with hard work, struggle and sacrifice" (189–204). Indeed, America and Italy share a common bond in strong women: both countries are made up of the "blood, tears and bodies of women who nobly died in forging it" (191). Moreover, the concept of woman's equality to man in America is totally different from that ancient concept found in Europe, and affects everything from marriage to family to divorce (192). The right to happiness for an Italian woman was an "enormous heresy, given the European and Latin conception of woman; indeed, it was subversive of the invulnerable and unwritten laws of custom" (192). Instead, in Italy, "we don't teach women their right, but rather sacrifice and submission to duty" (199). Here Sarfatti appears at her most critical not only of Fascist Italy, but Italy in general. Sarfatti suggests that the cultural roots of Fascist thinking about women derived from stereotypes already present in Italian culture, from Catholicism to nationalism to futurism. In constructing its images of women, Fascism in large part recycled the traditional images of women found in the fabric of Italian culture and society. While American women pursued the right to happiness, in Sarfatti's view, Italian women pursued the "right" to sacrifice.

In her second chapter on women, "More Power to Woman," Sarfatti returned to one of her most important subjects in the days she wrote for *La Difesa delle Lavoratrici*: women's work. During meetings with female college students in Washington, D.C., Sarfatti insisted that "all schools are open to both men and women and that non-political professions and jobs are accessible to women" (209). Debates during the late 1920s and 1930s centered not only on what material to teach women, but also on whether or not to educate women at all outside of home economics and those areas that privileged the cult of domesticity. Sarfatti failed to mention that, beginning in 1926, Fascist laws were introduced to force women out of schools and teaching positions. That year, a law was passed barring women from teaching subjects such as Latin, Greek, history, and philosophy in the *liceo* and *ginnasio*, and from holding major positions of authority in both middle and technical schools (De Grand 1976, 949). In 1928, university tuition doubled for female students (Saracinelli and Totti 1983, 120). Sarfatti pointed out that, in America, women were seen "in every kind of occupation," which created an immediate female "solidarity" no longer found in Europe (210). From the Daughters of the American Revolution to society women, from stewardesses to secretaries, Sarfatti saw an equality and a freedom for women unparalleled in the world, evident in American women's literature. In the end, American women "are capable of creating great things" by their own hard work (215).

While *L'America* may perpetuate Fascist economic and social inaccuracies, Sarfatti also suggests that Fascist policies were not beneficial for Italian women. For instance, she deconstructs pervasive stereotypes in Italy that deny women equal rights, applauds women's increased mobility and freedom in the United States, and valorizes American women's work in a variety of fields unavailable in Italy. By comparing Fascist Italy to the democratic United States, Italy is diminished in these examples vis-à-vis women's rights. Sarfatti now challenged, rather than perpetuated, the Fascist feminine model whose "right" meant only submission and sacrifice. Moreover, Sarfatti implicitly critiqued her own right-wing ideology, which predicated a so-called "natural" gender order that identified masculinity with the public sphere and femininity with the private sphere of home and family.

After the war, Sarfatti wrote two major works, *Mussolini as I Knew Him* (originally titled *My Fault: Mussolini as I Knew Him*) in 1945 and *Acqua passata* (*Water under the bridge*) in 1955. Mussolini provided Sarfatti with a passport after the institution of the Racial Laws in 1938–39. She went into exile first to Paris, then

Uruguay, and finally to Argentina, where she lived out the war. As an exile in Paris, Sarfatti tried to identify as a Jew, but was largely marginalized by the Jewish community, which remembered that she had acquired power and prestige from her long-standing association with Mussolini's Fascist regime (Cannistraro and Sullivan 1993, 520ff). Sarfatti returned to Italy in 1947 and died there in 1961. She is buried at Cavallasca, Como. Sarfatti's Fascist past made it impossible for her to publish her postwar biography of Mussolini in English or Italian; she was able to publish it only in Spanish. In her second biography of Mussolini, Sarfatti exculpated herself from her Fascist past by taking some historical responsibility for her role in the development of Fascism and in helping to create the myth of Mussolini in *Dux*. But her postwar *apologia* received little critical attention.

In her final memoirs, *Acqua passata*, Mussolini is the absent presence.[17] *Acqua passata* chronicles the period from Sarfatti's childhood in Venice to her 1934 visit to the White House. The spirited writer tells of her childhood, vividly recalls the cultural climate, but makes no mention of her intimate relationship with Mussolini. This is especially surprising because the two-hundred-page-plus book literally contains a cast of thousands, socialists and politicians, actresses and artists, friends and enemies, but no Mussolini. In *Acqua passata*, Fascism is mentioned only three times in the book, all in one chapter on the pivotal salon of socialist leaders Anna Kuliscioff and Filippo Turati. In this chapter, Sarfatti suggested that the "Fasci di Combattimento" (or the earliest local cells of the Fascist movement) attempted a material, as opposed to a spiritual, revolution (68); she notes how she petitioned the Fascist government for a pension for an ex-government official (70); and she argued that in February 1921 "Fascism in Milan brought together the almost unanimity of popular forces" (83). As in *Dux*, Sarfatti disregarded actual Fascist violence. As Bosi Maramotti has noted, Fascism is largely erased by Sarfatti: "about the Fascist period and the men who made it: cancelled, eliminated by writing, something that never existed. The woman who received much from Fascism and who gave much, through her official participation, through her political culture in Italy and abroad, forgets it, 'skips over' it, like a youthful and ephemeral adventure" (1982, 112).

Sarfatti's own self-portrait is as interesting as Mussolini's absence from it. Critics have emphasized the book's inaccuracies and lack of self-criticism, despite the postwar environment.[18] Sarfatti presents her own position in Fascist history as unproblematic. Regarding her Fascist past, Sarfatti simply claims that she was not bound to any one position: "but my Venetian humor did not permit me to yoke myself to any cart. I see the clay feet in the idol whose head I worship" (81). Harrowitz argues that Sarfatti's "claim regarding her ability to see the defects of her idols can only be read as revisionary, given her role in developing Fascism and her own attachment to Mussolini" (1996, 147). Of the years under Fascism, Sarfatti wrote instead about growing up in Venice, attending socialist meetings, and holding court as salon mistress and art patron. She takes no true responsibility for her own role in Italy's Fascist past.

It is difficult to categorize *Acqua passata* in terms of traditional narratives of self. Sarfatti's narrative moves from the traditional first-person "I" to the omniscient third-person narrator. While the "I" participates in parties and meetings, the third-person narrator describes important events. The traditional narrative "I" is eclipsed by a third-person narration, complete with serpentine dependent clauses, which functions to distance Sarfatti from the problematic interwar years.

Sarfatti considered *Acqua passata* a book of memories, rather than a memoir (Cannistraro and Sullivan 1993, 558). By doing so, perhaps Sarfatti would rather be accused of having a bad memory, rather than remembering badly. In the end, *Acqua passata* is neither an apology of nor rationale for her earlier writings. Nor is it a confession. In *Acqua passata*, as in her previous works, Sarfatti takes on multiple subject positions.

In life as in art, Margherita Sarfatti emerges as a powerful presence. In one obituary, Sarfatti was remembered primarily for her biography of Mussolini: "More than her articles on art, in which she supported the *Novecento* group, her memory is tied to her controversial *Life* of the Fascist leader, for whom she was devoted friend" (Geraldini 1961, 8). But Sarfatti was also an influential figure in her own right. Renewed interest in Sarfatti is evidenced by her appearance in the 1999 film *Cradle Will Rock*, in which she is portrayed by Susan Sarandon. As one of the most powerful women in Fascist Italy, she helped to legitimate the regime and helped to promote modern art. Through her salon, political contacts, and innumerable writings, Sarfatti tackled issues ranging from voting rights to the novel and painting to the modern state. One of her most pressing concerns was women's rights. As I have attempted to show, in some of her most important works, Sarfatti tried to reconcile feminism with Fascism. Although seemingly impossible to achieve in practice, Sarfatti sought to cross the lines between support of women's rights and support of a repressive regime, or at least to conjoin them. Sarfatti does not seem to display the sharp contradictions of identity that some critics have perceived. Rather than reinforce our own fixed categories of fascist or antifascist, feminist or antifeminist, Sarfatti challenges us to rethink critical categories of identity, to reformulate historical paradigms of fascism, and to redefine contemporary notions of feminism.

Notes

Research for this article was carried out under the auspices of a College of William & Mary Faculty Research Grant.

1. De Grazia (1982, 149; 1992, 230) and Nozzoli (1988) define her as an "organizer of culture." Philip V. Cannistraro and Brian Sullivan offer one of the most comprehensive studies to date with *Il Duce's Other Woman* (1993).
2. See Bosi Maramotti (1982, 110) and Pieroni Bortolotti (1978, 171–172). Simona Urso defines Sarfatti's feminism as "superficial" and secondary to her interest in creating a new ethical state founded on heroic individualism (1994, 158).
3. See, for example, Bock 1984, and Bridenthal and Koonz 1977.
4. See Gallucci and Nerenberg, 2000; Gabrielli 1999; Addis Saba 1998; Slaughter 1997; Jeansonne 1996; Cutrufelli et al. 1994.
5. See Addis Saba 1988; de Grazia 1992; Gallucci 1999, 1995; Gallucci and Nerenberg, 2000; Mondello 1987; Pickering-Iazzi 1995, 1997; Pinkus 1995; Spackman 1996; and Stone 1998.
6. Urso argues: "In spite of her presumed feminism, [Sarfatti] seems more interested in exalting the role of the woman-mother (even during the Libyan war): female suffrage seems to be a secondary problem for her, absolutely subordinated to the new order. If feminism was often seen by these same suffragists as the praising of difference, Sarfatti goes even further. She subordinates it to the preservation of the race and hearth. Sarfatti is already building the foundation for an ethics of female responsibility within the nation" (1994, 158). Urso does well to contextualize Sarfatti's early period, but may overlook the historical referents in the rhetoric of the suffragists.
7. Cannistraro and Sullivan may themselves be accused of perpetuating stereotypes of

women with this assertion on Sarfatti's feminine wiles over Mussolini: "Over the next decade, as Mussolini adopted increasing anti-feminist policies toward women, Margherita abandoned any illusions she might have had that her feminism was compatible with Fascism. . . . Privately she found herself forced to use against Mussolini the weapons of flattery and manipulation that she had been taught as a girl in patriarchal society. She had long since recognized the strategic benefits of assuming stereotypically 'feminine' roles in order to secure advantage and power: as hostess of a literary and artistic salon, as cultural activist, as 'mother of a war hero,' and, of course, as mistress to a leader" (1993, 307). Harrowitz argues that after the voting rights debacle, when it became clear that Mussolini (and the Fascist regime) was not going to support women's rights, "She eventually shut up about women's rights and feminism by the mid to late twenties when it became obvious to her that it was no longer politically acceptable to support these positions" (1996, 145).

8. Arturo Marpicati (1933, 398). See also Cecchi (1926, 245).

9. Sarfatti, *Dux*, 298; *The Life*, 338. See also *Dux*, 282, on "squadrismo" (the armed force of Fascism).

10. Anonymous, 1926, 464; Tonelli 1929, 251; Cecchi 1926, 244; Ruinas 1930, 102; Sarfatti, *The Life*, 346.

11. Bellonci 1929, 8; Panzini 1929, 3; de Grazia 1982, 153–154; Bosi Maramotti 1982, 101–112; Gramsci 1971, 181.

12. In interviews with the Sarfatti family, Cannistraro and Sullivan (1993, 337) find all the major players present in this "perversely autobiographical" novel: Fiorella is Sarfatti herself as the name suggests (both Fiorella and Margherita are flowers in Italian); Sergio is Sarfatti's husband, Cesare, who died in 1924; Neri is Sarfatti's son, Roberto, who was killed in the war in 1918; and Manlio is Mussolini.

13. Roberto Farinacci, editor of the Fascist daily *Il Regime Fascista* from 1926 to 1933, led a series of public attacks on Sarfatti. Even so, in the regime's series "Figure del tempo mussoliniano," Margherita Sarfatti figures prominently "in this extraordinary historical period, for her complete adherence to all the vast movements of thought, be they literary, political and artistic" in the brief biography by Orazia Belsito Prini (1934, 5). See also *Enciclopedia Treccani* (1936, 870).

14. In *Dux*, on a narrative level, Sarfatti weaves together a mixture of voices, from the intimate first-person singular and plural to the more traditional, "objective" third-person singular, the latter expected of a traditional biography.

15. The U.S. ambassador to Italy, Breckinridge Long, called her "probably the best-informed woman in Italy" (Cannistraro and Sullivan 1993, 431). See also "Italy-America Party Honors Donna Sarfatti" (1934, 11) and Dolly Cameron, "Reception at Sulgrave Club for Eminent Italian Writer and Critic" (1934, 14).

16. Sarfatti, *L'America*, chapters 14 and 15, and Pieroni Bortolotti (1978, 382–383). While acknowledging Sarfatti's renewed interest in women, some critics think her last book written during Fascism does not go far enough. Although Sarfatti does rethink her own feminism, Victoria de Grazia argues that she does not analyze the condition of women in Italy or the reactionary policies of the regime in any depth. This is "above all due to her isolation where she was voluntarily relegated in order to manage those crumbs of power which were reserved for her as woman of the Fascist regime" (1982, 154).

17. I would like to thank Paula Blank for discussing this idea with me.

18. See Bosi Maramotti 1982, 112; Cannistraro and Sullivan 1993, 558; de Grazia 1982, 151–154; Harrowitz 1996, 145–148.

2

Female "Fanatics": Women's Sphere in the British Union of Fascists

Julie V. Gottlieb

Founded by the former Labour M.P. Sir Oswald Mosley in October 1932 after the electoral defeat of his New Party, the British Union of Fascists (BUF) (1932–1940) achieved only limited success in recruitment and never managed to have any of its members elected to public office. Membership estimates suggest that the movement recruited no more than fifty thousand members at its height in 1934, dwindled to only a few thousand by 1938, and saw a rise in activism, if not numbers, when it launched its antiwar campaign in 1939 (Webber 1984, 575–605). In 1940 the British Union (the BUF was renamed the British Union of Fascists and National Socialists in 1936) was outlawed, its publications banned, and 747 of its members—including ninety-six women—interned under the British government's Defence Regulation 18B (1a) as suspected Fifth Columnists (Griffiths 1980).

Historical memories of the British Union of Fascists tend to evoke images of a marginal movement, making a strong appeal to ex-servicemen, and drawing support from anti-Semitic elements in London's East End,[1] with columns of *male* Blackshirts marching in step to vainglorious calls for a "Greater Britain." This general impression of the BUF as a paramilitary organization motivated by a macho ethos has been reinforced by inevitable sideward glances to the models of Fascist Italy and Nazi Germany. We might then expect that the BUF faithfully replicated the existing fascist regimes in Europe and that the movement was male chauvinist ideologically, and sexually discriminatory in terms of women's political participation. Yet, the British Fascisti, Britain's first interwar fascist movement, was launched by a woman in 1923 (see Farr 1987), setting a precedent for the visibility of women in the politics of the extreme Right in Britain. During the 1930s, 25 percent of the members in the much more influential British Union of Fascists were women (Gottlieb 2000, 46–47).[2] While the BUF first took its inspiration from Italian Fascism, and from 1936 increasingly took its ideological marching orders from German National Socialism, Mosley consistently claimed that his fascism was a thoroughly British movement, born of a British political tradition of dissent and uniquely equipped to confront the crisis in the British polity. In Mosley's understanding, fascism "is the new faith born of the post-war period in the last decade. It is not the product of Italy, nor of any other foreign country" (Mosley 1933), and the BUF—in common with all fascist movements in which the imagined community is the nation writ large—resisted the charge that it had imported Mussolini's creed. BUF members were required to sell British fascism with the stamp "Made in Britain." Part and parcel of the BUF's quintessential Britishness was a curious reverence for the revolutionary moment represented by the British suffragettes, and a continued commitment to women's political participation. Indeed, this ideological linkage with prewar British feminism distinguished the BUF from the rigid gender politics characteristic of Nazism.

This chapter will argue that the BUF appealed to a range of politicized women in Britain, even to some women who had a feminist background, by recasting women's political belligerence and militancy into fascist fanaticism. However, BUF women identified themselves as fascists first and foremost. They joined with their male counterparts in the construction of a political demonology in which the national government, "Reds," antifascist "warmongers," and Jews together sabotaged British imperial interests; lay idle as "Merrie England" suffered under the burden of mass unemployment, the exploitative practices of "international finance," cultural decadence, and the wanton neglect of the countryside; and failed to appreciate the socioeconomic panacea offered by Mosley's utopian corporate state of the fascist future. BUF women united with their male counterparts in Jew-baiting activities, joined in reciting the racist mantra by singing chants of "the Yids, the Yids, we've gotta get rid of the Yids!"[3] and agreed with their white male "protectors" that the predatory Jew exploited women workers in the sweatshops, perpetrated sex crimes, and was responsible for disseminating indecent and anti-Christian literature (Gottlieb 2000, 129–132). Theirs was not a struggle against patriarchy in any of its guises, and they were not concerned to arm and educate women qua women in a sex war of identity politics. As women of the far right they must be distinguished from feminists agitating for women's rights and the empowerment of a female collectivity. Their exclusionary racism transcended and, indeed, negated any vague commitment to the advancement of their sex.

Britain's fascists denied that they organized women according to the Continental Fascist or Nazi model, and it was with pride in the distinctiveness of the British fascist promotion of female participation that Mosley claimed:

> We have a higher percentage of women candidates than any other party in this country and they play a part of basic equality. We are pledged to complete sex equality. The German attitude towards women has always been different from the British, and my movement has been largely built up by the *fanaticism* of women; they hold ideals with tremendous passion. Without the women I could not have got a quarter of the way [my italics].[4]

Although Mosley chose to emphasize his movement's divergence from the Nazi prototype, he still strongly echoed the *Newspeak* of generic fascism, and, in particular, the fascist transformation of the term "fanaticism" from pejorative to positive.[5] This new idiom was a necessary correlate to the development of fascist civic-religious liturgy, and Mosley's women followers were also attracted by this political aestheticization of quasi-religious fanaticism. Nellie Driver, the BUF's women's district leader in Nelson, recalled how the fascist movement had "plenty of romance in the form of drum corps, salutes, standards, emblems, uniforms and impressive demonstrations which made a strong appeal to me. From henceforth politics and social reform were to be my religion" (Driver n.d., 20). Certainly the BUF mimicked the political nomenclature and aesthetics of fascism and national socialism. However, what is striking is that Mosleyite fascism's own particularism and responsiveness to the British historical situation meant that the BUF distanced itself from foreign models for the role and treatment of women.

Locating Women's Agency in their Fascist Fanaticism

Claudia Koonz has observed that "the women among Hitler's followers have fallen through the historian's sieve, unclaimed by feminists and unnoticed by men" (1987, 3) Until recently, Mosley's women supporters were similarly conspicuous for their absence from the historical narratives of the far Right in Britain. It is incontrovertible that fascism "failed" in interwar Britain, but this failure has by no means diminished historical interest in Britain's comparatively slight contribution to the history of fascism (see Cronin 1996). While prolific, the historiography of British fascism has traditionally been gender blind, focusing instead on the relationship between the liberal-democratic center and the extremist peripheries; the patterns of membership and what can be gleaned from geopolitical area studies of the BUF; moments of political violence and the ramifications of fascist racism; and the relations, both formal and intellectual, between Britain's fascists and their Italian and German counterparts (Brewer 1984; Lewis 1987; Linehan 1996; Skidelsky 1975; Thurlow 1998).

The work of Martin Durham and others has introduced a new wave in the historiography of British fascism by paying much needed attention to gendering the movement's membership and the BUF's propaganda by coming to terms with some significant links between the British suffrage movement and fascism, and by challenging the convenient formula that fascism is "by definition, an antifeminist movement devoted to the removal of women from the labour market and their return to a life of domestic servitude and the unceasing production of children" (Durham 1998, 4; see also Durham 1992, 513–527; Gottlieb 1999, 31–47; Kushner and Lunn 1990, 1989).

Broadly speaking, since the 1960s the historiography of women and fascism in Italy and Nazi Germany has evolved from a consensus around the victim status of women under fascism, through a view that women were "fooled" into lending their support to their dictators, to a heated debate as to whether women should also be acknowledged as the perpetrators under fascist regimes.[6] As it has developed, the extensive body of scholarship on women and fascism has provided theoretical and methodological models through which historians of "failed" fascist movements can evaluate the degree of agency exercised by these women and can contextualize the unique form of female dissent expressed through the politics of the extreme Right. We can now measure the male leadership's repression and manipulation of female spaces and women's sexuality, and gauge levels of female participation in order to evaluate the institutionalization of their gender ideologies. We can transcend the conundrum of women as victims or as coconspirators of fascist forms of patriarchy, male supremacy, and racial exclusion to postulate that fascist women were both victims *and* perpetrators. Arguably, this ambivalence can be illustrated very effectively through the active roles women played in fascist movements that occupied the margins of political legitimacy, movements in which women exercised their free will and zealotry *against* the political establishment.

In nations where fascist parties ruled, segments of the female population embraced fascism enthusiastically, voluntarily and willingly, and exercised a degree of free will in the *intensity* of their commitment to their dictators. In contrast, membership in the BUF was not the ticket to mass approval. To support Mosley in the Britain of the 1930s was a radical, unpopular choice that went against the political grain. Not by any means were BUF women compelled to join the movement; nor was it common for women to follow their fathers, husbands, or sons into the BUF. In fact, the BUF identified women as the instigators of fascism, and the ones who brought fascism into the home. In this vein, the *Fascist Week* proclaimed that "Fascism in Britain knows that it is a woman's influence that has converted so many of its male members" (17 November 1933). Louise Irvine (née Fisher), a young teacher trainee who had lost both her parents in adolescence, joined the BUF after hearing Mosley speak at Crewe and eventually rose to the position of women's district leader in Birmingham. Irvine said recently that "the mere fact of becoming a member was a striking blow for independent thinking. Subconsciously when I joined the movement I may have felt that I was even doing something slightly daring and out-of-step (correspondence with the author, 8 May 1996).

Patterns of BUF adherence underline this spirit of female initiative, as the female membership was marked by class, regional, generational, and familial heterogeneity (Gottlieb 2000a). The BUF drew mostly middle-class and working-class women, but some members were upper-class women, including Unity Mitford, the Viscountess Downe, and Lady Pearson. The BUF's appeal to youth attracted some women in their early teens (a number of whom admitted that the spectre of so many lithe young men in uniform aroused their interest in the BUF), but it also drew mothers who joined with their sons or daughters, and middle-aged women both married and unmarried. While the center of BUF activity was London, some of the most active women members were based in Lancashire, the Midlands, Bournemouth, and in rural areas. While the profile of women joiners was eclectic, it is significant that a number of the leading activists gained their formative experiences as members or even leaders of the Conservative Party, underscoring the fact that the movement was able to appeal to politically experienced women as well as to starry-eyed young recruits drawn to the movement due to the personal charisma and sex appeal of Mosley, the "Rudolph Valentino of Fascism."[7] For instance, Muriel Whinfield (former chair of the Alton Women's Conservative Association) relinquished ties with the Conservative Party when she joined the BUF in 1936, and Dorothy Viscountess Downe (former chairman of the King's Lynn Conservative Women's Association) "left the Conservative Party in disgust . . . and joined the BU, in which movement she saw hope for the future of Britain, which she could not see in any other Party" (*News Chronicle*, 23 April 1934).

Women and Masculine Fascism

In his 1932 fascist manifesto, *The Greater Britain*, Mosley prescribed that "the part of women in our future organization will be important, but different from that of men; *we want men who are men and women who are women*" (Mosley

1932, 41). In 1936 A. K. Chesterton (1899–1973), editor of the BUF's journals and, later, the first leader of the National Front, wrote "Let us smash the matriarchal principle and return to the grand object of manhood" (*Action*, 9 July 1936). Both ideologically and structurally, British fascism championed the resurgence of "the masculine principle" as a means to purge the state of the effeminate "old men" and "old women" who personified postwar decadence. The BUF institutionalized male supremacy by organizing young men in the all-male compound in London, the Blackhouse, and in paramilitary formations intended to reenliven the esprit de corps of the trenches, and only men were able to rise to the highest echelons of the BUF's leadership.

However, alongside these male-identified formations and antiwoman assertions, BUF women were given a forum in which to express even feminine and feminist concerns. The movement addressed women's political and social interests, and it developed a coherent if not radical ideology of women in fascism, competing with interwar feminists by proposing equal pay for equal work, the abolition of the marriage bar (a policy whereby women had to relinquish their jobs upon marriage), and improved provisions for postnatal care and child welfare, and by emphasizing the urgent necessity for greater female representation in the governing institutions of the nation. Both male and female journalists commented on the peculiarly British character of the BUF's policies toward women by recognizing that "there can be no stronger characteristic of the British nation than its recognition of the equal partnership of men and women" (*Blackshirt*, 8 January 1938). This sentiment was reiterated when Anne Brock Griggs, the chief women's organizer, said that BUF attitudes could not be likened to German Nazism because "a differing racial tradition in their attitude toward women makes comparison between the two countries impossible" (*Fascist Quarterly*, July 1935, 164).

Spaces for Women in the British Union of Fascists

How did women exercise their agency within Britain's fascist movement? In a parallel universe to the male quasi–storm troop divisions, the male leadership assigned women to their own all-female public spaces, in the Women's Section (1933), Propaganda Patrol (1933), the paramilitary Women's Defence Force (1934), the Women's Drum Corps (1937), and in their own speakers classes and camps. In public, women acted as Blackshirts and stewards at political meetings, were involved in violent confrontations, spoke at meetings, raised funds, sold newspapers, marched, canvassed, organized children and youth groups, filled BUF posts of paid employment, and stood as candidates in elections the BUF contested.

Furthermore, the BUF furnished an image-oriented and ritualized sphere for women, complete with the women's uniform of black shirt and gray skirt, clips and brooches of the fasces and the BU's own lightning symbol, and dolls dressed in the traditional Blackshirt. The movement added a fascist touch to every stage in the life cycle, including weddings and christenings. For instance, when Mosley acted as best man at the wedding of his deputy Ian Hope Dundas to Pamela Ernestine Dorman in 1933, the collar of the bride's dress was "trimmed with golden Fasces" (*Fascist Week*, 22 December 1933).

Female political violence was similarly stylized. Members of the elite Women's

Propaganda Patrol held the St. John's Ambulance certificate, which trained them to provide first aid at meetings. Women blakcshirts were trained in jujitsu, fencing, and techniques to deal with opponents at meetings. However, they did not bear arms. "No male member of the BUF is permitted to use force upon any woman; and women Reds [communists and socialists] often form a highly noisy and razor-carrying section at fascist meetings. Thus we counter women with women" (*Fascist Week*, 17–23 November 1933). Sanctioning violence between women seemed to appeal to women as much as it must have transfixed the male gaze and aroused the male imagination. In 1934 a large number of women volunteered to receive this training, but only fifty were chosen (*Blackshirt*, 1 June 1934).

The movement took great pride in the fact that ten of its first one hundred prospective parliamentary candidates were women. When Mosley presented former suffragette Norah Elam to her putative constituents at a meeting at the Town Hall, Northampton, in November of 1936, he "said he was glad indeed to have the opportunity of introducing this first candidate, and it killed for all time the suggestion that National Socialism proposed putting British women back into the home" (*Action*, 28 November 1936). Although the BUF hoped to over-throw democracy by democratic and constitutional methods, it offered women greater representation than the other parties. In the 1935 general election, 10 percent of BUF prospective candidates were women, compared with only 3.2 percent of Conservative candidates, 6.3 percent of Labour, and 6.8 percent of Liberal candidates.

Although BUF propaganda paid lip service to sexual equality, the movement's sections were still divided according to gender. Furthermore, the party streamed women into certain traditional female political tasks, from canvassing and spreading fascism "by word of mouth" to keeping the branch premises in orderly condition. By mobilizing women to perform these quotidian functions for the party, the BUF was no more and no less bound to tradition than the Liberal, Conservative, and Labour parties in this same period, each of which likewise created hybrid spaces for women in which the domestic sphere was politicized. The BUF's gender hierarchies mirrored those of the democratic parties. Nonetheless, this gender sequestering of political functions in the BUF has led some historians to confound gender segregation with female subordination to the male leadership, and compare female and male power at face value (Durham 1992, 513–527). How did women themselves understand their own experiences and subjectify their place within the structures provided for women's participation?

By comparing Mosley's recollections with those of one of his women followers, it can be seen how the puzzlement concerning the position and the reception of women in the BUF has emerged. Mosley recalls male comradeship and female subservience, while BUF women retain very different memories. In one passage, Mosley writes, "I joined in free discussion of politics which always prevailed among us, in the sports to which our spare time was often given, in the simple club room gatherings where we would drink beer together and cups of tea prepared by women blackshirts" (1968, 305).

Louise Irvine remembers, however, that women members "weren't just tea makers, you know." In the Birmingham branch, men and women Blackshirts worked together, despite the division of the sections (Cullen 1996, 49–59). Nellie Driver, the very energetic women's district leader in Nelson, wrote "The men treated me as one of themselves, as a good comrade, and the only time they seemed to realize I was a woman was when danger threatened, and they put me in the middle for protection" (n.d., 30). In addition, women took charge of a branch in the absence of a willing male recruit, as in the case of the Bournemouth branch, where three women ran the show by organizing events, speaking at local meetings, taking care of all the administration and correspondence with national headquarters (NHQ), and renting and managing the shop space for the branch headquarters.[8] By acknowledging women's consent and even enthusiasm at being made to inhabit a woman's world within the movement, and by taking into account the personal experiences of BUF women, we can avoid perpetuating the BUF leadership's own rigid paradigm of gender compartmentalization.

The Dysfunctional British Fascist Family: Organization and Sexual Disorder

The Women's Section of the BUF was first established in March 1933, half a year after the formation of the movement in October 1932. The Women's Section was originally under the titular leadership of Maud Mosley, Sir Oswald's mother. In March 1934, the Women's Section began fortnightly publication of the *Woman Fascist*, an "enterprising little paper which will deal with news and problems peculiar to women members" (*Blackshirt*, 22–29 March 1934).[9] In April of 1934 Mary Richardson replaced Esther Makgill, chief woman officer in the Women's Section, who was suspended and forced to resign when caught embezzling funds from the Women's Section. One of Richardson's early initiatives was the creation of a National Club for Fascist Women, which opened on 24 April 1934. The first sign of the ebbing away of the independence of the Women's Section came in December 1934 when the women's headquarters were moved from its own building to a former chapel adjoining the BUF's national headquarters. By that same autumn the *Woman Fascist* ceased publication, and it was promised that women's news and views would be integrated into the BUF's main publications. By July 1935, with the first round of reorganization of the executive structure of the movement, Neil Francis-Hawkins, director general of propaganda, temporarily assumed charge of the Women's Section.

What did all these moves suggest about the status of women in the BUF? The loss of the Women's Section's own premises was a symptom of the decline of the BUF's fortunes after 1934, as well as a result of the role women played in exacerbating personality conflicts and internal dissent among the male leadership of the movement; it also indicated the gradual retrogression of fascist women's independence vis-à-vis the male membership.

The instability and turnover of female leadership paralleled the nature of conflict among the male leadership at the national headquarters.[10] The government's intelligence establishment began to monitor the activities of Britain's extreme-right movement starting in 1934, and, according to the resulting Special Branch reports, it is clear that women left their mark on the national BUF organization by contributing to the management and, indeed, the mismanagement of the movement.

The first scandal to agitate the Women's Section was when Esther Makgill was caught embezzling party funds. A chartered accountant had to be engaged to examine the books and go through various transactions.[11] Sex scandals complemented this strain of "criminality" and demonstrated the obvious double standard of male privilege. In April 1934, for instance, the reputation of women fascists was tarnished by allegations of sexual licentiousness at the Brixton Branch, which had to change its address "in consequence of complaints lodged respecting the loose character of members of both sexes attached to the Branch. The Brixton Road address was in filthy and unsanitary condition, and it was reported to the landlord that men and women fascists were habitually sleeping there together."[12] It is significant that four women were expelled from the movement because of their conduct, while the men, who must by necessity have acted as accessories to their offenses against propriety, were not expelled.

In a similar case, the BUF's national headquarters was shaken by scandal when it was reported that E. H. Piercey, a high-ranking officer at the NHQ, was having an affair with Mrs. Joyce, first wife of William Joyce, the man who became known as "Lord Haw Haw" when he broadcast for Nazi Germany during the war and was hanged in 1946 by the British.[13] While women members could be expelled for sexual misconduct, Piercey was tactfully reappointed as chief inspector of branches to avoid any further scandal.

Within the BUF and among its critics, male sexual promiscuity did not call forth censure, while similar behavior on the part of women remained an obvious target of contempt and caricature. The 1934 Labour Party return of a questionnaire on fascist activities claimed that in Stoke "loose women appear to be plentiful ... it only wants a red light on the door!"[14] Before the disastrous publicity spawned by the violent debacle of the BUF's Olympia rally on 7 June 1934 (at which antifascists staged an organized counterdemonstration that was met with Blackshirt brutality and many bloody incidents),[15] the tabloid press exploited to the full the sexually charged image of young women in uniform, trained in physical fitness and self-defense. One *Sunday Dispatch* headline read "Beauty Joins the Blackshirts," accompanied by images of women engaging in actual physical confrontation while practicing their jujitsu, with others of women performing fencing demonstrations. In 1934 Lord Rothermere's *Daily Mail* even organized a beauty contest for women Blackshirts, and the *Sunday Dispatch* offered prizes for the photograph of the most attractive woman in Blackshirt uniform. This seemed to be taking things in the wrong direction, however, and as Mosley was relieved to point out, Rothermere "was staggered not to receive a single entry; and I was embarrassed to explain that these were serious women dedicated to the cause of their country rather than aspirants to the Gaiety Theatre Chorus" (Mosley 1968, 344). That fascist women were seen as the sex objects of a gang of Blackshirt hooligans was further exemplified by the common insult directed at women members selling the *Blackshirt* on the streets: "Mosley's whores" (Cullen 1987, 100).[16] This comment reflects the popular perception that far from representing the vanguard of a movement of women politicized from the extreme Right, BUF men exploited BUF women for personal pleasure. However, BUF women did not accept this sexually exploitative and suggestively pornographic use of their image; instead, they attempted to develop an image of feminine sternness and fearlessness to complement their fanatical devotion.

Rather than serving as the sex toys for a gang of thugs, the nature and intensity of conflict in the Women's Section in 1935 exemplify the inclusion of women in the BUF's internal government. Their implication in the movement's internal discords emphasizes the active roles they played in the high politics of the movement. By January 1935 Maud Mosley and Mary Richardson were at odds over the latter's appointment to take charge of part of the Lancashire area. Lady Mosley threatened to resign if Richardson was not withdrawn, appealing to her son to understand that "then came Miss R. with her dishonest inefficiency, later backed by Miss S. and Miss A.—in sullen opposition to me. I was a stumbling block to collaring the machine and all its resources" (quoted in Mosley 1983, 91–92).[17] By the end of 1935 both Lady Mosley and Mary Richardson had left the BUF. Their clash was just one of the chronic feuds within the dysfunctional British fascist family.

Maud Mosley's last words on the atmosphere of the Women's Section during her tenure made clear the urgent necessity for a purge of disreputable elements: "Intrigue the whole time. Insubordination from people whose word you preferred to take to mine and who would disappear from the movement by your instructions. No, Tom [son], it is not quite good enough. There is a limit to one's endurance" (Mosley 1983, 92). The challenges to one's endurance exacerbated by mixing family life and politics were avoided thereafter: Mosley's second wife, Diana (née Mitford), was never an active member of the BUF, and Mosley's three children from his first marriage to Lady Cynthia were intentionally secluded from his fascist politics. The gloss over the leader's status as father and husband tended to accentuate his virility, and the fact that private domestic concerns were not to impede his single-minded commitment to revolutionary activities.

The BUF underwent frequent reorganization: in 1935, in 1937 as a response to the Public Order Act, and again in 1939 because of financial difficulties. With each subsequent stage in the restructuring of the movement, women's leadership was redefined and increasingly eclipsed within the hierarchy of the movement itself. However, the women's organization also received a boost in that the reorganization placed a new emphasis on building an electoral machine, and women were expected to take charge of canvassing, stand as BU candidates, and contest both the London County council and ward elections the BUF fought in 1937. While they had lost their independent status within the movement following the closing of the Women's Section's headquarters, from 1936, as candidates and canvassers, they were nonetheless meant to remain representatives of an enlightened British fascist view on the representation of women in the public sphere and in the nation's governing institutions.

The Radicalization of the Fascist Women for Peace and in War

The participation of women grew significantly from 1938 to 1940 when the BUF became increasingly an antiwar movement. As the leadership structure disintegrated progressively due to further retrenchment, the desertion of leading figures, and the eventual military draft of many male members, women members came into their own in new ways; they took over from the men and established a virtually all-female pressure group for peace. BU women differed from women in the mainstream parties by preparing to resist intervention at all costs, by accepting that violent tactics might be employed to support that end, and by constructing their antiwar mission as a revolutionary one against the power and prestige of the parties that represented the "old gang." Anne Brock-Griggs stressed that it was the business of fascist women to take charge of a street block system and "to bring and to maintain in the homes of the people the responsibility for their country's destiny. . . . The revolution is won on the streets and maintained on the streets" (*Action*, 9 April 1938). Brock-Griggs incited women's defiance and conducted street-level revolutionary and racist agitation. The war already in progress, she was arrested in November 1939 and charged under the Public Order Act with using insulting words, obstructing the police, and endeavoring to influence public opinion in a manner likely to be prejudicial to the "defence of the realm" (*Daily Herald*, 7 November 1939).

Alongside some relatively benign appeals to protect mother and child, BU women planned to infiltrate other organizations as a means of spreading Mosley's four-point plan for peace (Mosley 1940). As subversive elements in other organizations, they turned appeals to sentiment on their head and spearheaded a campaign that can only be described as peace mongering. Their instructions were as follows:

> In shops, with Parent's groups at school, in Co-operative Societies, in ARP, Women Citizen's Associations, Women's Institutes, as a member of any local organization, a woman has endless opportunities to inspire a solid resistance to the narcotic of false sentimentality. . . . Letters to the local Press are of great importance and even more opportunities will arise in the next few months, as the flow of Jewish refugee children increases and nauseating sentimentality is poured out from Press and pulpit. (*Action*, 28 January 1939)

The mobilization of fascist women against the "Jew's war" culminated in the launch of their Women's Peace Campaign in February 1940.[18] Building on the momentum of female initiative and aggression unleashed by their peace campaign, during the early stages of the war BU women began to replace men in leadership positions, and some even graduated to the post of district leader, which had previously been a male preserve. When the detention of BU members under Defence Regulation 18B1(a) went into full gear in May 1940, the women were entrusted with increasingly covert tasks (such as holding party funds and paying salaries), leading the authorities to surmise that "perhaps the most serious cause of disquiet is the continued activities of the wives of pro-Nazi Fascist leaders after their husbands have been rounded up."[19] Although women were not supposed to rise to generalized leadership positions, the original design was sidestepped when the real crisis of war emerged: the fixed ideology of male authority became defunct in the face of necessity. Certainly the fact that ninety-six BU women were interned under Defence Regulation 18B(1a) as suspected Fifth Columnists and as threats to national security further substantiates the assertion that they were far more than the submissive underlings or the benign bedfellows of their male leaders.

Stranger Bedfellows: Feminism and Fascism in Britain

How did British fascist women reconcile their fascist fanaticism with their gender identity? What reassured them that the BUF did not intend to turn the clock back on women's emancipation in Britain? The equivocal relationship between women and fascism in Britain is attributable in part to the early harnessing of the militant spirit that had characterized the prewar British women's movement, particularly the suffragettes.[20] Mary Richardson, Norah Elam, and Mary Allen had all been activists in the Women's Social and Political Union (WSPU) before the Great War. By the 1930s, with the suffrage movement defunct, these former suffragettes found a new outlet in the BUF, transporting with them the legacy of female militancy of their feminist struggle, as well as their growing disillusionment with the postwar condition of the women's movement in the aftermath of female enfranchisement. We may be reassured that only a very few ex-suffragettes transferred hero-worship from Emmeline Pankhurst to Mosley, and yet the political course from feminist militancy to fascist revolutionary fanaticism was not without its own subjective rationale. As Mary Richardson explained to her former sister-in-arms, Sylvia Pankhurst, Emmeline's daughter: "I was first attracted to the Blackshirts because I saw in them the courage, the action, the loyalty, the gift of service, and the ability to serve which I had known in the Suffragette movement" (*Blackshirt*, 29 June 1934; and Gottlieb 2000b, 105–125). Explaining her transfer of loyalties, Elam said, "Fascism is the logical, if much grander, conception of the momentous issues raised by the militant women of a generation ago" (Elam 1935, 290–298).

In recompense for their noteworthy support, the BUF gave a prominent place to the suffragettes in formulating its own prehistory. The suffragettes were claimed for fascism and as it did not seem too "far fetched to suggest that just as before the war the anti-parliamentary movement of Ulster Loyalists had within it the germ of a Fascist revolution, aborted by the war, so the women's Suffrage movement might, uninterrupted by the same cause, have been the direct inspiration and forerunner of the Fascist movement in Great Britain" (*Action*, 4 January 1939).

While Richardson, Elam, and Allen represented a reassuringly distinct minority among former suffragettes to embrace British fascism, each nonetheless transfused the extraparliamentary methods and militancy of her suffragette struggle to the BUF and, along the way, became convinced that the female franchise was "an empty vessel" (*Blackshirt*, 22 February 1935) and democracy a sinking ship. Moreover, Elam condemned postenfranchisement women for "having allied themselves to the very parties in the state which have treated them with such unprecedented contempt. They once again wear the primrose of the Jew Disraeli, the rosette in honour of Sir Herbert Samuel, the red emblem in commemoration of Karl Marx" (*Action*, 26 March 1936). It is very clear that Elam's prior proven commitments to feminism made little substantial difference in the degree of her espousal of anti-Semitism and her implied advocacy of the denial of citizenship rights to "others," a sign of personal eccentricity and considerable intellectual acrobatics.

While we are accustomed to National Socialists using the term "feminism" disparagingly by identifying women's emancipation with Jewish decadence (see Durham 1998, 22), it is noteworthy that rank-and-file BUF women continued to apply the term to describe their own ends. In praising the provisions made for women in the new Nazi Germany, BUF member Eileen Lyons stated that

> naturally their greatest effort is motherhood of the race. Why not? No matter how much the rampant "feminist" (the writer is one) may forget or deny it, the majority of women of every country are wives and mothers. . . . If National Socialism can dignify motherhood and develop a healthier race for Germany, then a Fascist Government can do it for England. (*Blackshirt*, 24 January 1936)

Lyon's viewpoint illustrates well the BUF's difficulty in reconciling praise for the Nazi regime with respect and affirmative identification for a British feminist heritage. BUF women made a concerted attempt to temper fascism's machismo by staking out a centrist position on the sexual-political spectrum. Olive Hawks, one of the BUF's bright young recruits, appraised that "after centuries of oppression, [women] are often going to unfortunate extremes to prove their independence from economic and moral custom. Fascism, in this as in everything else, upholds neither the reaction or the anarchy" (*Blackshirt*, 1 April 1933). By 1936, the movement was relieved to announce that its women's administrative organizer (northern), Olga Shore, belonged to the "generation of women who have turned from the ties of Victorianism to the wider world of business." The article went on to say that although Shore "is not an 'ultra-feminist,' in that she would not demand equality for women in spheres in which they are not suited, she is a strong supporter of the idea of feminine emancipation" (*Action*, 21 November 1936). Even as they evoked the colorful history of women's suffrage in Britain and occasionally borrowed the label "feminist" to connote female stridency, British fascist women adopted the militant methods of the suffragette movement to disseminate the Mosleyite gospel of British social, economic, and racial regeneration. Looking back on what motivated her political activities, Louise Irvine said, "I was by no means a feminist. . . . But I do believe in being accepted as an independent, free-thinking individual and when I joined the BUF I think that was how women were accepted" (Letter to author, 5 June 1996).

Conclusion

The BUF was most at ease with this idea of women's emancipatory aspirations in this more limited sense. The movement accepted that women should achieve representation in the future corporate state and have a voice in spheres concerning their welfare; their political activity was essential to the propagation and nurture of the British white Christian "race." They were appreciated as female activists but struggled, achieving inconclusive results, to integrate and reconcile what might be defined as feminist debates into the dialogue of the movement. Their success, if it can be called that, was to assert that women should not be excluded from the fascist exaltation of nationalist fanaticism. Through their enthusiasm for the revolutionary methods of the extreme right, their fearlessness in the face of the law, and their unquestioning commitment to their leader, they convinced the male leadership that female political engagement in the public sphere could be harnessed for fascist militancy, and thereby fertilize the palingenetic revolution of the British race and nation. In image, word, and deed, women in the British Union of Fascists proved themselves to be faithful female fanatics, and underscored the point that women on the extreme right can be politicized without constructing their politicization as a feminist project.

Notes

1. The East End of London has traditionally been the area of the city where new immigrants have settled. In the interwar period it was largely a Jewish area.
2. According to the statistics gathered by Special Branch, women represented 28 percent of participants.

3. Quoted in a letter from Eugenia Wright to the author, 6 May 1997. In the British fascist imagination, the Jew was always male and in a position of authority over British women (there were significantly few evocations of the image of the Jewish woman).

4. Advisory Committee to Consider Appeals Against Orders of Internment. Witness: Sir Oswald Mosley, 3 July 1940. United Kingdom, Public Records Office, HO 283/14/2–117.

5. "The word *fanatic,* which had a negative connotation earlier, was now [after the First World War] used as an adjective to signify heroism and the willingness to fight" (Mosse 1940, 178).

6. For a more detailed survey of the historiography, see Gottlieb 2000. Works that tend to cast the woman under fascism as victim include Friedan 1963 and Millett 1989. Macciocchi 1969 argues that women were duped into supporting Mussolini. Sontag 1980 points to women's complicity in developing the Nazi aesthetic. Stephenson 1975 points to the continuity in policies toward women throughout the interwar period in Germany; de Grazia 1992 offers a modulated view of women's agency; Passerini 1987 explores forms of (passive) dissent in everyday life. For the current debate on women's status as victims or perpetrators see Koonz 1987; Bock 1996; von Saldern 1994; Gordon 1987; Grossmann 1991.

7. *News Chronicle.* 23 April 1934.

8. Saunders Collection, Special Collections, University of Sheffield Library, File A.4.

9. No copies of the *Woman Fascist* are known to have survived.

10. See "Private Document—For Personal Used and Information Only." Robert Saunders Collection, University of Sheffield Library, A.2.

11. United Kingdom, Public Records Office, HO 144/20140/250–52.

12. Ibid.

13. United Kingdom, Public Records Office, HO 144/20144/242.

14. Labour Party Questionnaire on Local Fascist Activities, National Museum of Labour History, Manchester, LP/FAS/34/16.

15. Vindicator [pseud.], *Fascists at Olympia: A Record of Eye-Witnesses and Victims* (London: Gollancz, 1934).

16. This taunt had special resonance because of Mosley's reputation as a notorious womanizer.

17. See also United Kingdom, Public Records Office, HO 144/20144/183–84.

18. See United Kingdom, Public Records Office, HO 45/22895/3–5.

19. United Kingdom, Public Records Office HO 45/25726.

20. In 1903 Mrs. Emmeline Pankhurst, together with her daughters, established the Women's Social and Political Union, and in 1905 they launched a militant campaign for the vote. The militants came to be known as the "suffragettes."

3

Hindu Nationalist Women Imagine Spatialities/Imagine Themselves: Reflections on Gender-Supplemental-Agency

Paola Bacchetta

One midsummer evening several years ago, I found myself seated on the back of a motorcycle, speeding through the streets of Ahmedabad City, Gujarat. The driver was Kamlabehn, a thirty-five-year-old, rifle-trained member of the Rashtra Sevika Samiti (hereafter Samiti), the women's wing of India's most expansive Hindu nationalist organization, the Rashtriya Swayamsevak Sangh (hereafter RSS). Kamlabehn and I had spent the day discussing the Samiti in her parents' home when she suggested we take a break. Our destination was her favorite tea stall near Ellis Bridge.

As Kamlabehn navigated skillfully through the streets, every fifty feet or so we passed the usual roadside tea stalls surrounded by men. I knew that everything about these men and this scene disturbed her: the men's leisure appropriated at hardworking wives' expense; the obstacle they collectively constituted in our path; their assumed ownership of the streets; how they rendered women there either invisible or objects of heterosexual advances. Kamlabehn had critiqued this to me before and had provided her own framework for understanding it: "The sisterfuckers have forgotten their identity. They think they own the entire nation."

Not far from our destination, we came upon a cluster of men so sizable it cut a semicircle into the flow of traffic. Suddenly, Kamlabehn shouted: "Hold on!" And, with a jolt we sped directly into the crowd. Grown men scattered, trying to avoid the wheels, cursing us, their arms waving in futile attempts to pull us down, and failing that, to flag us down. But we just sped on. When finally we arrived at our destination, one very content Kamlabehn halted the motorcycle, dismounted, and announced: "You see, the streets do not belong to men only. You want to know about the Samiti? This, too, is the work of the Samiti."

Kamlabehn, Feminist Scholarship, My Arguments

This mow-down-the-men-in-the-streets-as-feminine-Hindu-nationalism inci-dent provokes questions about how Hindu nationalist women inseparably imagine spatialities/imagine themselves, and, about how their agency, or ability to act, is produced as effects of their imaginings and of spatialities. The imme-diate conditions for this mowing-down are Kamlabehn's production of gendered spatialities in flux across scale: the body, the streets, the city, the nation. They are constituted in a constantly shifting oppositionality. To confront the collective masculine body in her path, Kamlabehn's feminine body is called into being (Althusser 1984) as fierce and determined. To co-gender the streets, the streets must be transformed into a make-way-for-women battlefield. The arrival of the feminine *HinduNation* requires the dispersal of the male *StagNation*. If Kamlabehn's mowing-down effected a reversal in gendered relations of presence/power, this was clearly temporary. For as soon as we disappeared, the streets reverted to the earlier male order (or, in Kamlabehn's view, "disorder").

More widely, this incident evokes questions about Hindu nationalist women's agency, Hindu nationalist spatialities, and about the political stakes involved in Hindu nationalism for women and men Hindu nationalists and their opponents. To address these, I exit the microsituational and examine wider sources: data from interviews I conducted with Samiti members (1988 to 1992, in Ahmedabad, Gujarat, and in Nagpur and Pune, Maharashtra), Samiti publications, and, for comparative purposes, RSS publications.

I will propose three interrelated arguments in this chapter. The first concerns Hindu nationalist women's agency. I would like to briefly situate it in relation to a numerically small but theoretically expansive spectrum of critical feminist scholarship on right-wing women over the past twenty years (see, for example, the diversity of positions across Dworkin 1978; Thalman 1982; Blee 1991; Koonz 1987; A. Basu 1993; Sarkar and Butalia 1996; Jeffery and Basu 1998). Feminist scholars have understood right-wing women variously as *victims* of right-wing men, living in false consciousness; as *actors adhering* to the right because it reproduces and clarifies ideas already integral to their dominantly situated social milieu: as *later converts* to the right; or as conscious, calculating *political agents* who proactively choose the right.

Across the feminist literature on right-wing women, two characteristics stand out. First, feminists studying right wings tend to focus exclusively on women. This is understandable to compensate for the mass of nonfeminist studies of the right that totally ignore women. Second, few conceptual tools exist to explain the specificity of right-wing women's agency, and studies of rightist women often rely on agency notions proposed in the much more ample research on feminist agency.[1] This situation has produced two theoretical positions. In the first, which I will call *agentic differentialist,* rightist women's agency is understood as different from feminist agency because their agentic *objectives* (their political projects) differ. In the second, which I will call the *agentic similitude* tendency, rightist and feminist agency is understood as similar and sometimes the same. Agentic similitude is further divided into two subsets, each focusing on different *criteria.*

Scholars in the first subset, which I will call *agentic modality-based similitude,* primarily foreground agentic *modalities* to argue that modalities of rightist women's activism *resemble* feminist activism (Jeffery and Basu 1998), that rightist women selectively *draw from* feminist activism (Sarkar 1991), or that rightist women can simultaneously *be* feminists (Karam herein). In contrast, in the second subset, which I will call *agentic objectives-based similitude,* scholars foreground agentic *objectives* to argue that some forms of self-designated feminist and queer politics are right wing. Thus, Winter (see chap. 14 in this volume) draws on Guillaumin's (1995) notion of "right thinking" to sustain that otherwise critical white Australian feminists (and leftists) uncritically take right-wing positions on certain issues.

My work is informed by insights from all of the above perspectives and inscribes itself at various points within these debates. However, a central concern of this chapter is to begin to delineate some tools for understanding the specificity of rightist women's agency. To do so, I shift the focus from right-wing women versus feminists, to a gender comparative approach: women Hindu nationalists versus their male countertparts.

In that light, I argue that Samiti members' agency, albeit individually variable (Bacchetta 1999a), is loosely understandable as *gender-supplemental agency* in relation to their RSS male counterparts. I use *supplemental* in the Derridian (1967, 203–234) sense to mean: *additive* (appending something to an already completed entity) and *substitutive* (replacing that completed entity with something else). The Samiti's gender-supplemental agency is *additive* insofar as it is configured as excess in relation to the already completed RSS discursive and practical project. Samiti agency is also *substitutive* insofar as given Hindu nationalism's gender separatism, the Samiti's version of Hindu nationalism sometimes, in certain times and spaces, replaces (for Hindu nationalist women) RSS discourse and practice with its own. Samiti agency is *gender* supplemental in that it inscribes women and femininities into the otherwise male and masculinist Hindu nationalist project both by accretion and time-bound replacement.

The Samiti's *agentic stances* in relation to the RSS are many: consent, acquiescence, resistance, insubordination, revolt and even (like Kamlabehn) transgression. Some of these stances contain possibilities for women's *equality* and even *liberation,* but these possibilities do not materialize because of Samiti structural and individual-subject subordination to the RSS. The highest ranking Samiti officer reports to the RSS's highest offices, and many individual Samiti members are RSS men's female kin, thus controlled through the heteronormative family. This subjection is reinforced by gender inequalities at other scales: in the economy, electoral politics, education, and so on. The Samiti's gendered subjection inhibits women's supplemental agency from producing a paradigm shift into gender equity (Stacey and Thorne 1993) in the overall Hindu nationalist project. But also, Hindu nationalism's fractionalization into separate men's and women's organizations prevents what Charlotte Bunch terms an add-women-and-stir effect in which women would be homogenized into an overall male project. Instead, Samiti women's supplemental agency, as additive and substitutive alike, retains gender differentialism and produces *gender equilibrium* (not equality) in the overall Hindu nationalist project. In turn, women's stabilization of the project reinforces women's subordination therein.

Second, I argue that spatialities (body, streets, city, nation) are pivotal actors to and within Samiti agency. That is, these spatialities are not passive, abstract, inert matter, nor simply a backdrop onto which Samiti agency inscribes itself (Smith and Katz 1993; Massey 1993; Pile 1996). Spatialities are constructed by humans but they also play active roles in human (here, Samiti) agency as producers, signifiers, and material effects of relations of power: between Hindu nationalist women and men, and between (polarly gendered) Hindu nationalists and their (polarly gendered) Others (especially Muslims). In what follows, drawing from Laclau's (1986) remarks about fascist discourse's capacity to bind contradictory elements, I point to spatialities, as sites where Hindu nationalism's many contradictions around gender and sexuality are concentrated.

Third, I bring my first two arguments together in the proposition that it is useful to examine the relations between agency and spatialities through the lens of scale (meaning spatialities of different dimensions from small to large, such as body, city, nation). If we understand at what scale Samiti agency can develop or gets inhibited by the RSS and how, then we should be able to see more clearly Hindu nationalism's limitations for women. And, if we can unpack the gender contradictions of Hindu nationalist spatialities, we might render dominant male Hindu nationalism vulnerable to Hindu nationalist women's critique.

In what follows I begin with some background on Hindu nationalism, the RSS, and Samiti. Next, I compare RSS and Samiti notions of the Hindu nation. Then, I discuss the link between these notions of the Hindu nation and Samiti agency in two sites in Ahmedabad, before arriving at some concluding remarks.

Hindu Nationalism, the RSS, and the Samiti

Hindu nationalism arose at the turn of the last century in opposition to *Indian* nationalism. Indian nationalism proposes secular pluralism, including Indians of all faiths (Hindus, Muslims, Parsis, Buddhists, Sikhs, Christians, etc.) in the citizen-body. In contrast, Hindu nationalism is a religious genocidal fraternarchal micronationalism of elites, in which exclusively (certain) Hindus belong in the citizen-body. Hindu nationalism is a political project that strategically mobilizes selected religious elements for political ends; it should not be confused with Hinduisms as faiths (Nandy 1990).[2] It targets internal Others (Muslims, other non-Hindus, and Hindus it rejects such as homosexuals) for conversion, expulsion, or elimination. Male Hindu nationalism is fraternarchal (not patriarchal), entailing elder-brotherly rule, or the rule of the Brotherhood in Saffron as one pro-RSS monograph (Andersen and Damle 1987) is unwittingly titled. Hindu nationalist ideologues, leaders, and members are primarily upper-caste, bilingual elites, although for electoral purposes since the 1970s they have tried to recruit lower-caste people to their cause. Not all elites, however, are Hindu nationalists: elites are found across the political spectrum including (numerously) in movements against Hindu nationalism.

The RSS was founded in Nagpur, Maharashtra, in 1925, during India's nationalist struggle against British colonialism, won in 1947. The RSS was absent from this struggle. It identified Indian Muslims and secular pluralist Indian nationalism as primary enemies, not British colonialism. The RSS is renown for its implication in the murder of Indian nationalist Mahatma Gandhi and in orchestrating violence between Hindus and Muslims. Today the RSS has 2.5 million members, branches in 47 countries, and 200 affiliates: trade unions for professions; identity-based groups for various social sectors; and issue-oriented groups. In 1980 the RSS established the Hindu nationalist Bharatiya Janata Party (BJP), which has held state power since 1998.

The Samiti was created eleven years after the formation of the RSS, in 1936, in nearby Wardha, Maharastra. It was established by Dr. K. B. Hedgevar, RSS founder and first *sarsanghchalak* (supreme leader) for life, and Lakshmibai Kelkar, a widowed mother of eight. Kelkar became *pramukh sanchalika* (intellectual leader, the highest Samiti office) for life. A former Gandhian activist, she learned of the RSS through her sons who were members. Her activism was not unusual: at the time women swelled feminist organizations and anticolonial movements (the Gandhian-led Congress, Marxist groups, and smaller revolutionary "terrorist" formations). For the RSS, the Samiti usefully deterred women from other activisms, thereby ensuring continued Hindu nationalist male control over them. While other movements were co-gendered, Hindu nationalism was gender segregated from the start.

The Samiti has two different founding myths: both illuminate its sexual, spatial, and class politics (Bacchetta 1996). In English texts for bilingual elites, the Samiti claims it formed to keep women out of the (religiously plural) Indian Women's Movement (IWM), which it sees as Westernized and anti(Hindu) national. But, in Hindi versions for nonelites it cites the need to defend working women from predatory middlemen, and all women from all male sexual harassment. Both renditions produce Other-Outsiders (to the Hindu nation) who potentially provoke Hindu women's distance, *dis*affection and *dis*appropriation from Hindu men. Both also reproduce the our-women-in-danger founding myth encountered widely in state nationalisms globally (Nast 1998), but with some variation. That is, the Samiti's threatening Others include males and females, a sign of Samiti anxieties around potential female homosociality across religious divides. And, where other national narratives hold up men as women's saviors, the Samiti proposes that women should save themselves from danger.

Today the Samiti has 1.5 million members and a presence in several diasporic countries where the RSS has branches (including the United States, Britain, Kenya, Australia). Many Samiti activities are similar to the RSS's, but the two organizations never convene together.

The Samiti's gender separatism has two important consequences. First, separatism disables the Samiti by assuring women's exclusion from top echelons of RSS power. Second, separatism enables and justifies Samiti control over its own homosocial space, discourse, and praxis. From the Samiti's inception, Dr. Hedgevar claimed he had "no experience or knowledge about women's life" (Samiti 1989, ch. 4), so Kelkar "herself sketched" the Samiti's "working plan" (Samiti 1988, 15). Since "the basic principles and philosophy of women's life" are "different from that of men" (Samiti 1988, 15), Kelkar had to forge a Hindu nationalism that would appeal to women. Indeed, the RSS generally reduces Hindu women to selfless mothers of RSS sons, an image that some Samiti members find appropriate but that others (such as Kamlabehn) find very limiting.

To configure a female-friendly Hindu nationalism, Samiti ideologues from Kelkar onward sometimes reproduce RSS representations, but interpret them differently. For example, the Samiti reads the RSS's ideal mother of brave sons as an army commander (Kelkar n.d. but post-1985), thereby indirectly implying her control over RSS men. At other times, Samiti ideologues draw from sources the RSS ignores to construct feminine identities beyond the RSS imagination. As a result, different aspects of the Samiti's discourse are coherent with, or a-symmetrically "complementary" to, or even directly antagonistic to, the RSS discourse.

The Hindu Nation

The RSS's MiscegeNation versus Its Hindu Nation

Both the RSS and the Samiti define the Hindu nation as having three component parts: the people or citizen-body, the territory, and culture/religion. But they interpret these components differently.

For the RSS, the citizen-body is composed of men, the "sons of the soil" (Golwalkar 1996, 447). The nation's territory is a maternal body, symbolized by the goddess Bharatmata, the mother of ancient King Bharat, a *kshatriya* (ruler and warrior caste). Here, the RSS represents the nation as a symbiotic son/mother relation. Hindu women are supposed to be like Bharatmata, raising brave warrior sons. For the RSS, "today, more than anything else Mother" (Bharatmata) "needs such young, intelligent, dedicated and more than all virile and masculine" men (Golwalkar 1996, 448). In this configuration, the daughter, wife, and sisters are absent, as are the father and husband.

For the RSS, in an ancient past, Bharatmata was pure, Hindu men militaristic, and the nation glorious. Then Muslim invaders entered, violated Bharatmata and Hindu women's bodies, thereby provoking the nation's downfall, which was consolidated through British colonialism (Golwalkar 1939). For the RSS, India's Partition (1947) signifies carving up Bharatmata's symbolic/material body (her limbs became Pakistan and Bangladesh). The RSS claims Indian Muslims consider devastated Bharatmata as "just a hotel," thereby evoking Muslim temporary residence, heterosexual misconduct, and Bharatmata as a site of destructive Hindu-Muslim MiscegeNation analyzed elsewhere (Bacchetta 1999a). Here, the RSS temporalizes Muslim Otherness, Muslim anormative heterosexuality, and Hindu male weakness in the face of enemies by confining them to the recent undesirable past/present, and spatializes Muslims by excluding them from the ideal nation. For the RSS, to revive the glorious Hindu nation, Hindu men must (again) develop militaristic masculinity necessary to eliminate the nation's enemies (Muslims).

This notion of the Hindu nation contradictorily both reproduces and resists colonial notions of culture, power, gender, and sexuality. The British tried to justify colonialism by claiming India was uncivilized and too disorderly for self-rule; the RSS responds by affirming the Hindu nation's ancient glory. The British utilized India as a "pornotropics" (McClintock 1995) or a screen on which to project desires deemed anormative; the RSS deflects abject desires (here hypersexuality) onto Muslim Others violating Bharatmata and Hindu women. The colonizers tried to discredit Brahmins, the caste of Hindus' spiritual leaders, by designating Brahmin men effeminate (Nandy 1985; Sinha 1997); the RSS counters by positing ancient/future Hindu militaristic masculinity. The British claimed Indian men abuse Indian women (they strategically globalized rare practices such as sati) without mention of British male abuse of British and Indian women; the RSS projects this onto Muslims victimizing Bharatmata. Finally, the RSS reworks the colonial gender-savior narrative in which "white-men-save-brown-women-from-brown-men" (Spivak 1994) such that Hindu-nationalist-men-save-Bharatmata-and-Hindu-women-from-Muslim-men.

To construct Bharatmata as victimized, RSS, ideologues selectively foreground or efface other Hindu territorial goddesses. For example, they draw on the devastated Bharatmata of Bankim Chandra Chatterjee's renown novel *Anandamath*, who is central to conflict between Hindu ascetics and Muslims (then the British). They similarly evoke Bhudevi (the Vishnavite sect's earth goddess), who in some mythologies is saved from demons by the god Vishnu. Here, Vishnu symbolizes Hindu nationalist men and the demon Muslims. In contrast, RSS ideologues discard the fierce, demon-battling goddess Kali, as conceptualized by the renown nineteenth-century saint Ramakrishna Paramahansa. This omission is significant because the RSS asserts strong connections to Ramakrishna, and

M. S. Golwalkar, a major RSS theoretician of the Hindu nation, claims early membership in Ramakrishna's religious order. However, for the RSS, Bharatmata's victimization is necessary to justify ideal militaristic Hindu masculinity. Here, the territory (Bharatmata) is produced as a symbolic and materialized effect of RSS male power.

The Samiti's Version: The Hindu Nation as InsubordiNation

The Samiti accepts the RSS Bharatmata but substitutively assigns her different characteristics. She needs no male protection. She is the "Supreme power of the universe" (Samiti 1988: 43). Further, the Samiti adds women into the RSS male citizen-body; it becomes co-gendered. Women citizens are "Bharatmata's daughters," and Bharatmata's "prototypes" (Samiti 1988: 50). Like Bharatmata, Hindu women have power "capable of destroying all the evil practices as well as tendencies," but they "must have the discrimination to use it in a way benevolent to our nation" (Samiti 1988, 55).

The notion that Hindu women require "discrimination" has multiple meanings. Denotatively "discrimination" means good judgment. Connotatively, it evokes a threat: an undisciplined woman might get out of (male) control. This threat indicates that Samiti agency has the potential to disrupt the RSS and Samiti's gender equilibrium. But no such transgression will occur because women *must* use their power "in a way benevolent" to the overall Hindu nation (ultimately dominated by men).

Finally, the Samiti reiterates that Indian Muslims violate Hindu femininity. But, in contrast to the RSS, the Samiti adds in a daily prayer that Hindu women have "never submitted meekly to anyone" (Samiti 1988, 43).

To construct an all-powerful Bharatmata, the Samiti substitutes RSS sources with goddesses from two Hindu texts. One is the *Devî-Bhâgavata-Purâna*, a text of the Shaktâ sect, dated variously as ninth and fourteenth century A.D. Shaktâs worship *shakti* (feminine energy) in the form of a powerful goddess. The second is the *Devî Mâhâtmya* (lit., the Great Goddess), which is part of the *Mârkandeya-purâna*, dated variously as circa third to fourth century A.D. and seventh to ninth century A.D. In both texts the most powerful divinity is an independent goddess without a male consort.

In the *Devî-Bhâgavata-Purâna*, the goddess creates all deities and demons from her inexhaustible energy. In the *Devî Mâhâtmya*, she overpowers demons. Samiti members I interviewed often narrated the same *Devî Mâhâtmya* episode: male demons threaten to destroy the world, and male gods, unable to stop them, call the Great Goddess. She first appears as the gentle goddess Pârvatî. But as she gauges the demons' power, she transfigures into fiercer forms, with corresponding names, to challenge them. After a bloody battle, she emerges victorious as the warrior goddess Kâlî, with the demons' skulls strung around her waist. The goddess' Althusserian-Butlerian (1984; 1990) interpellation performance, through physical transformation, are operative in Samiti imaginings of its organizational goddess, Ashtabhuja, and ultimately Samiti members' individual bodies.

Against the RSS's somewhat monolithic conception of today's Hindu women as victimized (like Bharatmata) son-producers, the Samiti puts forth serial feminine subject positions: loyal wives, supportive sisters, but also powerful mothers, rulers, warriors, *pracharikas*, and saints. (For a full overview see Bacchetta 2002.) Some are locked into gendered binary relations, wherein women are subjected to individual men, such as: wife/husband, or younger sister/elder brother. However, the Samiti provides positions outside individual subjection, by pairing women to acceptable entities such as: the woman ruler and warrior linked to the (co-gendered) Hindu people; the *pracharika* (who according to Kamlabehn is "married to the nation, not to any man"); and female saints bound to religion.

To imagine women's identities, Samiti ideologues select symbolic referents (goddesses, female principles, mythological figures) primarily from Hinduisms-as-faiths, reinterpret them, and hold them up as models. Kelkar created the Samiti's goddess Ashtabhuja (lit., "Eight-Armed Goddess") as a symbolic support for this purpose. Ashtabhuja is a name for Durga, a fierce *Devî Mâhâtmya* goddess, worshipped across castes. Iconographically, Durga often rides a lion and, like Ashtabhuja, carries weapons in her eight hands. However, the Samiti describes Ashtabhuja not as Durga but rather as "an integral combination of Mahakali, Mahasaraswati, and Mahalaxmi" symbolizing, as these three well-known goddesses do, "Co-ordination of Strength, Intellect, and Wealth" (Samiti 1988: 4).

Ashtabhuja illuminates the Samiti's contradictory submission and resistance to RSS dominance. The Samiti concedes to limit Ashtabhuja to three goddesses, thereby curbing her range of characteristics. For example, Ashtabhuja excludes the Sat Mâtrikâs (Seven Mothers), powerful goddesses in the *Devî Mâhâtmya* and local Maharashtrian popular Hinduisms-as-faiths. But, Ashtabhuja also challenges RSS dominance: her presence defies RSS erasures of women; she contains the warrior goddess Kali's fiercest form (Mahakali); and she spans all classes at a time when the RSS remained elitist.

Further, Samiti members use the threefold goddesses in Ashtabhuja, Hindu notions of *bhavas* (emotions) toward goddesses, and the *Devî Mâhâtmya*'s interpretive possibilities to stretch Ashtabhuja's meanings for themselves. Elsewhere Martin and Kryst (1998, 208) point to "mimesis and both sympathetic and contagious principles" characterizing female devotees' relations to the Virgin Mary. Samiti *bhavas*, too, can be mimetical (woman as like goddess) as stated above (Bharatmata as Samiti members' prototype). But Samiti members also relate to the goddesses as friend-friend (*sakhya*), child-parent (*vatsalya*), or protected servant–protecting master (*dasya*). In interviews in Ahmedabad (Bacchetta 1999b), I found that some individual Samiti members mimetically consider themselves Kali-like warriors (it will surprise no one to know that this is the case with Kamlabehn). Others identify as Mahalakshmi-like wives, protected by Mahakali, but capable of becoming Mahakali if required. Others see themselves as Mahasaraswati, but with Mahalaksmi and Mahakali capacities. In all these imaginings, Samiti bodies, like the goddesses, are produced as materialized effects of gendered power relations: as threats are progressively felt, women can transform into fiercer forms. The presence of a spectrum of goddesses as referents within Hinduism allows for a wider range of femininities (not female masculinities) than in Western Judeo-Christian contexts.[3]

A second central Samiti symbolic referent is Ahalyabai, of the epic *Ramayana* (Samiti 1990). As the story goes, Ahalya, desired by the Vedic god Indra, is instead given to Gautam for his good deeds. One day, the disappointed Indra disguises himself as Gautam, enters Ahalya's chambers, and rapes her. Gautam arrives, discovers them, and castrates Indra (fear not: his phallus is subsequently surgically restored). Gautam forces the now impure Ahalya to undergo penance. She meditates in an ashram so intensely that she becomes like stone. Eventually the god Rama enters, touches her with his foot, thereby purifying her, and she becomes animated again. For the Samiti, Ahalya signifies Hindu woman's (and Hindu society's) rape by an outsider. Above I mentioned the Samiti maintains that Hindu women have "never submitted." The Ahalya narrative confirms insubordination (Ahalya thought she was having sex with Gautam) but admits rape did indeed take place. Ironically, here the Samiti equates Indra, a major god in upper-caste Hinduism, with British colonizers and "Muslim invaders," but also with Hindu men. This contradicts the RSS idea that only Muslims and Others intrude and violate.

In yet another Samiti sexual violation narrative, this time centered on Muslim males, the sixteenth-century Moghul Emperor Akbar enters the women-only space of Meena Bazaar in Delhi dressed in drag as a veiled woman to abduct women (Kelkar 1988, Discourse 10). Akbar unknowingly abducts the niece of Rana Pratap Singh, a Hindu king who fought Akbar and whom Hindu nationalists consider a Hindu nationalist hero.[4] The niece humors Akbar, gets him drunk, and plans to kill him. But ultimately she spares him, an act the Samiti interprets as signifying Hindu nationalist women's decency.

I want to stress two main points about these violation narratives. First, in both the Samiti represents women's victimization spatially. Hypersexual males intrude into spaces that are supposed to be safe: Indra enters Ahalya's home, and Akbar enters the female space of the market. Second, for the Samiti, women either are instrumental in saving themselves (as Ahalyabai through meditation) or do so without Hindu male assistance (as Rana Pratap Singh's niece). Thus, Kamlabehn's disgust for male bodies (across faiths) occupying Ahmedabad's streets and excluding women, takes on deeper and wider meanings, as does her sudden enactment of mow-down-the-men-as-Hindu-nationalism.

Ahmedabad: The City-in-Process (of Hindu Nationalization)

Here I briefly discuss Samiti agency in relation to Samiti imaginings of two sites in Ahmedabad: the park and the commercial district.

First some contextualization is necessary. Ahmedabad is the eastern state of Gujarat's most populous city, with 4.8 million inhabitants. The region has long been inhabited, including by civilizations that traded with ancient Sumer and Egypt. In the third century B.C. the area was integral to Ashoka's empire. Ahmedabad was founded in 1411, by Sultan Ahmad Shah; thus its name (*bad* means "city of"), which Hindu nationalists desire to change, in the Hindu nationalization process, to *Karnavati* (after the queen of Chittor who in 1535 fought Moghul Emperor Bahâdur Shâh). In 1572, Emperor Akbar conquered Ahmedabad. It remained a business center of the Empire until Emperor Aurangzeb's death in 1707. From 1818, the British called Ahmedabad the Manchester of India: it housed (British-usurped) textile mills. Today, Ahmedabad remains India's textile capital. In 1915 Mahatma Gandhi, born in Gujarat, founded his Sabarmati Ashram in Ahmedabad, making the city central to anticolonial struggle. Today Gujarat is the only state in which the Hindu nationalist party, the BJP, holds power without a coalition, but Mahatma Gandhi's presence continues to be felt very strongly. Even the local BJP selectively incorporates, often distortedly, some of his ideas. In the postcolonial period, several Ahmedabad streets were named after Gandhi, and he remains iconographically present in statues (one is a favored place for antistate demonstrations). Gandhian principles inspire several organizations, such as the Self-Employed Women's Association (SEWA), the world's first and largest autonomous women's trade union. SEWA is comprised of members across classes, religions, and castes, and organizes in the informal sector (among sweepers, snackmakers, construction workers, domestic workers, rag-pickers, etc.). SEWA has a major presence in Ahmedabad's particularly active women's movement.

Gujarat is one of India's most urbanized, economically intense, and media- and communications-saturated (with newspapers, TV, radio, telephones) states (Sheth 1998, 12). Ahmedabad has the largest sector of castes involved in commerce in the country. Since the 1970s, the city's Muslim population has grown to more than 15 percent of the population and has entered the political process, while lower classes have expanded in the inner city through rural exodus (Sheth 1998: 84). As women have won new rights, women's suicide rates have declined in Gujarat and in Ahmedabad since the mid-1980s, but remain among India's highest, as is the rate of deaths related to Hindu nationalist and Islamist violence (Sheth 1998: 127).

The Park: Law Gardens

The first site I will discuss is Law Gardens, a central park contingent to Ahmedabad's Law College. It shares some characteristics with other (past and present) parks in India. As Kaviraj (1997) notes, historically Indian city parks were sites of colonial spectacles of power.[5] Colonial power was manifested in parks through colonial state pageantry, military assemblies, segregation for colonizers' exclusive use, iconographic representations such as famed colonizers' busts, and sometimes in the naming of parks to honor notorious colonizers. Parks are also sites of anticolonial resistance through acts such as legal and illegal demonstrations, public hunger strikes, and daily "trespassing" in defiance of segregation laws. After colonialism, parks became sites of representations of postcolonial state power through state pageantry, military assemblies, replacement of colonizers' busts with those of celebrated nationalists, and their renaming. Today parks are simultaneously sites of postcolonial democratization. People of all classes, religions, castes, genders, sexualities, languages, and regions inhabit and traverse them, sometimes at different moments. And public events such as festivals and protests are held there.

Law Gardens is inhabited differently at different times. At night, it belongs to otherwise homeless individuals and families, to sex workers, heterosexual men seeking sex workers, illicit heterosexual lovers seeking privacy, and men seeking men. During the day, various working poor install their portable businesses there: the clothes washer and ironer, the tea seller, the snacks hawker. In the evening, business people insert stalls at Law Garden's borders, transforming it into an open market for crafts, artworks, and household items. At times, co-gendered religious events, marriages, or political protests take place there. All the while, the postcolonial state provides male (and some female) police protection.

The Samiti regularly disrupts the state-protective, co-gendered, heterofamilial, hetero-extrafamilial, and men-only scenarios of the park, as it holds one-hour *shakha* (neighborhood cell) meetings there daily. Samiti members clear the space (not so violently as Kamlabehn's mowing-down operation) and assemble in paramilitary formation. They listen to their leaders lecture on Hindu nationalism, and they train in paramilitary skills (in wielding a *lathi* or a long stick weapon, archery, or karate). This paramilitarization operation calls to mind colonial and postcolonial state power spectacles, especially those achieved through bodily performance. It evokes the *akhara* or the wrestler's gymnasium attached to temples, with the variation that *akharas* are male spaces (Alter 1992). The Samiti produces the park as paramilitarized, Hindu nationalist, feminine separatist space, through the female body.

The type of female Hindu nationalist body produced in and by the park is fierce, alert, and determined. In turn, the fierce female body leaves its trace in the park: no men would dare interrupt the homosociality of Samiti space. Thus the *shakha* is a moment of the power-of-association in the sense of Arendt (1975), a power rooted in mutual action. John Allen (1999, 211) reminds us that this form of collective empowerment generally requires public space. But for the Samiti, there is no private/public dichotomy. Instead inner and outer spatial instances are relational within a continuum as home and world (Kaviraj 1997). All are Hindu nationalist spaces (becoming). Thus, for the Samiti, collective empowerment occurs in many sites and through multiple processes: Samiti bodies produced in the park are carried over to other sites while those produced in other sites (home, the market, the Internet) are carried over into the park that transforms them. This multinodal, processual production, invoked symbolically through the form and name-changing *Devî Mâhâtmya* goddess who informs the Samiti goddess Ashtabhuja, illuminates Kamlabehn's mow-down-the-men-in-the-streets-as-Hindu-nationalism. For Kamlabehn, inserting women into male streets requires a fierce feminine body, the conviction that the streets should ultimately belong to the entire citizen-body composed of both women and men, and the notion that men's exclusive occupancy is illegitimate. Kamlabehn's action, then, can be understood as an effect of her notion that all spaces must be produced as (bigendered) Hindu nationalist spatialities.

Commercial District

Let us shift to Ahmedabad's major commercial district in the center of the old city. It is a site of intense local-to-global flows: of capital, goods, services, people (of all classes, faiths, castes, genders, sexualities, regions) and of information. The middle-class Samiti members I have spoken with traverse this space regularly as individual consumers. Some also oversee Samiti projects such as *namkeen* (fried snacks) sales by lower-caste women whom the Samiti has recruited. The sellers make these snacks themselves in a Samiti income-generating project ironically modeled on income generating projects of feminists whom the Samiti condemns as "Westernized."

From time to time, the Samiti transforms the commercial district into an anti-Other symbolic battleground. For example, in 1988, following up on RSS claims that Saudi Arabian Muslims provide local Muslims with capital for their businesses, the Samiti organized a picket and boycott of "Muslim cloth" stalls. The Samiti's notion of "Muslim cloth" is paradoxical: in Ahmedabad weavers of this cloth are both Hindu and Muslim, and SEWA, too, includes women weavers across religions.

Local *shakha* leaders generated the anti–"Muslim cloth" actions, beginning within their own middle-class Hindu neighborhood. One leader, Ratnabehn, told me she called neighborhood women to her home, explained the Samiti position on "Muslim cloth" and requested that they join the boycott and walk the picket line. Initially she drew about fifteen women. But, she remarked, this effort could not be sustained because most middle-class Hindu women are "more interested in buying fancy cloth than in serving the nation."

Notwithstanding their apparent failure, the picket and boycott are particularly significant interventions. They attempt to achieve Hindu nationalism's *religioned cleansing* at a site where Hindu and Muslim social and capital flows intersect. Moreover, these actions try to recall, albeit in a highly deformed manner, traces of earlier Indian nationalist anticonsumption struggles centered on cloth, around which flowed discourses of gender, sexuality, and the (Indian) nation. That is, as early as 1908, in his *Hind Swaraj* (India's self-rule), Mahatma Gandhi identified cloth produced in Ahmedabad's British-owned textile mills and cloth imported from Britain as central effects of colonial exploitation and impoverishment (Gandhi 1927, 407). Responding to union organizer Anasuyabai Sarabhai (foremother of SEWA founder Ila Bhatt), Gandhi led Ahmedabad mill workers' strikes for higher wages (Gandhi 1927, 355). He urged middle-class Indians to boycott British cloth and to revive the *chakhra* (spinning wheel) to spin their own cotton. Masses of women were first politicized in the national movement when, in 1919, Gandhi appealed to them to join the *swadeshi* ("own country," meaning Indian production and use) movement against British cloth (Bald 2000). Gandhi linked spinning to chastity: women producing their own cloth would not need to work outside the home where they risked sexual harassment to pay for foreign cloth. All the while, he urged men to emulate characteristics he equated with Indian femininity: courage, right ethics, chastity, and nonviolence (Katrak 1992; Patel 1987; Kishwar 1985a, b).

In its actions against "Muslim cloth,"the Samiti drew upon these prior struggles, reworking them into a Hindu nationalist frame. But, whereas Gandhi had addressed women *across faiths*, the Samiti called only upon Hindu women. And whereas Gandhi worked against mass impoverishment and middle-class consumption, the Samiti's action encompassed no such critique. In fact, Ratnabehn told me she did not care if (Hindu) women bought cloth to their heart's content as long as it was from *Hindu* merchants.

The Samiti targeted "Muslim cloth" stalls because it imagined them as foreign (invading) sites of penetration into Hindu nationalist space. The Samiti's penetration imaginings rely on equations with its other spatialities: the commercial district as victimized Bharatmata, and excessive Muslim capital and "Muslim cloth" symbolizing the hypersexed Muslim male body (of the Samiti's Indra and Akbar narratives and elsewhere [Bacchetta 1999b; 1994a]). For the Samiti "Muslim cloth" is inappropriately, too closely, connected to the hypersexed Muslim male body (he sells it) and the Hindu woman's body (who wears it). The Samiti desires to disrupt this exchange because it too corporally connects these figures to each other (but in the process the Samiti also foregrounds the connection and exchange). The Samiti can propose female resistance by relying on

Ashtabhuja's fierce aspects and on the all-powerful Bharahmata as models. Ultimately the Samiti's attempt to produce the commercial district as a Muslim-free zone demonstrates how landscape, gender, and sexuality intersect in Hindu nationalist relations of power.

Concluding Remarks

To conclude I would like to make three points. The first is about this very local study. Kamlabehn's mow-down-the-men incident can be understood as part of a wider set of collisions, primarily between Hindu nationalist women and both Hindu nationalist and Other men. The collisions appear in antagonisms between the RSS and Samiti imaginings of the nation's territoriality (wherein RSS's victimized Bharatmata versus Samiti's Bharatmata as all-powerful), its citizen-body (wherein RSS militaristic males only versus Samiti bigendered citizens including powerful females), and in the Samiti's Ahalya and Akbar narratives that present male invaders. Samiti members collectively and materially expand these collisions as they take over Law Gardens and work to remove Muslim male flows from Ahmedabad's commercial district. Finally, Kamlabehn extends the collisions individually in her mow-down-the-men street action. In all of these collisions, Hindu nationalist women temporarily substitute female Hindu nationalist spatialities for male spatialities, marginalizing both Hindu and Muslim men. However, ultimately, given the Samiti's structural gendered subordination to the RSS, this substitutive agency is merely additive. That is, just as Kamlabehn's mow-down-the-men action only temporarily disrupts male spatialities by adding women into them, so do the Samiti's discourse and actions only temporarily disrupt the ongoing flow of RSS dominance.

My second point is about the possible wider implications of the gender comparative method. It revealed points of antagonism between women and men's same right-wing project, and helped pinpoint where women's agency can develop or gets blocked. Given that this women's version of a right wing project has the capacity to empower women (providing them self-confidence, a worldview, transforming their bodies, allowing for greater spatial mobility since they can protect themselves), revealing its limitations for women might be useful to resist it. A certain portion of right-wing women, such as Kamlabehn, if they became aware of the full scope of such antagonisms and blockages, might stir up some major gender trouble to make the overall project more woman-friendly, and failing that, might think about leaving the right altogether.

My third point is about the wider implications of a focus on spatialities and scale. I have examined Hindu nationalism not only as an imagined community (Anderson 1983) but also as an imagined gendered geopolitical entity that entails many interrelated spatialities across scale. Smith (1992) insightfully remarks that typically political power is exercised by "jumping scales." We saw above that claims to power established at one scale (for example the Hindu nation) can be expanded to other scales (such as a city park, commercial district, or street) and vice versa. If we wish to resist right-wing movements, it will be useful to know what spatialities they conceptualize and at what scales they operate. It is only then that we can figure out when and where, at what scale, it would be most effective to intervene.

Notes

I am indebted to Margaret Power for invaluable feedback on this essay. I am also grateful to Anjali Arondekar, Paula Chatterjee, Laurence Cohen, Mona Domosh, Rosemary Marangoly George, Gayatri Gopinath, Tamar Mayer, Radhika Mongia, Heidi Nast, Geeta Patel, and Parama Roy, for insightful feedback on an oral version.

1. This observation emerged dialogically in discussions with Margaret Power and belongs to both of us. (Thank you Margaret).
2. I pluralize Nandy's concept to foreground multiple positions, interpretations, and reinterpretations, within "Hinduism."
3. See Halberstam's *Female Masculinity* (1998). If masculinity implies characteristics assigned to males in gender/sex systems and female masculinity their shift to females, then Samiti fierceness cannot be read as female masculinity.
4. In one of their most renown confrontations, the 1576 battle of Haldighati or Gogunda Singh's army was led by a Muslim general, while Akbar's was led by a Hindu general.
5. For a discussion of London produced of its own imperialism, see Driver and Gilbert 1998.

4

Framing Volksmoeders:
The Politics of Female Afrikaner Nationalists, 1904–c.1930

Marijke du Toit

For the past several years, a framed photograph has accompanied me, to be propped on my desk or hung in one study or other. A figure stands on the edge of a railway platform. A shapeless coat and hat hide the apparently female body from easy perusal. Next to the woman are two suitcases, strapped shut. Light glances off her face, outlines a mouth that seems unsmiling—contemplative? Her body, the turn of her head, her eyes seem to follow the strong diagonal of the railway lines as they recede, or advance, beyond the frame. My gaze follows this path, is drawn back along the tracks to where they narrow into the distance, and I note the landscape opposite: small whitewashed houses, a fence, a field or *veld*, a sloping horizon. What brought the traveler to this deserted place? What is her destination?

But the meanings I have invested in this image hinge on the locations where I first encountered it, and on that narrowing of place and identity that my spatial and verbal framing may bring to the play of light and shade that is a photograph. In Cape Town's state archives where I was researching women's part in the advance of Afrikaner nationalism, the figure is identified as "M. E. Rothmann, organising secretary of the ACVV." The acronym refers to the *Afrikaanse Christelike Vroue Vereniging* (Afrikaans Christian Women's Society), founded in 1904. Its members, most of them middle-class townswomen or farmers' wives, combined cultural nationalist projects with charity for *armeblanken* (poor whites) in most towns and districts of the Cape. I found another print in Rothmann's autobiography, similarly described. *My Beskeie Deel* (My modest contribution) chronicled her life as journalist, author, and key player in this Afrikaans women's welfare organization—the part she played in the endeavors of her *volk* (people).

Since childhood I have occasionally taken a weighty volume from a shelf in my father's study. The *Gedenkboek van die Ossewatrek* (Commemorative book of the Ox-wagon trek) chronicles the centenary celebrations of the Great Trek, held in 1938. The embossed leather cover, textured with ox wagons, indigenous flowers, and the emblems of Afrikaner nationalist cultural organizations, elicits a mixture of boredom and fascination. These pages hold the heavy weight of constructed tradition, chronicle the success of a countrywide pageant that drew those pale-skinned Afrikaans speakers designated "Afrikaners" into a celebration of their pioneering forebears. The celebrations were the culmination of some thirty years' work by Afrikaner nationalists to construct and popularize a history of their *volk*; they also reflected a new ability by ideologues to centralize power and stage a

Figure 4.1 M. E. Rothman, Organizing Secretary of the ACVV.

successful, countrywide cultural spectacle. Leafing through the numerous visual records of people "reenacting" the *voortrekkers'* triumphant progress into the African interior, the strongly gendered nature of "traditional" dress is particularly striking. In one photograph, women wearing pure white dresses, stern faces scarcely visible beneath their bonnets, fly flags against receding mountains, a tall sky. The caption leaves no room for ambiguity: "United Front: Women from De Rust symbolise the action and outlook of the Afrikaans Woman." The figures are anonymous: it is enough that these are Afrikaner women.

Perhaps it was the contrast with pictures such as these that drew me so strongly to Rothmann's image. If snapshots of women in their flying machines, apparently liberated from the strictures of gravity, would soon grace the pages of South African newspapers, this framing of an Afrikaans female traveler—earthbound, but not treading the imagined spoor of ox wagons—was still unusual and evocative. Here, a female figure was juxtaposed with railway tracks.

In the context of Southern African history, railways are themselves a potent symbol—of imperial triumphs and settler ambitions, of the incremental advance of market economies into rural spaces. By the 1930s, the proximity of iron tracks often signaled "racially mixed" slum areas in South African towns and cities. As apartheid planners transformed urban geographies in the 1950s and '60s, the fenced lines of metal and gravel upon which segregated coaches traveled would often separate "blanke"[1] and "black" spaces. From the early decades of the cen-

Figure 4.2 "United Front: Women from De Rust symbolize the action and outlook of the Afrikaans woman."

tury, organized Afrikaans women also frequently discussed rail travel. When the ACVV held its annual congress to discuss safeguarding the morals of the *volk*, plans for promoting "their" language, culture, history, and measures for extending help to *arme blanken*, many delegates traveled by train from home villages, towns, and farms. Hence, perhaps, the regular demands for racially segregated coaches among the resolutions brought to vote.

From the 1920s, ACVV members in Cape Town, alarmed at "racial mixing" and an apparent tendency among the recently urbanized to leave the traditionally Afrikaans Dutch Reformed Church (hereafter DRC), visited homes in poor neighborhoods that crowded close to inner-city railway lines. It was in Cape Town's central station that a concerned Rothmann listened to a working-class "white" girl chatting in Afrikaans. To Rothmann's ears, she sounded like "a coloured of very inferior class . . . so rough, so ugly, so typically coloured." Around 1935, it was in a railway carriage that leaders of the four provincial women's welfare societies held an emergency meeting to strategize against the DRC synod's attempts to make them cede their organizations' independent status. In spite of long-standing and close cooperation with the DRC, they were determined to maintain separate structures.

The photograph itself was probably taken on one of Rothmann's journeys as organizing secretary of the ACVV. From 1928 and throughout the 1930s, she traveled toward far-flung rural destinations by train (changing to motorcar or wagon for the final stretch), advising branches on official policy and ascertaining the extent to which they understood the ACVV's Afrikaner nationalist and philanthropic aims. Very likely, the suitcase of this contributor to Carnegie-sponsored research on the "poor white problem" (published in 1932) also contained notes and letters detailing the painful, multiple childbirths of isolated (Afrikaans, "white") women, the lack of modern medical services for maternity care, and plans for a network of rural maternity clinics.

But what exactly could the striking framing of images in that other photograph of anonymous, white-clad women signify? Indeed, Anne McClintock (1995, 369) uses the picture from 1938 to illustrate a discussion of "the gender component" of "Afrikaner Nationalism . . . synonymous with white male interests, white male aspirations, and white male politics," an "imperial gospel" with "the contradictory figure of the *volksmoeder,* the mother of the nation" at its center. In its new surroundings (where it is shown together with several more pictures of the Tweede Trek), the picture has a somewhat different—yet related—function from that in the *Gedenkboek.*

In the latter volume it is difficult to contemplate the print (cited as first published in the Afrikaner nationalist daily *Die Burger*) without reading praises to the "determined courage" of the *voortrekker* women—"shoulder to shoulder with her husband she clears the way." The speech that washes against the edges of the photographic frame was by Judith Pellisier, president of the sister organization of the ACVV in another province. She sang the praises of foremothers who left behind their spacious homes: rebuilding wagons, watching over wounded menfolk, crossing mountains, loading guns . . . sowing lovely, threadbare patchwork quilts. By implication, the *voortrekker*-garbed women captured by the camera's lens embodied such heroism intertwined with homeliness. Elsewhere in the volume, perhaps provocatively and in more tenuous relationship with this image, a speech by Rothmann claimed ACVV women as early "feminists."

In McClintock's article, the picture, now captioned, "Gender and the National Fetishes," served to visually affirm a discussion of the gendering of nationalisms in which Afrikaner women were constructed as *volksmoeder* figureheads—visible in public when acting out their place in a patriarchal order. The costumed women's "starched white bonnets signifying the purity of the race, the decorous surrender of their sexuality to the patriarch, and the invisibility of white, female labor." Ox wagons and their occupants (arranged into patriarch-led families) "symbolized woman's relation to the nation as indirect, mediated through her social relation to men, her national identity lying in her unpaid services and sacrifices, through husband and family, to the *volk*" (370–371).

McClintock asserts that the "social category" of the *volksmoeder* was not an ideology "imposed . . . on hapless female victims" but "a changing, dynamic ideology rife with paradox, under constant contest by men and women" (378). But in her account, nationalist men invent a *volksmoeder* figure that celebrates women as apolitical, suffering, and self-sacrificial. The icon of the *volksmoeder* is paradoxical because it recognizes "the power of (white) motherhood" while functioning as "a retrospective iconography of gender containment . . . of domestic service" (378). Drawing on the work of Isabel Hofmeyr (1987), McClintock argues that "women played a crucial role in the invention of Afrikanerdom." However, "white women's activism" took place "within the economy of the domestic household," where "the cultural power of Afrikaner motherhood was mobilized in the service of white nation building" (379).

Had McClintock read Pellisier's speech, she might have paused at her call to men and women to urgently address national questions, "particularly the poor white question." But she relied on previous accounts of "Afrikaner" women's conservatism that assumed women's absence from the "public sphere" while attempting little primary research on the nature and extent of women's participation in the construction of Afrikaner nationalist discourses and political mobilization. Her reading of the photograph's denotative meaning—and of the symbolic role play in the *Tweede Trek*'s staged spectacle—is certainly convincing. However, the picture (together with other, similar pictures from the *Gedenkboek*) also serve as visual illustration for the only public political action of nationalist women discussed by McClintock. In this regard, its use approximates the limited ways in which Afrikaner women feature in androcentric works on Afrikaner nationalism (Moodie 1975; O'Meara 1983) that had little or nothing to say about female Afrikaner nationalists' activities and emphasized the power of exclusively male political organizations (McClintock 1995, 369). More pertinent, perhaps, she relies on essays by feminist historians that drew conclusions about Afrikaner women's attitudes toward "the political" from particular, male-constructed strands of *volksmoeder* discourse and that claimed "the near-total absence of female voices . . . in the construction of Afrikaner womanhood." Female Afrikaner nationalists were "man-made women" who accepted a *volksmoeder* ideal constructed by men (Brink 1990, 281). They were figures of silent conservatism: "male cultural entrepreneurs" had shaped the image of Afrikaner motherhood emphasizing "nobility, passivity, virtuous nurturing, and protection of children" while the women remained "silent as in their stereotypical portrayal" (Gaitskell and Unterhalter 1989, 60)

What prompts my preference for Rothmann's photograph should now be more obvious. Mine is a choice and reading "against the grain" of other choices, other readings. Afrikaner women exercised more agency than McClintock imagined. Indeed, many were vocal in the construction of Afrikaner nationalist maternalist discourse and active builders of a nationalist movement. In order to elaborate such claims—and further structure my own interpretations of these photographs as contrasting visualizations of female bodies in public spaces—I now invite you to a foray into the libraries and archives housing records of the work and words of female Afrikaner nationalists.

If you typed the obvious categories that come to mind into the database of the South African Library, your yield would very likely include A. P. van Rensburg's *Moeders van ons Volk* (Mothers of our people). His words of wisdom: "In essence the Afrikaner woman has never been a political person. She comes into her own with charitable and welfare work, in education." Published in 1966, this book belongs to a well-established nationalist genre praising Afrikaner woman (see L. Kruger 1991). For the seeker of women's words, Van Rensburg's pronouncement about female Afrikaners' propensity for charity is a useful pointer. In fact, Elizabeth Roos, first president of ACVV, would most probably have agreed with his pronouncements. Certainly, her carefully archived speeches and the minute books of ACVV branches—the first of which was founded soon after the devastating war between British forces and Boer republics (1899–1902)—detail philanthropic objectives and day-to-day charitable practices. The context was hugely increased poverty, also among Dutch-Afrikaans whites. From 1904, increasing numbers of organized women handed out old clothes, visited the poor, provided medicines.

Were these activities nonpolitical? Constructs of national identity rely on notions of difference and exclusion (de Groot 1993, 58), and ACVV leaders never doubted the whiteness of their *volk*. Regardless of cultural identity or church affiliation, people with skins of darker hue were imagined outsiders to this community. By definition, blacks had no claim on urgent help—in fact, they were the threat from which *arme blanken* (poor whites) had to be rescued. Work among the poor had long been accepted as ideally suited to women. Before the war and like many of their sisters in the DRC, Roos and several other leading ACVV women were already involved in charitable ventures. Now, Christian charity began to be fused with a nationalist mission. At the grass-roots level, such messages were absorbed to differing extent. Rural branches were sometimes slow to develop a sense of community that extended beyond their parish—a few were also slow to absorb the message of racial exclusivity. But others accepted the righteous task of demarcating racial borders with alacrity, reporting the removal of "our poor whites, who lived in locations among coloureds" to more appropriate lodgings.[2]

For Roos and her fellow founding members of the ACVV, their organization's task also extended beyond caring for the poor. Its constitution urged the promotion of all that was "pure Afrikaans." Executive members explained the need to popularize the history and language of their people in Dutch cultural journals and newspapers. ACVV members from affluent western Cape towns and more isolated villages employed a variety of strategies to promote the use of Dutch at school, home, and public occasions.[3]

Brink had claimed a lack of women's voices in the articulation of a "notion of idealized Afrikaner womanhood" (1990, 273). But from its earliest years and well before cultural entrepreneurs (male and female) elaborated a pervasive Afrikaans domesticity, discussions in the ACVV's monthly columns (published in Dutch-Afrikaans cultural journals) centered on motherhood. In this respect, the ideas articulated in these pages reflected women's rootedness in a religious worldview first articulated in the 1870s. Then, male-dominated evangelical publications (supported by key ministers of the DRC) celebrated maternal piety, women's duties, and their responsibility for children's souls. Now, over several years after the ACVV's founding, Dutch-Afrikaans women began to mesh religious and nationalist discourse. The promotion of "church, *volk*, and language" (the ACVV's slogan) involved a crucial reshaping of older conceptions of maternal duty: women should rear children for the community of the church while building a people defined by language.[4] In a context in which the mother tongue was increasingly claimed as *blank*, this was also a racially defined identity.

The older religious discourse and the new, more overtly nationalist messages shared one central trait: both idealized maternal duty centered in the privacy of home. Perhaps this emphasis, and the familiar sight of women practicing charitable work, explains the apparent acceptance of the ACVV's efforts to extend and publicize women's actions beyond this domain. For while concerns articulated by ACVV members affirmed women's adherence to "tradition," they certainly proclaimed their moral guardianship publicly. "Resolutions" (which often reflected the women's commitment to the morality of a "Christian" *volk* as guardians and their self-proclaimed role as moral guardians) were annually drawn up by branches, published in newspapers, and debated at an ACVV congress that also received detailed coverage. Indeed, the ACVV soon established for itself a com-

fortable and respected public niche in Dutch-Afrikaans society. But the new organization was hardly perceived as a firebrand by Dutch newspapers. Small wonder,
when early public addresses by Roos were preceded and followed by the prayers
and speeches of eminent men. When ACVV leaders invited members of the DRC
synod and their wives to join them for lectures on the role of women, *De Zuid-
Afrikaan* reported approvingly that members did not speak in public—instead,
church ministers spoke on their behalf. Speeches reminded women of their
allotted sphere. They were "house-mothers" with duties "as woman, as mother, as
Christian."[5]

The urge to explicitly praise instances of ACVV members' proper silence and
to remind them of their maternal duty suggests an uneasy acceptance of female
public activity. With the advent of local campaigns for female suffrage, such messages became more frequent and urgent. When the ACVV was first launched,
the idea that women should vote was not a point for discussion and debate in the
Dutch-Afrikaans press. But in 1907 the newly launched (largely English) branch
of the Women's Enfranchisement League successfully used debate in parliament
to thrust female suffrage into the center of public debate. Lengthy and intense
discussions in the Dutch-Afrikaans press followed—dominated by men who
largely opposed female suffrage. Of the few women who participated, most
agreed that "unbiblical" suffragettes threatened "domestic life."[6]

The urgent tone of discussion revealed an unprecedented interest in women's
apparently changing role in society. Indeed, new public concern that the separate spheres of femininity and masculinity were being challenged went beyond
opposition to suffrage. The specter of the New Woman crystallized a broader
concern with changing gender roles. Writers lamented that some women were
highly educated and entered careers previously held by men: "In other countries
women control almost everything." Woman was a "formidable opponent" who
would soon dominate every profession—the "fearful" prospect of equality for
men and women would lead to "social chaos." An essay by *Worcester's Christelike
Jongelings Vereniging* (Christian Young Men's Society) asked whether women
should be allowed to speak in public—and answered "emphatically no and yet
again no." Ministers from the DRC also explained that female subordination was
divinely ordained—for women, worshiping God entailed obedience to men and
silence in public.[7]

Speeches by the churchmen annually invited to the ACVV congress also
reflected alarm at the actions of the New Woman. Previously content to celebrate
motherhood and women's domestic destiny, Rev. Steytler (husband of a leading
ACVV member) now enumerated for his audience those activities not sanctioned
by God—being advocates, doctors, "feministen," public speakers, members of parliament, and church functionaries of any description. Others pointedly addressed
ACVV members "as mothers, not as citizens" or reminded them that they were
"no so-called modern women" who worked to undermine men's rights.[8]

How did the ACVV respond to such expressions of anxiety about female
transgression beyond accepted boundaries? From 1907 Roos carefully positioned
her organization and its actions against the *stemregvrouens* (suffragettes). Indeed,
the ACVV could soon be cited as proof that Afrikaans women did not want to
vote. At the 1907 congress, Elizabeth Roos dismissed the suffrage movement as
foreign to Afrikaans women, emphasizing that they had "never yet felt . . .
restricted, and have never yearned for more freedom and power." If men were at

pains to demarcate female territory, Roos's speeches at ACVV congresses and "sisterly letters" in *De Goede Hoop* (Good Hope) also copiously explained the role of women in church and *volk*. She warned against those who wanted to share "platforms" with men—or even strove to outdo them. Mothers had to teach their daughters their true, domestic destiny, or future generations would no longer be content to remain at home. And women's true destiny, God-given and glorious, the sphere of duty in which they could exert a powerful moral influence, was "home, lovely home."[9]

But while the organization distanced itself from suffragettes it also justified its actions to those who believed that women should not act in public. In these early years of the ACVV's existence Roos was acutely aware that it was moving onto new terrain—and this especially when it held public meetings. Her defense against critics who objected to the ACVV's publicly held congresses held no fundamental challenge: Roos explained that unusual times necessitated such unusual action. Postwar poverty and dislocation forced female nationalists to step outside their homes to help rescue their people.[10]

Even so, the ACVV was outlining a legitimate place for women in public. By 1909, a portrait in *De Goede Hoop* did so with confidence. The woman in the photograph sits with ringed hands clasped on her lap, her body turned sideways, her face to the viewer. The angled lighting highlights and shadows her grave expression. A dark dress covers her body—its cut and complicated pleating emphasizing shoulders and bosom, white frills encircling her throat. Above the picture, her identity is spelled out in familial terms: this is Mrs. Margaretha de Beer, born Bosman, wife of Rev. De Beer, mother to Miss E. De Beer ("Bachelor of Arts"). Below, political credentials are ennumerated. ACVV's treasurer, she is an assertive nationalist "in word and deed," able public speaker at erstwhile wartime protest meetings, "a woman who recoils at nothing when the interests of her Language, Nation, and Church are at stake." Moreover, she is feminine, not feminist, "a truly feminine woman, and has no sympathy with the suffragette movement."[11]

While the ACVV was at pains to demarcate the limits of its departure from "tradition," its leaders carefully maintained the organization's independent status. Before the war, missionary support societies and philanthropic societies to which such women as Roos belonged were directly answerable to a church entirely controlled by men. Now the ACVV alone decided on all practical, policy, and financial matters. Not only brothers in the church but also husbands at home were excluded from the dominion that women were creating for themselves in a society that afforded wives little control over personal property and finance. Indeed, a decade after its launch, the society was already accumulating property—not least the premises of its "housekeeping" schools for poor white girls. Occasional requests by church representatives that the ACVV cede its independence on financial matters were neatly sidestepped. While Roos cast the "newfangled women" demanding suffrage as threats to a gender hierarchy that she approved, the ACVV carefully maintained its independence from one of the most powerful institutions of male power in Dutch-Afrikaans society.[12]

But what of Rothmann, my enigmatic figure waiting for her train? While Roos and other ACVV founders debated their first constitution, Maria Elizabeth Oakshot, twenty-nine, separated from her money-squandering husband but not yet rid of his surname, lived in a western Cape village and worked as a teacher to support her two children. As this English-educated university graduate and wagon maker's daughter later recalled, the South African war had profoundly shaped her political consciousness. While her brother fought for the Republics, Rothmann spent time under house arrest as a suspected Boer sympathizer, painting the names of Boer generals on hat ribbons. For the first sixteen-odd years of the ACVV's existence, Rothmann, although apparently not involved in welfare work, promoted the use of Afrikaans in Anglophone schools, joined a society that promoted Afrikaans, and published Afrikaans children's poetry (thus launching a distinguished literary career). In 1913 Rothmann was also among the thousands who witnessed the unveiling of the Vrouwenmonument (women's monument)—Afrikaner nationalists' first significant attempt to commemorate women as victims of the South African War.

It was in 1922, a year before Roos died, that Rothmann's distinctive voice became a feature in the Afrikaans press. On Tuesday mornings, women readers of the newspaper *Die Burger* (The citizen) could henceforth turn to their "own" page—where she not only promoted female Afrikaner nationalists' party-political and welfare projects but also reflected upon gender roles in society. Now resident in Cape Town, she launched a new career as journalist and activist. Her *Vrouesake* (Women's issues) column provided extensive cover for the ACVV's activities. Together with a group of women—some married to men prominent in the Afrikaans press or the DRC, others forging careers for themselves as social workers—she proceeded to mold and publicize ACVV policies. Rothmann and most of her colleagues on the ACVV executive committee were voteless but politically committed women. They launched a National Women's Party (hereafter NVP) in the Cape, and Rothmann copiously promoted its activities in the newspaper that served as its mouthpiece.[13]

Rothmann's predecessor in the women's page had styled herself a preserver of the "old values" and never broached political or contentious issues. Like her contemporaries in cultural and women's magazines, Rothmann occasionally contributed to the construction of a modern, Afrikaans feminine fashion through essays on, say, the phenomenon of "passing fashions" or the dubious attraction of "nude stockings." Apparently, her minimal interest in fashion did not include the *voortrekker* dress patterns promoted in *Die Boerevrouw* (The farm woman); the domestic skills promoted in this recently launched women's magazine were mostly relegated to another part of the newspaper. Her *Vrouesake* page claimed other subjects as appropriate material for female discussion. Writing "as a woman," guest writer E. C. van der Lingen (also executive member of the ACVV and NVP), asserted that the public press failed to represent "all the activities and concerns of a nation . . . in no paper do we find a reflection of the spirit of the South African woman." She argued that newspapers neglected women's public activities and interests—and proceeded to discuss the work of various women's organizations.[14]

From the beginning, women's party-political activities featured prominently. In fact, Rothmann's ideas about women and politics contrasted sharply with the viewpoints expressed by Roos only a few years before. Careful justifications of why women were publicly active were replaced by an impatient dismissal of conservatism: "Those who think women's work should be limited to looking after their husbands at home themselves acknowledge that saying this makes no difference; regardless of this, the women organize outside and tackle issues per-

taining to the *volk*." Rothmann's original brief—as she explained sardonically—
had not included writing about politics. ("'And Madam, please no politics!'")
But women's entry into party politics made this impossible. "Can we still ignore
politics in the women's columns? And what will we do now that it is election
time? Will we really stay as removed from the struggle as we pretend to do?"
Unlike the previous generation of ACVV leadership, Rothmann, as a newer
leader, challenged the distinction between party-political and welfare work. She
pointed to the inevitably political and nationalist nature of Afrikaans women's
philanthropy: "The despised politics is in fact nothing other than matters of
national interest. . . . And our women are already busily studying matters of
interest to the *volk*. The ACVV and similar organizations see to that. The ACVV
may itself be unaware of this, but for the last sixteen years it has educated women
in nothing less than politics."[15]

On Rothmann's page, a range of issues pertaining to welfare, economy, and
politics were claimed as *vrouesake*. Political know-how ("What do the ministers
do?") and discussions on education for underprivileged Afrikaans children featured far more prominently than fashion. Her support for the ACVV was
reflected in frequent articles on poverty in Cape Town. Above all, she wrote as a
committed *Nasionale vrou* (National woman): she copiously reported and
explained the NVP's activities, and often sought to give direction to NVP policy.
She paid particular attention to efforts to encourage reading among Afrikaans
speakers. A founding member of the (female) *Handhawers* (Upholders) group,
Rothmann also promoted their determined efforts to have Cape Town shop-
keepers serve Afrikaans speakers in their own language.[16]

Vrouesake reflected a broad interest in women's position, public activities, and
political attitudes. Rothmann discussed women's role in society in such diverse
essays as "How Are Women Doing in Politics?" "The Business Woman," "Farm
Women School Councils," and "Women as Ministers of the Church." Throughout
the 1920s, she also published pieces on local attitudes about women's suffrage
and features on the "women's movement" in countries where women's right to
vote had apparently given them more power to influence state policy: "It really
gives food for thought, how women in other countries have been able to change
conditions, and how far-reaching their influence is." If she first preferred not to
emphasize her own pro-suffrage views in *Vrouesake*, Rothmann always covered
the suffrage debate with the implicit assumption that it was simply a matter of
time before women had the vote. As female suffrage gained increasing acceptance
in the NVP of the mid-1920s, Rothmann's own pro-suffrage views were openly
advocated and explained.[17]

In this respect, and like most Afrikaans women addressing a female audience
on political matters, Rothmann wrote in a pervasively gender-specific way, characterizing the National Party as the *mansparty* (men's party) and discussing the
issue of the day among "us women." But she was unusual in her frequent, publicly
expressed, and often perceptive comments on the gender dynamics between men
and women activists as females blurred the boundaries of "separate spheres."
When the NVP was launched, she emphasised the need for (and women's commitment to) cooperation between the sexes. Whether in separate organizational
structures or "together with the men in one party (when women have the vote),
our purpose and theirs is in any case, cooperation." She also insisted on the good
relations between Afrikaner men and women. But as she explained two years

later, in spite of their good intentions, men failed to understand the "plan" of cooperation and to accept women who acted as their equal: "They still regard us as a different sort of human being" explained Rothmann. "And they prove this by constantly praising us, and telling us, and repeating, and telling us again, how good and bright we are, and how much better than themselves. . . . Do the men also praise each other like this? . . . It is of course extremely pleasant to hear all the lovely appreciation; one feels so flattered and so good, so noble and so ideal; but when you get home—where nothing has changed—then you don't really know." When Rothmann chided women for an "unnecessary respect" for men's political knowledge (they shouldn't take over from men but could also learn to participate), she criticized men for their "friendly contempt" of female expertise. Not surprisingly for a woman who liked to philosophize on male-female relations, Rothmann found much to admire in Olive Schreiner. Afrikaans women with their growing political consciousness and keen eye for injustice could identify strongly with this champion of victimized women.[18]

Rothmann therefore expressed strong views on the inevitability of Afrikaans women's political participation, Afrikaner men's inability to accept women as their equals, and clearly supported suffrage for (white) women. But hers were the variations of an assertive woman on the *volksmoeder* theme. Speaking to fellow NVP members in *Die Burger*, she emphasized Afrikaans women's "independent spirit." As men's partners, their primary role was related to the family—a *volksaak* (national issue) often undervalued and unrecognized. NVP members' adoption of the designation *burgeres* ("citizen-ess or female citizen) indicated that for them, women's civic identity was based on their essential difference from men. If Rothmann claimed her rights as "citizen-ess," she simultaneously and primarily spoke as a mother working for the good of the *volk*: "Now, more than ever, we women must educate ourselves, so that we can judge well and sensibly and really serve our people, as female citizens as well as (in the first place!) mothers."[19]

Together with other prominent female Afrikaner nationalists (see L. Kruger 1991), Rothmann constructed a maternalist discourse that drew on mainstream notions of women's primary role as mother and did not fundamentally challenge the idea of separate spheres. But this "language of social housekeeping" claimed responsibility for nonfamilial social spaces, extending women's mothering role beyond the home, to forge "a new, more inclusive definition of the political" (Boris 1993) and to claim some direct power for women in a redefined public arena. When Rothmann asserted that nothing had changed at "home" in spite of men's praises, she very likely spoke in metaphoric terms. As with (for example) North American and European women in earlier decades, Afrikaner women participated in a distinct female political culture that "extolled the virtues of domesticity" (Koven and Michel 1990, 1097) while expanding "the environs of the 'home'"(Baker 1984, 631). The state was a household where women should exercise their (apparently superior) skills to create order: "We women are now realizing that the State, like the home, can get very disorderly, that our Afrikaans State is at this moment very disorderly, and we suffer because of this. . . . And we very much want to tidy up."[20]

Rothmann's interest in women's issues, like that of her colleagues in the NVP and ACVV, was also firmly circumscribed by the prerogatives of ethnic nationalism. Her interest in women's lot was firmly entwined with commitment to a racially defined *volk*. From the mid-1920s, *Vrouesake* covered such burning issues for Afrikaner nationalists as efforts to legislate against "immoral intercourse between whites and natives ... we women feel very strongly about this issue." Extensive coverage of her ACVV branch's work to combat poverty in Cape Town focused on "poor white" Afrikaans speakers and the dangers of their living in mixed-race inner-city slums. Indeed, this was the context for her concern at the "white" girl's demeanor in Cape Town station: "The child's language, her whole way of thought, was that of a coloured of very inferior class. It made one shudder." Rothmann frequently voiced such concerns—so did numbers of ACVV members. Afrikaner culture, defined in middle-class terms, was *blank,* belonged to "whites" in the logic of the racial, ethnic politics of Afrikaner nationalists—and the uncertain edges of whiteness had to be assiduously protected. The threat was poorer whites forgetting their true nature.[21]

At the time when the photograph was likely taken (c. 1930), Rothmann was still regularly contributing to *Die Burger* but had given up her post as editor as full-time "organizing secretary" of the ACVV. As Afrikaner men (especially through the *Broederbond*) began to organize the hitherto loosely affiliated Afrikaans cultural organizations into a more hierarchical and centralized structure, and as male academics and church dignitaries began to pay more urgent attention to the "poor white problem," Rothmann and her colleagues were making their own, more comprehensive plans for state support to combat poverty, convinced that turning *armmoeders* (poor mothers) into *volksmoeder* (nation-mothers) was key to the survival of the *volk* (du Toit 1992). For Rothmann, women's wisdom was essential to the success of "family welfare." In the early 1930s, the ACVV and its sister organizations worked for a political alliance that would recognize female expertise when formulating state social welfare policy. As Rothmann explained to ACVV members in the society's recently launched journal, the women's organizations, the state, and the church could combine powerfully to combat poverty among Afrikaners. Of this threesome, the women should speak with authority on the "domestic" aspects of this issue: "We must never forget that of these three powerful allies in social work, none can act so authoritatively as the Women's Societies."[22]

Roos had insisted that Afrikaans women desired no more freedom—while she carefully asserted the necessity of public action. Rothmann yearned for a "rebirth" in which females would be accepted as leaders who would put the "household of the state" in order.[23] But while Rothmann's activism coincided with Nationalist Party leaders' recognition of the benefits that female suffrage held for Afrikaner nationalism, the ACVV's hopes for a new partnership with men would soon become an area of struggle. Rothmann and her colleagues accepted patriarchal prerogatives, but attempted to redefine the boundaries of women's sphere. Men in state departments were willing to accept women as "practical" workers, but formulating policy was a different matter. Moreover, hopes for "cooperation with government" in which "capable women take the lead, and not necessarily the [DRC] ministers"[24] were steadily eroded as churchmen proved intent on forging an exclusive partnership with a newly established state social welfare department while forcing the women's welfare organizations to submit to the their authority.

Now that a selection of Roos's and Rothmann's words has been extracted from microfilm and archived papers, the figure at the station is perhaps less mysterious, and the logic of my choice more obvious. McClintock described "a changing, dynamic ideology rife with paradox, under constant contest by men and women" in her article (McClintock 1993, 71). But she did not substantiate this tantalizing and ultimately correct assertion, and accepted that women's work for nationalism was confined to home and family. In this respect she drew on the work of historians who failed to realize the extent to which Afrikaner women actively constructed nationalist discourse and asserted themselves as political activists—and sought to widen the legitimate sphere of "mothers" in the early decades of nationalist mobilization. Indeed, it was when (in the early 1930s) ACVV leaders argued that women—mothers with years of experience in philanthropic work—should formulate state welfare policy that powerful men in the Dutch Reformed Church contested their vision.

McClintock's use of the photograph from 1938 could be read as troping Afrikaner women into the figureheads of a male-constructed nationalism. The photograph she chose is indeed powerful, not least in its association of Afrikaans femininity with the ox wagon—a resurrected mode of transport signifying adherence to "tradition," a return to "the old ways." The framing of these women suggests participants' total immersion in a dramatic past. Seemingly, this is how women appeared in public: silent participants in a spectacle that limited their power.

Comparison with older photographs of *voortrekker* dress from ACVV columns in *Die Huisgenoot* suggest a shift from darker, printed fabrics to a pure, surely symbolic white—strengthening McClintock's argument of costume signifying racial purity.[25] However, her reading betrays ignorance of the women's work that made this very image possible, and of the extent of Afrikaner women's political agency. Those women from De Rust may well have been exposed to, or participated in, the many ways in which female Afrikaner nationalists shaped and promoted nationalist discourse. In sum, historians who take this image at its word—or fail to look beyond it—echo a version of *volksmoeder* discourse that cast women as visibly silent.

My photograph—of a female but almost neutrally gendered figure in a public space associated with the possibility of movement in a modernizing age— but also with peculiarly South African histories of dispossession, segregation— involves a different troping that stands in opposition to the fusing of nationalist-generated, predominantly male *Volksmoeder* stereotypes with assumptions of an apolitical or house-bound Afrikaner femininity. It stands for the construction of Afrikaner nationalist discourses crucially, often differently, shaped by female nationalists. The figure stands in enigmatic isolation, and in some ways Rothmann was indeed an exceptional individual—she certainly voiced analyses of gender politics within the nationalist movement with particular irony and insight. But she was an eloquent and important member of a larger, influential group of nationalist women who came into their own during the 1920s and led party political, cultural, and philanthropic organizations at this time. Rothmann and her colleagues embraced motherhood while seeking to extend their sphere of action to actively participate in formulating and executing a social policy entrenching racial privilege. The juxtaposition of woman and railway line in the photograph becomes a metaphor (more disconcertingly, an alternative iconography?) for the ways in which female Afrikaner nationalists pushed beyond ideas of whether and how they should take political action, and the particular politics of women intent on building a *blanke* Afrikaner people.

Notes

1. This Afrikaans word carries historical connotations of racial purity, the sanctity of "whiteness" and the weight of publicly legislated racism that the English "white" and the more neutral Afrikaans "wit" do not convey.
2. *De Zuid-Afrikaan*, 16 November 1907. *De Goede Hoop*, October 1906; September 1905, p. 66. Cape Archives (hereafter CA), A1953 (ACVV Collection), Add 1/12/5/1/1/1, 9 March 1918. For a more detailed discussion, see du Toit 1996.
3. CA, A1953, 1/1/1 (ACVV congress reports) 1905; *De Zuid-Afrikaan*, 21 September 1907; 19 November 1907.
4. *De Zuid-Afrikaan*, 21 September 1907. See also du Toit 1996.
5. *De Goede Hoop*, November 1906, p. 16; CA, A1953, Congress report, 1905. See du Toit 1996 for an account of the ACVV's efforts to promote the DRC and its commitment to this institution's Protestant morality.
6. *De Goede Hoop*, March 1909. Also October 1908; *De Zuid-Afrikaan*, 20 June and 1 August 1907.
7. *De Zuid-Afrikaan*, 27 June 1908; 12 December 1908; *De Goede Hoop*, May 1908; *Het Gereformeerd Maandblad*, December 1907.
8. *De Zuid-Afrikaan*, 11 April 1907; 14 February 1907; 15 April 1909.
9. *De Zuid-Afrikaan*, 5 April 1909; *De Goede Hoop*, September 1909, p.66; CA, A1953, 3/2/1, 1907; 1910. For a broader discussion of ACVV members' attitudes, see du Toit 1996.
10. CA, A1953, 3/2/1, 1906.
11. *De Goede Hoop*, July 1909.
12. CA, DRC, V21, 1/1/2; V21, 1/5.
13. Rothmann was forty-seven in 1922. See du Toit 1996 for more on the new leaders of the ACVV, some of whom were much younger and others of Rothmann's generation.The National Party (launched 1913) defined *volk* as white and Afrikaans. The South African Party (in power until 1926) saw the *volk* as white but English and Afrikaans.When, in 1931, white women received the vote in order to increase white voting power against a limited number of enfranchised blacks in the Cape, the women saw no reason to continue working in a separate organization and dissolved the NVP.
14. *Die Burger*, 26 August 1924.
15. Ibid, 2 June 1925; 15 April 1924.
16. Ibid., 4 August 1925; 14 April 1925; 15 July 1924; 30 March 1926; 19 February 1924; 6 Jan 1925; 14 April 1925; 16 May 1925; 12 January 1926.
17. Ibid., 29 December 1925; 14 April 1923; 27 April 1926; 15 May 1928; 23 January 1925; 6 May 1924; 8 April 1924; 22 April 1924; 26 July 1927; 26 February 1927; 31 December 1927.
18. Ibid., 9 May 1922; 15 April 1924; 13 January 1925. Schreiner (b. 1855) is perhaps best known for her books, *The Story of an African Farm* (1883) and *Woman and Labour* (1911). Rothmann's reference to her as a champion of women's rights was made with the latter publication in mind.
19. Ibid., 29 December 1925.
20. Ibid., 26 August 1924.
21. Ibid., 11 May 1926. For comparison with the racialized maternalist rhetoric of Afrikaner women's contemporaries in the United States, see Boris 1993.
22. *Eendrag*, November 1932, p. 4.
23. USDC, MER, 55.1.K.11 (51), Rothmann to Geyer, 19 July 1933.
24. Ibid. See also du Toit 1996.
25. *Die Huisgenoot*, January 1918. Discussing *Die Boerevrou's* of "correct" replicas of *Voortrekker* costumes, L. Kruger points to the gradual success of the *kappie* (bonnet) as a symbol of the past.

5

Whose Virtue Is This?
The Virtue Party and Women
in Islamist Politics in Turkey

Ayse Saktanber

By examining Islamist party politics on women in general, and Islamist women activists' position within the Fazilet Partisi (Virtue Party, hereafter VP) in particular, this chapter shows how Islamist party politics in Turkey have been symbolically feminized. Women operate within the confines of conservative patriarchal cultural codes and use gender complementarity rather than gender equality to participate in party politics. By symbolically feminizing right-wing politics in Turkey, parties secure a modern, liberal, democratic public image without, however, developing a program to improve women's situation. Women activists of the VP mobilize other women to work and vote for Islamist politics by reinterpreting their gender roles and identities and incorporating aspects of their domestic roles into the VP's politics and platform. Cultural codes of gender complementarity, legitimized within an Islamic discourse on gender construction, determine the ways in which women's participation in politics is construed both by women and by society. Women following the Welfare Party/VP line are expected to make great public efforts to promote the party without, however, compromising their private-sphere Muslim identity as devoted and pious mothers and wives, for which they have never been fully rewarded.

My information is gathered from interviews with prominent members of the Ankara Greater Municipality Ladies' Commission of the VP and its predecessor, the Refah Partisi (Welfare Party, hereafter WP), and with some female VP members of parliament, as well as from the parties' publications and from media coverage.

Changing Social Status of Women and the Head Scarves of Islamist Women

At the turn of the twentieth century Turkey chose to becomer part of the Western world and a modern nation. An aim of the Republic (1923) was to modernize Turkish society through secularization. The emancipation of women was one of the most ambitious projects of the new regime and central to the secularization of society. Women were to become equal citizens with men, and as enlightened mothers of the nation, they were expected to raise the future generations of modern Turkey. Accordingly, a series of reforms was initiated that directly influenced both the structure and the organization of everyday social life. These reforms radically changed the status of women in society and established a modern, secular social order. They helped to erase the influence of Ottoman Islamic rule and led to the Westernization of society. The Turkish Civil Code of February 1926 replaced Islamic law and abolished polygamy, provided women equal rights in matters of divorce and inheritance, established the equality of parents in child custody (although in disputed cases the husband had priority), and guaranteed free choice of marriage partner, marriage by civil contract, and a minimum age for marriage (fifteen for women and seventeen for men). Education was secularized and women were encouraged to seek higher education, work side by side with men, not wear the veil, and engage in all areas of social life.[1] Finally, women obtained full voting rights in 1930.

Women's ability to access and understand their legal rights, as well as their experience of them, varied according to their status and background. Moreover, the legal equality women achieved concealed important inequalities and failed to ensure them full participation in public life. For example, married women needed their husband's permission to work outside the home. In the 1980s women waged campaigns to promote gender equality in the Civil Code and succeeded in changing or abolishing some articles in the 1990s. In 2001 the Grand National Assembly continued to debate the issue of gender equality and the Civil Code. However, women faced additional obstacles in their efforts to improve their social status.

According to the 1990 census data, 30.7 percent of Turkish women were illiterate. In 1993, 65.3 percent of the total women's labor force worked in agriculture, compared with 13.3 percent in industry and 21.4 percent in services. In 1994, 34.3 percent of all civil servants were women. In 1996 women constituted only 27.46 percent of all upper- and middle-level managers in the public sector.

In addition, women are highly underrepresented in politics. Patriarchal moral code limit the scope of women's political participation as independent individuals. Women's public identity is defined within the confines of familial or kinship role models. They participate in local party politics as yenge[2] (sister-in-law) or abla (older sister) and even if they engage in politics on their own behalf, they develop role models either as "mother woman" or "asexual-puritan woman" (Güneş-Ayata 1995). Such an identity shield prevents women from being perceived as potential sexual partners while they are working alongside men and thus allows them some personal autonomy within the confines of deeply ingrained codes of chastity, virtue, and honor; the head scarves of women Islamic activists perform the same function.

Although women's social situation was far from acceptable, and violence against women, including domestic violence[3] and honor killings, were prevalent, in the last two decades the head scarf of Islamist women has been presented as the most important problem faced by women. Secular forces have defined covered women's participation in public life as one of the biggest challenges to the republican project of civilization, which foresaw the emancipation of women as the most indispensable characteristic of modernity (Abadan-Unat and Tokgöz 1994; Göle 1996; Özdalga 1998).

Although the Republic encouraged women to participate in public life, it never forcefully removed their veils as, for example, Reza Shah Pahlavi in Iran did (1926–41); he made unveiling compulsory (Najmabadi 1991, 72–73, n. 24). The women who supported the republican ideals unveiled themselves, seeing it as a sign of their emancipation. Nevertheless, Turkish women who covered their heads in private or only during prayer were not seen as strange. Covering the head in private was held to be a habit that would disappear as modernization evolved. Thus, in the 1980s, when urban, modern female university students began to cover their heads as part of a rising Islamist activism, the secular forces of society were alarmed, seeing this development as a sign of the political use of religious beliefs, a force that could jeopardize the very principals of the secular republican regime.[4]

The founders of the Republic did not want to eradicate Islam from society; they opposed the backward-looking religious tradition that they thought suffocated the masses and prevented modernization. Religion had to be relegated to the private sphere, and experienced by people as a matter of private conscience. After the establishment of the multiparty system (1946), Islamic political forces participated publicly in politics and were thus contained by the secular parliamentary system (Ayata 1996; Heper 1981; Mardin 1973, 1983; Toprak 1981). More important, socioeconomic changes experienced between 1950 and 1980 integrated the masses into the political and economic processes and, through mass education, affected the perception and aspirations of a wide section of society. As Mardin (1989b) argues, the most important consequence of the spread of education was the creation of a new type of elite, raised traditionally but educated in the new secular universal educational institutions. This elite later became the producers and supporters of the new Islamist ideologies. It successfully formed political cadres who espoused right-wing religious ideals and created channels through which these ideals could be communicated; and it formed the new generations of Islamic intellectuals, activists, and lay sympathizers (Mardin 1977, 1981, 1989b; Meeker 1990, 1994; Sanbay 1985; Sunar and Toprak 1983).

Yet, as Mardin has shown in his various studies on the place and meaning of religion in Turkish society, Islam has always been one of the most significant sources from which the cultural tissue of society gained its patterns (Mardin 1969, 1989a). As I have argued elsewhere (1996, 171), the endurance of patriarchal ethics and moral control clearly illustrates this. Islam also shaped gender identities: equality between men and women established by the legal codes regulated the public sphere, but was not fully maintained either in legal or civil terms in the private sphere. Here, the Islamic discourse of gender complementarity, sentiment, and intimacy has dominated the "everyday philosophy" of the majority, making it difficult to discriminate between secular and Islamic moralities, especially in the formation of gender relations and family life. It can be said that Islamist politics has always taken advantage of this situation and successfully appropriated secular gender codes, albeit selectively. Women's right to education, to economic independence, to choose their own spouses, as well as to initiate divorce and seek alimony are among the most salient of these. They accompany an acceptance of women's equal rights with men in child custody, sharing of family responsibilities, and having authority in family matters (though the husband has ultimate authority over the wife). These rights are accepted on condition that they do not harm Islamic rules and customs. However, none of these issues were discussed and written down in the Islamic party programs. Both the VP and the WP espoused the conservative family values ideology of the right while giving the impression that they believed the progress of women would be inevitably maintained by the establishment of a just Islamic social order. To a certain extent, other right and center-right political parties have also wanted to reconcile religious values with the modernization of women, but so far no other party has been as successful as the WP and the VP in promoting women's activism.

The history of pro-Islamic party politics in Turkey started with the establishment of Milli Nizam (National Order Party) in 1969. The Constitutional Court banned the party in 1971; it continued under the name Milli Selamet (National Salvation Party) from 1972 to 1980, when it in turn was banned as a result of a military coup. It was subsequently restarted as the WP in 1983 and took its current form with the establishment of the VP in 1997. These parties followed similar political lines under the leadership of almost the same cadre of leaders. Except for the VP, the Constitutional Court banned them all as a consequence of the military takeovers in 1971 and 1980 or for violating the legal code that forbids the use of religion for political purposes. The reduction of women's status has always been seen as one of the most crucial threats posed by the rising Islamist activism.

The Islamic revivalism of the last two decades, however, has made important contributions to shaping the discourse on women's freedom. It has forced the different political actors to rethink the meaning of modernization, secularization, and democratization, and the indispensable relation of women's issues to these processes. Naturally, it cannot be said that such reevaluations have always had positive results, particularly in terms of bringing about a much more democratic social system and maintaining gender equality. However, the WP's capacity to mobilize women (which became especially significant in the 1990s), and the unprecedented attempts by the VP to elect one covered and two uncovered women to parliament in the 1999 general elections prompted much speculation. Was it possible that democratic trends, including gender equality, could predominate within Islamic party politics and become the norm? Or was the newly gained visibility of women within the party only temporary, the consequence of a combination of certain sociopolitical and cultural conditions?

An Overview of the "Symbolic Feminization" of Turkish Right-Wing Politics

Throughout the 1980s, the Turkish women's movement gained a new impetus and constituted one of the most salient pioneering movements toward a civil society following the 1980 military takeover. The women question was reheard and rethought extensively in the changing context of the country, especially by drawing public attention to domestic violence and the need to broaden women's civil rights (Tekeli 1986; Sirman 1989). This activism could not be channeled rapidly and efficiently into party politics in part because men resisted women's participation in politics and their participation in decision-making processes. In addition, many feminists started to be much more critical of the parties' sexist organizational structures and discriminatory attitudes toward women. Also, after the 1980 military intervention, all political parties were banned, and the 1981 constitution prohibited any future parties from organizing women's and youth's branches. In 1983, when the parliamentary regime was reestablished, political parties started to organize women and youth into different party commissions, which, at least initially, were not as effective as the former auxiliary party branches.

However, as Yesim Arat points out (1998), from the mid-1980s, feminist and Islamist activist women succeeded in bringing about political change in Turkey by questioning the prevailing structures of power. Although the feminists did so in pursuit of women's human rights, and the Islamists to accomplish divine rule, they both challenged state authority over individual human rights. As I have argued elsewhere (1996), Islamist women activists mainly followed ways first employed by feminists in the struggle for the empowerment of women.

Thus, with the 1987 general elections, the participation of women in party politics was seen as the symbol of democratization for the political parties. Echoing this perception, Islamic activists targeted women, in spite of the fact that the right of veiling, which the official, modern, and Westernized elite rejected, appeared to be almost the only important demand of the Islamist movement for women. Toprak reasons that the gender question, as connected to identity politics, has become the distinguishing mark of the Islamist movement and if the movement were stripped of this concern, "little would remain to separate it from other contestants for power" (1994, 295). However, since the demand for the right of women to cover their heads in public institutions and universities was sought against the secularist principals of the republican regime, it also constituted one of the most severe conflicts between religious and secular forces since the inception of the Republic (Acar 1990; Y. Arat 1990; Göle 1996; Olson 1985; Saktanber 1994; Toprak 1994).

The overall consequence of these developments from the perspective of women's activism was the new and rapid politicization of provincial middle- and lower-middle-class women who first and foremost called themselves Muslims and wanted to lead their lives in line with Islamic rules governing modesty. Most of these women had not previously taken part in political activities. Others, particularly younger generations of Muslim women from modest social backgrounds who had had the opportunity to be educated in secular republican educational institutions and were thereby equipped to take part in public life, greatly encouraged the development of this new activism. Until the emergence of these Islamist activist women, almost all female politicians and political activists, except for some ultra-leftist and radical feminists, seemed to feel the need to revere the memory of Mustafa Kemal Atatürk, the founder of the Turkish Republic, who initiated radical reforms and enacted the civil and political rights of women. This mobilization fostered the emergence of a new type of female political activist who, unlike both her right- and left-wing equivalents, did not necessarily declare herself as *Atatürkist*. Beyond creating a shared target of hatred among the secularist sections of the Turkish polity and society and alarming them into organizing around NGOs in order to struggle against Islamic activism (Ayata and Güneş-Ayata 1998, 115–116), the emergence of these Islamist activist women created problems for the other political parties in terms of women's representation. These women claimed that they represented the silent majority of the female population who had dutifully performed their social roles as devoted housewives and mothers and their traditional religious duties. In addition to fulfilling their traditional role, they also displayed a new image of a Muslim woman who could be quite active in public life without harming the fabric of Islamic faith. This perfectly overlapped the social expectations of ordinary Turkish people with their century-old longing for becoming modern without losing their assumed cultural essence. The mobilization of Islamist women activists thus led other right-wing political parties to remember women's old symbolic importance in the building of a national society that is both modern and also independent, sovereign and thus "authentic."

The symbolic feminization of Turkish right-wing politics started as a result of

the new liberal economic policies of the 1980s. In this period economic liberalism opened almost every layer of Turkish society to the world economy and
liberalized private lives, which allowed for a relatively free display of ethnic, religious, and gender identities. The Motherland Party (MP), which spearheaded
these changes, also began to mobilize urban populations. This change forced
other right-wing political parties to develop new strategies to compete for the
urban votes and renew their public images. For example, in 1993, the TP, one of
the oldest center-right political parties of Turkey, elected a woman, Tansu Çiller,
as party leader to replace Süleyman Demirel, the party's former leader. This
choice was a strategic one; it opened the path for Çiller to become the first
woman prime minister of Turkey. Demirel was a conservative politician who had
been seen as *baba* (father), the paternalistic leader of the nation. He designated
Çiller, who was good-looking, well-educated, highly Westernized, urban, his
protégée, and "symbolic" daughter, to replace him.

The media covered practically every move made by the "beautiful" new prime
minister (Küçükkurt, Güz, and Anik 1996). She was hailed as the modern face of
Turkey, especially in the face of rising Islamic revivalism. Yet, as the leader of a
center-right political party she also appealed to the conservative rural and urban
sections of society and the new urban right. Çiller symbolically projected a balanced image by using chic and expensive scarves and foulards not to cover her
head but to complement her modern clothes. She also took great care to ensure
media coverage included pictures of her embracing and kissing covered women.

The WP took another path. As Öncü (1994) observes, in the 1991 election campaign the WP avoided using overtly religious idioms, symbols, and Koranic quotations and instead transformed its public image from that of an inward-looking,
traditionalist religious party to that of a mass party addressing a heterogeneous
audience. The party used seven female faces in its advertisements, only one of
which was that of a covered young girl who had been expelled from the university
for wearing a head scarf. This conveyed that no woman would be discriminated
against if the WP gained power (1994, 24). The WP swept the municipal elections
of March 1994, becoming a mass party. Its candidates were elected in twenty-eight
cities, including Istanbul and Ankara. Women, who had worked with endless
energy and devotion in the poorest outskirts of the big cities to persuade other
women to vote for the WP, received much credit for this success (R. Çakir 1994).
When this success was repeated in the 1995 general elections, the women of the
WP became almost an instant legend. Although women had no place in the upper
echelons of party organs, and were not included in decision-making mechanisms,
they continued to work unselfishly for their party (Talash 1996, 119; Yaraman
1999, 113). The head scarves of these women became the banner of Islamic
activism in Turkey as in other parts of the Muslim world (Ahmed 1992; Haddad
and Esposito 1997; Keddie 1991; Nader 1989), and the women themselves were
seen as the symbols of the hidden social power of the WP.

A Party of "Love" and "Affection": The Virtue Party

In early 1998, the WP was banned, and its leader, who then was prime minister,
seventy-year-old Necmettin Erbakan, was prohibited from participating in active
politics for the next five years. Members of the WP established a new party,
Fazilet Partisi (the Virtue Party) in order to continue its presence in parliament.

Since 1993, the whole country had been rocked by economic and political scandals allegedly involving impropriety; the party name fit the claims of the former WP that it was the most "correct," "honest," "just," and "virtuous" political movement in Turkey. However, this name has another important feature: Fazilet is a girl's name.

The party faced a considerable number of ironic comments because of the WP's reputation as a movement with a restrictive ideological stance toward women. For the secular media, first and foremost this choice of name illustrated the party's hypocrisy. In addition, Turkish politics is perceived as a man's activity, and ascribing qualities assumed to be feminine to any manly activity has always raised an unconscious aversion in men, leading them to devalue the activity or mock it.

The emblem of the new party, a red crescent, a red heart, and five red headless arrow-like stripes between them, also provoked humorous comments. This emblem often appears in white on a red background, the colors of the Turkish flag. The emblem might be more appropriate as a design for cheap stationery; it is not really in keeping with the presumed sobriety of a religiously oriented political party. However, the party ascribed the following meaning to the emblem: "The crescent represents our national identity, history, traditions, and culture. The heart expresses our feelings of affection, fraternity, and love, what we need most as a complete nation in this particular period. The lines express our five basic objectives: Peace and Serenity; Freedom; Justice; Welfare and Prosperity; Respectability" (*Fazilet Partisi* 1999, 10). The party's discourse reflected this theme of tenderness. Both women and the party are addressed by the names of flowers and are associated with poetically formulated characteristics. For instance, the head of the central committee of the women's commissions of the party addresses women as chrysanthemums. She uses poetic comparisons to describe the party's female supporters; they are "as nice as the butterfly on the prophet flower," "as affectionate as the holy light which drips from the prayer door." She also associates them with historic Turkish Muslim female saints (*Fazilet Partisi* 1999, 29). One of the party's two well-educated, uncovered female members of parliament who was elected in the 1999 general elections, Nazlı Ilıcak, describes covered young university students as "the colorful butterflies who run toward the light of science" and suggests that those students with head scarves be seen as a "field of flowers composed of beautiful girls" (*Fazilet Partisi* 1999, 78). The other uncovered female deputy, Oya Akgönenç, conceptualizes the party itself as a "snowdrop," a small but beautiful precious white flower that grows out of snow (read difficulties) in winter (*Fazilet Partisi* 1999, 70–71).

Nevertheless, neither within the party nor in society were the political situations of women who worked for the WP or the VP as gentle and pleasant as the formal discourse of the party described them. They had to work hard but in return had to be content with minimal rewards, at least in worldly if not in moral terms.

Political Success and the Hardships of the "Virtuous Woman"

There was no doubt in Turkish public opinion that women were the hidden force behind the victory of the WP in the local elections of March 1994. Tayyib Erdogan, who became the mayor of Istanbul in 1994, had foreseen the importance of women for the party and had established the women's commissions at the end of 1980s. Despite initial opposition from the party, women close to WP circles and friends and relatives of the men in the administrative organs of the party nevertheless started to form women's commissions in 1989, later called ladies' commissions (Y. Arat 1999, 8, 14–15). At first, the party merely planned to capitalize on the intellectual potential of educated covered women (Eraslan 2000, 223–224). After the mid-1980s, women played a more important role, mainly as a result of the head-scarf dispute. The commissions also embraced other women who hungered to go out and do something for the good of Islam and for the establishment of a better, more virtuous social life for everyone.[5] According to Yesim Arat (1999, 16–19), the ladies' commissions held a unique position within the party establishment because they were vertically organized and horizontally tied to the central organs of the party. The structure of the commissions ran from top to bottom at the provincial, district, county, quarter (*mahalle*), and even electoral precinct (*sandik*) level. In addition, in some cases women were organized at the street level and in apartment buildings in units up to four floors.[6] At each level, the administrative councils of the commissions attended weekly meetings and participated in monthly meetings at the next level higher, thus providing a flow of information from bottom up and vice versa. These meetings also enabled the party leadership to supervise commissions at the lower ranks of the organizational structure. Written reports to the higher levels of the party administration were required from each level.

Through this elaborate organizational scheme, the ladies' commissions were eventually established all over the country (in seventy-nine out of the eighty-one cities); in about six years, approximately one million women registered with the party. Both the propaganda and public relations activities of the ladies' commissions as well as their organization required very detailed planning, personal initiative, and hard work. For instance, as Yesim Arat reports (1998, 124), during the March 1994 local elections, Sibel Eraslan, a graduate of the Istanbul law faculty who chaired the Istanbul ladies' commissions for several years, worked with eighteen thousand women to mobilize other women, and in one month they personally met face-to-face with two hundred thousand women. However, as she was also critical of the party, declaring herself to be "a feminist with faith," a rare self-identification among Islamic women activists of the WP and VP, she was not given any position within the party organization.

Eraslan is not the only WP member who was treated unfairly. Before the 24 December 1995 general elections, the WP's board of directors declared that no women would be allowed to appear on the candidate lists; they even removed the names of previously registered women. This met with tremendous public reaction and was held to be an overt manifestation of the WP's hidden intentions to relegate women to the private sphere. Although this decision by the WP was fiercely criticized, other political parties on both the left and right ran only a few women candidates. Still, none of these parties banned women from participating in elections. In view of the public reaction, the WP's justifications of its decision seemed inadequate and unconvincing. The party issued statements saying that its followers were not ready to send their women to parliament, implicitly alluding to parliamentary dress code regulations that did not allow covered women to attend. The party also argued that the party delegates, not the party administration, had failed to promote women as candidates, implying that it was the women's own fault that they did not get the support of party delegates. Ironically, despite the severe criticism leveled against the WP, this situation relieved many, especially those who had claimed that an Islamic party would neither conform to the rules of the democratic system nor maintain the legal and civil rights that women had already gained through the republican reforms.

Some women members of the WP, though, were quick to approve the party's decision. To admit women to parliament would be untimely given the political context (the ban on head scarves in public institutions in general and the parliamentary dress codes in particular). The women planned to work for the success of the party even harder than before. The eagerness of those WP women who wanted to be candidates was attributed to the increasing number of the people in the party, particularly women, who had joined the party after its outstanding success in the 1994 municipal elections without fully comprehending its real cause. It was also said that women registered their own names without waiting to receive an invitation from the directors of the party.[7]

In the April 1999 general elections, Merve Kavakçı, a young, covered computer engineer, a divorcée with two children, educated in the United States and head of international relations of the ladies' commissions, received an invitation from the VP's leadership cadre and was elected to the parliament together with two uncovered women: Nazh Ihcak, a well-known right-wing journalist, and Oya Akgönenç, an associate professor of international relations and political science. Another covered woman, Nesrin Ünal, a medical doctor who was elected to the parliament in the same election from the ultranationalist Milliyetçi Hareket Partisi (Nationalist Movement Party), stated that she would uncover her head when she went to parliament because she respected both the principals of the Turkish state and its founder, Atatürk, but would continue to cover her head outside parliament.

Merve Kavakçı did not uncover her head and aroused an enormous reaction when she took her parliamentary oath in May 1999. The Democratic Left Party's members, who held the majority in parliament, protested her appearance for twenty-five minutes by continuously clapping their hands and shouting "out, out, out" until she was forced to leave the Grand National Assembly. She was thereby prevented from taking her oath and legally becoming a member of parliament.

For months Merve Kavakçı remained in the media and political spotlight. The volume of press coverage on her alone could be the subject of a separate study. Each of her previous relations and actions were reviewed by the media, and before long it was discovered that she was also a citizen of the United States who gave speeches there at international conferences about Islamic *cihad*.[8] Ultimately, she was prevented from becoming a member of parliament, and was stripped of her Turkish citizenship. Former President Demirel labeled her a separatist and a provocateur. She was seen as both a symbolic pawn of Islamic forces, and as a political actor: a militant who managed to be a provocative trigger for the problems of Islamism, secularism, democracy, human rights, freedom of individual expression, citizenship rights, women's rights, the boundaries between the public and private spheres, and the countless others that constitute the basis of political and social life. She gave an edge to the ascendancy of what I call the symbolic feminization of Turkish right-wing politics: the gaining of political credit both by and over women, hence guaranteeing an image of being modern, liberal, and democratic.

Ideological Bases and the Forms of the Political Attachments of Islamist Women

The women who support Islamic ideals in general, and the political ideals of the WP-VP line in particular, do not constitute a monolithic entity. They are diverse in terms of their levels of education, class and status, cultural background, and their social expectations and future aspirations. Yet, when they come to grips with the question of "life politics" (Giddens 1991)—that is, the question "How should we live?" they seem likely to share certain ideals, particularly concerning the basic premises of gender roles, which took their ultimate form within the boundaries of a given imagination regarding Islamist gender relations. This becomes especially true insofar as the discursive elements of that imagination are perceived as indisputable components of Islamic faith. This faith dimension of Islamic politics not only provides legitimacy to the WP-VP but makes its followers vulnerable to certain types of political ploys that can hardly be challenged as long as the religious loyalty of its followers is mobilized for political ends. Thus, working for the party's ladies' commissions can become a matter of service to God, a highly legitimate cause that others cannot easily compete with, as well as a matter of gaining personal autonomy: being Muslims, they see no deity or power over them but God. However, it is one thing to encourage women to interpret religion in order to gain individual autonomy and to break with their traditional bonds and participate in political activities. It is quite another to expect them to comply with party discipline and be loyal to its rules and ideological principles once they have joined.

Although in Turkish political life, submission to party discipline and hierarchy is expected behavior, the ways in which Islamist women activists perceive their attachment to the party and seek their place both in the party and everyday life show considerable differences. First, as I have observed (Saktanber 1994, 1997), women activists do not organize and participate in cultural and political activities in order to compete with men on the basis of individualistic concerns, but rather because they believe in supporting men willingly in both public and private life. They do this without, however, undermining the importance of obtaining the status of "person," having been recognized as women who can play a significant role in the advancement of their community in addition to the role that they play in the family. Here "community" may refer to the immediate social environment or to some larger social unit such as Islamic *ümmet* (the community of all Muslims), as well as to any kind of social ties that provide these women with a sense of belonging. It does not necessarily refer to a religious order or a specific religious community. In the course of their political action, they deliberately avoid construing themselves either as asexual comrades or manlike individuals. On the contrary, they feel themselves responsible for preserving their identity as Muslim women, which they hold to be enjoined by their religion. The dialogic boundaries of this identity are defined within the Islamic discourse on gender complementarity, according to which men and women are created with different natures or *fitrat* (innate characteristics) in order to fulfil different functions on earth. Since women are created with motherly qualities, they have the elevated attributes of sensitivity and affection that make them not only highly compassionate creatures as compared to men but also enable them to sacrifice themselves for others. This discourse on selflessness also determines their conditions in the party. It differs from the usual discourse on selflessness adhered to by the followers of other political ideals to the extent that the women in question assume it as the natural extension of their identity, not something to be cultivated in the process of becoming an active member of a political movement. Although selflessness is generally considered to be a necessary quality for those working for any political ideal, to the extent that women associate it with their gender, it determines their understanding of their participation in public life and politics. Moreover, contrary to the assumptions of those who oppose Islamic ideals, this natural attribute of women does not entail passivity; rather, it calls for extreme patience.

In their political endeavors, women utilize their talents and experiences gained through what might be called a "women's culture." This background allows them to build face-to-face contacts with other women on easy terms, listen to their problems in detail, be sensitive to the difficulties of their daily problems in the family, show sympathy for their hopes and fears for their children, find practical solutions to their immediate problems rather than give unachievable long-term advice, and share their problems about their married lives. All these skills become extremely important for ordinary women who, because of their secondary position in society, usually have to take things as they are and try to make the most of them. Much of what I have described here as the talents of female Islamic activists are not alien to any other populist way of forming political policies, or to women's politics in the context of what Waylen calls Third World politics, where the politicization of the private sphere entails the entry of women into the public sphere (1996, 17). What distinguishes them is that they also manage to provide a sense of trust: their political endeavors are undertaken only for the mercy of God since they also lead their lives as devoted Muslims. Thus, it becomes possible to convince others that they strive exclusively for the mercy of God and help people lead their lives in comfort following the "true path."

However, these new women activists do not limit their political activities to the dictates of an assumed common culture of womanhood. The university or lyceé graduates among them also organize seminars, panels, and discussion groups at the national and international levels and work with Muslim women's NGOs. Furthermore, they set up charity meetings and fashion shows and organize tours to different institutions to show their consideration for others' causes. They often make personal visits to targeted potential allies. They build close relationships with many Muslim youth and student organizations to mobilize them to take active roles in Islamic politics. Their overall success comes from their ability to mobilize women from different social classes and cultural backgrounds who, above all, like to see themselves as devoted, virtuous Muslims. In all these activities, what women aim to achieve is not gender equality between men and women, nor is their primary purpose to question the moral premises of patriarchal codes, be they secular or Islamic. Rather, they hope to build an Islamic society in which not equality but equity between men and women will be sustained according to the rules of an assumed just Islamic order, an order that would conform to the conditions of what many people expect from a democratic system.

Some Concluding Remarks

The political experience of women following the WP-VP line differs with the place they occupy in the party ranks and according to their interpretations of religious ideals. For example, the uncovered VP female members of parliament seem to be extremely far from seeing the religious cause of their party in terms similar to those that I depicted above. Perhaps because the VP had to erase its image as a religious party in the face of legal prosecution that threatens its existence, in an interview that I conducted with her on 28 February 2000, parliament member Oya Akgönenç insisted that the VP is not an Islamic party and has nothing to do with religion. In her view, "the VP is a completely new center-right party that is nationalist in the sense of protecting national values, respectful of religion as long as it remains a cultural characteristic of this society, and social democrat in economic terms." She said she joined the VP both because the leader invited her and because the party seemed to be a place where she could realize her democratic ideals while also being on the side of the "underdog." She avoided making detailed comments on the case of Merve Kavakçı except to say that society was not ready to deal with it. To my surprise, she also added that she had warned her party not to follow the "fashionable trend" of putting women to the forefront politically, a tendency that had become quite widespread among all political parties. On the other hand, Nazlı Ihcak seems much more familiar with the religious discourse of her party, coming as she does from a right-wing tradition. She explains she joined the party to protect the rights of conservative sections of society who are exposed to unjust treatment (Ihcak 1998, 197). She also actively supported Merve Kavakçı. Nevertheless, all the women in the VP agree that the overall situation of women in society is unacceptable and in dire need of improvement; but again, they believe that human rather than gender rights are prime. This understanding parallels what Eraslan (2000, 220) calls the "solemn silence" (*hikmetli sessizlik*) that prevails among the Islamist women political activists: that is, women comply with party discipline instead of forming a "women's opposition." All the evidence shows that this understanding will continue to prevail in the foreseeable future of the VP, but how long the symbolic feminization of right-wing politics in Turkey will last is quite another matter.

Notes

1. Contrary to widely held belief, there have never been any laws prohibiting the use of the veil in universities or elsewhere in modern Turkey; but other forms of regulation pertaining to certain restricted areas and public institutions were valid. Therefore the ban on Islamic head covering has always been an issue for the public institutions and universities. However, the consensus that interpreted the ban on Islamic attire in universities as an extension of the constitutional principles related to secularism was broken after the acceptance of a more democratic constitution in 1960. It was only after 1982 that the first outright prohibition against the Islamic head scarf was made by the Turkish Council of Higher Education under pressure from the NSC. The rule was softened in 1984 and 1987, repealed in 1989, and reinstituted in its most severe form after the 28 February Decrees of 1997.
2. In Turkish culture, for a woman to be an unknown man's *yenge* has a moral importance because it puts a sexual distance between them; he sees her in the same way he would view the wife of his brother.

3. The Family Protection Law was accepted in 1998 to protect women and children from domestic violence.
4. See Keskin, chapter 17 of this volume.
5. Personal communication with Halise Çiftçi, the chairperson of the Ladies' Commission of Ankara Greater Municipality, 12 August 1996.
6. Personal communication with Taciser İçyer, who was responsible for the Public Relations Unit of the Ladies' Commission of Ankara Greater Municipality, 10 August 1996.
7. Personal communication with Halise Çiftçi, Taciser İçyer and Lale Lüleci (Lüleci worked for the International Relations Unit), 10–12 August 1996.
8. Alternately translatable as "holy war," "religious endeavor," and also "warfare against the self," but here meaning a fight for Islamic social order.

6

"And We Ate Up the World": Memories of the *Sección Femenina*

Victoria L. Enders

The historiography of women on the right is fruitful ground for those theoretical and methodological debates that have enlivened and enlarged the field of women's history for the last two decades. The emergence of Spanish women's history has coincided with a major historiographical revolution in the larger narrative of Spanish national history—itself occasioned by the death of Franco in 1975. Thus, previous categories and assumptions have proved doubly inadequate to explain the reality of women's experiences in Spain. A case in point is the record of the Women's Section of the Spanish Falange during the period of the Civil War. The Spanish Falange was a hybrid political product of its time: it was formed in the 1930s on the model of Mussolini's fascism, but with distinctive Spanish features. The Women's Section of the Falange, or its *Sección Femenina*, shared with their male colleagues these hybrid characteristics: female Falangists claimed loyalty to both what they termed the "revolutionary" doctrine of José Antonio Primo de Rivera, the founder of the Falange, and to what they claimed to be the "eternal essence" of Spain. This they found concretized in the historical tradition of Isabel I and in Spanish Catholicism, which was best represented for them by Saint Teresa of Avila. In fact, they claimed devotion to apparently contradictory principles drawn from both sides of a divide that had bifurcated Spanish history from the time of Napoleon, most violently during the Civil War of 1936–39. How could they have maintained this position?

Spanish women's studies—and particularly the groundbreaking work that brought gender analysis to the historical study of the Spanish Civil War—have generally employed Marxist and feminist theory and focused attention on working women and their anarchist, communist, and socialist political sympathies, recuperating their experiences for Spanish history and asking questions related to gender and class consciousness. These pioneering gender studies understandably reflect the political climate of the post-Franco transition to democratic restoration. This same leftist sympathy infuses the work of such scholars as Sheelah Ellwood, Giuliana de Febo, María Teresa Gallego Méndez, María Inmaculada Pastor, Rosario Sánchez López, and Geraldine Scanlon, all of whom turned their focus to women on the right. Here, present political categories are reified in a historical analysis, which to a degree reduces and thus obscures the complexity of women's experience. Historical agency—or the exercise of conscious choice—is harder to recognize when political motivations are impenetrable to the observer; in these works by historians of the left, historical agency is more often denied women on the right, while their claims of agency are labeled "false consciousness." More recently, however, studies of women and fascism are looking more closely at the lives of fascist women and reveal an unexpected diversity and complexity in their motivations. The work of Martin Durham (1998) on Englishwomen and Ralph Leck (2000) on German women exemplify this more detailed and fluid reading of the concerns and motivations of women who joined the right. The present study of Falangist women is a contribution to that larger effort to examine the experiences of women on the right in Spain, based on their own words, as they recall their motivations of a half-century before.

Between 1987 and 1991, I interviewed a number of women who had played important roles in the Women's Section of the Falange. I spoke with these women, including Pilar Primo de Rivera (1910–1991), in the last years of their lives; they were looking back—during a time when the left dominated both Spanish politics and culture—and reflecting on the rationale that had determined the contours of their lives. From these interviews, which are relatively rare and which will become part of a much longer work on memory and ideology, I am culling a small selection that focuses on their reasons for joining the Falange. My objective here is to set these choices in the context of the time: to probe the surface of political choice to the underlying impetus and ideology that informs it. By considering these accounts of their experience, which they claim assimilated elements of both left and right, the goal is to transcend a rigid categorical divide, with all its accompanying associations, and advance a more nuanced discussion of the difficulties of identifying, categorizing, and explaining the experiences of women on the right (Enders and Radcliff 1999, 1–16, 375–397). The present study fills in an area of modern Spanish women's history that still remains largely blank: an account of the motivations of these rightist women as they remember their early experiences with the Falange, in their own voices.

The *Sección Femenina* was created in 1934 to give aid to Falangist prisoners and assistance to the families of fallen members during the troubled years of the Second Spanish Republic. The Falange, an uneasy blend of revolutionary syndicalism and authoritarian nationalism, with fascist trappings reminiscent of Mussolini's corporative model, was the offspring of José Antonio Primo de Rivera. A young Andalusian aristocrat, José Antonio's charisma and revolutionary ideology captured the imagination of a sector of youth, and in particular the loyalty of his younger sister, Pilar. Under his influence, Pilar Primo de Rivera undertook to organize the female sympathizers, at first mainly sweethearts and relatives of Falangist members, into a support organization, the *Sección Femenina*. The original group numbered seven. At that time, the Falange was one of a number of rightist parties.

Following Jose Antonio's "politics of synthesis," the Falangists believed that the divisions inherent in parliamentary government and liberal doctrine could be overcome, and Spain united, under Christian doctrine and the Falangist spirit. Recovering its imperial essence, Spain would rediscover its path, establish social justice, and achieve its *"destino en lo universal."* This uneasy blend of traditional Catholicism and revolutionary syndicalism in Falangist ideology hindered its ability to win adherents, and the Falange remained a small, politically ineffectual party at the outbreak of the Civil War. The arrest of José Antonio in the spring of

1936, and his execution behind Republican lines in November, deprived the party of the sole leader capable of maintaining its tenuous unity. The subsequent history of the Falange reveals a continual unfolding of factions and rivalries, coups and countercoups among its leaders. On April 19, 1937, at the height of these intraparty tensions, General Franco, having declared himself generalissimo and head of state of nationalist Spain the previous October, staged a preemptive coup against the Falange leadership and incorporated the party into the hierarchy of command under his control by proclaiming a new national party. The *Falange Española Tradicionalista y de las J.O.N.S.* was an unwieldy amalgam of the Catholic and monarchist "Traditionalist Union" and the already joined Falange Española of the Juntas of National-Syndicalist Offensive. Some resisted, and others among the *camisas viejas*—the party "old shirts"—decided to bide their time and work for their aims within the state, grumbling their discontent and nursing their dreams of revolution.

This period of consolidation in 1937 is an interesting moment in which to look at the *Sección Femenina:* founded three years before by the original group of Pilar Primo de Rivera and six of her friends and relatives, the organization grew to about three hundred in 1934 and to about eight hundred in 1935 (S. F., *Misión,* 10). Statistics from the *Sección Femenina* are sometimes inconsistent but they do give an indication of developments. According to its published accounts, membership jumped to nine thousand in 1936 and to two hundred thousand in 1937, doubling again in the next year (S.F., *Consejos,* 45). Civil war had broken out in Spain in July of 1936, and these numbers, of course, reflect the drastic imperatives of war conditions as the *Sección Femenina* organized women for war relief. Of those four hundred thousand members, three hundred thousand belonged to the Auxilio Social. These nonpolitical volunteers provided food, clothing, and shelter to widows, orphans, and the destitute, and taught them to "love God and understand the Falange" (S. F., *Misión,* 11). The *Sección Femenina* set up sewing centers to produce uniforms, and mobile laundries at the fronts to care for the needs of the soldiers. Eight thousand of its members were nurses. By 1939, the number of affiliates is said to have risen to 580,000 (Payne, 1961, 203).

Upon the victory of the Franco forces in 1939 and the establishment of Franco's dictatorship, the *Sección Femenina* became the sole state organization with authority over women from 1939 till the death of Franco in 1975. Pilar Primo de Rivera remained at its head and as a member of the Council of State exercised her mandate to form Spanish womanhood for the next thirty-six years. Every women who desired employment with the state—which included any teaching post—or who wanted to obtain a driver's license, a passport, or the like, was obligated to serve six months with the *Sección Femenina:* three months of instruction and three months of voluntary service. It was a massive organization through which almost every female in Spain—willingly or unwillingly—was eventually channeled.

Pilar was born in 1910, one of six children of General Miguel Primo de Rivera–José Antonio being the firstborn—who was dictator of Spain from 1923 to 1930. Death from childbirth, at the birth of Fernando, claimed their mother, Casilda Saenz de Heredia. Left with six small children, Primo de Rivera, then a lieutenant colonel, summoned his mother, two sisters, and a brother from Jérez de la Frontera to Madrid to establish a household and attend to his children. The combination of these factors—an absent mother, an authoritarian father often distanced from his children because of his career, the religious influence of the aunts, the economic constraints of a nonmonied military family, the patriotic and heroic values cultivated in a male-dominated household—left an indelible mark on Pilar, and subsequently on the organization she created. Also as a result, there developed an unusually high degree of trust and reliance among the children, so close in age. Pilar, who had revered her father—"the person most admired in the world, because in our case he was really admirable" (Pilar Primo de Rivera 1983, 18)—transferred her loyalty to her older brother José Antonio. As she said, "He saw that Spain was going nowhere ... and it occurred to him to found the Falange on the principles of the authenticity of social justice, the unity of Spain and the truth of Spain ... and I followed him" (author interview, 9 January 1989). Dionisio Ridruejo, a former Falangist, attests to the purity of the Women's Section's fidelity to José Antonio's Falange:

> The only part of the new party that maintained the identity of the former party was the *Sección Femenina* of the Falange, and that was so for the simple reason that its leadership was embodied by a sister of José Antonio who, as a result, remained as if sacralized by the militants and as if untouchable.... For the time, being, the *Sección Femenina* ... will be the collective vestal of the ancient cult. (As quoted in Martín Gaete 1987, 56)

Pilar remained unmarried, dedicating her life to the memory of José Antonio and to his mission.

My conversations with Pilar and some of the women who had held positions of responsibility in her organization explored why they had chosen the Falange and how it had held their loyalty for the better part of their lives. Again and again in these conversations, I heard three themes repeated. First, they believed that the Falangist ideology fashioned by José Antonio—which they regarded as a truly revolutionary ideology—had offered them a meaningful choice not offered by the major parties contesting for power in the new Republican political arena. They faulted the conservative Catholic Spanish right because it had no program for social reform, and they considered the left and its parliamentary politics to be unnatural to Spain and dangerously linked with international "godless" communism. To them, Falangism offered a corporative model of government that not only addressed the situation of the poor and desperate in the Spain of the 1930s, but was also firmly based on the family and Spanish Catholicism. Second, they reiterated that a central inspiration in their life projects had remained José Antonio—who had formulated and embodied those ideals— closely seconded by his sister Pilar. Finally, I found that these aging women of the right had evaluated their lives—devoted over decades to the *Sección Femenina*—and found them to be rich in fulfillment, in fellowship, in meaning, and in agency. That is, they believed that they had been meaningful historical agents of their time.

The case of the Women's Section of the Falange clearly figures among those paradoxical cases of organized activist women exhorting the majority of their sisters to return to their traditional roles. The women of the *Sección Femenina* accepted the gender system of their society, based on a Catholic view of woman possessed of a separate nature, which prescribed for her a separate sphere of activity. Women's importance in this gender system is identified with her role as wife and mother, her proper sphere of activity: the family. As the preserver and transmitter of religious and social values, her purity was essential and her self-denial required. A silent and self-disciplined submission to hierarchy, whether religious, familial, or governmental, figured as the central operational code in her decision making. Number twenty-five of José Antonio's "Twenty-Six Points" of Falangist doctrine had declared: "Our movement incorporates Catholic feeling—of a glorious and prevailing tradition in Spain—within the national reconstruction" (S.F., *Consejos*, 10). Thus the Falange and its Women's Section acquiesced completely in a patriarchal gender code.

It is the continuity of this gender code that María Teresa Gallego has emphasized in her study of the role of the *Sección Femenina* in the consolidation of the Francoist state (Gallego Méndez 1983, 151). In her argument, traditional Catholicism, Falangist fascism, and the Franco regime accentuated the primacy of and worked in concert to enforce the submission of women. However, if one takes 1937 as a focus for analysis, one is attracted by other possible interpretations. The propaganda of the time makes an appeal to a particular kind of submission: of women not to authority per se but to their *duty as women*. The change in emphasis suggests that it might be this subtle difference that influenced the increase in adherents to the *Sección Femenina* and to the regime. The publicity of the *Sección Femenina* served Spanish women an ideological brew that was a blend of religious models, historical precedents, and Falangist inspiration. In different styles, they communicated the same message: women were to fulfill their female duty. It was this call to fulfill their essence, not to disavow it, that drew women in such numbers.

The use of religious models and religious vocabulary in the formulation and diffusion of doctrine was a powerful legitimating factor for the *Sección Femenina* in a country where the index of religiosity among women was traditionally much greater than that among men (Gallego Méndez 1983, 143). For example, the Second Congress of the organization's leaders met in 1938 in Avila, the city of Santa Teresa. This association was made by design: the *Sección Femenina* claimed Teresa as its "celestial saint," the model on which members were to pattern themselves (S.F., *Consejos*, 10, 24). Adherents were advised that if they imitated Teresa's strength, an "interior castle" would fortify them and enable them to carry out their duty. Their own propaganda likened the members' blue shirts to "soldiers' uniforms" or "nuns' habits," which recalled the "ascetic and military sense of life proposed by José Antonio" (S.F., *Consejos*, 30). Fittingly, membership in the *Sección Femenina* required an oath of loyalty to the "sainted brotherhood" of the Falange, reminiscent of the Catholic Hermandades, or Brotherhoods, of the Reconquest.

The rooting of Falangist precepts in historical precedent (as with the Hermandades) also served to present the propaganda of the *Sección Femenina* in familiar and acceptable form. The Falange had adopted the yoke and the arrows of Ferdinand and Isabel as a symbol of religious and territorial unity. These symbols, which represented Spain on the threshold of a new state and of imperial greatness, clothed the Falangist doctrine of unity and empire in ancient and revered significance. Isabel I, "one of the purest in history," whose service, sacrifice, and discipline were symbolized by the yoke in the Falangist emblem, was celebrated as the ideal earthly model (S.F. *Consejos*, 76). The leadership cadres of the *Sección Femenina* were exhorted to accept the authority of their position, as Isabel had.

If the women of the *Sección Femenina* would take on the yoke (of duty), as they should, they would regain an "interior freedom" lost for two centuries (S.F., *Consejos*, 76). As in the above cases, submission is dictated, but it is a submission based on strength.

There is no doubt that the *Sección Femenina* subscribed to patriarchal values and was to play the leading role in a systematic effort to indoctrinate those values into two generations of Spanish women. (For an important, recent study on the gender ideology of the Franco regime, see Aurora Morcillo 2000). Its spokeswoman, Pilar, was unequivocal and unapologetic in her endorsement of these values. In this canon, woman's sacred duty was to be a mother and to be a complement to her husband. Pilar Primo de Rivera reiterated that woman was by nature submissive, that she realized herself most fully through self-abnegation (Primo de Rivera 1983). Proscribed from competing with man, or attempting to replace him, woman was to act in the well-defined and restricted world appropriate to her qualities within traditional patriarchal culture.

What was the appeal? Why would young women be drawn to a political organization that urged such restrictions on them? First, it needs to be recognized that the adherence to patriarchal values was not an exclusive characteristic of women on the right, but part of a wider conservatism of the time. "To understand the popular appeal of this conservatism (as opposed to its usefulness to political elites), its attractiveness needs to be seen as a product of anxiety," Helen Graham has pointed out. "Whether overtly articulated or not, the reinforcing of traditional gender divisions was clearly felt to be one of the keys to stabilizing societies in flux, along socially and economically traditional lines" (Graham 1996, 100; for a comparison to France, see Roberts 1994). This force was strong in Spain of the 1930s, during conditions of acute political and social instability, and was reproduced across the political spectrum, with leftist parties reinforcing gendered spheres even while they dispersed a rhetoric of equality. According to Shirley Mangini:

> The most valuable quality of women on both the left and the right, according to all treatises on the subject, was "abnegation": self-sacrifice, self-denial, giving up oneself, whether for the revolution, for the family, for the church, or for some other cause. In summary, selflessness was the prescription for females in Spain. Ibarruri[1] pleads for abnegation—as does, unwittingly, her reactionary counterpart, Pilar Primo de Rivera . . . head of the Feminine Section. (Mangini 1995; 43)

At a time of increasing insecurity, according to Graham, the right "proffered a vision of a separate sphere where the familial and religious values and structures which shaped women's identity would be cherished and perpetuated" (1996, 105). The gender retrenchment evidenced in the rhetoric of *Sección Femenina* was hardly exclusive to the right or to Spain.

Nevertheless, the apparent contradiction remains: the women I spoke with experienced their participation in the *Sección Femenina* as empowering, despite the rhetoric. Elsewhere I have suggested that one means of resolving that apparent contradiction was development of a matrix of symbols and saints that integrated nationalism and feminism (Enders 1992). The Sección Feminina adopted the "Y" of Isabel as its personal symbol because, as one tract elucidated, "the creator of an Empire, as an unending fountain of enormous energy and as the exemplary demonstration of constructive will, paired with the sweetest attributes of wife and mother, Isabel of Castile, wife of Ferdinand, presides spiritually over the abnegating labor of the national-syndicalist women" (Ballesteros Gaibrois n.d., 15–16). Saint Teresa of Avila, the religious counterpart to Isabel, was chosen to be their patron "because," Pilar explained, "you, comrades of the *Sección Femenina*, have, like her, the mission of being founders. You have to teach through all the lands of Spain the longing for our Revolution. . . . But in a quiet manner, without exhibitions and without speeches, because those are not appropriate to women—but simply, as Teresa did" (G. Di Febo 1987, 107).[2] An activist woman defending "true" Spanish values was thus not contradictory, but internally coherent.

If we turn to the voices of the members of the *Sección Femenina*, those who played leadership roles in the organization, we hear women who had subscribed wholeheartedly to the values of the Falange. Some were there at the original founding of the party, and through their voices we hear that it was the doctrine of the Falange—distinctive and unique to these women at the time—that drew them. "What moved us was the political idea of José Antonio. That was what most moved us," said Concha, as she stated the leitmotif of all the interviews (author interview, 13 January 1989). The women I spoke with had held positions of responsibility in the *Sección Femenina*, and remained active in the organization for a long time. José Antonio's doctrine, the "Twenty-Six Points of the Falange" introduced in 1934, formed the initial inspiration and remained the ideological core of the Women's Section for forty years.[3] Concha explained that the Falange offered something unique to people caught between conflicting political claims:

> We had a political dissatisfaction: we weren't of the left, nor were we of the right. The right seemed to us to be to blame for many things that had happened in Spain. We didn't have a close rapport with the left because communist ideas weren't for us: in general, we upheld a Catholic concept of life and a concept of respect for the family, of family tradition, of customs. But of infantile behavior [blind exaggerated religiosity]: we didn't like this business of the very inflexible right. (author interview, 13 January 1989)

The Falange shared the concern with the left that it was essential to address the needs of the poor and landless in Spain in a more responsible way than traditional charity or prayers, and they rejected the parties of the right for not responding adequately to Spain's needs. In the accounts of all these Falangist women, the quintessence of their doctrine—and what they found to be missing in the traditional right—was its call for "social justice."

Lola, one of the seven founding members of the *Sección Femenina*, explained what social justice meant to the group:

> Social justice is that each child at birth has the same possibilities before him. The same rights and the same possibilities that other children have, without privilege— or whatever—playing a part. It was José Antonio's principle, and it was ours, social justice before all. And education, because a child who is born can have the same rights, but if he doesn't have sufficient formation or sufficient education, he will always be on a lower level. Thus for us, social justice begins with education. (author interview, 19 June 1989)

Lola argued that the enterprise of the Falange was "the fight for a new Spain in which social justice would triumph: the unity of her men and her lands." She continued: "All of us have fought with our best arms: the disinterested surrender, honesty, the fight for a new Spain in which social justice would triumph, the unity of her men and her lands. . . . And no, they weren't trite expressions; they were ideals for which we were as combative as we could be" (Lola, as quoted in Palacio 1981, 23).

The women of the Falange were convinced that their goal was a new, still-Catholic Spain for the betterment of all, including the poor, and not just a defense of privilege against the revolutionary threat of the left. Contrary to the other parties of the right that were monarchist, the members of the Falange had hoped that the "New Spain" would accompany the advent of the new Republic in 1931. Concha describes how:

> in my house also, like José Antonio, we were happy that the Republic should come. We weren't in any way monarchists, nothing to do with Alfonso the Thirteenth. Besides, look, then you had the aristocracy. He was a very sympathetic king, very affectionate with the people, very popular. But the people had so many needs, with so many differences, with so many problems. And it was truly an atrocious crisis. As soon as the Republic arrived we all hoped that it would equalize things, that it would establish justice. . . . But, in general, the Republic was a disaster—for all of us who believed in it. In my house, of course, we were all republicans. For this reason, then, we embraced the Falange, all of us, because . . . we weren't of the right, but neither were we communists. So it was necessary to search for balance: to take the good part of communism, the sense of a social program, and as well, the good part of the right, with its sense of the *patria*, of religion, of the family, and of tradition, of course. It was about uniting the two things. (author interview, 13 January 1989)

Thus the Falange offered a revolutionary social program in answer to the critical social needs of Spain, but unlike the "foreign imports" such as Marxism or even liberalism, it reinforced the position of Catholicism and professed support for a more traditional role for women in Spanish life. The threat of change inherent in any social transformation—even theirs—was balanced by an emphasis on Spain's "eternal values."

José Antonio had defined the essence of Spain as Catholic, and the members of the *Sección Femenina* were careful to stress their faithful adherence to Spain's official religion. But it was faith in Jesus Christ [Dios JesuCristo] that inspired their respect, "not the forms of religion, nor religious congregations, nor the Vatican," specified Lola. "For us, the idea of religion is Dios JesuCristo" (author interview, 19 June 1989). José Antonio had underscored that:

> the way to respect woman is not to remove her from her magnificent destiny and hand her over to masculine functions. . . . True feminism should not consist of wanting for women the functions that are deemed superior today, but in surrounding feminine functions with increased human and social dignity. (Balletbó 1982, 7)

Accordingly, they chose Saint Teresa "as an example of a courageous woman, a strong woman, a woman who tried to clear away obstacles to achieve the ends that she considered worthy," explained Tomasa, another comrade. Teresa of Avila was a "revolutionary—in the mystical sense—who also broke many molds in her time" (author interview, 9 July 1987). Again, in their choice of patrons, the women of the Falange chose to harmonize, to reconcile ostensibly opposing values, this time embodied within the comprehensive image of a female saint.[4]

Consistent with their identity as Falangists, members of the *Sección Femenina* took pains to differentiate themselves as believers from other groups of Catholic women. They considered the women of the Carlist or Traditionalist Communion,[5] for example, to be "conservative persons and very to the right, too much to the right," declared Tomasa. Then she elaborated, noting that after Franco had unified the Falange with the Carlist Traditionalists in 1937, many of the Traditionalist women had continued meeting independently, and, "as they liked other things—did not join in with the Sección Femenina. But," she added, "many valuable women came from that group." As for the more mainstream Catholic Action (Acción Católica): "The Catholic Action didn't understand us. Catholic Action was completely made up of very retrograde women. Next to them, we came out very progressive and very advanced. . . . And the Catholic Action were, well, very inclined to the religious type of things: spiritual formation, moral formation."[6] Tomasa pointed out that many women from Catholic Action had joined the *Sección Femenina*. The *Sección Femenina* had in turn respected their religious concerns, as evidenced by the religious component of the courses they offered. "But," she concluded, "the spirit of the Women's Section, and the goals of the Women's Section, were wider." The courses offered by the *Sección Femenina* had included religious formation only as the spiritual part of a larger "human formation"—"not," she emphasized, "because our goal was religious work" (author interview, 9 July 1987).

With pride these former members of the *Sección Femenina* remembered being perceived as "advanced" or progressive, to the point that male members of the Church even considered their activities improper for good Catholic women. Tomasa recalled that:

> in those times, some twenty, thirty years ago, and in Spain especially, there were many bishops who did not look upon us with benevolent eyes. And many religious people who didn't look upon all this with benevolent eyes. In fact, they would say to us, that we were perverting the youth! But this didn't matter to us, because we also had our religious advisors and were authentically religious.
>
> All my life, I had been a person of firm religious conviction, all my family. . . . I have a Jesuit brother, three religious sisters. A religious family! I even had to go through one occasion when a priest who had confessed me said to me that if I didn't remove myself from the Women's Section, my soul was in danger [*si no me borraba de la Sección Femenina peligraba mi alma*]. For sure, I didn't ever return to confess with that man again. (author interview, 9 July 1987)

The members of the *Sección Femenina* remembered that others "saw us as revolutionaries." And what was the revolution? "Simply to promote women in all areas" summarized Tomasa (author interview, 9 July 1987). Repeatedly, these Falangist women underscored the revolutionary content of their cause, its focus on social justice, with added emphasis on women and children. Clearly, that element of Falangist doctrine figured centrally in their motivational world.

Accompanying the refrain of Falangist ideology was a second motif that ran through the testimonies of the Falangist women: they all described in glowing terms the overwhelming impression made by the presence of the siblings José Antonio and Pilar Primo de Rivera in the early days of the Falange. Numerous personal records among the male Falangists document the strong power of attraction of José Antonio, a magnetism made up of considerable physical, intellectual, and spiritual force. More than a half-century later, the young women who joined the *Sección Femenina* still recalled his influence on them and their friends. Concha remembers:

> He was a physically very handsome man: very attractive, serious, even timid. He wasn't very open. He had a great sense of responsibility and of justice, with an extraordinary intelligence. Besides that he was a poet. There is a phrase of his that says, "No one has ever affected the nations more than the poets, and woe is the person who does not know how to raise up against the poetry that destroys, the poetry that promises."[7] He was wonderful. His whole concept was a kind of poetry—very related to Spanish tradition, to what Spain had signified in the history of Europe and the world. (author interview, 13 January 1989)

But it wasn't just the poetry that attracted people to him, Concha stressed. It was "everything. His complete personality."

For a few years, José Antonio Primo de Rivera was the idol of an entire cross section of Spanish youth, and no one idolized him more than his sister Pilar. To her he was "a profound intellectual . . . a brilliant lawyer. He had read, he was very well educated." When we learn that they were taught by their father that they must "provide justice to the social being," it becomes easier to understand their close collaboration. Pilar mused about her father's influence: "Perhaps his life of contact with all the problems of Spain awoke in him this sense of justice." He passed this mission on to her: "I realized all this with the Falange; with what I had heard (about social justice) from my father" (author interview, 2 June 1987).

José Antonio also revered his father. In fact, his desire to vindicate his father's memory motivated his entrance into politics. Concha recalls the impression and excitement caused by José Antonio's first appearance:

> The first that I knew of José Antonio, being very young, was that we were very disgusted . . . with the politics of the right and the politics of the left, and suddenly there was a poster in the street of Madrid that said, "a seat in the Cortes to defend the holy memory of my father." His personality was something extraordinary. He was socially avant-garde, a defender of the simple and humble classes face-to-face with his own. Because he was titled: the Marqués de Estella. He wasn't understood by many beneath him, because he was a *señorito* of the aristocracy; and the aristocracy repudiated him for being socially advanced, someone who defended the worker. He struggled between two negative forces, but many people followed him, many. If only he had lived a few years more! (author interview, 13 January 1989)

We are accustomed to hearing such declarations about the brother: "He was a marvel, José Antonio." Yet, Concha extends the same attraction to the whole family. "The whole family Primo de Rivera. It's astonishing. It's a lineage. The father was a marvelous person" (author interview, 13 January 1989).

And, listening to the voices of the *Sección Femenina*, we can also discern the playing out of a strong but complex role for Pilar in the organization. Her brother, José Antonio, would say of her: "This Pili . . . is very dull [*deslucida*] but she is very talented (Lola, author interview, 19 June 1989). "Timidity" and "simplicity" are the words Lola used to describe Pilar. Nevertheless, as national delegate, she controlled an organization that at times numbered in the hundreds of thousands. And she appears to have been in many ways a model for many women of her generation.

As one might expect, many young women joined the Falange through family connections, usually brothers, or friends. Concha looked back on her initiation into the Falange and the importance of Pilar's example:

> I remember very well when my *novio* [fiancé] and my brother joined the Falange. I said to them, "I want to join. If you two are going to, I want to join too. I like this idea. I like it." Then, in order to keep me from joining—so as not to involve myself in problems, in danger—they told me, "No, there are no women in the Falange." So I told them, "But the sister of José Antonio is there, and that I know." "OK, she helps him, as you can help the two of us." And so, I didn't join then, but I helped them just the same. (author interview, 13 January 1989)

"At that moment," recalled Pilar, "we were all around twenty-some, or thirty years old, we were all young, and the girls came because they liked it" (author interview, 2 June 1987). Lola also described the pull of Pilar on her original small group of friends:

> We were basically the ones that she (Pilar) called. When she knew a woman, a girl, who she thought would be able to serve, she called her and gave her a function, an office or post in her organization. Already in 1933, I had heard Pilar say that the women of Spain still were not big fans of participating in things. Really, it wouldn't occur to anyone to belong to a women's organization. And then it was Pilar who gathered them all together, and was calling us, and giving us orders—norms—by which to do things. (author interview, 19 June 1989)

From the beginning, Pilar was the nucleus around which the organization coalesced. "In those moments," continued Lola, "all the women, even those who had not done anything, were full of enthusiasm, of the necessity of doing something, of contributing, sacrificing, of whatever was needed. And then, if there was a call from Pilar, certainly, many came who never before had dreamed of having these activities, or of doing anything" (author interview, 19 June 1989). Pilar's beliefs, ideals, and organizational methods were fundamental to the character of the organization. "We did not dissent much among ourselves," recalled Concha, "but if we did, the idea of Pilar predominated. Not that she imposed her ideas on us, but we explained our ideas in the committee—each one could have an opinion, though we didn't have a democratic vote. She carried us to conviction, and we all ended up convinced" (author interview, 13 January 1989).

The third main theme that I found emphasized when I talked with these women was their conviction that their lives had been unusually active, meaningful, and satisfying. In a variety of ways the former activists recounted the benefits that, in their minds, accrued to them as a result of their affiliation with the female Falange. According to two women, provincial leaders from La Coruña: "We achieved many benefits, because our [cause] was to provide justice and . . . yes, we did many things for women." And satisfaction? "Well, then, the fact of having served Spain. As we could, and no more. The fact of having served Spain in that which Spain asked of us at the moment, sometimes more easily, other times less—that gave many compensations and satisfactions" (Carmen, author interview, June 1989). And Lola repeats that satisfaction came from having served Spain: "Those of us who worked in the *Sección Femenina* [it was] as if it were a task so exciting, so exciting [to be] at the service of Spain. To establish social justice was an obsession" (author interview, 19 June 1989).

Concha echoes these testimonies, emphasizing that the principles of José Antonio—the Falangist ideals—had been the medium of an experience she describes in almost spiritual terms: "I found myself completely penetrated," she recalled.

> With the death of my fiancé (we were just about to marry), I was left completely destroyed. Then, thanks to my work in the *Sección Femenina*, I was able to work for the ideal for which he died, and to work for my country, and to speak with such a marvelous person as Pilar; and [to do these things] within the extraordinary ambience of the *Sección Femenina*, which never brought us a lucrative thing—money—because we made almost nothing. It was [the experience of] working to construct a Spain that had been destroyed, materially and morally. Then, I believe, that in the *Sección Femenina*, a new woman emerged. Because, in the *Sección Femenina*, the old taboos, or all these prejudices, were broken. A new woman emerged, brave, open, free, but with a great concept of religion, of the *patria*, of duty—then that mixture formed us. The *Sección Femenina* formed us, all of us who passed through. (author interview, 13 June 1989)

"It was an apostleship, a reason for living," she concludes. "It was to fill one's life."

This sense of apostleship and its inner meaning is reiterated by Margarita, another early affiliate: "We were fighters, battlers," she recalled,

> with such grand illusions, with such a great optimism. It seemed that we were going to eat up the world, and yes, we ate it up, many times. Don't believe we didn't. Because we achieved so many things, so many things. . . . There was always a current of relationship, of confidence, friendship, . . . tremendous. . . . And there were no quarrels nor huge discussions. Well, arguments [*polémicas*] to discuss matters, many, many. Tremendous. But in the sense of opposition, one against another, of mistrust . . . to try to put one above the other—of this, nothing. This didn't exist. It was a special current. For this, many people would say that it was a special thing that we had. And no doubt about it. But, the thing is that we started from a center . . . from some important principles, do you know? Later, we situated ourselves in a society that was in need . . . we fought for it. And then, naturally, we discovered we were like fish in water. We found ourselves enchanted with life. And with no remorse for anything, anything. (author interview, 16 January 1989)

Lola reiterated: "It was a giving of oneself—wholly, totally" (author interview, 19 June 1989).

Collective memory in the profoundly disrupted and traumatically discontinuous political world of the past century is, of course, ultimately at issue in the memory of the *Sección Femenina* women. The recurring themes in these memories—the strong pull of José Antonio's Falangist ideology, the power of the personalities of José Antonio and Pilar Primo de Rivera, and the personal fulfillment that rewarded their crusade for social justice in Spain—place this study at the center of current historiographical debates on memory and identity. In Peter Fritzsche's recent article, "The Case of Modern Memory," he underlines the importance of collective myths in the shaping of social identities and "their power to explain political motivations" (Fritzsche 2001, 89). Propelling the young women of the *Sección Femenina* was not only the constructed political myth of the Falangist future, but also a constructed historical myth of the Spanish past—embodied in the larger-than-life constructions of the women Isabel I and Teresa of Avila.

Fritzsche also offers the balancing argument, that historical circumstances themselves are the inescapable seedbed of social allegiances. The intense, even traumatic, experiences of these young women during the years of civil war produced in them a "generational consciousness": they were, in the words of Pierre Nora referring to another revolutionary generation, "a group united by age and dominated by the revolutionary event [that] discovered not just history as man's production of his own existence but also the power of collective action and social germination and the role of time in the unfolding historical process" (1996–98, 515). Leaders of the Women's Section thus conceived of themselves as active agents, the recognition of rupture and discontinuity in history and tradition opening up a place for "unprecedented activity" (Fritzsche 2001, 97). They became a "national cohort" and created their own narrative and memory system that enabled individuals to recognize their own, mute, experiences in this wider articulation (Fritzsche 2001, 108).

The *Sección Femenina* has been determined from the start to shape its own history: from organizing annual national congresses to formally commemorating its own martyrs; from restoring sites such as the Castilla de la Mota—to bolster its own historical narrative—to the recovery of traditional songs, dances, and cuisine. After the dissolution of the Women's Section, concerned members coalesced into a new group called *La Nueva Andadura* (the New Path). Their mission was to recover their history, which had been appropriated by the left in the new post-Franco culture. Insisting that their history be told as they remembered it, they archived their papers and their memories; they became a "memory cult." In so doing, still on crusade, they became once again the "priests and soldiers" of the Spanish Falangist "memory nation" (Fritzsche 2001, 99).

Notes

1. Dolores Ibarruri Gómez, a leader of the Spanish Communist Party, in 1933 created the Group of Anti-fascist Women (*Las Agrupaciones de Mujeres Anti-fascistas*) and later headed the Republic's Women's Auxiliary Commission (*Comisión Auxilio Femenino*) that organized women in antifascist war effort. She became the almost mythic heroine "La Pasionaria" in the battle for Madrid during the Civil War.
2. G. Di Febo posits the existence of an alternative "Christian Feminism" as a kind of "antagonistic model" to the Republic's efforts toward women's legal emancipation.

3. Stanley Payne has described the Falangist program as a "palingenetic project" for Spain. For a description of the ideology of José Antonio, see Payne 1999; especially 144–148.
4. For more on Saint Teresa as the patron of the *Sección Femenina*, see G. Di Febo 1987.
5. The Carlists, or Traditionalists, were forced into an uneasy shared identity when Franco merged the groups into the Falange Española Tradicionalista y de las J.O.N.S. in 1937.
6. Author Interview, 9 July 1987: *"La Acción Católica no nos entendia. La Acción Católica entonces, era—la componian toda mujeres como más retrogradas, nosotras a su lado resultabamos muy progresistas y muy lanzadas.... Y las de Acción Católica eran pues, como más inclinadas a la cosa de tipo religiosa, de formación espiritual, de formación moral, pero no con.... Pero el espíritu de Sección Femenina y de las metas de la Sección Femenina eran más amplias."*
7. *"A los pueblos no los han movido nadie más que los poetas y ay del que no sepa levantar frente a la poesía que destruye, la poesía que promete."*

part II.

Right Activisms and Racialized/Classed/ Religioned Others

7

The Gendered Organization of Hate: Women in the U.S. Ku Klux Klan

Kathleen M. Blee

Among all right-wing extremist groups in U.S. history—that is, groups far outside the political mainstream that favor violent means to achieve anti-egalitarian goals—the most successful in recruiting women members have been those that call themselves Ku Klux Klans (KKK). In the 1920s, KKK-affiliated women's Klans brought an estimated five hundred thousand women into the politics of virulent racism, anti-Catholicism, xenophobia, and anti-Semitism, forming what arguably was the largest extremist right-wing women's movement in U.S. history. Today's racist, anti-Semitic, and homophobic Klan is greatly reduced in size, numbering no more than twenty thousand (less than 1 percent of its 1920s membership), but probably at least one-quarter of these members are women.

Given women's significant involvement in the Klan, it is ironic that few political movements have been so active in promoting masculinity as a political virtue. From the all-male gangs in the mid-nineteenth century to the gender-integrated groups today, the KKK has presented itself as a vehicle for challenging threats to the social, economic, and political power of white U.S.-born Protestant (later, Christian) men. Indeed, the Klan explicitly identifies itself as a fellowship, or clan, of besieged and enraged white men. Despite this intense emphasis on masculine political power, however, many women have enlisted in the Klan's white supremacist crusade.

The participation of women in the Ku Klux Klan not only illustrates an interesting paradox in the history of U.S. racist politics, but also permits an examination of more general propositions about gender and the far right. In this chapter, I focus on three related issues. First, I examine the gendered nature of women's *participation* in the Klan in the 1920s and today and its implications for women's involvement in other extremist right-wing movements. Second, I explore the *motivation* of women who joined the Ku Klux Klan, how women are mobilized into right-wing movements that do not reflect, and are even antithetical to, their gendered interests. Third, I consider the *gender ideologies* of the Klan, focusing on how rhetorics of women's rights can support agendas of racial, religious, national, and sexual hatred and bigotry.

As a secret organization, the Klan does not make available its documents or membership lists. Thus, data about the participation, motivations, and gender ideologies of women in the Klan come from a variety of more indirect sources.

For the 1920s Klan, I used public and private collections of documents published by the Klan and secondary documents about the Klan. These were supplemented by oral history interviews that I conducted during the mid-1980s with a number of elderly former Klanswomen in Indiana. Information on today's Klan is from my life history interviews in the mid-1990s with women Klan activists, part of a larger project about women in the contemporary U.S. racist movement. This is supplemented by my observations at Klan events and analysis of propaganda issued by every existing Klan group over a one-year period.[1]

Women and the Far Right

Scant scholarly attention has been paid to the role of women in racist or extremist right-wing movements in the United States. This dearth of scholarship can be attributed to three conceptual shortcomings. The first problem is the assumption that right-wing extremism is best understood by focusing on its leaders and spokesmen. Due to both the difficulty (and danger) of obtaining reliable information from rank-and-file members of far-right groups and to an assumption that authority in the extreme right is always male dominated and top-down, scholarship on right-wing extremist movements is based almost entirely on written propaganda or interviews with (often self-proclaimed) leaders. This has skewed information on the far-right toward the pronouncements of those who are most visible to the public and away from members who are less open about their participation, resulting in biased data on participants in right-wing extremism.

Relying on the statements of those with organizational titles ensures the invisibility of women in mixed-gender groups of the extreme right. Very few women are official leaders or public spokespersons in the Klan or other such mixed-gender groups in the United States. This is not surprising, given the far-right's emphasis on the importance of men in racist politics and the vitriolic misogyny expressed in the propaganda and political agendas of virtually all right-wing groups in the United States. Yet the absence of women from leadership and public spokesperson roles in the far-right in the United States does not mean that women are not numerous, and even important, rank-and-file members of these movements. Indeed, women are often particularly sought as members by right-wing extremist movements precisely because they are less visible to outsiders, thus helping to shield groups from outside scrutiny and allowing better access to potential recruits. Moreover, the lines of authority in the Klan can be complicated, with leadership (in the sense of providing strategic direction, attracting and socializing new recruits, and organizing internal cohesion) exercised by middle-level leaders, including women, while formal, titled leaders, generally men, may command the allegiance of fairly few followers.

Second is the conceptual blinder of regarding even those women who hold official public or leadership roles in extremist right-wing groups as simply proxies for more powerful men. Thus, major figures in the history of the far-right in the United States such as Alma White, a Quaker preacher who became a defender of the KKK in the 1920s, or the influential American Nazi devotee of the 1930s, Elizabeth Dilling, have received far less scholarly attention than comparably situated, less influential male figures.[2]

Moreover, U.S. scholars commonly overlook the significance of women as members of right-wing movements, even when the extent of that participation is known. As an example, the existence of numerous women's chapters of the KKK in the 1920s was known to many historians, but without a gender-sensitive lens of analysis, Klanswomen were assumed to be the political or personal pawns of Klansmen, and scholarly attention was directed exclusively at the Klan's male members.

Third, the absence of women as subjects in scholarship on the extreme right is due to a belief that right-wing movements are intensely and uniformly patriarchal in both their ideologies and their practices. Certainly, support for the social, economic, and political privileges enjoyed by white, or Aryan, men is an outcome of virtually all extremist right-wing politics and an explicit goal of most far-right groups in the United States. However, the gender politics of groups in the far-right also can be complicated. Far-right groups at times have supported gender rights, although always narrowly conceived as the rights of white, or Aryan, women. Such support generally has been a tactic to recruit women members or to broaden the group's appeal to the political mainstream.

Further, the members of right-wing extremist groups can vary in their views about women's rights. Many women in right-wing extremist groups in the United States, including the Klan, espouse views about gender issues that are markedly different from those found in the propaganda of their groups or expressed by male leaders. In the 1920s, for example, a number of prominent women members of the Ku Klux Klan demanded gender equity within the larger Klan movement, over the objection of male Klan leaders. Today, some women in the Klan privately support women's access to abortion or governmental efforts to promote women's advancement at work, even as their groups strenuously denounce women's reproductive rights and state policies like affirmative action. Such complexities of gender ideology within the far-right in the United States are invisible to researchers who do not simultaneously scrutinize the rhetoric of organizational propaganda and the views of rank-and-file members.

The Ku Klux Klan

The Ku Klux Klan is a historically discontinuous series of four waves of organized racist activity in the United States. At each period of Klan activism, a number of discrete and often antagonistic Klan groups have claimed to be descendants of the original Klan. Although each Klan is distinct in its leadership and membership, the groups are unified in an agenda of hatred toward African Americans and members of other racial, religious, ethnic, and now, sexual minority groups. They also use similar organizational names, clothing, and rituals. The four most significant waves of Klan activity occurred in the 1860s, 1920s, 1970s, and from 1980 to the present (Bennett 1988; Chalmers 1981).

The initial Klan arose in the mid-1860s, at the end of the Civil War. Born as a violent response by southern whites against efforts at racial and political realignment within the U.S. South during Reconstruction, the first wave of the Klan loosely linked gangs of impoverished rural white male southerners, wealthy plantation owners, and industrialists who feared the loss of their political and economic supremacy. Women did not participate as members in this initial Klan, although white southern women were evoked as symbols of the tradition of racial and sexual supremacy that Klan men were expected to protect. This wave of the Klan was intensely violent, fomenting a bloody sweep of lynchings, assaults, arsons, and destruction and expropriation of property across the former states of the Confederacy, directed at freed African-American slaves, northern representatives of the Reconstruction government, and whites thought to be sympathetic to the new racial order. The first Klan collapsed in the mid-1870s in the face of federal pressure and as a new structure of white supremacist laws, agricultural sharecropping, and a racially exclusive political system shored up the racial structures formerly enforced by the system of slavery (McLean 1994; Blee 1991).

A second wave of the Klan emerged in the mid-1910s and gained strength through the mid-1920s in the period of high immigration from southern and eastern Europe and large-scale migration of African Americans from southern to northern states of the United States. Most scholars estimate the membership of the 1920s Klans at between 2 million and 3 million members, of whom about a half-million were women, making it the largest Klan and perhaps the largest extremist right-wing movement in U.S. history.

Unlike earlier and later waves of the Klan, the second Klan was stronger in many parts of the Midwest, East, and West, including such states as Indiana, Ohio, Oregon, and New York, than in the South. It took root both in large urban areas that were absorbing new immigrants and in racially and religiously homogenous small towns and rural areas that were experiencing few population changes, and it enlisted a substantial proportion, even a majority, of the white, native-born, Protestant population. This Klan drew members from a range of social classes, enlisting small-business owners and professionals together with those from the working and lower classes and, in many areas, was reputedly financed by local wealthy benefactors. In addition to racism against African Americans, the 1920s Klan mobilized sentiment against Catholics, Jews, non-U.S. born immigrants, labor unions, Mormons, and other minority groups (Blee 1991, 57–65).

Women participated in a number of women's Klan groups in the 1920s, the largest being the Women of the Ku Klux Klan. Like male members, Klanswomen came from a range of social positions. They were married and single, employed for wages and housewives, long politically engaged and new to public politics. Although the women's and men's Klans had similar political and racial agendas and rituals, there were outbreaks of conflict and hostility between them, generally over the disbursement of Klan dues. In a few cases, tensions between men's and women's Klan groups became public, spilling over into lawsuits and even physical confrontations between male and female leaders and members. In the states of Arkansas, Michigan, and Pennsylvania, women's and men's Klans battled in court, charging each other with financial mismanagement and illegal practices. Women from an Oregon Klan attacked a male Klan leader when he tried to interfere with their group. This wave of the Klan collapsed precipitously in the late 1920s, as the result of a series of internal financial and sexual scandals and the passage of severe immigration quotas, which undercut one of the Klan's most visible political issues (Chalmers 1987).

The third wave of the Klan appeared in the late 1960s and early 1970s during the turbulent period of social and school racial desegregation in the South. This Klan recruited largely from populations of poorly educated and economically marginal white men in the rural South and unleashed a wave of violence and terror against African Americans. Women played only minor roles in this Klan wave, which had become insignificant by the late 1970s.

Today's Klans emerged in the late 1980s, as part of a broader upsurge in racist activity. This wave of organized racism was fueled by economic restructuring and decline in certain sectors of the economy, notably small-scale agriculture and industrial work, as well as by the increased use of xenophobic, racist, and homophobic rhetoric by politicians from the conservative political mainstream. The Klan and other racist groups also grew in the 1980s because of internal factors within the racist movement. Most important were alliances between previously antagonistic racist and neo-Nazi leaders, made possible in part by decisions by several Klan leaders to deemphasize anti-Catholicism and even to welcome Catholic members along with their traditional base among Protestant fundamentalists. Also influential were efforts by right-wing extremists in central and eastern Europe to forge a transnational "pan-Aryan" movement that would champion the interests of all non-Jewish whites (Aryans) and oppose Jews and all nonwhites, incorporating anti-Semitism into an international racist agenda. A final factor was the growing influence of ideologies of "Christian Identity" in the racist movement that served to cement ideological alliances across racist groups. A pseudoreligion imported to the United States from England, Christian Identity is viciously anti-Semitic and racist, teaching that Jews and African Americans are the offspring of Satan and that white Christians are the true lost tribe of Israel (Barkun 1994; Betty and Shanks-Meile 1997).

Most of the several dozen or so groups that now bill themselves as Ku Klux Klans remained small during the 1980s and 1990s, many declining even further in the face of federal investigations of the extreme right after the bombing of the Oklahoma City federal building in 1995. Despite their dwindling size, some contemporary Klan groups, especially those allied with neo-Nazi groups, have become significant players in an amalgamated racist movement. All groups in this movement predict an apocalyptic racial war between African Americans and Aryans. Some groups also advocate race war as a way of undermining racial minorities, while others, who view both Africans American and Aryans as under the grip of powerful but invisible Jewish conspirators, fear that race war will ultimately benefit only Jews.[3]

The composition of the modern Klan is more gender diverse than any Klan since the 1920s. Women are full-fledged members in most Klan groups. In some, they have even become public, although low-level, leaders. Women constitute an estimated 25 percent of the membership of some Klan groups and may make up 50 percent of the new recruits. Like women in the 1920s Klan, today's Klanswomen come from a variety of social class and family statuses. Although it is impossible to determine the exact characteristics of Klan members as a whole, it is clear that both married and nonmarried women, mothers as well as those without children, the employed and those without waged jobs, have joined the Klan in recent decades.

Despite, or perhaps because of, the increasing number of women members, Klan groups, perhaps more than any other segment of the modern extreme right, have experienced conflict between male and female members. Privately, a number of Klanswomen point to disparity between the messages of gender equity espoused in the recruiting materials of some Klans and their treatment as the handmaidens of male members in the Klan. Although all Klan groups maintain the Klan's traditional adherence to moral conservatism, including opposition to divorce and a belief that men's authority should be respected in politics and the home, many of them insist that women are treated as equal to men within the racist movement, including having opportunities to advance to leadership within the Klan. One male Klan leader told me that, "Without women, we wouldn't have the Klan,"[4] and at least one Klan features women on its Internet page to demonstrate its gender inclusivity. A major Klan chapter insisted, evidence to the contrary, that "women hold a very high and exalted position in the eyes of the Ku Klux Klan."[5] Further, it claimed to "still believe that our women find their greatest fulfillment as mothers of our children," even though "international finance" [i.e., Jews] has "retarded the advance of white women in this country," who purportedly are pushed into poorly paid jobs when Jewish bosses or bankers make it impossible for white non-Jewish husbands to sustain their families.

In their life histories and private communications, however, Klanswomen say that they regard the gender messages expressed in Klan recruitment materials as a cynical means of bringing women into an organization that does not support women in its internal practices or public politics. They object to what they perceive, but do not label, as a "glass ceiling" in the leadership structure of the Klan in which women are prevented from assuming positions of actual decision making in most Klan groups. As one Klanswoman told me, "The Klan is male oriented, totally sexist. The men still run it, as far as the offices go." Although one woman has received some prominence in one of the major Klans and may even advance to leadership in the near future, she is the daughter of the current Klan head, and many women dismiss her, correctly or not, as her father's political puppet. For their part, Klansmen complain about the increasing presence of women in the Klan, claiming that women are usurping the authority that is rightfully theirs (Coppola 1996, esp. 127–128; Blee 2000, 93–110; Blee 2001).

Gender and the Ku Klux Klan

To understand the involvement of women in the Ku Klux Klan, I focus on the two periods in which women were most active: the 1920s and today. These time periods also had active Klan chapters in both northern and southern states. It was in these time periods, too, that the Klan had the most elaborate ideologies, specifying not only ideas about race, but also about nationhood, gender, religion, historical change, sexuality, and political leadership. By examining women's participation and motivations and the gender ideologies of these Klans, it is possible to discern more general patterns of women's involvement in extremist right-wing organizing.

Participation

Women's participation in the 1920s Klan was confined to all-women Klan groups that proclaimed their separateness from the male Klan, very different from women's participation in today's mixed-sex Klan groups. Yet the nature of women's involvement in these two waves of the Klan reveals similar, gendered patterns.

One similarity is that both Klans recruited women for strategic purposes. The

1920s Klan was organized at the peak of activism on behalf of women's suffrage. When women were given the right to vote in U.S. federal elections in 1920, they constituted an attractive recruiting pool for Klan leaders. Such practical considerations outweighed the general reluctance of male Klan leaders to enlist women in a male racist fraternity, although they did not quell the antagonism of many men to the intrusion of women into this formerly all-male sphere of politics and violence. Responding to the Klan's appeal, women joined the 1920s Klan to preserve and extend their rights as white Protestants, rights they feared would be eroded by immigrant, African-American, or non-Protestant voters. Indeed, many Klanswomen earlier supported women's enfranchisement in order to counteract the votes that had previously been won by African-American and immigrant men. For them, the transition to Klan politics of racial and religious bigotry and xenophobia was an easy one.

In today's Klan, women are recruited for different, but no less gender-specific, reasons. Faced with declining memberships, Klan leaders have turned to women to bolster the size of their groups relative to those of competing Klans or to stave off organizational collapse. Too, some Klan leaders regard women members as effective in recruiting their sons and husbands to the Klan's cause. Others see women as more stable and less legally vulnerable than men, pointing to women's lesser propensity to engage in nonracist criminal activity that could attract the attention of law enforcement to the Klan.

Women's involvement in both of these waves of the Klan provoked negative reactions from male Klan members and gender conflict within Klan groups. In the 1920s, the incorporation of women into the Klan, even in gender-segregated Klan groups, was met with derision and hostility by many Klansmen who saw the Klan as a bulwark against all forms of "immoral modernism," including the expansion of women's rights. Male Klan members chided women members, and KKK leaders battled their counterparts in the women's Klans over money and authority. This disdain for women in the Klan was shared by some anti-Klan activists, who ridiculed the KKK for bringing women into politics, out of the home where they rightfully belonged. A prominent anti-Klan newspaper editor from Muncie, Indiana, for example, attacked what he termed the "bob-haired Amazons" of the Klan, chastizing women who "abandoned" husband and children for Klan politics and ridiculing the husbands of Klanswomen who had relinquished their role as family "boss" to their wives (Giel 1967; *Muncie [Indiana] Post-Democrat*, May 23, 1924; Blee 1991, 65–69; Blee 2001).

The modern Klan, too, has experienced internal conflicts over issues of gender in its ranks, although these have seldom spilled over into public view. In my interviews, a number of Klanswomen expressed discontent about the condescending and hostile behavior of many male Klan officials and members. These women see Klansmen, in the words of one woman, as "Joe Six-Packs," unable to deal with women as equals. They are particularly critical of men who assume that women are the sexual possessions of men or who expect women to be in the background of racial politics. A Klanswoman complained to me about her husband, saying, "He's been at more rallies than I have. But, you know, I have to work, and I can't really be there and work at the same time. And the bills have got to be paid." Another woman decried what she regarded as the limited vision for women in the Klan, commenting, "Klansmen see women as breeders, and most women in the Klan feel they should produce babies for the white race."

Despite their own commitment to the Klan, these women conclude that they will never encourage their daughters to join such a group. As a Klanswoman told me, if her adult daughter joined the Klan, "there wouldn't be anything for her to do. She could go to a few rallies or picnics, but wouldn't be allowed to go to the real meetings." Once having learned the racist ideas of the Klan, these women see themselves as having a responsibility to the white race to continue in the racist movement, but, surprisingly, they feel no comparable need to instruct their daughters to join racist groups that do not treat women well. Clearly, this is a source of future fragility in a Klan movement increasingly reliant on women recruits. Moreover, as some women continue to rise, although slowly, through the ranks of lower- and middle-level Klan leadership and make claims for positions as Klan spokespersons and leaders, these gender tensions are likely to become a greater source of conflict within the Klan (Blee 1991).

In both of these waves of the Klan, women were involved in activities that served to extend the virulent racism of the Klan, although the nature of these differed. In the 1920s, Klanswomen rarely participated in overt terrorism like night-riding and physical assaults on Klan enemies as Klansmen did, but they were vicious and effective perpetrators of economic, political, and social terrorism. Through organized networks of gossip and boycotts, Klanswomen in Indiana worked to destroy the livelihoods and community acceptance of those they deemed unacceptable in the Klan's vision of America. The jobs and stores of Jews, Catholics, new immigrants, and African Americans were especially vulnerable to such pressures. Across the state, Catholic schoolteachers, Jewish store owners, and African-American workers, facing Klan terror, fled their communities, abandoning careers and businesses in search of safety. In the Klan's campaign to rid Indiana of racial, religious, and national minority groups, the organized effort of Klanswomen was crucial. Women in the Klan spread negative rumors about members of these groups, encouraging others to boycott their stores and shun them personally.

Similarly, Klanswomen today rarely are visible in public violence or terroristic activities in the Klan, but they are active advocates of these actions by Klansmen and work hard to create the organizational strength, effective propaganda, and attention to the recruitment of children and retention of members necessary to continue the Klan over generations.

In one significant way, however, the participation of women in the 1920s differed from that of the modern Klan. In the 1920s Klan, women were brought into all-women's groups that mixed support for the overall Klan agenda of racism, anti-Semitism, anti-Catholicism, and nationalism with ideas of rights for white, Protestant, U.S.-born women. Since this Klan gained strength at the peak of women's suffrage and social reform activism, it recruited many women who combined racist ambitions with substantial histories of involvement in religious, civic, women's rights, and political organizations. These organizational skills and resources, garnered in other social movements, not only made these women effective advocates for the Klan and able to mobilize large numbers of women into its political crusade, but also allowed them to successfully press the Klan to express some support for the political and economic rights of (white, Protestant, U.S.-born) women.

Contemporary women join a very different Klan, one that is small, politically marginal, gender mixed, and in which men hold a firm monopoly on positions of power, titles, and influence. In the decades after the collapse of the 1920s Klan, subsequent waves of Klan organization were virtually all male. Women were incorporated only in background, supportive roles as the wives and girlfriends of Klansmen and the helpmates of the Klan movement. By the 1980s, however, Klan groups started recruiting women directly into the Klan. This strategy has been successful, bringing many women into the Klan, but few have substantial prior involvement in other political movements, and almost none have been given leadership or public roles. As a result, they have relatively little influence over Klan politics and propaganda.

Motivation

The participation of women in the male-supremacist Klan suggests that women can be mobilized into racist movements that seem antithetical to their collective interests. Indeed, far-right agendas—based on appeals to individualism, antiegalitarianism, nationalism, and moralism/traditionalism—appear to offer little to women as a group. Few women would benefit from the patriarchal nature of right-wing agendas, at least to the extent that white class-privileged Protestant men might. Yet, women do join Klan groups and a variety of other extremist right-wing movements. Why?

Evidence from the 1920s and the life history narratives of today's Klanswomen indicate that, like their male counterparts, women are drawn into the Klan in a search for answers to problems they consider pressing in their lives or in society as a whole. But this is a gendered process. In the 1920s, the traditional expectation that home and family life were the province of women provided the Klan a way to attract women members, by presenting itself as a bulwark against the destructive forces of unchecked vice and alcohol on family life. In the propaganda of the 1920s Klan, vice (such as frequenting dance or pool halls, prostitution, gambling, and sexual promiscuity) was associated with Jews and African Americans, and alcohol with Catholics and immigrants. The Klan's focus on vice and alcohol was similar to appeals used by other reform movements of the early twentieth century, including progressive reform movements, but the Klan tied issues of morality to those of race and religion. This is a common and powerful tactic of racist groups, who assert their credibility by focusing on issues of general public concern, then move these in a racist direction.

Today's Klan uses a similar tactic, recruiting women members by emphasizing issues like the declining quality of public schools, then attributing blame for school failure to racial minority and immigrant students, Jewish teachers, and a Jewish-controlled government. One woman explained to me her decision to join the Klan by saying that she got "fed up" that she could not get her children educated properly, adding only as an afterthought that their poor education must have resulted from the presence of Hispanic children in their classroom. Another Klanswoman cited the problem of latchkey children, arguing that "the children of the world now are lost. Mother is having to work now and support them, and they have to sit on the doorstep a couple of hours before their mother ever gets home."

Race, religion, and nationality become simple, concrete solutions to social and political problems that people feel otherwise powerless to correct. Swelling the ranks of the Klan, therefore, are not only women who are motivated by racism, elitism, or bigotry, but also those worried about the effects of crime on themselves and their families, the escalating rate of family dissolution, or the decline of city services—concerns that cannot be easily described as inherently reactionary or progressive (West and Blumberg 1990, 1–40).

Women structure their political opportunities differently than men suggesting why, as West and Blumberg note, women's protest activities—on the left and right alike—are more likely than men's to be linked to issues of economic survival, national/racial/ethnic conflict, humanism/nurturance, or women's rights.

Although the 1920s and 1990s Klans emphasized very different sets of issues, both presented their agendas as consistent with women's interests as mothers, wives, or female citizens. Temma Kaplan's concept of *female consciousness* as the process whereby "recognition of what a particular class, culture, and historical period expect from women, creates a sense of rights and obligations that provides motive force for actions" (1982, 545) is a useful way to think about how women's daily life experiences can be manipulated to bring them into right-wing politics, a process exemplified by the Klan's efforts to position itself as the bulwark against social decay.

Gender Ideologies

The ideas about gender found in the propaganda of Klan groups are surprisingly complicated. This is true both today and in the early-twentieth-century Klan. Throughout its history the Klan has been regarded, correctly, as an organization that fosters male supremacism as an integral part of its racist agenda, guarding the privileges of white men against perceived encroachment by white women and minority group members. What Martin Durham in his study of the British fascist National Front terms its "overwhelming masculinity" has been true of the Klan even during periods with significant female membership (1995, 277; citing Mosse 1985).

Despite this historical constancy, however, the propaganda about gender issues issued by the Klan has changed over time in response to changes in the larger political environment. The Klan's ability to combine support for white supremacism with varying positions on gender is attributable to its embrace of what historian George Mosse terms a "scavenger ideology," a system of beliefs formed by annexing pieces of other ideologies (Blee 1991; Koonz 1987; de Grazia 1992).

Thus, in different periods, the racist and anti-Semitic core of the Klan has been surrounded by ideas as disparate as those of alien invasions, animal rights, and temperance. In such an ideological milieu, a variety of contradictory ideas about gender equity also have been able to coexist with dedication to hard-core racism.

Women from groups that the Klan sees as its enemies—racial minorities, Jews, progressive and communist movements, labor unions, immigrants and, in the 1920s, Catholics and Mormons—always have been portrayed by the Klan in demeaning and brutalizing ways, as animalistic, sexually aggressive (or, conversely, asexual), predatory (or, conversely, passive victims of domination and cruelty by nonwhite, non-Aryan, non-Protestant men), and duplicitous, irresponsible baby breeders (Ware 1996, 79).[6]

The Klan's ideas about white women are more variable. One way that white or Aryan women are depicted by the Klan is as *racial victims*. This idea is captured aptly in scholar Vron Ware's description of the "enduring image of a seemingly passive, but wronged white femininity." The notion of white women as victims is central to every Klan, presented to justify assaults on minority-race men in retaliation for the threat they are declared to pose to innocent white women.

A main claim of the original Reconstruction-era Klan was that it would protect the wives and daughters of Confederate soldiers from retaliatory attack by newly freed African-American men. In the 1920s, the category of those seen as posing danger to white women was broadened to include Jewish businessmen, labor union bosses, and Catholic clergy, together with African-American men. How women were victimized was broadened as well, to include economic and political exploitation. This took many forms, including lurid tales of Catholic priests or Jewish factory owners preying sexually on innocent white Protestant girls, stories of violence inflicted on white women in cities with growing populations of African-American men recently dislocated from the U.S. South, and propaganda that stressed the exploitation of young working women by corrupt labor union officials.

The Klan's message about racial danger to white womanhood has continued unabated over time.[7] Like its predecessors, the newspapers, fliers, websites, and other propaganda of the contemporary Klan proclaims messages about white women's vulnerability to predatory racial minority and conspiratorial Jewish men. Typical and common are cartoons such as those that portray white women as defenseless in the face of vast numbers of nonwhite men streaming across the southern border of the United States from Latin America, anxious to experience the sexual paradise they anticipate in the United States by foisting themselves on young white women, or that depict African-American men as sex-obsessed beasts waiting to spring on vulnerable white women.[8]

The contemporary Klan, much like Klans of earlier years, combines sexual prudery and sexual titillation to nest admonitions to white women against interracial sex in sexual graphic images, decrying, for example, "young [white] women who fondle these black greasy ballplayers."[9] Klanswomen concur with this message. One Klanswoman told me that "the Klan could do a lot of good, especially with young white girls who keep falling for black guys." The Klan and other racist groups also warn that white women who become involved with racial minority men will be responsible for the "death of the white race."

As one flier, widely distributed across the racist movement, instructs:

"Whiteman, look at the beautiful woman you love. Whitewoman, think about the future for your children. WHITEMAN, THINK. The decision is for this generation. Your children will be outnumbered fifty to one, by colored people who have been inflamed to hatred of our people by the JEWMEDIA . . . YOUR FIRST LOYALTY MUST BE TO YOUR RACE, WHICH IS YOUR NATION!"[10]

Second, the Klan emphasizes white women's responsibilities as racial *wives* and *mothers*.[11] The focus on white motherhood is central to all racist movements because of concerns with racial destiny, racial reproduction, and socialization into racial identities. In her study of France, Claudie Lesselier finds that "at the heart of every racist and/or nationalist system the same function is assigned to women: they are called upon to transmit the blood, tradition, language, and be prepared to fight if necessary" (Lesselier and Venner 1988, 175).

In the 1920s Klan, motherhood was heralded as a status that positioned white women to assume the task of repairing the nation. Drawing on ideas of mothers as the natural housekeepers of the community and the nation, the Klan argued that white native-born Protestant mothers had both the insight and the responsibility to undertake the political work required to restore America to a former glory of white Protestant domination.[12]

As one grand dragon of the Klan declared in 1923, "no longer will man say that in the hand of woman rests the necessity of rocking the cradle only. She has within her hand the power to rule the world."[13] To this end, women were urged to join the Klan to rid their communities of any obstacles to white supremacism. Many women responded enthusiastically to this call, claiming that as mothers of children, they needed to expel Catholic schoolteachers, Jewish-owned businesses, African Americans, and immigrant populations.

In today's Klan, the emphasis on white motherhood largely takes the form of calls for white Aryan women to bear many children. Such pro-natalist rhetoric, reserved exclusively for white non-Jewish women, reflects the Klan's fear that the white race is on the brink of demographic destruction because of high birthrates among minorities and the involvement of white women in interracial affairs. Since the procreative abilities of white Aryan women are seen as the means of securing numerical advantage for the next Aryan generation and safeguarding the purity of Aryan bloodlines, virtually all Klans churn out propaganda stressing Aryan childbearing and endless images of Aryan women as mothers of dependent and innocent family members, especially infants, young children, and older girls. Older boys are rarely depicted in this way as they are not seen as equivalently helpless. The racial procreation entrusted to white women is portrayed as essential to the racial struggle, although still decidedly secondary to the activism of white racist men. As mothers, white women do not have to take conscious racist action. Rather, they safeguard the racial future through their passivity and adherence to conventional gender norms of family life.

Third, at some points in its history, the Klan has found it politically expedient to add issues of *women's rights*—the rights of white Aryan women only, of course—into its ideological stew. The 1920s Klan was organized at a time of heightened political involvement by women. Ever opportunistic, the Ku Klux Klan seized on the rhetoric of the suffrage and reform movements to promote itself as the guarantor of good government and expanded rights for white, U.S.-born, Protestant women. Its chapters championed higher wages for white Protestant working women (although not wages equal to those of white men), billed themselves as opposed to the effects that bootleggers and government corruption had on women and family life, identifying these as the result of Catholic influence in municipal government and police departments, and even urged women to maintain an identity separate from their husbands by keeping their maiden name after marriage. Chapters of the women's Klan even campaigned for an eight-hour day for mothers, suggesting that motherhood should be regarded as work and thereby deserving of social recognition and social regulation (Comer 1923).

The modern Klan has a more ambivalent rhetoric about women's rights, as it is caught between the social conservatism of its recruits and its desire to bring more women into the Klan. It consistently denounces the feminist movement, declaring it the product of Jewish and lesbian leaders who seek to ruin white Aryan family life. Yet various Klan groups also declare themselves in support of increased rights for white women, both in the racist movement and in society as a whole. To an extent, this is meant to target Klan enemies, by posing white women as beleaguered by affirmative action programs and lenient immigration policies that help racial minorities, supposedly at the expense of white women. But there is also some consideration of white women's rights more directly, seeking to include women in the political campaign for white supremacy as active, if not equal, partners with white men. At present, however, the Klan's emphasis on the importance of women to its mission is more rhetorical than real, and Klanswomen express considerable frustration about their subordinated position in Klan groups. One Klanswoman confided to me her disillusionment with the gender politics of her group, saying that "they acted as if women were equal [to men], but once you are inside the Klan, women are not equal at all."

Conclusions

What does the case of the U.S. Ku Klux Klan tell us about the mobilization of women into extremist right-wing politics more generally? How might we use this knowledge to counteract the appeal of far-right groups to women? There are three implications from the study of the U.S. Klan. First, research on the far right cannot ignore the participation of women. Scholarship has been distorted by the exclusive focus on men, especially those who proclaim themselves the leaders of the right. Looking more closely at the women who populate rightist groups reveals a wider range of experiences in racist groups. Men and women are recruited in racist groups through different sets of appeals. They have a different relationship to racist group leadership. And they may have strikingly different political views, at least on issues of gender. It is important to understand these gender differences in order to design strategies to prevent the recruitment of women by the far right or to lure them out of extremist right-wing groups. Too, the experiences of discord in racist groups may provide useful insights into how the cohesion of far-right groups could be shattered.

Second, there is a difference between the propagandistic messages of right-wing groups and the motivations that bring women into their ranks. While bombastic and vile attacks on African Americans, Jews, and others are the obvious messages of racist groups, many of their members are attracted by much more mundane concerns, like education, physical safety, and family life. Yet it is also clear that such issues do not need to be the province of the far right. Protecting schools, family, and personal safety are issues that can, and should, be addressed by feminist and progressive movements. This is the best means of ensuring that they do not becoming a mobilizing force for the far right.

Finally, rightist ideology can be dangerously multifaceted. The far-right is able to broaden its appeal to new audiences by incorporating the rhetoric of political agendas, like those of women's rights, that generally are antithetical to the right. Although this is not common in the extreme right wing, it shows the striking ability of the right to manipulate issues in order to attract recruits. Feminists and political progressives need to recognize the complex ideologies found in right-wing groups to develop an effective counterstrategy and to make more explicit the links between feminism, antiracism, and transnational efforts to safeguard human rights and dignity.

Notes

1. Greater detail about the methodology of this study can be found in Blee 1991a, 596–606; and in Blee 2001.
2. Some biographical information on Alma White can be found in Blee 1991b. The one full biography of White (Stanley 1996) does not fully explore White's Klan activity. Jeansonne 1996 includes a discussion of Elizabeth Dilling, but the lack of feminist analysis in this book limits its discussion of gender issues in right-wing politics.
3. From interviews and observations. Also see Cochran 1993, and Ross 1995, 166–181.
4. This quotation, and subsequent quotations from Klansmen and women, are from oral histories and other interviews I conducted in 1994 and 1995. Since the interviews were confidential, no names or identifying details, including dates and places of the interviews, are provided in this chapter.
5. "Women and the Ku Klux Klan," *White Patriot* (1987), 1.
6. An excellent discussion of the role of sexual and gender imagery in another right-wing extremist movement can be found in Bacchetta 1994.
7. There are a large number of Klan publications in which these messages appear. Collections of Klan materials are available at Tulane University–New Orleans Special Collections, the University of Kansas–Wilcox Collection, and the Anti-Defamation League of B'nai B'rith–New York.
8. From untitled fliers distributed by Ku Klux Klan groups.
9. From an untitled flier distributed by a Ku Klan Klan group.
10. Capitalization in the original. From an untitled flier distributed by a Ku Klux Klan.
11. Blee 1997.
12. See, for example, publications by the Women of the Ku Klux Klan, including *Ideals of the Women of the Ku Klux Klan* (n.p. 1923); *Constitution and Laws* (1927); *Women of America!* (n.p., c. 1924); Comer 1923, 89; Graff 1924, 7.
13. See *Christian Century*, May 21 1925, 177–178; *Fiery Cross*, July 6 1923, 23; and *Imperial Night-Hawk*, September 3 1924, 6.

8

Charity and Nationalism:
The Greek Civil War and the Entrance
of Right-Wing Women into Politics

Tasoula Vervenioti

A civil war is fought not only between opposing soldiers on the battlefield but with civilians as both combatants and targets, and women are crucial in establishing its specific form and agenda. In the Greek civil war, which was fought between the left and the right, some elite right-wing women engaged in politics, even though they did not have formal citizenship rights. They mobilized individual women, women's unions, Christian and charitable organizations, and initiated an international campaign to rescue children—and hence the nation—from the communists and to give children the "right" national education. They founded institutions called Childtowns to shelter the children. The umbrella that covered their actions was individual charity and not the State's Welfare Ministry; it was the Queen's Fund. Twenty upper-class women, the so-called Commissioned Ladies of the Queen's Fund, pulled the strings. They, as biological and ideological reproducers, as "cultural carriers" of the Greek nation (Yuval-Davis and Anthias 1989, 7), superseded the government in matters of internal and external affairs very effectively in the "save the children" enterprise and played an important role in the eventual campaign for women's suffrage.

Right-wing women in Greece (a European but not a Western country) displayed features and contradictions of both First and Third World women's agency, identities and strategies not as naturalized and totalized categories, but as "historically specific differences and similarities between women in diverse and asymmetrical relations, creating alternative histories" (C. Kaplan 1994). They lobbied as citizens without political rights, using their family relations, as in countries where family affiliations and structures, especially within the elite, can determine political relations; thus the apparent paradox of female prime ministers in states with minimal women's rights (cf. Yuval-Davis 1997, 81–92). On the other hand, while the white suffragist leaders in the United States used the expedient strategy of the "double" difference (first between men and women; second between white and black) (Mink 1990), the right-wing women in Greece converted the difference between white and black into the right and left. The left-wing women's unions had been dissolved, and left-wing women could not be public servants; nor could they have a driver's license or a passport—because of the civil war.

The paradox is that right-wing women demanded the right to vote and the right to occupy political office, and at the same time insisted that a woman's place was in the home. Lina Tsaldari, one of the Commissioned Ladies and the first woman minister, in her preelection speech to the women's unions (11 February 1956) stated, "A woman's first duty is to her family" and "You must not consider that women who participate in political life are going to abandon their homes and their families, as some women have enjoined us to do in the past" (FALT 18).[1] Tsaldari did not argue "equality" but "difference": she argued that a woman is first a woman and then a citizen (J. W. Scott 1996, x; Sen 1993, 233), and not only did she invoke "nature" and the "difference" between the sexes, but by implication also "difference" from "other" women—the women of the left wing. This difference-based feminism perfectly fit within a nationalist framework, making it an acceptable part of nationalist ideology (P. Cohen 1996, 724).

This chapter argues that right-wing women in Greece entered the political scene in an emergency situation (the civil war) as members of powerful families. They used their male relatives' influence and their own connections with men in power to achieve their goals. They converted their earlier practice of charity work into a political cause that served to both undermine the left and place them in a position where they could obtain the vote. In that sense, they did not really struggle for their rights as women per se, but for their right as right-wing women to defend the nation as they defined it. Although they mobilized women's unions to save the children and the nation from the communists, they did not do it to gain women's suffrage. Anticommunism and their version of nationalism propelled them to undertake political action. Moreover, they relied on notions of naturalized sexual differences with men and chosen political differences with left-wing women. A civil war overrides common gender identity and even gender interests.

The Women's Unions: Charity and Nationalism

Established at the beginning of the twentieth century, Greek women's unions were closely connected to charity and nationalism. Both charity and nationalism clearly expressed right-wing women's agency. Charity was a socially acceptable channel through which upper-class women could enter the public sphere and exercise power. Nationalism is generally rooted in an idealized past where women as mothers are "the guardians of the traditional order" and cultural identity (Mosse 1985, 17; Blom 1995). However, charity is, in many respects, unlike social welfare; it usually assumes the dependency and passivity of those given the charity, and the rights of the recipients exist only at the behest of the givers. Bourgeois volunteers performed charities, and poor women received them; there were also poor women who worked for a wage in charitable institutions.

The oldest and the largest women's union was the National Council of Greek Women. It was a federation of fifty associations that mainly exercised charity on poor women and children, established in 1908. The Lyceum of Greek Women, founded in 1911, had nationalistic goals: to revive the glorious Greek past and to rescue Greek traditions. It never had more than five hundred members and eleven branches in the large urban areas. In the middle war period (1920), a feminist union, the League for Women's Rights, located exclusively in Athens, was established. The league attempted to denounce charity in favor of political activity; it advocated political rights, mainly women's suffrage (Varikas 1993; Avdela and Psarra 1985).

In 1936, the dictatorship of Ioannis Metaxas, blessed by the king, was established. The Metaxas regime envisioned an ethnically and politically homogeneous state: to that end, communists and suspected communists were imprisoned or exiled, and the slavophone minorities of Northern Greece were persecuted. It also envisioned the nation as a home, and it glorified women as mothers. Because the Metaxas regime opposed women's unions, it dissolved the League for Women's Rights and forced the National Council to act only as a charity union. It cooperated with the Lyceum of Greek Women on its folk festivals and worked with the National Council to establish a welfare state so as to delimit the communist threat. Individual charity supplied what state welfare could not.[2] Nevertheless, it generated new images of femininity especially for young women; they could not be frail and helpless but strong and vigorous (Rupp 1977). Three hundred thousand girls were enrolled in its youth organization. Moreover, some new women's charity organizations, were founded: the Working Girls' Club offered shelter to poor working girls, and the Children's Wardrobe (CWR) provided clothes and shoes to pupils. After a decade, women in charge of both organizations became Commissioned Ladies of the Queen's Fund.

In 1940 Greece entered into World War II and as of 1941, the Germans, Italians, and Bulgarians (the Nazi-led triple alliance) occupied Greece. During the Occupation (1941–1944) a broad resistance movement developed, as in other southern European countries (Italy, France, and Yugoslavia). Greek women entered into the public sphere en masse through the resistance—the National Liberation Front, which was dominated by the Communist Party. As Hobsbawm has observed, during the antifascist struggles in Europe the left gained control of national identity from the right (1990, 203–207). In Greece, the National Liberation Front fought for national liberation and social reform, for a new society—People's Rule—in which there would be gender equality (Mazower 1993), but it accepted a gendered division of labor. Women formed the majority of the National Solidarity, the welfare organization of the Resistance, but women also accounted for almost 10 percent of its armed branch. Most women members of the National Solidarity were poor, rural, and middle-aged. Their main effort was to provide the Resistance fighters with clean clothes and food. They considered these activities as supporting the nation's liberation, not charity. Young women and girls did not restrict themselves to welfare activities and engaged in political action (Vervenioti 1994).

Just as periods of social upheaval and crisis often act as vehicles for the expansion of women's role, their ending frequently results in woman's return to their "traditional duties" (see Higonnet and Higgonnet 1987). This process of enforced domestication was especially painful in postwar Greece due to the civil war that erupted between the left and the right soon after the war. In the first year after the war, the Resistance vision of a new society was still vivid. Women's unions mushroomed all over the country. Women Communists and the feminist League for Women's Rights founded the largest ever women's federation in Greece, the OGE, with 120,000 members. The Federation was established in February 1946; some months later, it dissolved. The key slogan of right-wing rhetoric—a continuation of the Metaxas dictatorship—was *ethnikofrosini*, which meant loyalty toward the nation and nationally-minded. This concept referred not only to the defense of the homeland from the communists, but also to the defense of traditional Greek values (Alivizatos 1984, 392). For women it implied a return to domestic tasks and submission to the rules of the patriarchal family. The right forced Resistance women back to their "traditional duties" not only through propaganda, but through raw violence. The right-wing terrorist bands, the police, and the army raped and tortured women or punished them with a "haircut" (MGA 31).[3]

The Greek civil war took place in the framework of a global war, the Cold War. The United States' intervention in Greece—on behalf of the right—was intended to stop the spread of Soviet influence in order to "protect American interests in the Middle East, for instance petroleum" (Whitner 1982, 107). Members of the American mission were stationed as advisors in all Greek Ministries. They gave "advice" not only on economic and warfare matters, but also on education and welfare. They practiced charity/welfare, too, through twenty-six organizations (UN, Welfare Mission 1950). They cooperated with the state, but mainly with the Queen's Fund, the most well-organized charity/welfare organization.

The "Salvation" of the Children

The end of World War II and the defeat of fascism had given rise to hopes for a better world, in which children, the future of society, would be privileged. Consequently, in the Greek civil war (1946–1949) the salvation of the children was one of the targets of the strategies adopted by the two opposing camps. Both armies rounded up children from the battlefields. The Government Army moved them to the Childtowns of the Queen's Fund, and the Democratic Army, dominated by the Communist Party, transported them to Soviet bloc countries (UN, A/AC.16/251 1948).[4] The Ministry of the Interior of the Democratic Government insisted that the actions of the official government of Athens, which was ruthlessly burning and bombing villages in northern Greece and blockading villages so that literally thousands of children faced starvation, made children's evacuation necessary (*Exormisi*, 3.15.1948).[5] Queen Fredericka took up the effort to save the children from the communists through her fund.

The Queen's Fund was established by Royal Order on 10 July 1947, after the queen had called a meeting of all charitable organizations. Of course, charity is a normal activity among European royal families, but in Greece the situation was rather different. Queen Fredericka enacted politics through charity. Fredericka used the fund to secure the status of the palace in the political arena of the civil war, as King Paul, her husband, was not a dynamic presence, according to popular opinion (Queen Fredericka 1971). She also used the fund to secure her position with the Greek people, who considered her a foreigner: antiroyalists accused her of having been a member of the Nazi Youth Organization in the prewar period; many royalists, like nationalists, disapproved of her German origins.

An executive committee (EC) of five men directed the fund, even though organization's members were mostly of women. The fund had the structure of the political parties of that time, based on patron-client relations. It established a network of committees all over Greece. Twenty upper-class volunteers, loyal to the palace and especially to the queen, the so-called Commissioned Ladies, were at the apex of the organizational pyramid. Middle-class women from the charities, Christian women, members of women's unions, volunteers of the Red Cross as well as Girl Guides, played an important role in local committees. The base of this pyramid consisted of rural and working-class women who were employed or sought employment. Unemployment was a very serious problem in postwar Greece and most of the staff of the fifty-three Childtowns were female. Furthermore, the young and pretty queen visited the destroyed villages. She promised rural women peace and gained a strong following. The fund was a female analogue of male patron-client structures, a network of personal affiliations with public power. Each of the Commissioned Ladies was responsible for a certain area of Greece. Fredericka empowered them and acquired power through their activities.

The fund was established for northern Greece, where the main battlefield of the civil war was. The headquarters of the Democratic Army was also located there, close to the borders of Yugoslavia, Bulgaria, and Albania, states friendly to the Democratic Army and the Communist Party of Greece. Moreover, the official government had evacuated the mountain villages of central and northern Greece, mostly because they supported the Democratic Army. Initially, the aim of the fund was to cooperate with the state for the welfare of these refugees, estimated to number between 700,000 and 750,000 (10 percent of the whole population). The queen and the Commissioned Ladies, as women-mothers, turned the focus toward children—the future of the nation. This agency might have become merely another link in the chain of women's charities, but it became a national issue.

In proposing the children's "salvation" enterprise to the government, Fredericka framed herself as "the first mother" of "mother Greece" (MGA, PM 66/9).[6] The Commissioned Ladies of her fund were conscripted to this national duty, which enabled them to conceive of themselves as political agents. They founded fifty-three Childtowns to shelter about eighteen thousand children (EOP: *Report for the decade 1947–1957*). They offered them the "right" national education; children prayed to God and to the king and queen nine times per day and ate five meals a day.[7] Right-wing propaganda labeled this enterprise *paidofylagma* (child protection) and the actions of the Democratic Army were labeled, by contrast, *paidomazoma* (child abduction).[8] The queen and Council of Ministers declared that the *paidomazoma* constituted genocide and a crime against humanity. They argued that communist bands violently kidnapped Greek children to denationalize them and to inject them with the communist virus, so that the children would fight against their homeland and for the "Slavic bloc" (FALT 9A).

The case of the "abducted" children was employed as part of the war strategy, a diplomatic tactic and a method of psychological warfare in the framework of the Cold War. The Commissioned Ladies created an "opportunity space" (Wilford 1998, 12) for entering the national political stage as well as for acting in international fora, even though they had no domestic political rights. The principal actors were two: Alexandra Mela,[9] the activist of the fund, and Lina Tsaldari,[10] who as the widow of a political leader had the greatest chance in a patriarchal context of becoming a political leader (Yuval-Davis 1997, 81; J. W. Scott 1996, 169). Both were anticommunists, nationalists, and royalists and had experience in charity. Their status enabled them to exercise power over other women, which also, in a system of patronage, affected their ability to influence the processes of formal politics. The sensitive social and political matter of the children's "salvation" from the communists was linked with the nation's salvation from the communists and the victory of the "free world."

One of the battlefields of the Greek civil war was the United Nations. The Commissioned Ladies managed to influence public opinion before November 1948, when the issue of the "abducted children" reached the UN General Assembly.[11] They used the women's unions in Greece and outside Greece, the Red

Cross and other international charity/welfare organizations as well. The National Council of Norwegian Women passed a resolution entitled "The abduction of the Greek children is a shame for our era"; it was the answer to the appeal of the National Council of Greek Women (FALT 8). The Conference of the International Union for the Protection of Children (Stockholm, 10–14 August 1948) as well as the International Meeting of the International Committee of the Red Cross and the League of Red Cross Societies (Stockholm, 20–30 August 1948) adopted resolutions sent to the United Nations demanding the repatriation of "abducted" Greek children from the Soviet bloc countries to Greece (Tsaldari 1967, 43). Lina Tsaldari participated in both conferences; the Greek minister of external affairs congratulated her for the "very successful resolutions" (FALT 8, 30.9.48).

Throughout the following year, 1949, the Commissioned Ladies continued their struggle for the repatriation of Greek children; they used the media, especially the radio and poster photography, to promote the queen's image as a national symbol: the "mother of the people and the army.")[12] They also organized campaigns in Europe and in the United States supported by the Greek Embassy and the Greek Orthodox Church. Their campaigns were well planned and effective. On 6 November 1949, while the discussion at the United Nations was taking place, Greek women's unions organized meetings of "mothers" all over Greece asking for the return of their children (newspapers: *Estia, Ethnos,* etc., 11.7.1949). Their resolution was sent to European women's unions. In 1950 and 1951, Lina Tsaldari, Greece's representative to the UN Commission on the Status of Women, also raised the issue, as the "Problem of Greek mothers whose children have not yet been repatriated" (UN 1950, Commission on the Status of Woman, Supplement No. 6).

The Commissioned Ladies had succeeded in changing the political climate of the UN meetings and public opinion on behalf of the official Greek government. While the Soviet bloc countries accused it of torture, executions, and concentration camps, on the issue of the "abducted" children, the communists were on the defensive. The Greek communists, as nationalists, insisted that they fought against foreign intervention—the United States'—and for national liberation, but they had transported children outside of the nation-state. The Cold War figured to the advantage of the queen and the Commissioned Ladies, who seemed to have a stronger argument than that of the communists. Thus, the UN General Assembly unanimously approved three resolutions for children's repatriation from the Soviet bloc countries to Greece.[13]

Nevertheless, the Soviet bloc countries refused to return the children, maintaining that there was no democracy in Greece, and furthermore, no child care (MGA/PM 118, 119). By the end of 1952 only 538 out of 25,000 to 28,000 children had returned (UN A/2236). All that were repatriated came from Yugoslavia, as General Tito was in conflict with Stalin. Once again the case of children was drawn into the political game of the Cold War. But in that same year, 1952, the Greek government stopped petitioning for children's repatriation. Its representative stated at the twenty-second meeting of the UN General Asembly that "after five years of communist indoctrination, those children must be well advanced on the road upon which the Secretary General of the Greek Communist Party had put them" (UN 1952); that is, the children had already become communists prepared to fight against their homeland. The children's fates were interconnected with the fates of the Democratic Army's fighters, who, after their defeat (1949), left Greece and remained political refugees in Soviet bloc countries. The exact number of children who were repatriated in the '50s and '60s is not known as yet, but those of Greek—not Slav—origin, as well as the Democratic fighters, were allowed to come back to Greece some thirty years later, when the junta (1967–1974) had fallen, Greece became a democracy, and the Communist Party was no longer banned. In 1989 the Greek Parliament passed a law against the consequences of the civil war—meaning that reparations would be undertaken, refugees repatriated, and so on. The Cold War was over.

The Commissioned Ladies and the Executive Committee of the Queen's Fund

Meetings of the executive committee of five men who directed the Queen's Fund took place at the Real Estate Bank, with the bank's assistant director in charge. The committee handled large amounts of money from taxes, which the Council of Ministers had approved. Nevertheless, the Commissioned Ladies took control of the fund slowly but steadily. At the beginning, while the male members of the committee stayed safely in Athens, the Ladies traveled all over Greece to make reports on the situation in the northern regions or to find buildings on the islands to shelter children. At that time traveling was no easy matter. Often the railway did not run and the Democratic Army from the mountain areas attacked the cities. This difficult fieldwork was the first step the women took in securing their position. The next was the establishment of the Ladies' Special Committee on the Childtowns, which happened only with the queen's support. The executive committee had to consult the Ladies Committee on every issue concerning the Childtowns (EOP: 17th Meeting). In 1948, during the sweeping-up operations conducted by the Government Army and in view of the emergency conditions on the battlefields, the Commissioned Ladies founded new Childtowns independently of the executive committee. Thanks to their hard work and solidarity, they gained responsibilities and authority.

The relationship between the EC and the Ladies was full of tension, which only got worse toward the end of the civil war. It resembled the relationship between a traditional Greek husband and his unemployed wife. The husband/ EC had the money, and the wife/Ladies asked for money for the children's food and education. For instance, in January 1949 the EC accused the Ladies of having given orders to some Childtowns to supply children with more olive oil than others had. The EC argued that in all Childtowns the children must have the exact same ration of olive oil in their meals; if the fund supplied all children with even 1 more gram of olive oil, the budget of the fund would be devastated. The Ladies insisted that a fixed sum be available for each child per day. Each Childtown should be free to adjust its rations according to local conditions and production. Neither the members of the EC nor the Ladies backed down; the discussion was postponed. At the same meeting the Ladies petitioned the EC to increase the salary of the Ladies Committee's secretary. The EC decided to give her half the sum the Ladies had requested (EOP: 52nd Meeting). There were also disagreements about children's education: how many and who should continue their studies. The Ladies were more generous with the poor and needy people and less restricted in accepting innovations and initiatives from below than the EC.

The Ladies appeared to occupy the position of the paradigmatic dependent wife; they had undertaken the most difficult, graceless, and undervalued tasks; they knew the problems of the children and the staff firsthand, clearly better than the EC. The difference was that they were both a collectivity and had patronage: the Ladies Committee and the queen's support. In June 1949—two months before the end of the civil war—the minutes of the meetings report new discussions about the fund's services and responsibilities, and the tension between the EC and the Commissioned Ladies transformed into conflict. Alexandra Mela resigned. The EC argued that it must make the final decision on all issues. The Ladies assumed complete responsibility for the Childtowns. The EC gave in to their demands, and Alexandra Mela retracted her resignation, but the Ladies had to admit the presence of a member from the EC at their meetings (EOP: 61st to 64th Meeting). They worked step by step and always accepted what was feasible for the time being. However, time was on their side. In May 1950, the armed conflict was already over, and two Ladies became members of the EC, in fulfillment of the "queen's will" (EOP: 91st Meetings). The male members of the EC did not act to appoint these women in recognition of their efforts, but only as a result of the expressed desire of the queen, who wanted to empower the Ladies.

At last, the Ladies gained control of the fund. In the summer of 1950 most of the children returned to their villages. Of the fifty-three Childtowns only thirteen remained, and those were for orphaned children or for those whose left-wing parents were imprisoned, exiled, or political refugees. The Ladies proposed and the fund began establishing "Children's Homes" and Technical Schools for the cultural and technical education of rural people. Solely a committee that consisted of five Ladies and one man oversaw all these activities (EOP: 101st Meeting). The Ladies gained ground along with the Queen's Fund. It controlled a portion of the state's welfare system and a portion of education, and ran these programs independently of the ministries, as a state within the state, an anomalous situation compared to most nation-states, which monopolize both services (Gellner 1983, 71–79). In 1956, the Queen's Fund was renamed Royal Welfare. At that precise time the Commissioned Lady Lina Tsaldari was minister of welfare, and Alexandra Mela became the director of Royal Welfare. The queen and the Ladies had successfully entered the political arena.

The Civil War, the Women's Unions, and Women's Suffrage

The Commissioned Ladies played an important role in gaining women's suffrage, but they began to argue for it only in the late 1940s. Other women's groups, since the 1920s, had struggled for the vote. In 1930, the government granted the right to vote in local council elections to literate women over the age of thirty. During the Resistance (1941–1944), the National Liberation Front granted women's suffrage. After World War II Greek women were not granted political rights as women had been in Italy and France. For a short period of time, just after the liberation, all women's unions in Greece cooperated to demand the right to vote. The largest of these unions, the Federation of Greek Women, was a coalition of feminists and communists. In 1946 Greece signed the UN Charter, thus gender equality had theoretically become Greek law. But because the civil war intervened, the League of Greek Women Scientists, as well as other women's unions, adopted the view of right-wing politicians that women should not yet be given suffrage (AGWL, 2/1946). In a civil war nobody can remain neutral; the women's unions had to choose sides. The official Greek government dissolved the left-wing women's unions as followers of the Communist Party, which was outlawed.

In 1948, the country was deeply divided; there were two governments and two armies. The left gave women the vote. It needed women, as they made up about 30 percent of the Democratic Army fighters and 70 percent of its personnel in support services.[14] Women fighters, in October 1948, established their own union, but the left was defeated by the right. On the right's side, near the end of 1948, the United Nations asked the official Greek government to send a delegate to the Commission on the Status of Woman. The women's unions took advantage of the "opportunity space" (Wilford 1998, 12) that the United Nations granted to them, established a Coordination Committee of Seven Cooperating Unions and started demanding the vote for women (Vervenioti 2000).

The Seven Cooperating Unions were the oldest women's unions, the National Council of Greek Women and the Lyceum of Greek Women, which had cooperated with the Metaxas dictatorship (1936–1940), as well as the Christian Union of Young Girls and the Panhellenic Union of Intellectual Women. It also included the League of Greek Women Scientists, which in 1946 had requested that women not yet be given suffrage. Even the League for Women's Rights, which the Metaxas dictatorship had dissolved (it was in the front line of the battle for women's suffrage) and which had cooperated with women communists, participated. The civil war placed a crucial dilemma before the League for Women's Rights, which had to choose a side; the right-wing women's coalition did contribute to its broader effort to obtain women's suffrage. The newest of the seven unions was the Greek Federation of Women's Unions, the Greek branch of the U.S. General Federation of Women's Clubs, founded in 1948 (Tsaldari 1967, 191–193, 196). Lina Tsaldari, its president, was appointed as the Greek government's delegate to the UN Commission on the Status of Woman. American influence was clearly crucial in making the link between the right-wing and the women's movement.

The Coordination Committee of the Seven Cooperating Unions neither demonstrated, nor petitioned, nor held public meetings, as the left-wing unions had done, to demand suffrage. Lina Tsaldari had made it clear that "Greek women" were not like left-wing women who "rejected everything Greek and everything womanly" and that the vote was a "national duty" (Tsaldari 1967, 244–247). The women's unions had to prove that their members were real Greeks as well as real women; therefore, in order to exert pressure they visited the prime minister, the vice president, the minister of the interior, along with the leaders of the political parties. They cooperated with the local and state authorities that would enroll women on the electoral registers. All these authorities were hostile to the left wing because of the civil war, and consequently friendly to the right wing. So, right-wing women could register to vote more easily. And thus the leadership of right-wing women provided a new electorate for right-wing politicians.

Another tactic used by right-wing women was to exploit the power of the male members of their family. Lina Tsaldari, before leaving for the United Nations, sent a letter (10 February 1949) to her nephew Konstantinos Tsaldaris, then minister of internal affairs. She asked for women's suffrage "so that those people who are disgracing Greece will stop taking advantage of this issue" (Tsaldari 1967, 165–166). Those who disgraced Greece were not only the communists (in the UN meetings they said that under the official Greek government that there was no democracy in Greece), but also some liberals who claimed that Greece was the only European country of the "free world" (except Switzerland) that did not grant women suffrage.[15] Konstantinos Tsaldaris gave Lina Tsaldari assurances, and she, in her speech to the Commission on the Status of Woman (Beirut, 21 March 1949), said that Greek women would be able to vote in the next elections.

But, the law of 29 April 1949 gave women the right to vote only in local council elections, and not in general elections. Two years later (April 1951), Parliament ratified the law by a margin of eight votes. The new constitution that was adopted on 1 January 1952 gave the right to vote to all citizens regardless of gender. However, the new electoral law included an amendment saying that women could not vote in the general elections that were to be held on 16 November 1952 because the agents of the Ministry of Internal Affairs had not registered all women electors. Clearly, the laws were at odds; the amendment was unconstitutional. Lina Tsaldari wrote again to her nephew on 27 September 1952: "I am deeply sorry that you voted against Greek women," and she reminded him of his promise to the Women's Committee, and to her personally (Archive of Dinos Tsaldaris, F 59). Moreover, the Women's Committee sent a memorandum to the government and to all political parties threatening to have the elections invalidated. The president of the League for Women's Rights took action to apply for ballots, but the other unions stopped her. Members of the right-wing unions, as nationally minded Greek women, once more sacrificed their right to vote for the benefit of their country.

In the beginning of 1953, in Thessaloniki (the largest city of northern Greece) a by-election took place. Women voted for the first time in general elections. Eleni Skoura was elected as the first female member of Parliament. She was a "volunteer assistant" of the Queen's Fund. In the general election of 19 February 1956, Greek women finally participated on equal terms with men. Two women were elected: the left-wing Vasso Thanassekou, and Lina Tsaldari from the right. She got more votes than any other male right-wing party candidate did, and she became the first ever woman minister in Greece, serving as minister of social welfare.

Lina Tsaldari's career clearly illustrates the trajectory from individual charity organizations to women's unions to formal state power; the influence of class, of the monarchy, of kinship in the development of some liberal democratic policies in Greece is also interestingly revealed. Lina Tsaldari was from an upper-class family: her father was a university professor, and her husband the leader of the right-wing party in the prewar period. She herself was vice president (1946–1950) and then president (1950–1956) of the largest charity/welfare organization for the protection of children and motherhood, which functioned under the auspices of the queen. From 1948 on she was also the leader of a women's union, struggled for women's suffrage, and became minister of social welfare. There is perhaps no better anecdote to support the intimate connection between private and public than the following: when Lina Tsaldari concluded her term as minister, she took with her, along with her own personal papers, the complete archives of the Ministry of Welfare, which remain part of her personal archives.

Conclusion

In Greece, while the entrance of women en masse into politics occurred through left-wing Resistance organizations (1941–1944), the first female member of Parliament (1953) as well as the first woman minister (1956) were both right-wing.

Both of them were Ladies of the Queen's Fund. During the civil war they had employed individual charity as a means to save the Greek children and hence the nation from the communists; they had mobilized women, women's unions, and Christian and charitable organizations, and had established Childtowns to protect children and to give them the proper national education. While Greek women had the legal status of minors, the right-wing women were crucial in establishing the specific form and agenda of Greek nationalism. Their campaign on children's salvation changed the political climate of the UN meetings and public opinion on behalf of the official Greek government.

Right-wing women in the framework of the Greek civil war and the Cold War functioned in the context of three identities—nation, class, gender—more or less in conflict with each other. In the heated atmosphere of the civil war, national identity took precedence; they sacrificed the demand for formal political rights when the nation was in danger. But gender and class identities persisted, intersecting one another and flavored/favored their nationalism. In the context of their charitable activities they undertook work inappropriate for women of their status, but suitable to their gender, such as providing recipes for children's meals or supervising the cleaning of children's toilets. Their gender as well as their class position enabled them to exercise charity; their families' affiliations enabled them to gain power. As there was no dichotomy between individual charity and state welfare, there was no distinction between private and public, family and state. Thus, the Ladies ran the campaign against the "communist crime" of "abducted" children, they participated in international conferences and the UN Committee, they took initiatives and acted as citizens and individual agents, while legally they remained under the protection of their fathers and husbands.

In order to gain political rights they proffered some very persuasive political arguments. They proved that in practice they were patriotic Greeks before they were women looking to enhance their own interests. While the armed civil conflict was in the balance, they refused to demand the vote. Their main argument for women's suffrage was that it would bring Greece into line with other Western democracies, and, given that the Communist Party had granted women's suffrage during the Resistance, enfranchising women would be a way of both practically and symbolically resolving national and political differences. This strategy asserted national unity and yet effectively worked against the left, invalidating the accusation that in Greece there was no democracy because half of the population had no political rights. Moreover, they convinced the men in power that voting rights would serve not the narrow interests of women but the urgent needs of the nation as a whole; the refusal to give women the vote would prove an international embarrassment. This approach helped convince male politicians and voters that women's votes would serve the nation by complementing, rather than challenging, men's and women's traditional roles.

The most surprising conclusion was that their best ally was in truth their greatest enemy: left-wing women. During the Resistance, they had been elected to local councils as well as to the National Council; they had fought for a society in which there would be gender equality. Ironically, they had provided the precedent for what right-wing women would achieve in practice: women's participation in the public sphere. Moreover, the expedient strategy of the double difference (between men and women and between women and other women) offered the paradox that she who declared that a woman's place was in the private domain was rewarded with a public office.

Notes

1. The consequences of the civil war continue today. Researchers have no access either to the state's or to the Communist Party's archives, which insist that they have not yet classified their material. Moreover, in 1989 the Greek Parliament unanimously voted to burn the police files. The diplomatic history of the Greek civil war has been written based on English and American archives (Richter 1986; Whitner 1982). During my research on the social history of the civil war, I discovered the unclassified archives of the Proceedings of the Children's Wardrobe (CWR), the Queen's Fund (Ethnikos Organismos Pronoias, hereafter EOP), of Lina Tsaldari (FALK, Konstantinos Karamanlis Foundation), Rosa Imvrioti (Omospondia Gynaikon Ellsadas, hereafter OGE), and the Greek's Women Lyceum (AGWL). I have also used the Modern Greek Archive at King's College, London (MGA). In addition, a Fellowship of the Program in Hellenic Studies at Princeton University made the transcripts of the United Nations on the "Greek Question" available to me.
2. In 1934 out of a total of 2,300,000 working people, only 210,465 were insured (Vellianitis 1934).
3. The Resistance punished women accused of having sexual relationships with the occupiers in the same way (Vervenioti 1994, 144–152). The same happened in France and elsewhere after the liberation (Laurens 1995).
4. There was a precedent for this during the Spanish Civil War (1936–1939) (Legarreta 1984).
5. *Exormisi* was the newspaper of the Democractic Army.
6. On the cover page of the pamphlet *Mother Greece and Her Children* there is a photo of Queen Fredericka surrounded by children; the caption reads: "The first mother of Greece with her children."
7. The fund fed twenty-five thousand to thirty thousand children, while the number of orphan children was estimated at 340,000 to 380,000.
8. The word *paidomazoma* evoked images of the "brutal" Turks, longtime enemies of the Greek nation. According to national historiography, during the four hundred years of Turkish occupation (1453–1821), Turks rounded up Greek children and made them Muslims ready to fight against the Greeks.
9. Alexandra Mela, president of the Working Girls' Club, was the daughter of the director of the Bank of Greece and married the son of a hero killed fighting for Macedonia's union with Greece. She held the strings that controlled all of the activities carried out by the fund which helps to explain why she became its first director in 1956.
10. For her career, see below.
11. At the UN discussion on the "Greek Question" started in 1946 (UN, Yearbook 1946–1947 and 1948–1949).
12. The title of a pamphlet (sixty-two pages) edited by the "Library for National Enlightment" [1949].
13. The first resolution 193C(III) 27 November 1948; the second 288B(V) 18 November 1949; the third 382C (V) 1 December 1950.
14. The left's opposition to the U.S. intervention had much in common with anticolonial struggle in China, Algeria, Vietnam, Peru, etc. (Nachmani 1993; Dombrowski 1999). In Greece, the left-wing women's feminist element was able to become a revolutionary force as in China and elsewhere, but right-wing women's struggles did not move beyond the sphere of limited and selected reforms such as the vote, which have little effect on the daily lives of the masses of women; nor do right-wing women address the basic question of women's subordination within the family and in society (Jayawardena 1986).
15. The *New York Times*, 28 August 1949, published a letter written by Dorothy Kenyon, U.S.'s representative to the Commission on the Status of Women, entitled "Freedom and the Woman's Status." She stated that in countries such as Greece where women had not yet been granted suffrage, democracy was in dispute (quoted in Tsaldari 1967, 164).

9

Far-Right Women in France:
The Case of the National Front

Claudie Lesselier
Translated from the French by Paola Bacchetta

The question of women's participation in antifeminist, nationalist, xenophobic, racist, and authoritarian regimes or political movements is not a new one, even if it has been considered against the grain of received opinions in feminist movements, which have represented women homogeneously as either victims excluded from power or as political rebels. I would like to pursue this question by focusing on women members or activists in France's most powerful far-right political party, the Front National (National Front, hereafter FN).

Founded in 1972 by Jean-Marie Le Pen, the FN remained a marginal movement until the early 1980s. At that time, it gained considerable weight in French political life, gathering strength from a national social crisis and the effects of globalization and economic liberalism, and mobilizing against immigrants in defense of "national identity."[1] In fact, the FN had a direct influence on both right and left governmental parties; fearing they would otherwise advance the far right's rise to power or hoping to recruit its voters, they hardened their policies against immigrants and foreigners seeking exile, and reproduced certain far-right themes or terminology in their own discourses (Tevanian and Tissot 1998). After winning from 10 percent to 15 percent of the votes (higher in some southern cities, in the Rhône valley, and the northeast) in legislative or presidential elections, the FN won seats at the municipal, departmental, and regional levels, as well as in the European Parliament. The FN became an umbrella organization for far-right tendencies that had previously been divided, and it claimed as its heritage multiple, diverse ideological traditions, from counterrevolutionary thought to fin-de-siècle nationalism, and from Vichyism to colonial racism (Bihr 1998; d'Appollonia 1988). But, if the culture of its leaders is relatively homogenized, that of its electorate or simple members is more heterogeneous, for it is the party's protest dimension that has made it successful, especially among some sectors of working-class people.

The FN's growth nonetheless had its limits, and its unity appears fragile. At the beginning of 1999, strategic differences and significant power conflicts caused it to split into the FN led by Jean-Marie Le Pen, and the Mouvement national républicain (National Republican Movement, MNR) led by Bruno Mégret. This division was sanctioned by a decline in votes, a loss of credibility and resources, and, at the organizational level, a serious crisis in the networks the FN had constructed to mobilize women, youth, and various categories of workers. Nevertheless, antifascists remain alert to the effects of far-right ideas on French society and political life, and their possible expression in other forms such as sexism, xenophobia, and nationalism, which are not particular to the far-right alone.

In France, feminist groups, feminist activists, and feminist academics have been engaged in the struggle against the far-right since it first appeared. They have analyzed the right's relations to sexism and racism, both of which are founded in a naturalist and differentialist vision of the world (Lesselier and Venner 1997). While there are numerous critical studies of the FN's ideology, studies on the FN's members and activists are more rare. There are some surveys of activists (Ysmal 1989, 1991) and studies based upon opinion survey and electoral results (Perrineau 1997; Mayer 1999), but gendered perspectives are not extensively developed (Orfali 1990a,b; Venner 1997, 1999; Bolter 2000).

The point of departure for my study will be an analysis of the ratio of women among the FN's leadership, members, and voters. A presentation of the FN's women's organization, the Cercle national femmes d'Europe (National Circle of European women, CNFE), will provide an example of women's action and ideology in the FN. Next, I will attempt to clarify the motivations and political trajectories that have led women to get involved in the FN. Finally, I will examine how women's political role is conceptualized and materialized in the party.

Women as a Minority in the Electorate and in the Organization

A Male-Majority Electorate

Voter surveys reveal a very significant gap between men and women's votes for the FN, or for Jean-Marie Le Pen. The FN's electorate, like that of other far-right parties in Europe, is 60 percent male (in contrast, the center-right's electorate is mainly female). In the last presidential elections (1995), 19 percent of men and only 12 percent of women voted for Jean-Marie Le Pen. In the last legislative elections (1997), 18 percent of male voters and 12 percent of female voters, chose the FN. While this gap is wide in the presidential elections (seven points in 1988), it is more variable in the legislative elections; in 1993 there was a one-point difference, and in 1988, five points.

All studies concur on the reasons for this gender gap in the vote. Janine Mossuz-Lavau (1998) and Nonna Mayer (1998) put forth that women value the rights they have won, such as the right to control their own bodies and their rights as workers, and that the FN's platform and traditionalist vision of women's role in society fail to attract women to the party. According to Nonna Mayer, moreover, women are less receptive to "the physical and verbal violence, which often has sexual and macho connotations, that surrounds the far right." Pascal Perrineau (1997) raises the issue of men's attraction to this political party and maintains: "beyond the nostalgic seduction of machoism in Le Pen's discourse, ever-prompt in manipulating references to an expressive virility, the extensive male vote for the FN can be explained by troubled masculine identity that has begun to lack confidence and has become perturbed by the significant redistribution of roles between men and women (105).

The FN's electorate is in fact very heterogeneous. It shifted from a middle-class electorate (especially independent professions) in the mid-1980s to an interclass vote with a large working-class component in the 1990s. The gender gap is particularly large in certain socioprofessional and age categories: in the

1995 presidential elections, among voters age 18 to 24, 19 percent of men and 10 percent of women voted for Le Pen; among students, 16 percent and 6 percent; among unskilled workers 34 percent and 20 percent, respectively. Janine Mossuz-Lavau noticed a persistent gap between male and female voters aged 18 to 24 (19 percent men and 14 percent women). This gap was was especially significant among the unemployed (20 percent men and 10 percent women), as well as those over age 65 (20 percent men and 6 percent women). But surveys that encompass the category of workers (as a whole) have produced one combined result of 24 percent for men and women. The working-class FN electorate is a complex phenomenon: it includes among its motivations hostility to immigrants, attachment to traditional values, as well as economic and social concerns and challenges to the political system that are not so different from those of left and extreme-left voters. In fact some of the FN electorate had voted for the Socialist and Communist parties in prior elections. Without trying to answer all the questions that these electoral questions beg, I will cite Nonna Mayer's analysis of the 1997 elections. She explains that more female homemakers vote for the FN than do wage-earning women. "Young women, with little education, who are poor and socially disadvantaged" vote for the FN in equal numbers with men. In contrast, "young women with college degrees, with mid-to-high level professional jobs, who are dedicated to defending women's rights and for whom the reactionary, antifeminist dimension of the FN's program is unbearable" vote left massively, and only 5 percent of them choose the FN. Finally, "older women who are practicing Catholics, who have a more traditional vision of women in society . . . have internalized the Biblical message of tolerance more than men, and their dedication to these values leads them to reject the FN." This group primarily votes for the center-right, giving the FN no more than 3 percent of its votes.

A Male-Majority Party

According to a study of delegates to the FN's congress in 1990 (Ysmal 1991), which included 1,002 participants, 82 percent of its delegates were men and 18 percent women. Half the women delegates had no professional training and were unemployed. Nevertheless, this male domination is not unlike the situation in other political organizations. Surveys on congress delegates from other parties in the same year revealed a male majority throughout: 76 percent in the Rally for the Republic, 81 percent in the Socialist Party, 71 percent in the Communist Party, and 70 percent in the Green Party.

There are even fewer women higher up in the FN's hierarchy. According to the FN's own party documents, nine of the 110 departmental and regional secretaries in 1998 were women (8.2 percent). Only two of its forty Political Bureau members were women (Martine Le Hideux since 1988, and Marie-France Stirbois since 1990). Also in 1998, an organizational chart of party leadership, which includes thirty-two people besides the Political Bureau and the Central Committee, reveals the presence of only three women: one of the FN's vice presidents (Martine Le Hideux), the national secretary for French overseas territories (known as the DOM-TOM) (Huguette Fatna), and the press director in Jean-Marie Le Pen's cabinet.

Far more significant is the absence of women from the development of the FN's theory and platform. There are only men on the Scientific Council and on the Editorial Committee of the theoretical magazine *Identité*. The editors of the FN's 1993 platform, created under the leadership of Bruno Mégret, were all men except for Marie-France Stirbois.

The proportion of women candidates at the time of elections increased slightly in relation to the FN's rapidly expanding electoral presence, which dates from the 1980s. However, a large number of these candidates have no chance of being elected! In the last legislative elections (1997), the FN presented 570 candidates (one in each district): 499 men and seventy-one women (or 12. 4 percent of the FN's total).[2] The only legislative election to permit FN members in the Parliament, which took place through proportional voting in 1986, reflected a similar breakdown: among the thirty-five deputies there was only one woman, Yann Piat from the Var, who was also the only candidate reelected after the dissolution of France's National Assembly in 1988. Shortly thereafter, Piat was excluded from the FN, and joined the Union pour la Démocratic Française (UDF, Union for French Democracy) again. In an autobiographical narrative (1991), she downplays her involvement in the FN, denouncing its cult of the leader, Le Pen's absolute power, and his anti-Semitic slurs. In 1989, a partial legislative election in Dreux (Eure and Loire), resulted in the election of Marie-France Stirbois, but she lost her seat in 1993. Finally, in the 1998 regional elections, in which 275 FN representatives were elected, women constituted only 17 percent of the total.

The FN's Heirs

In the last European Parliament elections of 1999, 20 percent of the candidates on the two far-right lists (Le Pen's and Mégret's) were women. The list led by Le Pen won 5.7 percent of the votes (but no woman was in an eligible position), and Mégret's won 3.3 percent (thus falling short of electing any European Deputies). As yet, no survey has been conducted on the gender division of these votes. However, males and females who were elected at other levels (municipal, general, and regional) are more or less similarly divided between the two parties that emerged from the original FN split. Among the 275 regional representatives, some resigned while others joined other formations; only 251 remain, out of which 130 are with the FN (including twenty-eight women) and 122 with the MNR (twenty-one are women). During the split, staff members tended to join the MNR, while most other members stayed in Le Pen's FN. This is why today the FN has more women in it than the MNR (the FN claims that 40 percent of its members are women). Since currently there is insufficient documentation on these two new parties, my study focuses on the FN prior to 1999.

Family Preference and National Preference: The CNFE, Backup for the National Front

From 1985, the FN constructed a network of "circles" and associations to guarantee its presence on a number of terrains and to mobilize diverse social milieux. Martine Le Hideux, who remained its president, founded the CNFE in this context in 1985. The CNFE boasts departmental delegations, brochures, and a newsletter that explains its ideas and publicizes its activities such as dinner debates and participation in FN demonstrations and anti-abortion movements. At the time of the CNFE's last congress in 1995, Martine Le Hideux claimed it had a thousand members. The majority of CNFE representatives supported Jean-Marie Le Pen at the time of the National Front's split. The MNR did not reconstitute a similar structure.

The CNFE's main preoccupation is restoring the family, "the basic unit of society," "the keystone of the natural order," organized on the "complementarity" of men's and women's functions as defined by the "natural order." For this reason, the CNFE believes that one must "promote marriage" and "restore honor to the family and the mother who stays at home," by means of paying a "maternal salary" to French women who stay at home. The CNFE's second concern is the struggle against the "fall in the French birthrate," which encourages "foreign invasion"; this includes repealing the law legalizing abortion, paying birth bonuses, helping "future mothers in difficulty," and condemning contraceptive measures. These concerns are not unrelated to the CNFE denunciation of "moral decadence" (AIDS, homosexuality, loss of parental authority), its accusations that public schools favor the disintegration of the family and the national community, and its stigmatization of the pernicious consequences of women's work. It is important to note, however, that over the years, the CNFE has worked to present its propositions in a more modern language better adapted to the reality of women's lives. In its most recent publications, it claims it wants to allow women "to choose" and "to reconcile work with family life." Today, the CNFE sometimes refers to the maternal salary as "parental income" or "family income."

The CNFE joins together two tenets of FN propaganda: "family preference" and "national preference." In a small CNFE brochure called *French Families First*, a title that echoes the FN slogan "The French First," the CNFE demands, as does the FN in its party program, that French families have priority in or exclusive rights to state family allowances, social aid, and housing. If the family is the basis of the social order it is also the basis of the nation. Thus, French women in this political project have a fundamental role to play in biological reproduction and cultural transmission in the service of defending and strengthening national identity against anything that threatens it.

For the CNFE, the sexual, moral, familial, and national order are closely intertwined, and anything that puts to question the base of this structure brings ruin to "the whole of Western civilization." To confront these threats it is necessary to restore "natural law" or "natural order," which includes the distinction between women's and men's roles. As the CNFE states in one of its newsletters, it intends to revalorize traditional feminine functions, "feminine specificity," against the grain of modernity that imposes a "masculine model" for women and new constraints on them, as women face the "pseudoliberation" that feminism proposes. For the CNFE, as an article in its newsletter maintains, "feminist movements consider relations between women and men as power relations. We think of them as complementary.... There is a natural harmony that must be conserved at all costs." Today antifeminism rarely takes the form of explicit opposition to women's equality. Instead it insists upon difference, the specificity of each sex and their complementarity, while obsessively denouncing the lack of sexual distinctiveness and women's power (Bard 1999). Another widespread thematic is that women pay the price of their emancipation. Finally, the CNFE denounces feminism as too radical a movement, as leftist or as lesbian—or simultaneously and paradoxically in vain or useless because women have already obtained everything they wanted.

Above all, the CNFE represents the FN's traditionalist Catholic current, its "bourgeois" wing and its older generation. Its vitality and activity are very limited; it has no autonomy in relation to the FN. The FN's male leaders are responsible for publicly communicating the FN's position on family policy or women's role, and for legitimizing the CNFE and women's meetings. Thus, at the CNFE's 1995 congress, male leaders presided over three of four commissions.

Women's Trajectories and Motivations in the National Front

Some sociological and political science based surveys, and some of the FN's own published biographical notes, allow for a limited analysis of the political trajectories and motivations of party members, activists, and staff. Oral testimonies contained in articles in the far-right press are of course not neutral and reveal the various patterns of political activism that legitimate women's political involvement.

Some High-Profile Women on the Far-Right

Among the FN leaders, there are only two high-profile women, and neither one has much power. Both are longtime extreme-right activists. Born in 1933, Martine Le Hideux became politically engaged in the 1950s, notably by working to defend French-colonized Algeria as an activist in an organization offering aid to repatriated French colonials and support to political prisoners of the Organization de l'armée secrète (OAS).[3] She has been a member of the FN since its creation, and is very close to Le Pen. She is the vice president of the FN and a member of its Political Bureau. From 1984 to 1989 she was a European deputy, in 1992 was regional representative of Ile de France, and since 1995 has been general counselor of Paris. Born into an upper-bourgeois Parisian family that is well known as rightist (her uncle was minister of industrial production under the right-wing Vichy government), she helped to obtain traditionalist Catholic networks' support for the FN. Interestingly, in spite of her married status, she kept her natal family surname.[4] Martine Le Hideux is also an honorable member of the Union des nations d'Europe chrétienne (Union of Nations of Christian Europe, UNEC). This organization, founded in 1986, struggles against abortion, communism, and the de-Christianization of Europe. It has networks in Germany, Poland, Ukraine, and elsewhere. Notably, in 1990 and 1991 UNEC organized pilgrimages to Auschwitz to denounce abortion as "genocide." This terminology clearly attempts to marginalize the Shoah, or even to negate it. In fact, this propaganda was part of UNEC's condemnation of Jewish activists in the struggle for free abortion in France (especially Simone Veil, Minister of Health who prompted the vote that legalized abortion in 1975). Martine Le Hideux's involvement is not limited to familial and demographic issues; during the FN's last "summer university" session (an annual FN ideological meeting), she presented a paper entitled "Immigration Lobbies: Let's Free Ourselves from Globalization."

The younger of the two, Marie-France Stirbois began her activism at the end of the 1960s in a far-right that opposed the student and worker movements of 1968. That is where she met her future husband, Jean-Pierre Stirbois, a revolutionary right-wing activist with affiliations to fascist and Nazi tradition. In 1977, Stirbois rallied to the FN, and eventually became its general secretary. He died in an accident in 1988. Marie-France Stirbois obtained a deputy seat in 1989 during a partial legislative election and was named to the FN Political Bureau. She recently drew attention when she made extremist antifeminist declarations during the FN's summer university in August 1998. There she made an appeal to "liberate women from feminism," a "sectarian" and "perverted ideology," tool of "lesbianic proselytism," "the avatar of communism," to which she opposed "femininity, an intelligence never stripped of good sense, close to reality." She concluded: Let us be neither men's "equals," "superiors," nor "inferiors," but rather "their indispensable complements who know how to comfort and support them but also sometimes overtake them."

Beyond the FN exist a nebula of newspapers, groups, and associations affiliated with the far right. Even in this network, women are few in number. A 1990 survey in *National Hebdo*, the "unofficial" FN newspaper, showed that 87 percent of its readers were men and 13 percent women. Indexes of historical books about the far-right in France register only a very small number of women's names among far-right activists or writers. One can surmise that, as in many organizations, their roles are barely visible but indispensable. During her survey of the right, Fiammetta Venner encountered Hélène Sabatier, who works at Alliance générale pour le respet de l'identité française et chretienne (General Alliance for the Respect of French and Christian Identity, AGRIF), a traditionalist Christian organization that legally pursues in court acts it deems motivated by "anti-French racism" or "anti-Catholicism." She is unknown to the public, as she stays in the shadows of the AGRIF President Bernard Anthony (who is also a FN leader), but according to Venner, she is the organization's most key worker. She comes out of the Organisation of the Secret Army (OAS) and far-right revolutionary-nationalist groups of the 1960s like other activists of her generation (Venner 1997). Also noteworthy are women in the far-right's press, such as Camille Galic, a "French Algeria" activist, and since 1983 the editor-in-chief of the weekly *Rivarol*, a newspaper of Vichy origin hostile to Jews and immigrants; Claude Giraud, publishing director and editor-in-chief of *Monde et Vie*, a traditionalist Catholic bimonthly publication; and Chard, who illustrates *Rivarol* and the national Catholic daily *Présent* with highly elaborate drawings stigmatizing a whole series of scapegoats and enemies—Jews, immigrants, youth of immigrant origin, and homosexuals—without any legal opposition.

Activists and Intermediary Leadership

In her 1989 study, Fiammetta Venner (1997) interviewed approximately fifty female members of the FN, the Front national de la jeunesse (National Youth Front, FNJ), far-right student groups, traditionalist Catholic groups, and radical nationalist groups in Paris. While the sample does not claim to be representative, it suggests that these female activists (none of whom has a primary role in the FN) are either young and single without children, or older than forty-five. With grown children, the older women can now become politically involved or resume a prior commitment. Venner found few women in the intermediate generation. She questioned the trajectories of these women who had no political background and found that many of them followed their men into the movement. This is consistently the case for young women in far-right "radical" groups (skinheads, revolutionary nationalists) whose only place in the group is as the partner of a male member. This is often the case of women in tradition-alist Catholic milieu: their activism, as voluntary activities oriented around concrete tasks (holding office hours and answering phones, taking care of mail, secretarial work) is part of familial organization wherein the husband, children, and wife each have a function. The wife generally has no professional training and her voluntary activities are an extension of her domestic role. Venner found activist women in the CNFE whose daughters are in the FNJ. But she also discovered women who joined the cause on their own, such as a policewoman whose active involvement in a police organization close to the FN led her to divorce her husband because he did not appreciate her spending so much time on her activities; she declared that she was happy to have divorced. Other young female members of the FNJ also became involved independently of any family ties, or even in spite of their parents' hostility. Female members of the Union nationale interuniversitaire (National Inter-University Union, UNI, which encompasses right and far-right student activists) claim to be in favor of equality between men and women in the family and at work. In the group of women Venner surveyed, the criterion of age seems essential. Young women affirm equality, the right to work, and moral freedom, whereas older women identify more with the role of mother, the role of women in the family, and the stability of marriage.

As described by Venner, women's motivations differ little from men's and are not unlike those of other activists across the political spectrum. Most of the women activists desire to be useful, and to have an impact on events. Their polit-ical awakening or commitment is rooted in political events or a global analysis of society, not in family preoccupations or in the FN's platform on women. Some of them, however, do not approve of all FN positions (for example, its opposition to abortion rights). When questioned about whether or not "as women" they felt particularly threatened by "insecurity" or "immigration" (these are FN propagandist themes), most say they have not thought in these terms. On the whole, however, most of these women express the same prejudices and ideas as FN men, whether favoring the death penalty, protesting the breakdown of values, or denouncing immigration as a cause of delinquency and disorder. Unlike the FN men, who stigmatize concrete enemies, FN women often limit themselves to general accusations or expressions of anguish about the changing world.

Birgitta Orfali (1990) analyzed the motivations of FN members by targeting mechanisms of adhesion to a minority group that aspires to speak for the ("silent") majority of the French, and gives its members a strong sense of iden-tity. She found little difference between men's and women's motivations. Still, she noted that women FN members often become involved through the membership of a man, father, brother, or husband. They assume their place in a "party as family," an orderly, sanctioned space of security whose hierarchy centers on the authoritarian and paternal figure of Jean-Marie Le Pen. Therein women participate in a strictly impersonal way without truly asserting their place; instead they reiterate the ideas and statements formulated by others. Their membership is based on a model of women's subordination to the father or the husband. Nevertheless, unlike their male counterparts, they are not very attached to the idea of a moral and family order, of a vision of an unequal and authoritarian world. According to Orfali, admiration for the leader and following family traditions play an essential role in female membership. Resentment is a strong stimulus for male and female FN participation; in women, however, it is manifested more often in terms of fear, confusion, and a feeling of inferiority, while men express more hostility and even hatred.

The women surveyed or portrayed in biographical material and interviews with women activists published in the FN press often insist on the continuity of their family heritage. To the extent that a far-right nationalist movement always refers back to traditions and to roots and not to innovation, can we say that this is proper to women? The veneration of the charismatic leader and attraction toward Le Pen, as seen in public demonstrations, are not solely women's characteristics, even if women express them more explicitly, especially in their most sensual and mystic dimensions. Le Pen's press attaché Ariane Biot declares in *National Hebdo*, in 1985, that "being near Jean-Marie Le Pen is, let's say, a sort of state of grace." In sum, the interviews and portraits shed light on a number of similarities between men's and women's convictions and motivations for commitment.

The survey carried out after the FN and MNR's split does not note any difference between the women of the two parties (Bolter 2000). None of the women spontaneously evoke their movement's family program, nor do they point to it as a motivation for their adhesion. As Flora Bolter underscores: "These issues often serve as sounding boards for other issues such as Islamism, and the claim that France is losing its identity because of immigration" (29). Her survey confirms Venner's findings on the relations between activism and maternal functions: more than half the women surveyed are childless, and only two are mothers who stay at home. Those who have children left their jobs, and ceased or reduced their political activities while their children were young. Bolter concludes that in the nationalist activist universe the main dichotomy is between mothers who are raising children and other people, and not between female homemakers and activist men.

Patterns of Women's Activism

Even if the motivations and trajectories of activist men and women are not fundamentally different, this does not diminish the facts that the far right and its hierarchy are overwhelmingly male and that its ideology is based on a notion of difference between men's and women's roles. As a consequence, women's activism is invested with certain meanings and inserted into a discourse that justifies it, legitimates it, and valorizes it in the name of party interests. Statements by or about activist women and female activism fall into several types of patterns and perform several functions that I will now examine.

A Fighter

Since 1987, the FN has held a demonstration every year on May 1, the day commemorating Joan of Arc, a figure who seamlessly combines religious, national, military, and feminine thematics, and thus introduces the idea of woman as a fighter. In the FN press, the notion of "front," not only as an idea of unity but as a line of combat and "resistance" (against foreigners), offers an inexhaustible repository of metaphors. When *National Hebdo* presented the FN's two women candidates in the November 1989 partial legislative elections, its headlines read: "Immigration, Women Take Up the Resistance," then "Marie-France Stirbois on the Frontline in Dreux," and "Marie-Christine Roussel on the Front in Marseille." In September 1989, a woman was raped and murdered in Avignon. Jean-Marie Le Pen himself led a street demonstration, presenting the victim (who, it is necessary to point out, was an FN member), as a "martyr of savage immigration," "fallen to the occupying power." In April 1999, a FN propaganda meeting for the European elections was similarly depicted: "European Campaign: Women Rise to the Frontline."

Giving the Party a Good Image

Party leaders claim the FN is not a "macho" party, and that it reserves a large place for women. At a very decisive moment, when the FN emerged from the shadows to conquer the electorate in 1985, Le Pen insisted in a interview on "women and politics" published in *National Hebdo* that "the responsibilities of some women in our movement completely invalidate our reputation, such as our devotion to the national heroine Saint Joan of Arc and the fundamental role we recognize in the mother." Feminine imagery is consciously evoked in propaganda such as the 1989–1990 poster, "the National Front, it's you," which showed a young woman clasping her two young girls. All three have long blond hair and blue eyes, and they are dressed in tricolor harmony, the colors of the French flag. The FN uses images of threatened Frenchwomen in its campaigns against immigration, Islam, and insecurity, while condeming women's "fate" in Islamic or African cultures, as a tool for racist anti-African and anti-Islam propaganda.

Activist women contribute to improving the image of the FN which feels it has been "demonized" by the media. One woman elected to the Regional Council of Languedoc-Roussillon, explained in an interview in *National Hebdo* in October 1999, that as a woman she offers a positive image of the FN that takes her adversaries by surprise and challenges received opinions. Jany Le Pen, the wife of Jean-Marie Le Pen, whom he married after his divorce, is also a member of the FN. Le Pen wanted to place her at the head of the list for European elections in 1999,[5] and she was supposed to play the same role. As she said in an interview "a warm, active and curious woman is susceptible to softening, you understand, my husband's image, and therefore, to participating with others in cracking the wall of demonization." Women are not the only ones to be put forward in this way; the (few) FN activists of African, Maghrebian, Caribbean, or Jewish origin are also tokenized in a completely systematic way. Huguette Fatna, the DOM-TOM secretary whose "island beauty" and "vanilla fragrance, coffee color" Le Pen never fails to mention, is thus a lively image of the patriotism of "little France at the edge of the world," as he said in the first public meeting for the 1999 European elections. A singer of Malagasy origin and wife of an FN sympathizer, Isabella, claimed in *National Hebdo* in October 1999 that she was warmly welcomed by the FN, where, she adds, "there is no racism"; on the contrary, she has been "boycotted by the [mainstream] media" for being a "singer of color proud of being French."

The Party-as-Family

Women's involvement is inscribed in the pattern of the party-as-family, wherein activists have the feeling they belong to a true "countersociety" with its own places, conviviality, customs, and language, and wherein very personalized relations are consolidated. In this way, women activists, especially those who are not well known, are portrayed as "the daughters" or "wives" of the more central male activists in the foreground. When Le Pen first made his list for the 1999 European elections public, each candidate who was the wife of an FN staff member was identified as such, and the presence of these couples was emphasized in his speech.

The role of Catherine Mégret (the spouse of Bruno Mégret, at the time second in the FN's hierarchy) remains among the more significant ones for an FN woman: in 1997, she ran for office in Vitrolles (Bouches du Rhône) in place of her husband, who was declared ineligible after the preceding ballot. In fact, he was the one who campaigned. His portrait was foregrounded on the campaign posters, and although he was not elected, he was seated behind her at the first meeting of the new municipal council.

The personalization of FN political life is particularly spectacular in regard to Jean-Marie Le Pen as a personality, and FN internal opposition denounced his nepotism. A special task falls upon Le Pen's two daughters. They are represented as his legacy in a high-profile, highly dramatized father-daughter relation. They are at his sides during demonstrations. He has appointed them to political positions within the party, and they receive part of the devotion that FN activists give to the leader-father. In 1984, Le Pen dedicated one of his first books, *La France est de retour* (France Is Coming Back), to his "Celtic lineage" and his daughters, "who will hereafter hold the responsibility of transmitting the flame of life." They are obliged to be loyal to him, and beware to she who betrays him! One daughter is the wife of Le Pen's close colleague and FNJ leader Samuel Maréchal. But the other took a position in favor of the opposition in 1998 at the time of the party crisis, when her companion was one of Mégret's assistants. Her father publicly denounced her on the major French television channel in December 1998 as being tied to a "sedition leader"; she chose the opposition side, he said, "under the natural law that leads girls toward their husband and lover instead of their father."

When Jany Le Pen's husband suggested she lead the campaign for the European elections of 1999, Le Pen's partisans began working to create a high-profile, positive image for her. That was the function of an interview with her conducted by Samuel Maréchal and published in an FN newspaper in September 1998. The interview represented Jany Le Pen as a woman of "remarkable modesty," who is "emotional, sensitive, profoundly touched by the unhappiness of her compatriots," led by "an idea of softness, harmony and beauty," a lover of nature and animals, and concerned about "distressed mothers who are left with abortion as the only way out." Jany Le Pen spent a substantial portion of the same interview praising her husband. As this project to designate Jany Le Pen at the top of the electoral list raised some protest within FN ranks, Le Pen justified his decision in *National Hebdo* (December 1998) thus: "To my mind, I don't see anything scandalous in such a move; when the sailor is at sea, or soldier at war, it is the wife who takes care of and runs the house."

Women politicians are judged in function of their adequacy (at least in appearance) in their role as mother, daughter, and wife. Activists who were interviewed reproduced stereotypes diffused in their movement's propaganda. One of the women interviewed by Flora Bolter and her research team, who had participated in organizing the MNR National Council on the family, emotionally evoked Madame Le Gallou,[6] Catherine Mégret, and their children: "These are women, real women" (Bolter 2000). Activists who stayed in the FN still feel that the split between Marie-Caroline Le Pen and her father is scandalous. One of the women interviewed declared: "She is the daughter of a very important man; she should not have turned her back on her father."

Loyal and Modest

Another pattern of women's activism is their indispensable yet discrete sense of devotion and work. First there is the "wife of the male activist," "mother and general steward of the family," "the one who keeps the rearguard together," "the one who gives a helping hand and above all who gracefully supports and accepts her husband's activities," as Nathalie Manceaux says in *Chrétienté-Solidarité* (November-December 1998). Next are the women activists cited in the *Activist Guide* published by *National Hebdo* in 1991: "these women are just as capable as men of handing out leaflets door-to-door and hanging posters, and if they would rather just clean their brooms, that too is an equally useful job." In this hierarchical party, rank-and-file activists, and men and women alike, must take on practical tasks and take commands. Neither men nor women are supposed to discuss or decide. Some women feel satisfied with these subordinate roles, having internalized the limits and constraints that prevent women from achieving more, while others, according to Birgitta Orfali and Fiammetta Venner, nonetheless tell of conflicts with boys who only reticently accept girls in street actions or in hanging up posters. Obviously the ones who desire to take on responsibilities equal to those of men are confronted with these contradictions, of which younger members are especially conscious. For example, one FNJ militant, interviewed by Venner, states that she believes she is equal to men. For her "there is no difference"; yet she recognizes that her movement does not exactly share these ideas. During the May 1, 1990, demonstration, Jean-Marie Le Pen greeted CNFE women who walked in procession with their children or pushed baby carriages (empty, to symbolize the decreased birthrate), with this announcement: "Women of Europe! You are charm and fertility!" Notwithstanding the political ambitions these women expressed, they were reduced to sexual and maternal roles.

From the Private Sphere to the Public Sphere

Yet another aspect of women's activism is the legitimization of public action through the private sphere. Thus, the CNFE calls for women to act in the name of their families or maternal responsibilities. During the first CNFE Congress, in 1987, the far-right journalist and activist Alain Sanders addressed the audience in these terms:

The National Circle of European women is exceptional for it includes women who have no fear of compromising themselves.... These are women who have understood that if they do not get involved in politics—truly, seriously, and completely—then politics would continue to interfere in their lives, and the lives of their family and children. This explains their involvement—daily, multiple, from all directions—in scholarly establishments, in workplaces, in associations for parents of students. This involvement is, admittedly, a departure from our traditional thought, which, by its very nature, discretion, and modesty, has long avoided having women put themselves forward, and in a word, "compromising themselves."

According to this pattern, we find women directing the FN's charity and social organizations, such as Fraternité française (French Fraternity, founded in 1990 to help French people in difficulty), Cercle national pour la defense de la vie, de la nature et de l'animal (National Circle for the Defense of Life, Nature and Animals, founded in 1985), "SOS enfants d'Irak," led by Jany Le Pen, organizations to help "future mothers" (against abortion), and for youth activities (Cendrine Le Chevallier, wife of the FN mayor of Toulon, directs the FN's youth organization there).

Women activists are supposed to demonstrate (especially in interviews or "portraits" published in the far-right press) that they can reconcile the traditional image of femininity and, when possible, motherhood, with a salaried job and political duties, as well as legitimize their political involvement as a family responsibility even when it clearly does not correspond to the reality of their motivations. Thus, the longtime, right-wing activist Marie-France Stirbois felt it necessary to declare at the time of her election in 1989 that "everything that I do, I do for my family and my children," adding that she "is taking up the guard to relieve" her husband. The far right does not have a monopoly on this scenario: all women politicians are confronted with questions about how they reconcile their feminine and political responsibilities. But perhaps it is more visible in the far right. Marie-Caroline Le Pen, the candidate in district elections in 1985, said she ran because "she was called" to do so. She said she believes women's privileged role as mothers requires that they devote themselves to their children's education in order to "counter the influence of school" and concludes: "In short, a woman's role is the 'repose of the warrior' in the noble sense of the term."

The most recent survey on women in the FN and MNR confirms that women electoral candidates or women with responsibilities in the organization all maintain that they have been designated. Flora Bolter (2000) writes: "They never stress that they have any will or personal initiative to have access to responsibilities."

Conclusion

Contrary to the claims of Alain Sanders, as cited above, women's involvement as activists in the far right is not a new phenomenon, but it has certainly increased in the past few years. It is part of a trend of growing participation of women in all areas of public life. However, in a far-right movement women's involvement can be a source of tension because activists' actions and ways of life are in contradiction with the feminine models their party wants to promote. Women, especially younger women, who become politically active and desire to take on responsibilities equal to men are obviously confronted with contradictions that they may even be conscious of. Nevertheless, these tensions seem to have been thus far controlled within the far right. This tension management operates by articulating the feminine and activist function within a nationalist framework, by distinguishing the ideal (mother who stays at home) and reality (the constraints or obligations pushing women to work and to become politically involved), by justifying women's activism as mothers' (or wives') responsibilities, and finally by integrating women's personal trajectories into the structuring models. The women who express themselves publicly in the FN's name appear to be perfectly integrated into it, and they reproduce the FN's discourse. The far-right also knows how to manipulate several registers of language, praising French women in their roles as mothers, as biological reproducers and transmitters of culture, and presenting them as victims of social ills, immigration, and the destabilization of the social and familial order, as well as political agents and fighters. The presence of women activists is essential to normalizing the image of the far-right and expanding its influence. However, these women hold secondary responsibilities and are few in numbers. This scant participation is not unique to the far-right: in this area too, the far-right is no exception. But women's lesser involvement, the fact that less women than men vote for the FN, demonstrates that women's reluctance and opposition toward the far right is greater than men's.

Notes

1. Foreigners constitute 5 percent of the population living in France. But the far right also rejects French citizens of non-European origin.
2. But there was not a single elected person, as the legislative elections with uninominal ballots in two rounds affect minority political structures unfavorably.
3. The defense of "French Algeria" simultaneously against the movement for Algerian independence from French colonial rule and against Charles de Gaulle provoked the reconstitution of a previously marginal far-right. Notably it gave birth to the *Organisation de l'armée Secréte* (OAS, Organization of the Secret Army), a terrorist organization that operated in Algeria and France in 1961 and 1962. A whole generation of today's far-right leaders and activists, including Jean-Marie Le Pen himself, was trained in this context.
4. Her husband, André Dufraisse, who died in 1994, was also a member of the FN from its inception and the leader of the Circle Entreprise moderne et libertés (Circle of Modern Enterprise and Freedoms), an FN group for CEOs and high-level staff of businesses. During World War II, he was a member of the Parti populaire français (French Popular Party, a group of collaborators with Nazism) and engaged in the Legion des voluntaires français contre le bolchevisme (Legion of French Volunteers against Bolshevism), an organization composed of French people who fought on the side of the German army on the Russian front.
5. In 1998, Jean-Marie Le Pen was threatened with being declared ineligible after having been sentenced for illegal use of excessive force (he beat up a socialist candidate during the 1997 electoral campaign). So, he proposed placing his wife at the top of the candidate list for the 1999 European elections, in fact, without letting her know about it in advance. This proposal provoked some opposition inside the party. However, the problem was solved as Le Pen was finally allowed to run as a candidate.
6. Jean-Yves Le Gallou, a prominent leader of the new right and formerly of the FN, is Mégrets' main assistant in the MNR.

10

Women in the Non-Nazi Right during the Weimar Republic: The German Nationalist People's Party (DNVP)

Raffael Scheck

Until 1930, the predominant party of the German right in the Weimar Republic was the *Deutschnationale Volkspartei* (German Nationalist People's Party, DNVP), which combined monarchist, reactionary, and anti-Semitic groups. In the early 1930s, the DNVP lost votes to the rapidly growing Nazi Party but remained strong enough to help this party gain power in 1933. Although the parties shared some ideological positions, such as an extreme nationalism and hatred of democracy and socialism, the DNVP differed from the Nazis with regard to women in politics. Whereas the Nazis excluded women from their parliamentary groups and higher party offices, the DNVP allowed women to occupy seats in parliaments and encouraged them to organize a National Women's Committee and regional women's committees from the start. The DNVP had several well-known women representatives in the *Reichstag* (national parliament) and the diets of many German states. By presenting the four most notable women from the DNVP, this chapter will trace their motivations for joining the party, the focus of their activities, and their ideologies. Each of these four women was in some way typical of larger groups that played a role in the party.

Research on DNVP women has just begun (Scheck 1997; Heinsohn 2000). With one exception (Käthe Schirmacher), none of the women presented here is known in Germany today. Yet, there is a body of literature dealing with the alleged affinity to right-wing positions of the majority of Germany's bourgeois women's movement. Scholars such as Richard Evans (1974) and Claudia Koonz (1987) have claimed that politically active bourgeois women increasingly focused on the community of the people and on separate gender spheres, with an emphasis on women's "inherent" maternal qualities. This is supposed to have prepared them for Nazism with its aim to consign women to motherhood and the household. This thesis has been disputed, however, by historians who argue that the stress on separate spheres for men and women was often combined with the claim for equal rights and that the emphasis on the community of the people did not imply Nazi racism. It has been argued that the concept of "spiritual motherhood," which was popular in the German women's movement, called for an extension of women's alleged "maternal" qualities to all of society, regardless of a woman's biological motherhood, and that this ideology often demanded equal rights even while claiming different gender spheres (Schaser 2000; A. T. Allen 1991). Whereas my contribution, dealing with women who were already on the right before 1918, cannot address the alleged increasing tendency of German bourgeois women to embrace right-wing positions, it can show that the separate spheres ideology—even in the right-wing spectrum—did not preclude equal rights demands and did not predetermine a restriction of women to the role of a mother and housewife.

The DNVP was formed out of older conservative and anti-Semitic parties in November 1918. It opposed the democracy being established after the abdication of German emperor Wilhelm II on 9 November 1918 and advocated an aggressive, confrontational foreign policy incommensurate with Germany's power. In the mid-1920s, the DNVP moderated its stands and participated in government together with moderate parties (Trippe 1995; Hertzman 1963; Liebe 1956; Grathwol 1980; Hiller von Gaertringen 1960). In 1928, however, the party elected as its chairman Alfred Hugenberg, an intransigent rightist. After a career in the top management of heavy industry, Hugenberg had built up a strong media empire. Hugenberg's financial contributions and support from his media had become increasingly important for the DNVP before 1928 (Holzbach 1981; Walker 1976; Leopold 1977). Under his leadership, the DNVP adopted an obstructionist policy and made substituting an authoritarian state for the Weimar Republic its primary aim. Hoping to integrate the Nazis and other radical right-wing groups into a broad opposition front against the Weimar Republic, Hugenberg repeatedly cooperated with Hitler and prepared the way for Hitler's appointment as chancellor on 30 January 1933.

The DNVP's votes came mostly from the small-town bourgeoisie and the rural population in Protestant regions, the very groups that in the early 1930s provided the Nazis with the bulk of their electoral support (Childers 1983). The DNVP attracted aristocratic landowners, civil servants, entrepreneurs, Protestant ministers, teachers, farmers and rural workers, housewives (both rural and urban), and a sizable group of blue-collar workers and lower-level employees. It competed for the vote of most of these groups with several other parties, including small special-interest parties. The DNVP started out with 10 percent of the national vote in 1919 but had doubled its share by 1924 (for all election results, see Falter, Lindenberger, and Schumann 1986). An uneasy balancing act between participation in government and opposition cut the DNVP's electoral support to 14.7 percent in 1928. Hugenberg's radical opposition then drove the more moderate groups out of the DNVP. Still, the party retained about 8 percent of the national vote even in March 1933, at a time when the Nazis were dominant and the DNVP's other competitors virtually wiped out. The DNVP formed a coalition government with the Nazi Party upon the appointment of Adolf Hitler as chancellor, but the Nazis soon excluded the DNVP from power and dissolved it on 30 June 1933 (Hiller von Gaertringen 1960, 609–616).

The introduction of women's suffrage in November 1918 encouraged the German right to intensify its efforts to mobilize women. The DNVP won the support of well-known women leaders and their organizations and ensured the election of women to the Reichstag and most state diets. Women usually had a share of 3 to 9 percent in the DNVP's Reichstag group, which was comparable to the other nonsocialist parties although lower than in the left-wing parties (Scheck 1997; Boak 1990). In the diet of Prussia, by far the largest German state, women for many years made up about 10 percent of the DNVP representation. The party also funded a newsletter edited by its National Women's Committee and sent to all local women's committees, many individual members, and the nationalist press (this was the *Frauenkorrespondenz für nationale Zeitungen,* renamed *Deutschnationale Frau* in 1931). Electoral analyses suggest that the DNVP usually got between 54 and 58 percent of its national vote from women (only the Center Party and its Bavarian sister party received a slightly higher share). At its electoral zenith in 1924, the DNVP thus must have been the choice of one quarter of the German women who voted. In the DNVP strongholds in the north and east of the country, this share may well have approached 50 percent (Falter et al. 1986, 81–85). Although the reasons for women voters to support the DNVP are difficult to assess, we can examine the motivation and thinking of those women who participated at the highest level of DNVP politics.

Paula Mueller-Otfried

Paula Mueller-Otfried was the longest-serving Reichstag member among the DNVP women. She represented the concerns of women in Germany's Evangelical Church. Her policies were conservative in matters of morality and reproduction, but she also insisted on the expansion of women's rights. Born in 1865 to a family of a high-level civil servant, she became a teacher, one of the few professions open to an intellectually gifted woman at the time. She remained unmarried. (Until 1919, women in state employment, including teachers, had to quit when they got married, but whether this compelled Paula Mueller-Otfried to remain single is unclear.) Mueller-Otfried gained a national reputation as chair of the Deutsch-evangelischer Frauenbund (DEF, German Evangelical Women's League), an organization that sought to mobilize women within the Evangelical (Lutheran) Church and, unlike the numerous charitable women's groups in the churches, emphasized women's rights (Reagin 1995). In 1908, Mueller-Otfried made the DEF a member of the predominant umbrella organization of the German women's movement, the Bund Deutscher Frauenvereine (Federation of German Women's Leagues). But the membership contract stipulated that the DEF did not have to support the union's call for women's suffrage. Mueller-Otfried herself advocated women's suffrage in areas where women were already involved (the churches and the local community) but not on the state and national levels.[1] (The reform of state suffrage threatened to open a can of worms for conservatives because most German states still had property-based suffrages that minimized left-wing representation.) In the last year of the First World War, the DEF left the union in protest against the union's vigor in calling for women's suffrage. To build a counterweight to the union, Mueller-Otfried then formed a new umbrella organization, the Vereinigung Evangelischer Frauenverbände Deutschlands (VEFD, Union of Evangelical Women's Leagues of Germany). Already before the war, Mueller-Otfried had joined the Conservative Party, the most important predecessor of the DNVP, and chaired its women's committee. When the DNVP was founded, Mueller-Otfried joined the party, as did many leading DEF and VEFD members (Scheck 1997, 37–39).

In 1920, Mueller-Otfried was elected to the Reichstag. As a member of the Reichstag, the National Women's Committee, and the DNVP Party Council, Mueller-Otfried was mostly concerned with public morality and social policy. In the early 1920s, she became instrumental in orchestrating the hateful racist campaign against the presence of black African soldiers in France's occupation army in the Rhineland.[2] The fact that the French occupation army in western Germany used soldiers from France's African colonies had triggered widespread outrage in Germany and concern in other countries as well. Some German newspapers reported that Africans had committed rapes and blew the few incidents out of proportion, presenting them as a deliberate policy by France to undermine the morality and strength of the German people. Mueller-Otfried was instrumental in drafting a protest note to the League of Nations that stated: "The French Government also forced several town administrations to the unheard-of measure of opening brothels with German women for the people of color, thus to lure black beasts with white flesh" (quoted in Scheck 1999, 27).

Mueller-Otfried also played an important role in drafting legislation restricting immorality in film and print and became the DNVP's most outspoken advocate of small rentiers, people who had lost their retirement savings during the inflation of 1923. Mueller-Otfried and her allies won some concessions for the small rentiers, a majority of whom were women, but they narrowly failed to pass a law that would have given the rentiers adequate compensation for their losses in 1928 (Hong 1998, 121–123; Crew 1998, 33, 67, 90; M. Hughes 1988, 22; Führer 1990). On some occasions, Mueller-Otfried also fought for women's rights. In the Reichstag, she opposed initiatives to reintroduce the celibacy clauses for women civil servants abolished in 1919 but insisted that a woman civil servant with an illegitimate child had to be dismissed.[3] In the course of deliberations on the right of women to serve on juries, Mueller-Otfried even voted against the majority of her party for a bill that would grant women full access to the legal professions.[4]

In August 1932, after having been reelected five times, Mueller-Otfried declared she would not run in the November election. The press hostile to the DNVP claimed that Hugenberg had forced her to give up her place to a lower-ranked man, but Mueller-Otfried herself, who had repeatedly expressed admiration for Hugenberg, denied these rumors.[5] Like most leading DNVP women, Mueller-Otfried watched the rise of the Nazis with ambivalence. Whereas she welcomed the destruction of the Weimar Republic and the Nazis' terror against the left, she worried about their antifeminist stands, their cultlike veneration of Hitler, and their contradictory attitude toward religion.[6] She consequently stepped down as chair of the DEF in February 1934 (she had resigned from the VEFD earlier) (Lange 1998, 104). She lived in retirement until 1946.

Mueller-Otfried represented the powerful symbiosis of evangelical and conservative political motives among the women and men of the DNVP. Prominent evangelical church leaders and many women from the DEF and the evangelical charity organizations participated in the DNVP. One of the most famous was Magdalene von Tiling, a teacher who had received an honorary degree in theology. Von Tiling succeeded Mueller-Otfried as chair of the VEFD and sat in the Prussian state diet (1921–30) and the Reichstag (1930–33). Mueller-Otfried and von Tiling represented conservative rather than radical right-wing positions. They detested the Weimar Republic, which they saw as an amoral state hostile to religion. They were deeply affected by Germany's defeat in World War I and the Treaty of Versailles and believed that their work for public morality would prepare the rebirth of a strong, united, and Christian Germany. They did advocate some women's rights, such as the right to vote and to be elected in spheres where women had long done most of the work (such as the churches), but they were uneasy in the company of the mainstream women's movement with its more democratic orientation. Von Tiling, in particular, advocated a corporate state built on authoritarian and religious values.[7] Although Mueller-Otfried played an important role in the campaign against the black soldiers in France's occupation army, DNVP women associated with the Evangelical Church were not at the forefront of the radical racism advocated by many other DNVP women. One such DNVP activist from the province of Hannover, Else Meyer, openly questioned this tendency in 1931: "Such a controversial issue as the race question first needs to be clarified carefully before it is made into an object of mass education. Otherwise it becomes mere phraseology."[8]

Margarethe Behm

Mueller-Otfried may have been the most important DNVP woman in the Reichstag, but Margarethe Behm clearly was the most popular one. She built up the DNVP's National Women's Committee and sat in the National Assembly 1919–20 and the Reichstag from 1920 to 1928. Behm was a leading DNVP authority on social policy. Her particular concern was the lot of preindustrial women home workers, who lacked the legal and social protection granted to workers in factories (Quataert 1979, 35–36). Yet Behm seemed less concerned with women's rights per se than Mueller-Otfried even though she voted with her for the bill granting women access to the legal professions. Behm wanted women to be religious and socially sensible educators of the nation and accepted a stereotypical hierarchy of gender roles: "Men should lead us [women] whenever reason has to decide, we want to lead them whenever reason becomes a hindrance for what is born out of feeling in us."[9]

Born in 1860, Behm was, like Mueller-Otfried, an unmarried teacher. She came from a wealthy landholding family from the border area between Germany and Poland. Behm gained a national reputation as leader of the Gewerkverein der Heimarbeiterinnen (Union of Women Home Workers). Supported by Empress Auguste Viktoria, Behm pushed the prewar Reichstag to pass a sickness insurance bill for the women home workers. Her interest in workers induced Behm to get involved in the Christian Social Party, another one of the DNVP's predecessors, whose founder hoped to woo workers away from socialism with a mixture of social welfare, Christian values, and anti-Semitism.[10]

As chair of the National Women's Committee of the DNVP, Behm was ex officio a member of the highest party committees. Until she resigned from the National Women's Committee in 1923 to devote herself more to her other duties, she was involved in all party decisions.[11] At the first national party convention in July 1919, she was given the honor of reporting on the DNVP's work in the National Assembly following the initial address by the party chairman. Behm appealed to the historic importance of that moment: "For the first time in Germany, possibly for the first time in the whole world, a woman stands up to report on the work of a parliamentary group."[12] Behm then called for the rebuilding of Germany in a national and Christian spirit and fiercely denounced both the Treaty of Versailles and the Weimar Republic. Behm won admiration across the political camps through her concern for socially disadvantaged women and through examples of open-mindedness. In her speech at the party conference, for example, she called for the party to be open to everybody willing to build a new and united Germany—including Jews.[13] Although she admitted to having anti-Semitic views before 1918, she argued that most Jews had proven themselves to be patriotic Germans and should be welcome in the DNVP (Striesow 1981, 114–128).

In the Reichstag, Behm's greatest achievement was the passage of a bill granting extensive insurance coverage for the women home workers in 1922. Her crucial role in this success was recognized when the press dubbed the law the "Lex Behm."[14] Unlike the rather serious and grim Mueller-Otfried, Behm displayed sharp humor in her speeches. Her responses to male hecklers in the Reichstag often caused general amusement, as when she justified her opposition to lowering the voting age in Germany from twenty-five to twenty in the National Assembly: "The male youth, in particular, is real cider in this age group, (very good! On the right) it can turn into beautiful wine, better than the one we get nowadays, (laughter and approval) but it still is only cider, (very true! On the right) and we have to wish that it turns only into the most noble wine."[15] Relating to her compassion for the lot of poor women in the cottage industry, she cultivated the image of a just and caring mother (or grandmother), so that she came to be called "Muttel" Behm (a tender version of "Mother Behm"). On her sixty-fifth birthday in 1925, she received an honorary doctorate from the medical faculty of the University of Greifswald.[16]

Behm died in July 1929 and thus witnessed only the beginnings of Hugenberg's party leadership. It remains open to speculation what she would have done had she lived longer. Suffice to say that several members of the Gewerkverein left the DNVP in 1930, including Behm's closest friend and successor at the helm of the Gewerkverein (Opitz 1969, 150, 178, 217). Like Mueller-Otfried, Behm and her Gewerkverein colleagues were conservative but not radical right-wing leaders. Ardent nationalism and a strong religious identification led Behm into the DNVP, and her social-mindedness was important in the party before the Hugenberg years.

Käthe Schirmacher

Although well acquainted with Mueller-Otfried and Behm, Käthe Schirmacher seemed to live worlds apart from them. She had a Ph.D. in French literature, had played a leading role in the left-wing women's movement before the war, and maintained a lesbian relationship until her old age. Her partner, Klara Schleker, for a short time served as DNVP deputy in the diet of the state of Mecklenburg and, at age sixty-eight, was appointed as the diet's president by seniority in 1920 (Walzer 1991, 26, 79; Rupp 1997, 96). Nobody in the DNVP was more outspoken about women's rights than Schirmacher. Though she moved to the right in the last years before the First World War, she never reneged on her strong commitment to women's rights. But Schirmacher also became a representative of extreme racist and anti-Semitic positions in the DNVP.

Schirmacher was born in 1865 in the east German port city Danzig (today Gdansk, Poland) as the child of a wealthy merchant family. She received a good school education and went on to study at the Sorbonne in Paris and later at the

University of Zürich, where she received her doctorate in 1895. She rose to high positions in the German and international women's movements, serving for many years as secretary of the International Council of Women. After 1900, Schirmacher displayed an increasingly fanatical and antidemocratic German nationalism. She became a prominent activist on behalf of the Germans in those parts of east Germany that had a Polish majority, defining their conflict as a racial struggle. At the same time, she expressed hatred of democratic practices, whose weakness and decadence she claimed to have observed in France and which she saw on the rise in Germany, too. By the outbreak of the war, Schirmacher had resigned, or been pushed to resign, from her positions in the women's movement (Walzer 1991, 66–68). During the war, she called for a compulsory women's service that would drill young women in housework, gardening, and child care and instill strict discipline and nationalist values in them. She stressed the national importance of housework: "The world war has taught us that cooking and housekeeping are a service to the country, a defense of the country, and a form of citizenship. Not only the sword is a weapon—in the 'hunger war,' the cooking spoon is equally important."[17]

The possibility of her home province falling into Polish hands after the war induced Schirmacher to join the DNVP and to rally Danzig's German majority in a spirit of national defense. She was elected as a representative of West Prussia to the National Assembly in 1919, but the DNVP did not give her a promising place for the Reichstag elections of June 1920 after her voting district had been separated from Germany (Walzer 1991, 89). (Danzig came under a League of Nations mandate, and the rest of West Prussia was awarded to Poland.) In the National Assembly, Schirmacher passionately protested against the transfer of ethnically mixed areas to Poland, claiming that the Germans in those areas faced cultural repression and economic ruin under their new masters. Hers was one of the angriest voices against the Treaty of Versailles, and she was among the first to attack the presence of soldiers from the French colonies in the Rhineland. She claimed: "The lust of white, yellow, and black Frenchmen for German women leads to daily violence."[18]

Schirmacher was active in the National Women's Committee and the party's committee on race, the Völkischer Reichsausschuß, until her death in 1930. In many articles and speeches, she developed paranoid scenarios of a Germany in the throes of a "negroized France" (an allusion to France's use of African soldiers) and an "animalistic Moscow" (her metaphor for "Jewish" bolshevism). To counter this threat, she urged the Germans to keep their race "clean" and to strengthen its Nordic elements, a task in which women as mothers and educators had to play a primary role.[19] There were (well-founded) rumors that Schirmacher and Schleker hid right-wing terrorists who had assassinated politicians of the Weimar Republic. With a fanaticism that raised eyebrows even in the DNVP, Schirmacher strove to keep alive a spirit of revenge for Versailles, stressing repeatedly: "There is no happiness before we have been avenged."[20] Shortly before her death, she called for support of a popular referendum submitted by the DNVP and the Nazis against a new settlement for German reparations: "It is exciting to say *no* in times of deepest national shame and national surrender—to resist, to fight. The Germanic people were always fighters; their sign was the light-spraying hammer. Be cheerful, optimistic—be Germanic! Swing the bright hammer of the referendum against the lie of Versailles, against tributary payments, against national decadence, against the spoiling of our present and our distant future. We can win, if we *want* to win. Want it!"[21] Yet, Schirmacher also demanded that women be allowed to participate in the national struggle as equal partners: "Each social, political, or national equation that fails to include women is wrong, unjust, and breeds misfortune."[22] Thus, Schirmacher claimed a direct connection between the liberation of women and the strength of the nation.

Whether Schirmacher's lesbianism was known in the party and hindered her DNVP career is impossible to say. Following some liaisons with men and perhaps women, Schirmacher met Schleker in 1903, at age thirty-eight. Schleker, an independently wealthy woman, was fifty-one and belonged to the same women's organizations as Schirmacher. After reading their private letters, historian Amy Hackett concluded that their relationship became erotic in 1906 at the latest. In 1910, Schirmacher moved in with Schleker. Schleker experienced the same political transformation as Schirmacher from a left-wing position to the far right (Hackett 1976, 289–291; Walzer 1991, 24–26). Given that women's friendships in the period tended to be more openly affectionate even without erotic background, it often happened that lesbianism was ascribed to women who were simply good friends or shared a household. By the same token, however, it is possible that Schirmacher's lesbianism was not widely recognized because of the more affectionate style of friendships between women (Hackett 1976, 290, n. 123). Hackett does not say whether Schirmacher's and Schleker's lesbianism was known in the women's movement before 1914; in the DNVP, nobody ever seems to have mentioned it.[23] In any case, Schirmacher's left-wing past and her outspoken insistence on women's rights were enough to give her an awkward position in the DNVP, although the Third Reich later venerated her for her nationalism and racism (Hackett 1976, 291).

Many men in the party, and many women, too, could not forget (or forgive?) Schirmacher's dazzling feminist career before 1914, and some DNVP women professed that her insistence on women's rights even after 1918 bothered them.[24] Yet Schirmacher was widely respected in her party, as the outpouring of admiring obituaries in the DNVP press shows, and she helped inspire a group of DNVP women, mostly intellectuals, who sought a similar synthesis of women's rights and fanatical, often racist nationalism. These women, sometimes called "*völkisch* feminists" (which is a questionable term considering their advocacy of rights only for women of a certain ethnic group), played an important role in the publications of the National Women's Committee. Most of these women preached a Nazi-style racism and anti-Semitism. Pointing at examples of gender equality among the Germanic tribes, they claimed that the subjection of women in Western civilization was the outcome of a Jewish intrigue and that a truly Germanic nation would recognize women as equals to men (H. Arendt, Hering, and Wagner 1995, 22–24). Had the Nazis allowed women a more prominent role in their party, it is possible that the *völkisch* feminists from the DNVP would have joined them. Yet, their positions were not unusual in the DNVP. The DNVP always had an anti-Semitic and racist wing, which even gained prominence in the last years of the Weimar Republic. But no matter how much resonance the racism and anti-Semitism of the *völkisch* feminists may have found in the DNVP, their advocacy of women's rights probably went too far for most men and many women in the party.

Annagrete Lehmann

As a personality, Annagrete Lehmann was less distinct than the three others, but she quickly emerged as a clever politician in the DNVP women's organization. In early 1923, she succeeded Behm as chair of the National Women's Committee and received a seat in some of the highest party committees. She also served as DNVP representative in the Prussian state diet and later the Reichstag. After 1928, she cultivated close contacts with Hugenberg and was even appointed as one of the vice chairs of the party.[25] It is probably to her credit that the DNVP did not roll back its commitment to women's issues in the last years of the Weimar Republic, when Hugenberg pushed the party to the extreme right. Lehmann, who was significantly younger than the three other leading DNVP women, gave strong support to racist views in the DNVP.

Born in 1877, Lehmann had worked as a teacher and played a role in women teachers' organizations before she joined the DNVP. She got elected to the Prussian state diet in 1921 and joined the Reichstag in 1928, where she remained until 1933. According to her own testimony, she was instrumental in mobilizing the support of academic women for the DNVP.[26] As a parliamentarian, Lehmann addressed an unusual variety of topics. She became notorious for her attacks against the left-to-center Prussian government, which ruled for most of the period 1919–1932. In 1927, she stood in the limelight after having been selected as her party's commentator on the budget of the Prussian Ministry of Science, Culture, and Education. Accusing Prussia's government of nihilistic mass worship, Lehmann extolled the virtues of a *Volk* constituted through "affinity of the blood, genetic heritage, community of culture, and community of fate throughout history."[27] In the Reichstag, she fought against the liberalization of abortion and the charge that Germany had started the First World War. This was definitely her favorite topic. Lehmann for many years cochaired a women's committee dedicated to fighting the so-called "war guilt lie." Pointing out that the war guilt charge introduced the article on German reparations in the Treaty of Versailles, Lehmann and her peers believed that they could unhinge the legitimacy of the treaty by consistently denying Germany's responsibility for the war.[28]

As a close confidante of Hugenberg's, Lehmann after 1928 justified his every move to the women in the DNVP. The DNVP women's newsletter in this phase often carried a Hugenberg quotation in bold type followed by a Lehmann article that interpreted the quotation like a minister preaching about a Bible passage.[29] Notes of the DNVP's top-level meetings from this phase, in which Hugenberg negotiated several agreements with the Nazis, show that Lehmann attended most meetings but hardly ever spoke even though many other DNVP women were afraid of the Nazis' antifeminism and openly said so (Weiß and Hoser 1989). Although Lehmann used her position to protect the women's organizational structure of the DNVP, she showed less concern for women's rights than Mueller-Otfried or Schirmacher. When unemployment inspired German politicians to tighten the rules on the employment of married women in 1931, for example, Lehmann stood at the forefront of those women who justified the new restrictions.[30]

Lehmann enthusiastically welcomed the end of the Weimar Republic, the bloody repression of the left by the Nazis, and the dawning of a state based on racial, nationalist, and—so she hoped—religious principles. A programmatic document issued by the National Women's Committee, still under Lehmann's leadership, in February 1933 defined the first task of the German woman to be a "guardian and cultivator of the race."[31] Lehmann expected that the Nazis would allow the DNVP to cooperate in the buildup of the racial state, but what she did after the dissolution of the DNVP is unclear. Like Hugenberg, she may have sat out the rest of the Nazi years in retirement. She died in 1954.

Lehmann was not only important as an efficient, if colorless, organizer but also as a link to the young generation. Her racism, in particular, was shared by many young DNVP activists at the end of the Weimar Republic. The two most notable among them were Alexa von Porembsky, a party activist from Thuringia, and Dr. Irmgard Wrede, an economist from Silesia. Both propagated the same racial eugenics that was at the core of Nazi race ideology. Porembsky even warned the Nazis in February 1933 that their predilection for submissive women would produce further racial decay because it induced Nordic men to marry racially inferior women; the precious Nordic woman, Porembsky claimed, was as self-assertive and bold as the Nordic man.[32]

Conclusion

Although the four most notable DNVP women cover a broad range of women's activism within that party, they leave open a few gaps. The most significant one is the absence of a housewives' representative. Housewife issues occupied an important place in the DNVP women's activities. As Schirmacher stressed, good housekeeping had become a national duty during the war. In "buy German" campaigns, DNVP women after 1918 stressed the power and responsibility of the German housewife as a consumer and producer. Several housewives and members of Germany's powerful rural housewives' union sat in the DNVP's parliamentary groups, yet none of them was famous for her party career (Bridenthal 1993). Another point to consider is that the four most prominent DNVP women, having built up or led independent women's organizations, entered the party from a position of strength. They knew how to deal with the hostility of men to the presence of women in politics. The situation was different for those women who lacked a prominent organizational role preceding their DNVP involvement. A telling example is Anni Kalähne, the wife of a professor in Danzig, who became the leading DNVP activist in this city. To get things done, Kalähne discussed her ideas with two powerful men in her party, inducing them to present her ideas as their own.[33]

In spite of these limitations, the four case studies show that the primary concerns of women who joined the DNVP were radical nationalism, often coupled with anti-Semitism and racism, and a religiously inspired conservatism. The women were generally able to assert their influence within the limits defined by the party statutes and broader ideological conventions, which assigned to them topics such as education, public morality, religion, and housekeeping. They occasionally protested if their share of parliamentary seats or funding for their activities was reduced, and male party leaders often lent an open ear to these complaints (Scheck 1997, 44–46). The limitation of women to fields that were deemed close to the work of housewives and mothers led to differences of emphasis between women's and men's stands in the DNVP. Still, no clear line separating their political stands in general exists, although it appears that DNVP women in the late Weimar years took more strongly to racist and anti-Semitic ideas than did activist men in the same period.[34] The gender-specific emphasis of women's political work was typical of all parties in Weimar Germany and was rarely challenged (Koonz 1976).

With respect to women's rights, different priorities emerged among the DNVP women activists. They certainly agreed that the push for women's rights per se was not justified in a national emergency such as it existed for much of the Weimar Republic. But some DNVP women activists welcomed women's rights primarily as opportunities for women to infuse German politics with a stronger nationalist and religious spirit. Others, such as Schirmacher, believed that women, despite their differences from men, should be granted full equal rights and that the national liberation of Germany even hinged on that. Unlike Western feminists, these women tended to justify equality not with recourse to the natural rights discourse of the Enlightenment tradition but rather through the invocation of an allegedly egalitarian Germanic past. Those DNVP women most interested in racial eugenics even constructed a racial foundation for this argument by claiming that the Nordic woman was by nature self-assertive and bold.

Given that all four leading DNVP women—despite some inconsistencies— were assertive about women's right (and duty) to participate in politics, however, this chapter contradicts the thesis that the gender-specific emphasis of German women activists was decisive for German women's affinities with Nazism. Equal rights, even if tied to gender-differentiated roles, was not something Hitler and leading Nazi ideologues were willing to grant, as shown in their refusal to admit women to their parliamentary groups and higher party posts (Scheck 1999, 32). It is important, moreover, that the leading DNVP women rejected the separation of public and private spheres that usually came as an analogy to the division of "male" and "female" spheres (Yuval-Davis 1997, chap. 4). The food crisis of the First World War had shown how important housekeeping was, and the sharp social tensions after 1918 demonstrated the relevance of the so-called female sphere in the political realm. At a time of near civil war and—real or perceived— moral decay, the social policies and the legislation on public morality articulated foremost by women appeared to be a matter of national importance. Finally, one should consider that those women who, like Schirmacher and the *völkisch* feminists, came closest to advocating a Nazi-style racism, were often the most outspoken DNVP women with respect to women's rights.

It is safe to say that the DNVP women helped to make Weimar legislation more conservative and that they demonstrated—for the first time in Germany and perhaps the world—that women could be trusted to represent right-wing causes in parliaments and in the wider public. Their impact on the rise of the Nazis and the Third Reich, however, is harder to assess. In their critique of the Nazis, DNVP women defended the right of women to participate at all levels of politics (Scheck 2000, 242–247). Their own antidemocratic stance as well as their stress on the primacy of women's role as housewife and mother, however, threatened to undermine their credibility. If one opposed a democratically elected parliament and advocated an authoritarian state, what sense did it make to defend the right of women to vote and to serve in parliaments? The Nazis, once in power, swiftly brushed the DNVP women aside and built up a women's organization untarnished by women's rights stands. The leader of the Nazi women's organization after 1934, Gertrud Scholz-Klink, a young mother of five children, was the widow of a Nazi martyr and had little political experience (Koonz 1987, xxxviii, 166–167). Still, the DNVP women's synthesis of religious concerns with racism and anti-Semitism may have helped pave the way for the Third Reich by preparing German women for the racism of the Nazis. Perhaps the definition of the German woman primarily as a guardian of the race, as expressed by the DNVP women in February 1933,[35] was the logical conclusion of a stand that rejected universalistic natural rights and democratic principles while embracing a racially underscored hypernationalism.

Notes

1. Paula Mueller(-Otfried), *Weltanschauung und Frauenbewegung.* Berlin, 1910.
2. Protokolle über den 2. Parteitag in Hannover, Oktober 1920, in Bundesarchiv Berlin, 60 Vo 2 DNVP, vol. 53 (films 45125/6), pp. 46–48.
3. *Verhandlungen des Reichstags,* vol. 354, p. 211, and vol. 355, p. 630.
4. See *Deutschnationales Handbuch,* vol. 8. Berlin, 1921, pp. 108 and 233. A different bill was passed in 1922 with the votes of the DNVP.
5. "Paula Mueller-Otfried," *Deutschnationale Frau (DnF),* 15 September 1932.
6. Paula Mueller-Otfried, "Waffen für den Wahlkampf," *DnF,* 10 July 1932.
7. See, for example, Magdalene von Tiling, "Der alte und der neue Staat," *DnF,* 23 and 30 October 1932.
8. Else Meyer, "Nationalsozialismus und Bildungswesen," *DnF,* 1 July 1931.
9. "Tagung der deutschnationalen Frauen," *Frauenkorrespondenx Für nationale Zeitungen (FK),* 6 November 1920.
10. Emma von Westarp, "Margarethe Behms Lebensgang," and Paula Mueller-Otfried, "Margarethe Behm im Parlament," both in *FK,* 8 August 1929.
11. On her resignation, see *FK,* 23 February 1923.
12. "Parteitag 1919," special issue of *Die Post,* July 1919, p. 2.
13. Ibid.
14. Reinhard Mumm, "Der Ehrentag Margarethe Behms," in *Der Parteifreund,* 15 April 1922.
15. For Behm's speech, see *Verhandlungen der Nationalversammlung,* vol. 327, p. 1266. See also Reinhard Mumm, "Weibliche Beredsamkeit," in *FK,* 12 March 1921.
16. *FK,* 7 January 1925.
17. Käthe Schirmacher, *Frauendienstpflicht.* Bonn: Marcus and Weber Verlag, 1918, p. 6.
18. See *Verhandlungen der Nationalversammlung,* vol. 341, interpellation no. 1898 (quoted), and vol. 343, interpellation no. 2771.
19. Käthe Schirmacher, "Frankreichs farbige Truppen," *FK,* 13 July 1925.
20. As quoted in Annelise Spohr, "Käthe Schirmacher. Zu ihrem Geburtstag am 6. August," *FK,* 24 July 1930. See also Walzer, 1991, 87.
21. Käthe Schirmacher, "Zum Volksbegehren," *FK,* 24 October 1929.
22. Schirmacher, "Margarethe Behms Todestag am 28. Juli," in *FK,* 17 July 1930.
23. A biography of Schirmacher published by her former secretary introduces Schleker merely as Schirmacher's "partner in struggle and life" (H. Krüger 1936, 131–37).
24. See Anni Kalähne, "Käthe Schirmacher zum Gedächtnis," *FK,* 27 November 1930.
25. Elisabeth Spohr, "Zehn Jahre Führerin der Deutschnationalen Frauenarbeit," *DnF,* 15 February 1933.
26. Annagrete Lehmann, "Der Frauenausschuß der Deutschnationalen Volkspartei." In *Der nationale Wille. Werden und Wirken der Deutschnationalen Volkspartei 1918–1928,* ed. Max Weiss, pp. 319–336. Essen: Wilhelm Kamp, 1928, p. 321.
27. *Verhandlungen des Landtags,* vol. 12, p. 18174.
28. Lenore Kühn, "Die Schuldfrage Deutschlands Lebensfrage," *FK,* 19 November 1921.
29. For examples, see *DnF,* 23 October 1932 and 15 November 1932.

30. Annagrete Lehmann, "Rechtliche Stellung der verheirateten Beamtin und Lehrerin," *DnF*, 1 May 1931.

31. "Was hat das bisherige System an moralischen Werten verwirtschaftet?" *DnF*, 15 February 1933. The article introduces a resolution by the National Women's Committee that includes the quotations.

32. See the summary of her talk "Woman and Race": "Die völkische Tagung am 4 und 5. Februar in Berlin," *DnF*, 15 February 1933.

33. "Lebenserinnerungen von Anni Kalähne, geb. Schäfer." Landesarchiv Bremen, Nachlass Dietrich Schäfer, vol. 7.21.

34. Whereas the DNVP women's newsletter after 1930 contains many racist articles, the general party newsletter (*Unsere Partei*) contained only one such article in the same period—written by Alexa von Porembsky ("Der völkische Gedanke in der DNVP," *Unsere Partei*, 1 September 1932).

35. "Was hat das bisherige System an moralischen Werten verwirtschaftet?" *DnF*, 15 February 1933.

11

Spartan Mothers:
Fascist Women in Brazil in the 1930s

Sandra McGee Deutsch

A suggestive story entitled "Integralist Mother" appeared in *Anauê*, the magazine of Brazilian Integralist Action (AIB), the Brazilian fascist movement of the 1930s. Shooting between communists and Integralists, and Integralist women at the barricade singing the national anthem, permeated the background. In the foreground, a young man informed his mother that a communist bullet had killed his older brother. The woman said, with some satisfaction, "They wanted to kill the Fatherland and he died for it. They wanted to destroy the family and he died for it. They wanted to insult God and he died for God." She had given him the "Brazilian blood" that flowed through her veins. Thus, when the communist hordes, "paid with the money of London and New York bankers," attacked Brazil, she did not have to tell him what to do. Grasping her meaning and the rifle she took from her martyred son, the younger man jumped into the fray. No longer holding back her tears, the woman sank to her knees and prayed to God to protect him (*Anauê*, Rio de Janeiro, no. 1 ([January 1935], n.p.).[1]

A man penned the fictional story, but women writing or quoted in this and other Integralist publications echoed its themes. The movement was engaged in a war of words and bullets with the left, and women were not always absent from these skirmishes. Integralists did not use the term "Spartan," but they probably would have endorsed it, for it epitomizes some of the desired qualities of an Integralist woman: brave, stoical, and warlike when emergencies arose. These traits departed from those generally prescribed for Brazilian women, ones which, in day-to-day life, Integralist women also were supposed to display. These included love, piety, morality, and self-sacrifice. Thus the AIB's ideal woman combined Spartan and conventional maternalist features. For the AIB she was a seamless whole, for it did not discern contradictions between the two sets of characteristics. The magnitude of the crisis that Integralists perceived justified Spartan traits, ones that proper mothers would shed when the crisis ended.

Male opinion makers still assigned women domestic identities in the 1930s, and most women accepted them. According to the census of 1920, only a small minority of women were wage earners, but this estimate probably was inaccurately low. Evidence suggests, however, that even women who worked outside the home tended to define themselves in terms of their labors inside it. The fact that most women's work was unpleasant and poorly paid helped determine their identities as mothers and helpmates. Nor did the increasing participation of privileged women in the labor force, as well as their usual church and charitable activities, contradict their devotion to domesticity (Hahner 1990, 102, 105; Besse 1996, 3–4,129–130, 151; Veccia 1997, 137).

Thus it is not surprising that, although women performed a variety of tasks in the movement, they and their male comrades generally saw their duties as motherly, beneficent, and wifelike: serving as model women, inspiring their menfolk, helping the poor, and raising stalwart children for the cause. These tasks resembled those of fascist women elsewhere. The AIB trilogy of "God, Fatherland, Family" had special resonance for many women because it addressed their roles in the home and church. Fearing that communism would destroy this trilogy, women flocked to the Brazilian variant of fascism. While mostly middle-class and Christian, Integralist women from a variety of backgrounds venerated family and motherhood and feared that a capitalist-communist conspiracy of international bankers (a euphemism denoting supposed Jewish interests) not only financed leftist mobs, as in the story above, but sought to destroy their homes. Under these circumstances, it was permissible for mothers to be Spartan.

Although these women composed roughly 20 percent of what was arguably the most prominent fascist group in Latin America (Broxson 1972, 197), scholars have devoted little attention to them. Yet these women were noteworthy in several respects. As in the case of the "Integralist Mother," at times they witnessed violence. Moreover, some of them were of African and indigenous descent. These characteristics made Integralists unique among fascist women in Europe and the Americas, and for these reasons alone they warrant examination.

Rise of the AIB

Although women had belonged to Catholic nationalist groups in the early 1920s (Deutsch 1999, 117–128),[2] Integralism was the most significant extreme rightist organization in Brazil to mobilize women before the 1960s. It arose in a moment of economic crisis and political flux. The Depression undermined the oligarchic republican structures and parties, and the revolution of 1930 replaced this old regime with the new one of Getúlio Vargas (1930–45, 1951–54), whose ideological orientation initially seemed vague and malleable. There was a sense that Brazilians had to move forward and forge new governing forms and philosophies to replace the liberalism that had fostered dependency and fragmentation. Hoping to influence the government and create the first genuine national parties with popular appeal, the AIB and other groups stepped into this political vacuum.

Founded in 1932, the AIB offered a fascist prescription for Brazil's future. Its initial rise was not so much a reaction against the left, which was weak at that time, but against the prevailing sense of national disunity and weakness. The AIB favored a strong, politically centralized, corporatist state that would regulate private property, oversee relations between workers and employers, withstand foreign companies and bankers, and control some essential industries. While many Integralists were Catholics, the AIB officially supported religious freedom and "Christian" ideals so as not to alienate Protestants, particularly those of the large pro-fascist German community of southern Brazil. Vertically organized under the command of "Chief" Plínio Salgado, an intellectual and politician from São Paulo state, this militarized movement was supposed to exemplify the hierarchy, unity, and social solidarity that would characterize the future Integralist State. Democracy, leftism, materialism, and liberalism were among its enemies, and, like other fascists, it tended to identify these things with Jews.

These beliefs and their anti-Semitic component drew from Catholic nationalist groups of the 1920s as well as European fascism. The rapid growth of the Jewish population—from about 6000 in 1920 to 55,666 in 1940—and the resentment over economic competition that it engendered during the Depression, also fueled Integralist prejudice against Jews. So, too, did the fact that anti-Semitism was in vogue in the 1930s, and not only among fascists (DellaPergola 1987, 101; Lesser 1995; Levine 1968, 45–48).[3]

As did fascists elsewhere, Integralists exalted male dominance and insisted that the woman's place was in the male-ruled heterosexually organized home (Payne 1995, 13). Yet they recruited many women, who composed about 20 percent of their estimated two hundred thousand members. The sizable number of women in Integralism related to its aim of creating a total way of life for its adherents. Intricate rituals and symbols played a critical role in this movement. Integralist men and women wore the green shirt or blouse and greeted each other with the fascist salute and an *anauê*, a word supposedly derived from the indigenous Tupi language. Plastic pictures of the Chief hung on walls, and the AIB insignia adorned coffee cups and other items in Integralist homes. Distinctive ceremonies marked the rites of passage in an Integralist's life (*Anauê*, esp. no. 20 (October 1937), 9; Sombra and Guerra, 1998). The AIB had its own sports teams, social gatherings, charities, and more than a hundred periodicals that supplied its view of the world, including articles written by and directed toward women. The creation of an all-encompassing lifestyle, which made participation meaningful to many who were new to politics, required women's involvement. Women took part in the rites, marched in parades, organized many of the social and philanthropic activities, bore and educated the children to be inducted into the movement, and disseminated Integralist symbols and ideas in the home. A way of life could not be total without both genders. Nor could this ambitious attempt to mobilize a broad popular base—one that paralleled the efforts of other fascist movements—succeed without women's participation (Blee 1991, 37–41, 59, 65, 128–129, 134–139, 162–170).

Electoral opportunities also helped account for the AIB's recruitment of women. Although it theoretically rejected partisan politics, the movement entered the political arena as a means of spreading its message and attracting support. Other than the frequently banned Communist Party, the other parties existed at the state level and served as vehicles for local elites and strongman figures. Ironically, the Integralists became the first nonproscribed, popular, nationally organized party in the country. Moreover, decades of feminist struggle had culminated in the acquisition of the vote in 1932. The fact that literate women could vote at all levels increased Integralist interest in mobilizing them.

The AIB, then, had practical reasons for persuading women to join; why women themselves decided to participate is another question. Integralist views on family supply insight into women's motivations. Carmela Patti Salgado, the daughter of a wealthy businessman whose participation in Integralism predated her marriage to Plínio, noted that while the French Revolution had declared that all men were equal, Integralism declared all families were equal. All had the right to earn enough to live on and attain a degree of material well-being; all had the duty of revering God and country and following Christian values. Within the family, she noted, the woman had the exalted task of serving as the "great guard of the virtues of the home," one that extended far beyond the walls of the household (*Provincia de Guanabara*, Rio de Janeiro, 1:3, 19 April 1937, 2).

Aurora Nunes Wagner, a dentist and chief of the Feminine Department of Porto Alegre, predicted approvingly that the Integralist state would judge women's duties to be as important as those of men (*Aço Verde*, São Paulo, 1:16, 7 October 1935, 2). Such statements demonstrated the AIB's high regard for family life and homemaking, which struck a favorable chord among many women. So, too, did the AIB's concern for the family's economic viability, given the context of the Depression and enormous inequalities in Brazilian society.

Its frequent warnings that communism endangered the family also found listeners, although the notion that this ideology represented any kind of threat by the mid-1930s was dubious. When Integralism arose, leftist groups were in disarray, but over time they took advantage of the political opening offered by the revolution of 1930. Many workers joined unions, and in March 1935 communists and other progressives created a popular front organization, the National Liberating Alliance (ANL). Between seventy thousand and a hundred thousand joined the ANL, whose militancy alarmed the AIB and the government. Advocating women's rights, its women's auxiliary attracted mostly middle-class urban members (Levine 1970, 74–75, 79; Hahner 1990, 175). After several bloody encounters between the AIB and ANL, the administration shut down the latter. The authorities easily stamped out communist-influenced army revolts in November, using them as an excuse to repress any manifestation of leftism and consolidate an authoritarian order. By late 1935 the communist menace was a chimera, even though sporadic fighting between leftists and Integralists continued. This bloodshed helped explain Integralist promotion of a "red scare," as did the Church's concerns that the anticlerical violence of the Spanish Civil War might spill over into Brazil. The opportunism of AIB leaders, who sensed an audience for their hyperbolic claims about the Soviet threat, also accounted for their anticommunist campaign.

Why Women Joined

Anticommunism was among the prime reasons men joined Integralism, according to Hélgio Trindade (1974, 160). Yet women's concerns about preserving the existing family structure may have made them even more susceptible to arguments about a communist threat. According to Nilza Perez, editor of the women's section of *Anauê*, the family rested on the bedrock of indissoluble marital ties, private property, and the parents' exclusive right to educate their progeny. The communist state, however, robbed parents, and especially women, of control over their children's education. By taking over private property, it hurled families into mass housing projects that reeked of promiscuity. Legalized divorce converted marriage into "officialized prostitution," a "banal meeting of persons who can separate after satisfying their animal instincts": an institution that failed to protect powerless women. Thus communism reduced "the first cell of society to an agglomerate without expression or social value" (*Anauê*, no. 21, November 1937, 49). Communism could hurt any family member, but women, whose identity and purpose primarily came from their roles as mothers and wives, stood to lose the most.

Like other Integralists, Perez identified most of what the AIB opposed with communism. Public education, divorce, sexual desire, and apartment complexes, however, were not uniquely communist, but were features of modern secular life. Female Integralists feared modernity as much as the "red menace," or simply conflated the two.

The AIB's anticommunism had class implications. Trindade found that the Green Shirts were largely of middle-class backgrounds, and one might conjecture that women members, many of whom were related to the men, were as well. About 22 percent of local male leaders and members, however, were rural and urban workers, and it is likely that a similar percentage of women shared these origins. The AIB's concern for private property and marriage resonated with middle-class women, who tended to be dependent on husbands and tied to the home. It might seem to have had less appeal for lower-class women, who usually lived in common-law relationships or served as family heads, and who had few possessions. Yet many women workers primarily defined themselves in terms of their familial roles and aspired to be full-time wives and mothers. Since the AIB recruited from the ranks of the upwardly mobile, as Trindade concluded, perhaps these women expected to fulfill their goals and identified with middle-class family values (Trindade 1974, 144–146, 150–151; Veccia 1997, 137; Weinstein 1997, 91–92).

As photographs indicate, many Green Blouses (and Green Shirts) had indigenous or African ancestry. While they rarely addressed the issue of race, Integralists accepted the fact that most Brazilians were people of color, and they sometimes criticized racial discrimination. Plínio Salgado praised the nation's mixed racial composition, and an AIB newspaper, *Ação*, claimed that the movement was an expression of the "*mestiço* masses." Although not all Integralists echoed these beliefs, the movement in general stood for racial tolerance. Integralist anti-Semitism, however, demonstrated the limits of such tolerance, as did the AIB's initial opposition to Brazil's first black party, the Brazilian Black Front, which arose in 1931 and espoused civil rights. The Black Front's activism encouraged divisiveness and even racial exclusion, according to AIB spokesmen, who evidently accepted general statements disapproving of racism, but not the political action required to overturn it. When a sector of the Black Front moved toward an anti-immigrant, rightist stance in 1933, however, the AIB embraced it (Sombra and Guerra 1998; *Ação*, São Paulo, 23 December 1936, 4; Salgado 1935, 40, 46, 51; *Ação*, 14 May 1937, 1; Andrews 1991, 147–155; K. Butler 1998, 119–123).

Despite the contradictions, such stances set the AIB apart from most members of the political elite, who were ashamed of the makeup of the Brazilian population. They also separated the AIB from most fascists in the world (Deutsch 1999, 170–171).[4] Indeed, the Integralists used their relative racial openness precisely to highlight these differences. They wanted to distinguish themselves from the former ruling class in order to emphasize their radical credentials. Integralists also pointed to these characteristics to separate themselves from German Nazis, whose paganism alienated most Brazilian Catholics.

Other factors also accounted for the AIB's racial ideas and multiracial composition. Its precursors had denounced the upward mobility of foreign-born at the expense of native-born, mostly non-white Brazilians. The AIB and its predecessors understood that the racist theories popular abroad—and among the local elite—condemned Brazil to an inferior status, and as nationalists they opposed such a ranking (*Ação*, 4 January 1937, 4). Integralist leaders also recognized that to create a genuinely popular and nationwide movement, they would have to recruit people of color, who constituted the majority of the population.

To what extent these racial views influenced women to join is unclear. What individual Green Blouses thought about race, aside from the "Jewish question," is also uncertain, for they did not write or speak about this issue. Their silence is revealing. Like many other privileged Brazilians, the middle-class Integralist women did not want to call attention to a racial stratification system that benefited them. More likely to be poor than the white women, the women of color in the movement probably thought the AIB's social justice platform addressed their needs. Perhaps they concluded that membership in Integralism could help "whiten" them, enabling them to climb the racial and economic ladder. Whatever their color or class, Green Blouses may have agreed implicitly with their male comrades that frank discussions of race could undermine the unity and strength they sought for their country.[5]

They did address the need to oppose communism, which they said was their main reason for donning the Green Blouse. A leftist attack on Integralists in the Praça da Sé of São Paulo, described below, shocked Margarida Corbisier, an eyewitness. Convinced that the AIB needed her to fight against communism, she joined immediately against the wishes of her brother, a prominent young AIB intellectual. Integralism could safeguard "our homes, beloved Fatherland, and saintly Religion," said Flor de Lis Dias Tavares (*Anauê*, no. 18, August 1937, 62).[6] These women became soldiers in a crusade.

The religious aspects of this crusade attracted Corbisier. She thought that her participation in the movement helped her become a better Catholic. When she campaigned for Integralism, its members offered her food, shelter, and companionship, just like the early Christians. Although she and other young women worked closely with male comrades, Corbisier claimed that they always treated each other with respect and purity. She believed that the AIB, which had borrowed much of its social program from Catholic doctrine, was the vehicle for putting her religion into action.[7]

An Integralist municipal councilwoman, Maria Bernadette Leme Bueno Romeiro, described herself as a fervently Catholic mother. By working through Integralism to promote God and Christian civilization, she and other Catholic women could keep atheism from spreading from places like Spain to Brazil (*Ação*, 7 October 1937, 13). For many women like Corbisier and Romeiro, anticommunism, religion, and Integralism went hand in hand. The faith that underscored many women's lives was another powerful motive for their affiliation.

So, too, was the influence of husbands, boyfriends, fathers, and brothers. Many Green Shirts told their wives and women relatives about the movement and helped persuade them to join (*A Offensiva*, Rio de Janeiro, hereafter *AO*, 1 January 1937, 4).[8] The belief in family harmony may have influenced reluctant women to wear the Green Blouse despite their misgivings. Corbisier's brother's resistance, however, also suggests that some men opposed women's involvement as unseemly or dangerous.

Dr. Irene de Freitas Henriques, the highest female official in the AIB, addressed the notion that politics was inappropriate for women. She credited the Chief with reviving a nation drugged by "internationalist banking Semitism and administered by a criminal and cowardly liberalism." Believing that this mission of countering Jews and liberalism was a male one, many women had remained apart. But Henriques thought that if women did not enter politics, the family was doomed, and with it affection, mutual aid, and happiness in general. Humans would become animals, as communists wanted. Female apathy in this dire situation was unacceptable to Henriques. She agreed that women should not enter politics as usual, for it might corrupt them, but they should enter the Integralist type, which sought to moralize the state, help the poor, and fulfill the AIB trilogy (AO, 11 October 1936, 15).

Those men and women who thought women's participation might be dangerous judged it correctly. Not only did women see their sons, brothers, or husbands killed or wounded by leftists (and, on occasion, police), but they sometimes placed themselves on the battlefield. While they did not necessarily participate in violence, they were present at such scenes, which sets them apart from most fascist women in the world.[9] The best-known incident took place in a rally in São Paulo on October 7, 1934. Early that afternoon, members of the Feminine Department gathered in the downtown Praça da Sé and climbed to the top stairs of the cathedral. They waited behind the platform where the Chief and his entourage would stand, thus affording protection for them, as Integralist planners may have assumed that leftists would not fire on the leaders and thus endanger women's lives. Jeering at the AIB leaders for using women as shields, members of a coalition of antifascist groups engaged in a shooting match with the authorities, later backed by male Integralists who marched into the square. In one of the breaks between volleys, the young Green Blouses dared the leftists by lifting their arms in the fascist salute and singing the national anthem, to the applause of onlookers. Thirty-four persons were wounded and six persons died, including two Green Shirts. No Integralist women were injured, yet the courage they had demonstrated inspired other women. Chief of the Feminine Department of the Federal District, Margarida Prestes Maia lauded her comrades' bravery and exhorted women to recount this story to their children. For Maia, it showed that when the time came, women knew "how to be Integralists" (AO, 11 October 1934, 1, 5, 7; Maffei 1984 esp., 98).

On other occasions women received injuries and direct threats. In July 1937 in Muguy, Espírito Santo, assailants described as communists broke into an Integralist function. Their shots severely wounded a Green Blouse, Serafina Bernarde. In August that year the columnist Nilza Perez faced down intimidation from the local government in Minas Gerais. The sister of a young Integralist shot by police in Maragogipe, Bahia, in June 1937 prevented the police from entering the house and disturbing his body (AO, 21 July 1937, 1; Anauê, 19 September 1937, 8, and 16 June 1937, 2–3). These brave militants, as well as those in the Praça da Sé, exemplified the Spartan traits.

AIB leaders frequently reminded Integralists of the men who had fallen to their foes and the sacrifices made by their mothers and widows. Such women received recognition in AIB ceremonies. One example took place during an important ritual, the annual "Night of the Silent Drums," in which Integralists around the country mourned the outlawing of their militia. The government had closed it down in 1935, and the AIB maintained the fiction that this armed body had disappeared, although surreptitiously it continued to exist. The Chief of each local chapter, or nucleus, initiated the event by handing the proceedings over to the humblest and poorest member. In São Paulo in 1936, the wife of a martyr of the Praça da Sé, Anna Spinelli, received this honor (*Ação*, 8 October 1936, 1).

Women's Tasks and Organization

In keeping with the martial image, an official Integralist statement urged the Green Blouse to fight against "all that seeks to enslave her." These enslaving forces included bourgeois ostentation, libertine sensual pleasures, and the dictates of fashion, an industry controlled by international Jewry. Poor women tried to emulate rich women, according to the AIB; since they could not consume to the extent the wealthy did, they felt humiliated and unfulfilled. Some became prostitutes in order to afford similar luxuries or in other ways rebelled against society. The pittances that male workers received pushed women into the labor force, where they also earned low wages and worked under terrible conditions. Integralists thought that leftist ideas that dismissed marriage, and false scientific theories that reduced life to sex and converted women into mere instruments of desire, also chained women. So, too, did immoral films, books, and bathing suits. To free themselves and other women, Green Blouses would set an alternative model of womanhood that combined Spartan and customary maternal traits. By promoting spiritual and domestic values and the cult of saints and heroes, Integralist women would moralize society. Within the home women would ensure that men were loyal Integralists, but they would also spread word of the AIB outside it, anywhere they were active. In the future Integralist state, women would occupy a status neither above or below that of men; their roles would differ because their natures differed, and the duties of one sex would complement, rather than conflict with, those of the other. The Integralist state would permit women to exercise any of the liberal professions, assuming they had the requisite ability and would not neglect their tasks in the home (*AO*, 13 September 1936, 16). Although the AIB envisioned women primarily as mothers and helpmates, it accepted and made use of their roles outside the household.

The means of organizing women to fulfill these ideals evolved over time. At first women belonged to the male Integralist cells, called nuclei. A few became officers of these male cells. In December 1933 women organized a "feminine Integralist militia" in Teófilo Otoni, Minas Gerais. Perhaps because it departed too overtly from the usual peaceful connotations of womanhood, the term militia was dropped, but the idea of segregated women's units caught on; by mid-1934 feminine departments arose in Rio de Janeiro and São Paulo, and other localities followed. The departments held meetings in nuclei headquarters at times planned to avoid male gatherings. The purpose of separating the genders was to meet standards of "proper" behavior and, possibly, to demonstrate the sense of order and hierarchy within the movement. Whether intended or not, however, this separation also permitted women the opportunity to run their own meetings and activities. This, in turn, may have lifted women's sense of autonomy and confidence in their own abilities (*Fon-Fon*, Rio de Janeiro, 30 December 1933, 36; *AO*, 24 May 1934, 8; 28 June 1934, 1; 23 August 1934, 8).[10]

A military-style structure of command is a feature of all fascist movements, and Integralism was no exception. Similar to the men, women owed allegiance to their municipal, district, and provincial Chiefs and to the national leaders, who were mostly male but included the Chief of the National Feminine Department, later called the National Secretariat of Feminine and Plinian Regimentation. Named for Plínio Salgado, the Plinians were the youth contingent, significantly grouped together with the women. Dr. Irene de Freitas Henriques was the Chief of the National Secretariat and also served in the Integralist Supreme Council. Iveta Ribeiro, editor of the AIB women's magazine, *Brasil Feminino*, and frequent contributor to the women's page of the main AIB news organ, *A Offensiva*, served in another governing body, the Chamber of 400, along with four other women (*AO*, 10 June 1937, 3). There were few women among the top-level leadership, and while they issued orders to the women below them, it is doubtful that they gave any to men. Even Spartan women were subordinate to their menfolk.

The National Secretariat organized women's activities. Sponsoring gymnastic and sports activities was the job of its physical culture division. The fact that it set up many such events demonstrates the AIB's concern for the health of mothers and their prospective children. The education division directed training in literacy, nursing, typing, home economics, civility, and child care, most of which related to women's domestic chores or customary means of earning an income. Education, sociology, and philosophy courses and lectures in other disciplines fell under the supervision of the study division. Finally, the social action division organized clinics, milk dispensaries, and other measures to help poor Integralist families. Female Plinians, who were separated from the boys, mainly received training in the domestic arts appropriate to their future roles as mothers (*Monitor Integralista*, Rio de Janeiro, no. 15, 3 October 1936, 13–14, 16–17).

As member Mariana Galvão de Queiroz Ribeiro de Castro noted, the future AIB state would provide for the poor. In the meantime, the Green Blouses helped alleviate their suffering. They founded schools, libraries, inexpensive restaurants, and free medical clinics. Nursing courses trained members to become bandeirantes da caridade,[11] who staffed the clinics and visited medical facilities and needy Integralist families. In the schools women handed out teaching materials and clothing to students, while at the annual "Christmas of the Poor" celebration, Green Blouses distributed candy and toys to children. When floods hit the state of Bahia, Integralist women set up a sewing room to make clothes for victims. By July 1937 the AIB claimed that in five years Integralist women had established more than three thousand schools, more than one thousand clinics, and hundreds of milk distribution centers, and that they had distributed goods to more than 5 million people. A few months later the AIB contingent of the state of Minas Gerais insisted that its 6,084 Green Blouses had founded 105 literacy, twenty-two domestic arts, fifty vocational, and thirty-five sewing schools, with a total of 5,006 women pupils, as well as eight libraries and fifteen milk distribution centers (*AO*, 18 July 1937, 12, 14; 13 December 1934, 6, 8; 3 January 1935, 1, 6; 3 January 1937, 15; *Brasil Feminino*, no. 38, November 1937, 24; *A Província*, Bahia, 1:17, 8 June 1935, n.p.).

The numbers probably were inflated, but the philanthropic work reveals how Green Blouses claimed to uphold a standard of womanhood that opposed bourgeois greed and frivolity. How these activities differed from standard bourgeois charitable endeavors, however, was unclear. It is also possible that middle-class Integralist women were altruistic at some moments, and greedy and frivolous at others.

Other activities were designed to mold Green Blouses into model women. Cooking, sewing, and home economics courses enabled members to become better homemakers. Learning to sew one's own uniform was a domestic task that could impart a sense of economic independence, said an AIB newspaper notice—whether from men or from foreign textile firms was unclear. Female participation in artistic exhibitions and literary and musical evenings enhanced women's "natural" abilities to create beauty and harmony. Involvement in sports strengthened women and their ability to bear healthy children; it also provided a manner of sublimating sensual urges that might otherwise be expressed in immoral dances—or worse. Female and male leaders lectured Green Blouses on how to inculcate their children with proper gender and Integralist notions and inspire their menfolk to be exemplary Green Shirts (*AO*, 29 November 1934, 4; 5 October 1937, 2; 17 January 1937, 13; 3 January 1936, 7). With their recipes and articles on child care, mothers' health, and, ironically, fashion, the women's sections of *A Offensiva* and *Anauê* reinforced these domestic and bourgeois messages.

Some activities, however, aimed at preparing women to think about and participate in politics. Men and women comrades regularly addressed women on such matters as AIB political doctrine, the supposed Marxist repression of women, and the Brazilian financial situation. One purpose of the AIB schools was to teach potential voters to read, as suffrage was limited to the literate, and AIB publications exhorted Green Blouses to instruct their maids as well. They also explicitly urged Integralist women to register to vote and take others to be registered. A few Green Blouses ran for office and several won city council seats. The priority, however, was to turn out the vote for men, particularly for Plínio Salgado's presidential campaign of 1937. Indeed, women also participated in the internal plebiscite that chose Salgado as the AIB's standardbearer, casting an estimated 6 percent of the votes. Since women composed 20 percent of the membership, however, their electoral participation was low (*AO*, 24 January 1936, 4; 11 October 1936, 15; 17 January 1937, 13; 4 November 1937, 2: *Brasil Feminino*, no. 36, June 1937, 25; Broxson 1972, 197; Deutsch 1999, 288–289).

Perhaps voting was too striking a departure from the past for many Green Blouses. The main factor inhibiting less privileged Integralist women, however, may have been their inability to read. Half of adult Integralists, according to Plínio Salgado, were unlettered (Broxson 1972, 198). We do not know whether this figure was accurate, or how many of the illiterates were women. At any rate, illiterate women may have decided there was little point in voting in the plebiscite, since they could not participate in the general election.

Women's involvement in three feminine congresses offered additional evidence of their Spartanlike commitment and militancy. For the first women's congress, in Rio de Janeiro in October 1936, Henriques invited provincial and local female Chiefs from the entire country, and delegates from at least eleven states attended. Delivered by men and women, the speeches concentrated on women's roles in the movement, the communist threat, education, and immoral films. Participants also attended local Green Blouse charitable works and Plinian formations. Not wanting women to assume too much prominence, even the AIB media downplayed coverage of such congresses. Nevertheless, they provided a forum for women from different places to meet, exchange ideas, and address large groups. Many women broke with custom by traveling long distances to attend (*AO*, 3 October 1936, 1; 16 October 1936, 1, 17 October 1936, 3; 3 January 1937, 15, 17 January 1937, 13).[12]

Women also broke with custom by participating in marches. Wearing uniforms, stepping in time, and giving the fascist salute gave women a martial and militant appearance. Yet at times the AIB stepped back somewhat from portraying women in this Spartan mode. On November 1, 1937, thousands of Green Shirts marched through downtown Rio de Janeiro to the Praça Duque de Caxias, where an estimated five thousand Green Blouses from Rio, São Paulo, Guanabara, and Minas Gerais awaited them in military formation, holding flowers for their male comrades. Then they marched together to greet President Vargas at Guanabara Palace. The bouquets softened the women's image, but they still looked like soldiers (*Brasil Feminino*, no. 38 [November 1937], 31; *Anauê*, no. 22 [December 1937], 19, 31; *AO*, 2 November 1937, 1–2.).[13]

Anauê described this women's activity as "the greatest and most splendid affirmation of genuine feminism" (no. 22, December 1937, 31). This curious observation indicates the Integralists' peculiar relationship with feminism. They frequently criticized it for setting women against men, overlooking the differences between men and women, and threatening to overturn what Iveta Ribeiro called the "formal government of the family" (*AO*, 11 October 1936, 15). Yet AIB leaders feared that some observers might regard the Green Blouses as dangerously feminist, and they needed to counterbalance this perception. At the same time, feminist advances in Brazil made it hard to simply dismiss the women's movement, particularly since the AIB wanted to attract the votes of middle-class women who might have agreed with some of the feminist platform. Thus Integralists tended to advocate a moderate form of feminism, one that praised women's familial roles yet accepted their political and civil rights. This was a "true feminism, Christian and Brazilian," (*Anauê*, no. 4 [October 1935], 29) suitable for Spartan mothers.

This "true feminism" did not differ greatly from the public positions adopted by the main suffrage organization, the Brazilian Federation for Feminine Progress. The bourgeois federation had insisted that voting would not remove women from their duties in the home, and it refrained from criticizing the Catholic Church. It advocated collaboration between women and men and between the social classes; indeed, it maintained that feminism would help stabilize Brazil. Unlike the AIB, however, the federation was not pro-clerical. Moreover, it regarded women's work outside the home more positively than many Integralists, and it openly opposed sexual discrimination, a matter which Integralists ignored. In general it favored women's autonomy much more fully and consistently than did the AIB. Outside the federation, there were feminist freethinkers who denounced the church, marriage, and the sexual double standard, and who regarded Integralism as anathema (Hahner 1990, 144–161; Besse 1996, 164–178; Alves 1980).

Before women could use their rights and cast their ballots in 1938 for the Integralist or any other presidential candidate, President Vargas canceled the election to perpetuate his rule. This was one of a series of measures designed to establish the dictatorship he had been building since 1935, with the AIB's encouragement. Thinking that his movement would become its base, Salgado supported the consolidation of an authoritarian regime, but the wily president dissolved Integralism as well. AIB leaders called off a poorly planned conspiracy against the government scheduled for mid-March 1938, and the second attempt, on May 11, ended in failure. The Chief and other leaders went into exile, some members were imprisoned, and others hid their beliefs. Integralism never recovered.

Conclusion

Still, this Brazilian variant of fascism left an important legacy of women's activism. Women's marches, militant and anti-Semitic speeches, and presence in armed confrontations revealed their Spartan side; their discourse of piety and love, as well as their charitable endeavors and training for domestic duties, manifested the more customary maternalist bent. The aim of raising children for the cause and inspiring their Green Shirt husbands and relatives indicated both. Male Integralists recruited women to help create a total way of life within the movement and mobilize a broad popular following, one that included men and women of all racial backgrounds. This racial diversity, as well as their presence at scenes of violence, distinguished Green Blouses from many other fascist women in the world. Women of varied class backgrounds joined the AIB, although most were of the middle. These women of the middle sectors—and some of the lower—believed Integralism was the best means of defeating what they saw as the communist threat to their faith and families. The perceived magnitude of this threat impelled Integralist women to assume Spartan qualities when necessary. The AIB appropriated the term "feminism" and made use of women's advances in society. It opposed the liberationist message of feminism, however, and its Catholic model of femininity contrasted with the secular feminist model.

Some of these characteristics resurfaced in the early 1960s, when many middle- and upper-class Brazilians perceived President João Goulart (1961–64) and his encouragement of popular mobilization as a communist threat. The military and rightist civilians organized to overthrow the left-leaning administration. Aided and financed by a businessmen's organization, the Instituto de Pesquisas e Estudos Sociais, women formed anticommunist groups in the major cities. These middle-class women and their upper-class leaders asserted the need to protect God, family, and country from communist assault, as had the Green Blouses before them. Marches in which they prayed with their rosaries emphasized the importance of religion in their campaign. While they upheld the Marian virtues and image, they also provoked and engaged in violence, manifesting a confluence of Spartan and conventional maternalist traits. The crisis that bourgeois Brazilians perceived seemed to justify the Spartan behavior. When the women planned a parade for the day of the coup, its leader, General Humberto Castelo Branco, suggested postponing the women's action. The head of one of the female groups warned the general not to interfere, and the march took place (Simões 1985; Starling 1986, 151–192; Dreifuss 1987, 294–299, Dulles 1970, 173, 180–181, 189–190, 261–262, 267–268, 275–278, 341–342). Like their precursors in the AIB, they, too, were fearless Spartan mothers.

Notes

I thank the University of Texas-El Paso, National Endowment for the Humanities, American Council of Learned Societies, and CIES-Fulbright for sponsoring the research for this article. I appreciate the editors' useful comments, and I am especially grateful to Margaret Power for her invaluable help in preparing this piece for publication.

1. For a similar story, entitled "Brazilian Mother," also written by a man, see no. 10 (May 1936), 11.
2. Unless otherwise stated, all background information on the Brazilian right comes from this book.
3. The AIB's interest in recruiting Teuto-Brazilians was not an important factor behind its anti-Semitism.
4. The Movimiento Nacional Socialista of Chile, however, praised the mestizo "race" and included many mestizos, who constituted a majority of the Chilean population.
5. Brazilians have long sought individual advancement up the racial ladder, or "whitening," through marriage to lighter-skinned spouses, education, or association. Silence on racial issues has characterized other groups and time periods in Brazil. See Skidmore 1985, 15–17.
6. Hélgio Trindade, interview with Margarida Corbisier, São Paulo, 1969–70, 2–3
7. Ibid., 3–5, 7–8.
8. Hélgio Trindade, interviews with Aurora Nunes Wagner, Porto Alegre, 1969–70, 1, and Corbisier, 14.
9. To my knowledge, the only other cases of extreme right-wing women in the interwar period participating in or being present at violent encounters were the British Union of Fascists and the Ku Klux Klan. See Durham 1998, 54–55 and Blee 1991, 40–41. Chilean radical rightist women engaged in and provoked violence. See Power 2002, 156–157, 221–222; Crummett 1977, 106; Davis 1985, 47, 154–155, 196–197.
10. Hélgio Trindade, interview with Corbisier, 2.
11. The bandeirantes were explorers from São Paulo who claimed territory in the Brazilian interior for Portugal during the colonial period. Through *caridade* (charity), these latter-day female bandeirantes tried to expand the AIB's appeal.
12. Other feminine congresses took place in Petrópolis (*AO*, 25 June 1937, 1), and Caruarú, Pernambuco (*Anauê*, no. 12 (September 1936), 13.
13. Other examples of women in marches are in *Fon-Fon*, 26 May 1934, 38–40; *AO*, 28 June 1934, 1, 23 August 1934, 8.

12

The Feminine "Apostolate in Society" versus the Secular State: The Unión Femenina Católica Mexicana, 1929–1940

Kristina A. Boylan

Catholic women's campaigns against the postrevolutionary Mexican state are cited as proof of their being reactionary and unquestioning in their allegiance to their church hierarchy, a portrayal that obscures the meaning of their mobilizations. Mexican Catholic women from diverse social milieus chose consciously to resist the state's reform program, instead militating for policies and practices more in line with Catholic precepts and with the conservative political movements reemerging in Mexico. After the Cristero Rebellion (1926–1929), the church hierarchy planned for the Unión Femenina Católica Mexicana (Mexican Catholic Women's Union, hereafter UFCM) to foment the "re-Christianization" of Mexico. But UFCM members did more than follow the hierarchy's plan to perpetuate and encourage Catholic practice in their homes and churches. Over the next decade, these women challenged the state's anticlerical laws and practices and its socialist education scheme, competed with state organizations to provide community services, and supported opposition social and political campaigns. Without Mexican Catholic women's grass-roots resistance, the practical suspension of much of the state's anticlerical campaign would not have been won.[1] This chapter presents these women's strategies, organization, and achievements in 1930s Mexico, which formed an integral part of the Catholic Church's recovery and the development of conservative social movements after the Mexican Revolution.

Although analyses of extraordinary females in the Catholic Church and of its gendered division and distribution of power are available, not as much work has been done on women remaining "in the pews" (Walter and Davie 1998, 640). Catholicism is often interpreted as being a "general anesthesia" for otherwise discontent peoples and providing a "psychological reassurance of legitimacy" for dominant social groups (Scott 68). Popular Catholic practices are also interpreted as being anti-intellectual or less doctrinally sound (Bamat and Wiest 1999, vii–viii). In the postrevolutionary Mexican case, it is unfair to dismiss the women who mobilized for the church in the postrevolutionary period as "cultural dupes," lulled into obedience via a false consciousness of paternalist Christian ideology or unsophisticated tradition. Such a conclusion overvalues the rhetoric of ecclesiastical leaders and critics of the church and undervalues women's contributions to their churches as well as the opportunities religious participation provides for education, decision making, and public activism (Walter and Davie 1998, 645).

Mexican historiography has failed to recognize the choices Mexican women made to support the church as their affirmation of a vision of social organization in concordance with their religion. Meanwhile, Catholic historiography has tended to consider Mexican women's activism as secondary to men's, whether ordained or lay. Yet in postrevolutionary Mexico, laywomen formed the majority of the Catholic community's principal vehicle for social mobilization, the Acción Católica Mexicana (Mexican Catholic Action, hereafter ACM), and their activism played a key role in its support for the church and actions against government policies.

Historical Background

As a consequence of previous church-state conflicts and conservative Catholic involvement with counterrevolutionary forces, the 1917 constitution aimed to eliminate the Catholic Church's broader cultural and spiritual hold over Mexico, not just the property and judicial privileges targeted in the previous two centuries. The 1917 constitution nationalized all church properties and declared the state's control over all education, the civil registry, and even the distribution and organization of the clergy in Mexico, by providing for ample legal restrictions and asserting the right of the individual states to mandate the number of ministers and sites of worship of all religions, according to population and local necessity.

Catholics protested against these constitutional provisions and their enforcing laws, passed at the insistence of anticlerical president Plutarco Elías Calles (1924–1928) in 1926. The laws prompted increasing protests from the church hierarchy, culminating in the cessation of all religious services within government-controlled church buildings. Catholic laypeople, mobilized in social action organizations, protested with a boycott of the goods and services of the government and its allied labor unions. Some chose armed resistance, joining the civil war known as the Cristero Rebellion. The government and the church hierarchy negotiated an agreement that became known as the "arreglos" to end the fighting in July 1929. However, these proved to be more of a temporary "arrangement" to restore social order than a real resolution of the conflict (Negrete 1988, 338).

In 1929, Calles founded the central government's political party, the Partido Nacional Revolucionario (National Revolutionary Party). During the 1930s, the Mexican government, led by this party, consolidated its control of political organization, labor, education, and social services. The state's new social programs were modernist, centrist, antireligious, and ideologically and behaviorally demanding. Nevertheless, the state won many people's support for its reform programs with its portrayal of workers and peasants as the makers and thus the beneficiaries of the revolution of 1910; the declaration of their rights within an inclusive, multiethnic, populist national culture, the promise of concrete benefits like land redistribution, inclusion and protection in state-sponsored unions and cooperatives, and a share in Mexico's nationalized resources. All these rights were enumerated in the 1917 constitution, alongside its anticlerical clauses, and appealed strongly to many. Both the revolutionary regime and radical organizers sought to harness women's support and made advances in some venues, such as rural women's associations, labor unions, and mobilization for political and social rights. However, these projects remained incomplete during the decade and were, more often than not, still predicated on women performing variants on traditional gender roles (Vaughan 1997, 190; Becker 1995; Macías 1982).

Throughout the 1930s, debates raged regarding government restrictions of religious practice, education, organizations, and activity, raising questions about Catholic attitudes toward Mexican law and the government's legitimacy. Federal, state, and municipal governments arrested, fined, and deported men and women who violated the laws, and also closed churches and confiscated property. Anticlericalism was incorporated into government school curricula and propaganda. Boycotts, demonstrations, riots, and new outbreaks of religiously motivated armed conflict led many to believe that the Catholic Church and the revolutionary regime could not coexist peacefully.

Yet by the end of the decade, it seemed that church and state leaders had finally reached an understanding, publicly signified by Archbishop Luis María Martínez counseling Catholics to support President Lázaro Cárdenas's nationalization of Mexico's oil industry in 1938. This resolution entailed a tacit understanding that outward conflict would cease and that each institution would cooperate in order to maintain law, order, and the peace in which to operate. However, this détente came about in a climate of gradual relaxation of the enforcement of anticlerical laws, itself produced by grass-roots organization and popular pressure that had begun years earlier (Reich 1995, 55, 72–72; Romero de Solís 1994, 481, 486–502).

The Catholic Alternative: The ACM

In Mexico, Catholic men and women had organized workers' associations and unions, mutual aid societies, cooperatives and credit unions, schools, and catechism programs for children and adults in the decades prior to the revolution. In the early years of the revolution, Catholic leaders consolidated social and labor activism into national organizations, among them the Unión de Damas Católicas Mexicanas (Union of Mexican Catholic Ladies) and the Asociación de la Juventud Católica Mexicana (Association of Mexican Catholic Youth). After the Cristero Rebellion, the Mexican government made it clear that it would not tolerate any Catholic political or labor organizing, especially if led by or associated with the clergy.

With Catholic civic organizations banned, the Mexican church hierarchy instead aimed to train lay leaders who could act in civil society in favor of the church. Developed in western Europe during the late nineteenth century, "Catholic Action" had been endorsed by several popes as the correct way for lay Catholics to contribute to their church. Lay Catholics would meet in Catholic Action groups to prepare themselves spiritually and intellectually. Then, *as individuals*, they could enter areas from which modernizing, secularizing governments barred the clergy, such as social and political contests and education, to uphold Catholic moral standards and goals. Catholic Action's proponents argued that the organization was by definition "apolitical" and defended its existence in climates that prohibited religiously oriented political parties or organizations.

In late 1929, the church's Secretariado Social Mexicano (Mexican Social Secretariat, SSM) drew up new statutes for the ACM, creating four suborganizations divided along lines of age and gender: the UFCM (reorganized from the Union of Mexican Catholic Ladies, UDCM) for women married or over thirty-five; the Juventud Católica Femenina Mexicana (Mexican Catholic Feminine Youth, JCFM) for young, single women; the Unión de Católicos Mexicanos (Union of Mexican Catholics, UCM) for men married or over thirty-five; and the Association of Mexican Catholic Youth (ACJM), purged of its ties to the Cristeros, for young, single men.[2]

Mexican Catholic Women's Organization, Old and New: The UFCM

Like the ACM as a whole, the UFCM coordinated from a Central Committee based in Mexico City. SSM organizers traveled across Mexico to establish UFCM chapters in its dioceses in 1929. The diocesan committees in turn encouraged local clergy and laity to found parish groups under their supervision. To provide spiritual and doctrinal guidance, a priest was assigned as an ecclesiastical assistant to each UFCM group, at every level of its organization. The statutes stipulated that the ecclesiastical assistants' role was to guide the UFCM, not to directly lead it; women would (and did) constitute the organization's leadership (Tromp 1937, 674).

Diocesan committees and parish groups were supervised by means of correspondence and visits from central committee members and ecclesiastical leaders. All members were encouraged to attend biennial General Assemblies. Dioceses and parishes held assemblies in alternate years to assess their work, hold seminars on doctrine and social action, and plan for the next two years. The central committee diffused information through circular letters and the UFCM monthly, *Acción Femenina* (*Feminine Action*), which began publication in 1933 (Méndez 1980, 29).

It is hard to generalize about the UFCM's social characteristics, as it kept no records or statistics of its members' race, ethnicity, or income level. The UFCM organized from diocesan cities outward. Chapters in rural areas were located more often in municipal head towns, usually also the locations of parish churches, than in outlying villages and settlements. Like Mexico as a whole, the majority of the membership was most likely of mixed ancestry. While middle- and upper-class women had more time and resources to volunteer, they were not the only members or contributors. Until regional and local groups are studied in more detail, it can be said only that the UFCM had a substantial presence in wealthier, whiter, urban areas, but also established groups in poorer neighborhoods, towns, and villages with mestizo and indigenous populations.[3]

At each level, UFCM groups were organized into "sections" in which members concentrated their efforts on a single issue or project. Initially the UFCM recommended that every chapter have four sections, focusing on the home and the church: religious instruction, support for priests and seminaries, mothers, and "enthronements."[4] Optional additional sections included Catholic schools, piety (religious introspection and personal conduct), and charitable works. As the church responded to developing ideological and social conflicts, the UFCM adapted these sections and created new mandatory ones, significantly those targeting rural and urban working women.[5]

During the early 1930s, federal and state laws restricted all "religious activity" to the interior of church premises, banned public display of religious symbols, and closed religious schools and convents. Some priests were legally permitted to minister by state governments, but they were assigned multiple parishes with numerous or dispersed populations and could not reach all their parishioners with any frequency. Other priests lacked legal permission to minister or lived in exile. Lay Catholic men were threatened by state persecution of ex-Cristeros and by anti-Catholic discrimination in employment and politics (J. Meyer 1973–74: 1, 344–346; Romero de Solís 1994, 341, 372). In comparison, lay Catholic women could circulate in their communities with less fear of reprisal or discrimination. Since women could not vote or enter public office, their claims that their work was apolitical worked more often—though not always—than similar claims made by their clerical and lay male colleagues. UFCM activists across the country aided priests and other church personnel still working in Mexico and represented the clergy where it could not act publicly.

At first, the UFCM closely followed the lead of the church hierarchy. UFCM activists aimed to extend Catholic practices beyond church buildings by visiting private homes and encouraging residents to dedicate them with an enthrone-ment, as this served as a visible sign of religious loyalty to both household residents and visitors. They were also meant to counteract the increasing presence of the state in private homes that resulted from the growing influence of state agents such as schoolteachers and agents of hygiene and sanitation pro-grams. The organization of unions, the formation of peasant, worker, and antialcoholism leagues, and the women's revolutionary auxiliaries and societies in their support also opened channels for state influence in the home as well as in public life (Vaughan 1997; Becker 1995, chap. 4).

During the 1930s, opportunities for Catholics to participate in the sacraments were limited because of the restricted numbers of clergy licensed to minister and of churches opened by the government for religious use. UFCM members orga-nized Masses and preparatory classes for children and adults to take the sacraments. The UFCM was especially concerned with legitimizing consensual unions, among which they included couples married solely by civil ceremony, through the sacrament of marriage. The UFCM encouraged women in such situ-ations to "legalize" their marriage (a significant choice of words, since the government had not considered religious marriages legally binding since the Liberal reforms of the 1850s), and in some cases paid the fees for those who could not afford church ceremonies.[6]

The uneasy deténte of the *arreglos* soured in late 1931, when Catholics fervently commemorated the four hundredth anniversary of the apparitions of the Virgin of Guadalupe.[7] In response, the state clamped down on Catholic social activity. Catholic women participated in acts of civil disobedience for the right to publicly practice their faith, as when Guadalajara Catholics were arrested in 1932 and 1933 for "displaying" crosses on their foreheads outside churches on Ash Wednesday. Led by women, Veracruz Catholics mobilized in 1937 after an adoles-cent girl, Leonor Sánchez, was shot and killed when government agents broke up a clandestine Mass in Orizaba. Thousands of angry citizens occupied churches across the state, forcing Governor Miguel Alemán to relax his anticler-ical policies, open churches and allow more priests to officiate. After years of wearing down local law enforcement, Catholics again were able to enact public religious displays and elicit little or no response. By 1940, the UFCM cited public acts such as the pilgrimage, procession, and outdoor Mass honoring Our Lady of Ocotlán (Jalisco) that occurred nationwide without repercussion.[8]

The UFCM versus State Education

Pope Pius XI (1922–1939) again warned Catholics of the dangers of worldwide trends to laicize education, which had been condemned since the *Syllabus of Errors* (1864), and inveighed even more against introducing sex-education programs (Pius XI 1929, 97–131). Mexican Catholics protested vehemently against the state's 1933 proposal for a sex-education curriculum with petitions, school boycotts, marches, and rallies. Although the campaign, coordinated by the Unión Nacional de Padres de Familia (National Union of Family Parents[9]), did not succeed in formally eliminating the curriculum, it convinced many public schoolteachers to tone it down, and generated enough negative publicity to force Minister of Education Narciso Bassols to resign. This campaign had a gendered edge; fliers asked parents, "Would you want your sons *and especially your daughters* to lose their good consciences?"[10]

In 1934, National Revolutionary Party radicals pressed for the amendment of Article 3 of the 1917 constitution to strengthen the ideological slant of public education. Rather than merely being "secular," the quickly amended article now mandated "socialist" education in all schools and prohibited confessional education in advanced as well as primary schools (Lerner 1979, 11, 70, 82). Former President Calles declared that Mexico's children belonged to the nation, not the family, and that the government should decide by what standards they should be taught. President Cárdenas declared the "freedom of conscience" and teaching that Catholics demanded to be "empty phrases" masking reactionary tyranny and clerical and capitalist dictatorship (Brown 1964, 205, 107). The church hierarchy protested the reform from its outset, and the UNPF, ACM, and other groups campaigned to boycott state schools and for the reform of Article 3 and other laws (Lerner 1979, 44–45).

The UFCM responded quickly to the Mexican government's plans to control education. Following the request of the Mexican Episcopate, the UFCM not only continued supporting extracurricular catechism programs but established alternative schools so that Catholic parents could comply with the injunction to withdraw children from socialist schools. Catholic teachers, mainly women, followed a curriculum that eschewed the state's anticlericalism and radicalism, instead incorporating church teachings.[11] Federal law required that all private schools with more than nine students be incorporated into the Secretaria de Educación Pública (Ministry of Public Education), to force the schools to comply with laws, use SEP curricula and textbooks, and pass government inspections (Lerner 1979, 39). UFCM activists first organized smaller home schools, but regardless of their size, these still contravened laws banning religious activity outside of church buildings. Thus, any homes or properties used for Catholic schools risked legal sanction, as did their teachers and students and others supporting them. In some regions, local officials actively sought the Catholics' clandestine schools and retaliated with arrests and confiscation of properties. Despite this, the UFCM was running approximately twenty-five hundred schools throughout Mexico by 1936.[12] The *New York Times* reported that not only upper-class *madres* joined this campaign, but that women's support of the church and of Catholic education was found at all levels of society.[13]

Maintaining the clandestine schools became difficult, if not impossible, and not only because of strict enforcement of anticlerical laws. There was always a lack of funds, space, and staff willing to be paid even less than their counterparts in public schools while risking arrest.[14] As a result, the church hierarchy opened loopholes for Catholics who wished to work in or attend public schools. In mid-1937, the church made a conciliatory move in declaring commendable the government's exhortations to teach respect for the laws and for the Mexican nation in public schools. Church leaders still forbade Catholics to take the SEP's pledges to "defanaticize" children or to uphold antireligious laws or curricula, even if they intended to ignore or circumvent them afterward ("Consultas" 1937, 366–367; "Instrucción Pastoral" 1937, 487–493). At the same time, the SEP, recognizing that the government did not have sufficient resources to educate all children, gradually became more permissive regarding private and confessional schools. The SEP also relaxed its demands on ideological purity for teachers, allowing the return of those who had left or lost their jobs earlier for refusing to renounce Catholicism. Meanwhile, popular pressure, which ranged from parent-led boycotts and protests to brutal attacks on and assassinations of teachers in rural areas—wore down the will of many teachers and administrators to enforce socialist education programs (Raby 1974). Although written educational law remained unchanged until the 1940s, the character of public education and regulation of private education changed sufficiently to diminish explicitly antireligious teachings and to allow for the presence of Catholic education, a practical victory brought about in great part by women activists' work (*Mexicano: Estaes* 1968, 24–26).

The UFCM and Working Women

Some historians have criticized the ACM as being solely composed of elites, isolated from much of Mexican society as well as the majority of Catholics (Reich 1995, 94–95; Lerner 1979, 46). However, the UFCM was, if not a complete cross section of Mexican society, more diverse than critics have portrayed it. The UFCM had a fairly clear perception of class differences and composition. At the UFCM's first General Assembly, María Luisa Hernández addressed the differences in organizational strategies, educational methods, and needs of women members from the proletarian, middle, and "elevated" classes.[15] Through the 1930s, the UFCM engaged in recruitment and increasingly politicized work to offset the Mexican government's growing influence with working-class and rural, peasant women (Vaughan 1997, 11).

The church hierarchy recognized that a growing number of women were leaving the household for salaried work, and expressed its concern that the "weaker sex" would be overworked, especially in industrial employment. However, leaders often interpreted outward changes in women's behavior as inward treason. They blamed the defection of working (especially working-class) women from the church solely on the fact that women had begun to work outside the home, ignoring needs that women had which were filled in the workplace or through unions and government programs, rather than in religious practices and venues (Leo XIII 1891; Pius XI 1931; Garibi Rivera 1936). Some UFCM members echoed these sentiments and took a reactionary stance toward women's work outside the home; one *Acción Femenina* author declared, "The woman who leaves [home] to work goes outside of her proper environment, of the place that Divine Providence has marked for her." Nor did they advocate women's organizing to radically change the workplace. Rather, they aimed to "bring to Christ the souls that are debating good and evil." UFCM members proposed programs to help impoverished rural women by "bringing the Gospel to the countryside" and encouraging them not to neglect their children's Catholic upbringing (Avila 8).

But in working with wage-earning women, some UFCM members became conscious of the needs they faced and began to advocate more practical plans for addressing them. Building on earlier Catholic and secular models, the UFCM started adult education programs, hygiene and health services, workers' associations, and social organizations. Mothers' sections sponsored day care for working women's children, and parish and diocesan groups founded adult education academies and night schools. UFCM members ran clothing and food drives for victims of catastrophic events (e.g., floods, earthquakes) and for the needy in poorer urban and rural areas, including the indigenous Tarahumara and Maya. While the UFCM's efforts constituted charity more than structural change, they sometimes provided important services, such as bringing financial support, food, and materials to areas where they were insufficient and were not provided by employers or the government.[16]

In 1937, Pius XI asked Catholics to devote "special attention" to the working classes, which Mexican Catholic women already had done. In 1934, the San Luis Potosí Diocesan Committee established the first UFCM Patronage for Women Workers and Servants. The 1936 General Assembly included a presentation on "The Working Class of the UFCM and the Peasant UFCM." UFCM sections in various parishes sponsored medical dispensaries and other distributive programs. Another *Acción Feminina* author called on Catholic women to be "conscious of social responsibility" and to promote grass-roots organizing among working women, giving descriptions of existing UFCM enterprises such as community gardens.[17] UFCM leaders treated the theme in more detail at the 1938 General Assembly. Belatedly adopting the language of the times, the UFCM now grouped its efforts into one section, Working Classes, subdivided into concerns for peasants, blue-collar workers, white-collar workers, and professionals. The UFCM recognized that many women—many in its ranks—needed and wanted to work, and it dispensed with the vision that women's salaried employment would cease.[18]

For the Future of Mexican Catholic Women: Sofía del Valle

In addition to its emphasizing "maternal" responsibilities toward the young, the UFCM sponsored the girls section of the ACM and took seriously its responsibility to uphold morals among young Mexican women. Encouraged by church leaders, UFCM members wrote articles condemning "immodest" fashions such as calf-length skirts and bobbed hair. Women's committees in Chihuahua patrolled church entrances to prevent "immodestly" dressed women from entering. The UFCM also collaborated with the Liga Mexicana de la Decencia (Mexican League of Decency), a social-civic group founded during the 1930s that monitored the contents of movies and other media. The league disseminated its media recommendations (to attend or boycott) in ACM magazines and in volunteer-distributed fliers.[19]

But Catholic women's activism on behalf of younger women went beyond concern about their hemlines and moviegoing habits. Catholic activist Sofía del

Valle repeatedly insisted that the church recognize that women were more than housebound daughters, future wives, and women religious. An early participant in the SSM, Del Valle first demonstrated her convictions in her efforts to organize Catholic women's unions during the 1920s (Del Valle 1972–73, INAH/PHO/4/11; Comité Diocesano n.d., 11–13; B. Miller 1981, 128–129; Hanson 1994, 363–364). She sat on the committee that rewrote the ACM statutes in 1929, traveled through Mexico and abroad to promote the ACM, and was the first president of the ACM's girls organization after the Cristero Rebellion. Under Del Valle's leadership, the JCFM mushroomed alongside the UFCM. Its membership increased rapidly, going from 8,601 in 1929, to 31,107 in 1934, and to 102,491 in 1942; branches existed in almost one thousand parishes, and members made up almost one-third of ACM membership. Del Valle was so effective that copies of her correspondence with Mexican bishops and Catholic activists filled state files on subversive Catholic activity and were used to accuse her of supporting a "clerical conspiracy."[20]

In deference to church leaders, Del Valle acknowledged the primacy of family responsibilities for women who chose to marry. But, proudly noting that the Instituto Superior de Cultura Feminina (the educational institution that the JCFM sponsored from 1926 to 1954) counted educators and politicians among its alumnae, she continued to emphasize women's need to study social problems and their duty to engage in social issues. Del Valle did not consider herself a *dama* (as she suspected many other women did not) and chose not to join the UFCM as she advanced in age; instead, she dedicated herself to providing alternatives for Catholic women (Del Valle 1972–73, INAH/PHO/4/11, 20–21; B. Miller 1981, 135–138). Though atypical among Catholic women (and indeed many other women) of her day, Del Valle was never ordered by church leaders to retract her statements. Her work was indispensable for cultivating committed women activists in diverse social classes and retaining the support of the growing number of women who diverged from church leaders' view of ideal womanhood.

The UFCM, Women Religious, Priests, and Seminarians

The UFCM was concerned with the effect that the Mexican government's legal restrictions would have on the number of Mexican priests and of vowed religious men and women. As the government enforced the constitutional prohibition on religious communities, the UFCM's work to support their seminaries, convents, and other institutions (schools, orphanages, hospitals) became illegal. In the early 1930s, state and federal law enforcers searched private residences, ostensibly to disband seditious meetings and discover arms caches, but really to locate hidden residences, seminaries, and facilities. For several years, strict enforcement of these laws resulted in the arrest, fining, and imprisonment of numerous women religious, as well as the confiscation of their property (Parsons 1936, 73–75, 120–122).

Part of the rationale for the closure of Catholic schools in 1934 was that their teachers were, in general, not state educated or licensed, as government regulations mandated. Some Catholic schools run by women's religious orders hired licensed, lay teachers, attempting to remain open by complying with this regulation.[21] However, even if they could find teachers willing to sidestep state regulations regarding religious content in teaching, etc., they often could not afford to pay their salaries. By 1935, even schools that employed only laywomen were closed for violating antireligious constitutional provisions and laws.[22]

The UFCM consistently concerned itself with the religious women who remained in Mexico, securing housing, classroom space, and supplies so that they could resume their schedules of prayer and work. Some religious women continued to teach, but enrollment plummeted because of the risks of attending clandestine classes. Consequently, many religious women lost their source of income while the laws were being enforced strictly, and had to turn to low-paying piecework or relying on charity.[23] Conditions for religious women did not improve until the next decade, when the relaxation of the enforcement of anticlerical laws allowed them to act openly on their vocations and resume their work in schools, hospitals, and other community projects.

During the early 1930s, the UFCM central committee ordered members to hold collections at their meetings and assemblies to raise funds to support both legally and clandestinely working priests. Because of the restrictions on religiously oriented higher education, it was nearly impossible to train seminarians within Mexico. This was part of an explicit attempt to reduce the clergy's numbers, for the 1917 constitution also prohibited foreign-born ministers from working in Mexico. The Mexican Episcopate appealed to the Vatican for an alternative seminary outside the country. Responding to their requests for help, the UFCM raised funds and collected supplies for the Montezuma Seminary, founded in Arizona in September 1937. Pending a relaxation in church-state tension and of laws restricting the numbers of priests allowed to officiate, these Mexican-born priests then would be constitutionally eligible to minister. Interestingly, Montezuma students did not constitute the majority of Mexican seminarians, which points to the resurgence of clandestine seminaries within Mexico during the 1930s, also supported and aided by the UFCM.[24] UFCM president Refugio Goribar de Cortina reminded members that more than raising money was needed to redress the priest shortage; parish groups should encourage vocations and sponsor at least one seminary student each.

A Catholic Woman Militant: Refugio Goribar de Cortina

Refugio Goribar de Cortina dedicated decades to the ACM while consistently advocating women's proper place as the home. Goribar de Cortina lived in Mexico City and was active in ACM women's leadership there beginning in the early 1920s. Although she played a behind-the-scenes role in negotiations between Cristeros and members of the Mexican Episcopate in early 1929, she publicly sided with the hierarchy, criticizing Catholic belligerents and recommending pious, restorative acts to strengthen the church and its members' faith (INAH/PHO/4/4, 41–43; Hanson 1997, 17–22; B. Miller 1981, 109).

From 1930 to 1932, Goribar de Cortina served as vice president of the UFCM central committee. At the first General Assembly, she declared the principal goal of the UFCM to be "the restoration of the family and of society." Goribar de Cortina revealed a *dama*'s class bias, stating that women of the "elevated," "directing classes" should lead this restoration. Yet this status also conferred responsibilities. UFCM activists should be like the "strong woman of the

Gospel"; having proven their moral superiority and capacity to instruct and lead in the past, they needed to do so again. She called Mexican men to task for neglecting their obligations to guide their families (and by extension, the country) in the Catholic faith. Women, in turn, were to use their influence on men to encourage this Christian direction for Mexican society.[25] Goribar de Cortina became UFCM president in 1932 and continued for two more terms (1934–1938), during which time UFCM membership quadrupled.

Goribar de Cortina launched campaigns in the public arena as well. In 1922, the newspaper *Excelsior* promoted the celebration of May 10 as Mother's Day, attempting to deflect calls for women's suffrage. Over time, endorsing the festivity gained political currency as evidence of interest in women and families. In the 1920s and 1930s, Catholics also seized upon Mother's Day as a new opportunity to fuse civic and religious cultural practice. Bishops encouraged priests to hold special masses on the day, and Catholics petitioned the government to allow for open-air, public Catholic celebrations honoring the "mothers of the nation's future."[26] Goribar de Cortina pledged the UFCM's support to continue to make Mother's Day a Catholic holiday in practice, if not in name; the "Madres" sections distributed thousands of fliers to this effect. In 1937, she gave the UFCM's Mother's Day efforts almost as much importance as its campaign for Catholics to comply with their annual sacramental obligations at Easter. She then proudly stated that "year by year [it] acquires a more spiritual aspect and becomes a more truly human holiday."[27] Goribar de Cortina espoused the conservative, Catholic stance on women's roles, but also encouraged women to manipulate their status within the home and the "political family" to create broader opportunities for religious practice.

UFCM Membership, 1932–1942

Through the 1930s, the UFCM grew steadily, despite harassment of Catholic activists by government officials and partisans and occasional legal repercussions. In 1932, the UFCM counted 13,465 dues-paying members, along with 17,124 other affiliated women. By 1936, counting only dues-paying members, the UFCM had 67,775 members, and by 1940 the UFCM had 149,514 active members. In comparison, membership in the left-wing coalition Frente Unico Pro Derechos de la Mujer (United Front for Women's Rights) peaked at about 50,000 in the late 1930s, at the height of its mobilization for women's suffrage and social reform.[28]

In 1942, UFCM membership stood at 177,677; more than 100,000 young woman were active in the JCFM and about 60,000 young men were involved in the ACJM. Even after ten years of ACM mobilization, however UCM membership did not exceed 25,000. During the 1930s, priests' periodicals published articles describing UFCM campaigns and the inquiries of its ecclesiastical assistants. These were paired with less optimistic articles suggesting means to get Catholic men to join the UCM in the first place ("Acción Católica"). Adult men's participation in the ACM was consistently low, reflecting both the risks associated with their open participation in Catholic groups and their lack of disinterest, and problematizing portrayals of laymen as the leading element in Catholic mobilization.

Conclusion

Women who participated in the UFCM during the 1930s had either witnessed the revolution or were the children of it; they realized that there would be no return to a prerevolutionary social order. There was room for adaptation in postrevolutionary Mexico, and Catholic activists insisted on creating a space for their religious practice in the new social order. In return for the relaxation or nonenforcement of anticlerical laws, Catholics curtailed their attacks on public schools and institutions.[29] At the same time, Mexico's gradual, uneven modernization, urbanization, and growing trade with other countries (especially the United States) prompted Mexicans to rethink cultural paradigms and strike compromises between spiritual and secular life in ways that diminished discord and violent conflict (Knight 1990, 227–264; Vaughan 1997, 195).

The UFCM developed strategies to work around the Mexican state's restrictions. They harnessed the "apolitical" roles assigned to women by the church and the state to publicize their demands and influence the organization and functioning of postrevolutionary society. In doing so, some UFCM members were able to circumvent the restrictions of prevailing gender roles within each system. In great part because of the Catholic campaigns of the revolutionary period, the church still plays a large part in Mexico's cultural and social life. Through the UFCM, Mexican Catholic women defended their values against the state's call to reject their religious heritage, responding to both global Catholic concerns and local loyalty to tradition. In doing so, they created an influential niche for themselves in their communities, their country, and their church.

List of Acronyms

ACM   Acción Católica Mexicana (Mexican Catholic Action)
ACJM   Asociación Católica de la Juventud Mexicana (Catholic Association of Mexican Youth)
JCFM   Juventud Católica Femenina Mexicana (Mexican Catholic Feminine Youth)
PNR   Partido Nacional Revolucionario (Revolutionary National Party)
SEP   Secretaria de Educación Pública (Ministry of Public Education)
SSM   Secretariado Social Mexicano (Mexican Social Secretariat)
UDCM   Unión de Damas Católicas Mexicanas (Union of Mexican Catholic Ladies)
UFCM   Unión Femenina Católica Mexicana (Mexican Catholic Women's Union)
UNPF   Unión Nacional de Padres de Familia (National Union of Family Parents)

Notes

1. This research is based on materials in the UFCM archive at the Universidad Iberoamericana (UFCM–Ibero), the Mexican national archives (AGN), the Secretariado Social Mexicano archive (SSM), and the Fideocomisio Plutarco Elias Calles y Fernando Torreblanca (PEC/FT) in Mexico City; from the Instituto Libre de Filosofia Archivo Cristero (ILF/AC) in Guadalajara; from the National Archives and Records Administration: United States Department of State Records Relating to the Internal Affairs of Mexico (USDOS) and United States War Department, Military Intelligence Reports: Mexico, 1919–1940 (USMIL); and the author's interviews with UFCM members and those of the Instituto Nacional de Antropología e Historia's Proyecto de Historia Oral (INAH/PHO). Also see Fowler-Salamini and Vaughan 1994, xxii.
2. SSM, *Episcopado–Informes, 1924–1931*, Miguel Darío Miranda, "Seis Años de Actividades del Secretariado Social Mexicano, 1925–1931," 13–16.

3. I base this conclusion on my own previous research. See Boylan 2000.
4. Enthronements were ceremonies popularized by the Jesuits in the nineteenth and twentieth centuries in which a household was consecrated to a specific image, such as the Sacred Heart of Jesus or the Virgin of Guadalupe. See McSweeney 1980, 49–50.
5. UFCM–Ibero, 4, 25, "III Asamblea General de la UFCM, Oct. 1936," "Informe del Comité Central."
6. UFCM–Ibero, 4, 25, "I Asamblea General" (October 1932): Refugio Goribar de Cortina, "Restauración Cristiana de la Familia," and María Luisa Hernández, "La Instrucción como fundamento de las socias de la UFCM."
7. The Virgin of Guadalupe is the Marian image seen by a Nahua peasant, Juan Diego, and reproduced on his cloak in 1531. Though initially discouraged as a local, syncretic crossover, devotion to her grew. Her image was gradually endorsed by the Archdiocese of Mexico. Nineteenth-century religious leaders emphasized Guadalupe as a unifying aspect for Mexicans, and the Vatican named her "Empress of the Americas" (1895). Guadalupe graced battle flags in the Wars of Independence and the Mexican Revolution and is ubiquitous today. See Lafaye 1976.
8. USMIL Report #3686, 18 December 1931, and Report #3697, 29 December 1931; USDOS RRIAM, 812.404/1074 (1931), and 812.404/1945–1950; NYT, various articles, February and March 1937; "La UFCM en Ocotlán," 12.
9. Parents founded the UNPF in 1917 to resist the state's mandatory education programs and other influences on children. Although not church sponsored, the Mexican Episcopate and the SSM praised its actions, and many Catholics were members. (See Torres Septien 1992; "Conclusiones aprobadas" 1935, 159–160).
10. PEC/FT, 12, 010806, exp. 21, inv. 7275, "Padre de Familia Lea Usted," emphasis in the original (also Lerner 1979, 41, 45).
11. UFCM–Ibero, 4, 25, "II Asamblea General de la UFCM, October 1934"—"Informe"; Episcopado Mexicano 1935, 26–41.
12. Miranda, "Informe"; III Asamblea General (1936), "Informe." These schools probably took in about 1 percent of Mexico's school-age children, though the lack of written records for clandestine schools make this difficult to quantify. Many more children did not attend school at all (Sexto Censo General 1942, 4).
13. NYT, 25 November 1934 (I, 18); USMIL (0022), Report #5677, 30 October 1934.
14. Teresa Michel de Barba (b. 1912), interview, Guadalajara, Jalisco, 27 May 1997 (also Lerner 1979, 110).
15. Hernández, "La Instrucción como fundamento . . . ," 9 and 11.
16. "Circular No. 8, 2 October 1936," Christus 2, 14 (January 1937) 14; III Asamblea General (1936), "Informe," 7, 9–10; UFCM–Ibero, 4, 25, "IV Asamblea General de la UFCM, October 1938," R. Goribar de Cortina, "Informe," 10–11.
17. Pius XI 1937a, 422–426, and 1937b, 393; M. del Valle 1940, 9–10; Peñalosa de Del Río 1940, 12–13 and 19.
18. II Asamblea General (1934), "Informe," 8; III Asamblea General (1936), "Informe," 9.
19. Hernández, "La Instrucción como fundamento de las socias de la UFCM"; "M." 1937, 643; Garibi Rivera 1936; III Asamblea General (1936), "Informe," 10; and IV Asamblea General (1938), "Informe," 7; María del Rosario Ortíz de Salazar, interview with the author, Guadalajara, Jal., 7 May 1997; USDOS RRIAM, 812.404/1912.
20. PEC/FT, 12, 010806, Exp. 1; Ruíz y Flores 1935, 4–6; El Nacional, 28 October 1934 (also B. Miller 1981, 133–134).
21. Consuelo Ardila, RSCJ, interview, Guadalajara, 16 November 1996; Maria del Rosario Alejandre Gil, interview, Guadalajara, 13 May 1997; also Parsons 1936, 121.
22. SSM, J Aviña L., "Datos sobre la actual persecución religiosa . . . ," 27 March 1935, and "Informe rendido al Excmo Sr. Vicario General acerca de las actividades docentes de algunas Casas Religiosas," 2 May 1935.
23. Aviña L., "Datos sobre la actual persecución religiosa . . . ," and "Informe rendido...".
24. Indicating its enduring influence, in 1989, thirty-nine of Mexico's 106 diocesan

bishops were Montezuma alumni (Vera 1998, 22–27; Parsons 1936, 254–257; Galindo Mendoza 1945, 22).

25. I Asamblea General (1932), Goribar de Cortina, "Restauración Cristiana de la Familia," 1–10; II Asamblea General (1934), "Informe," 1–2; III Asamblea General (1936), "Informe," 3, 11; IV Asamblea General (1938), "Informe," 1–2.

26. Orozco y Jiménez Circ.15–30 and Circ. 16–30; AGN-Gobernación, exp. 2.340(11)-10; ILF/AC, Carpeta "Defensa de la libertad de enseñanza sin fechas," Exp. "Educación," document "Día de las Madres." Also Tuñon 1999, 100; Macías 1982, 119–121.

27. Refugio Goribar de Cortina, "Balance del Año," AF3, 11 (December 1987), 1–4.

28. II Asamblea General (1934), "Informe," 3; III Asamblea General (1936), "Informe," 12; InterDocumentation Company (Leiden) microfiche #2347—"Congresos. Asamblea General 5 de la UFCM (1938–1940), 1–5 October 1940," 23 (also Méndez 1980, 29, Macías 1982, 121).

29. IV Asamblea General (1938), "Informe," 3.

13

Foreign Women in Spain for General Franco during the Spanish Civil War

Judith Keene

During the Spanish Civil War women outside Spain, from the right and the left, traveled to the Iberian Peninsula to work for the victory of their own side. Their actions were compelled by a strong political impulse which in turn was buttressed by personal independence and a sense of adventure. Most numerous and well-known were women of the left. As part of the International Brigades, whether serving as nurses, doctors, drivers, or translators, they have left a rich record of their wartime experiences on the Republican side (Fyrth and Alexander 1991; Keene 1998, Fyrth 1986).

The foreign women who worked for Franco's victory are far fewer and comparatively unknown. Probably numbering no more than thirty and making their way to Spain as individuals, they have left a detailed, if fragmentary, record of their efforts to promote Franco's victory. Like Franco's other foreign volunteers, the women supporters were drawn from the array of European right-wing groups that flourished in the decade before World War II. Whether they were monarchists, traditional Catholics, crypto-fascists, or outright admirers of one or other of the interwar dictators, there was considerable dissonance between their own actions as political activists and the place of women in the new state that Franco was creating.

Recent studies have attempted to map the everyday activities of female membership in right-wing movements in order to produce a more complex picture of their internal workings and the place of women in them (de Grazia 1992; Durham 1998; Passmore 1999). The present study maintains the focus on the day-to-day in order to fill out the details of the lived experiences of foreign women in Franco's Spain during wartime. They constitute a significant part of an understudied segment of the Spanish Civil War and the European interwar right. Their narratives highlight the general paradox that confronted activist women in right-wing causes between the world wars in that they were committed to the victory of a political system in which independent and adventurous women like themselves would have no place.

Historical Background

On 17 July 1936, a group of Spanish generals led by Francisco Franco staged an uprising against the government of the Second Spanish Republic, triggering a bloody civil war that dragged on until April 1939. During these terrible and wearing years the Nationalists, as the insurgents came to be called, began from positions in the south and west and moved eastward across Spain until they had reached the northeastern seaboard, eventually taking control of the whole country. By the end of the war, half a million Spaniards were dead, and thousands of Republicans had fled into exile.

From the beginning, Germany and Italy supported Franco. Germany sent the crack airborne squadron of the Condor Legion, composed of experienced pilots and technicians, to support him. Italy dispatched more than one hundred thousand troops to fight alongside Franco's army. On the Republican side, the International Brigade, comprising some sixty thousand volunteers of left-wing democrats and communists, enlisted in Spain with the help of the Comintern. In the course of the Spanish Civil War international relations were reconfigured into the pattern of future allies and opponents that faced each other in World War II.

In the 1930s, right-wing movements shared a broad agreement that strong nations were grounded in a social order in which men were soldiers and fathers, and women were nurturing and fecund mothers. And whether framed in terms of the complementarity of the sexes, as in Mussolini's Italy, or in a Nazi patriarchy that privileged male power, there was no argument that a vital population required clearly delineated gender divisions.

Nationalist Spanish ideology was an amalgam of traditional Catholic values grafted onto an amorphous fascist corporatism. Added to this was the particular Spanish leaven of military discipline that came from Franco's own military model of how an orderly society should be run. At the head of the state, with overriding authority, was the caudillo. Below him were generals and administrators and, at the bottom, like obedient military conscripts, were the citizens carrying out the orders. In the parallel realm of family and private life, the pyramid of authority was replicated with fathers at the head of families exerting an unchallenged authority over women and children.

Women were marginalized in the very process by which the new Nationalist state was conceptualized. The cultural anthropologist Giuliana di Febo (1987) has argued that women in Franco's Spain were offered the "model of the beehive" in which females carried out constant and essential labor for the whole community, but within the hive, out of sight and in silence (p. 208). In the symbolic order of Franco's New Spain, men were configured as heroes in a crusading military tradition, and women were relegated to the "Reconquest of the hearth" (p. 208). In the process, maleness and military values were foregrounded as representing all that was "authentically Spanish," which, in turn, was contrasted with the "un-Spanishness" of the Second Republic (p. 208).

As is frequently the case in wartime, women in Nationalist Spain were drawn into war work. The objective, however, was to assist victory, not to disrupt the existing gender order. For example, although the Falangist Women's organization, the *Sección Femenina de la Falange Española,* recruited young women for public service, the movement's leaders always emphasized that their aim was to strengthen the family within a "New Spain" (Barrachina 1991; Enders 1999). There were some contradictions. Frances Lannon has highlighted that female leaders of the *Secciones* led busy public lives preaching the need for women to stay at home (1991, 225). In general, though, Spanish women's wartime activities never challenged the clear gender delineation in Nationalist Spain. In Franco's New Spain women were firmly shunted out of the public sphere and into the obscurity of family life (Roura 1998; Morcillo 2000).

In 1931 under the new constitution of the Second Republic, Spanish women had become full citizens, which for many traditionalists constituted the hallmark of a degenerate state. Indeed it was exactly from this sort of progress that Franco had proclaimed he would "save" Spain. Within the Nationalist zone, the figure of the New Woman of Republican Spain was held up as a symbol of the disorder of the Second Republic. Even worse, in Nationalist terms, were the Republican *milicianas*, the women who in the early months of the war took up arms and went off to the front to fight alongside their male comrades. In Nationalist propaganda, these women were castigated as epitomizing the corruption of Spanish womanhood in the Republican zone.[1]

Single, foreign women in Nationalist Spain, even though promoting Franco's victory, violated *franquista* conceptions of the demeanor of respectable women. These foreigners were away from their families and traveling unchaperoned in pursuit of their own projects. Because their business was with the war, they were highly visible in militarized public spaces. Whether coming and going in army headquarters to obtain passes to travel, or driving on roads that were crowded with trucks in convoy, they stood out as transgressive figures in a public domain that was masculine. As a consequence, it is probably not surprising that as in other cases of women in wartime, the closer they came to the front, the less acceptable their female presence became (Darrow 1996).

Franco's Foreign Women Volunteers

Against this background it is interesting to track what happened to five individuals among the foreign women in Nationalist territory. Their strong commitment to Franco's cause had brought them to Nationalist Spain in order to make their individual contributions to his victory. Some collected material to use in Franco's cause outside Spain, while others worked directly at the front in order to aid the military victory.

Among them were several upper-class women who had taken the opportunity offered by the war for a little battlefront tourism. In a study of travel between the world wars, Paul Fussell has argued that the British traveler went equipped with a "national snobbery" that was engendered by "two centuries of wildly successful imperialism" (1980, 74). Their general disdain for outsiders provided a thick skin that made English males (and, in our case, females) intrepid travelers in foreign places. Similarly, Europeans from more industrialized societies traveling in regions that were less industrialized often perceived themselves as bearers of a more civilized way of life. Many of the accounts by foreign women in Nationalist Spain during the Civil War speak with relish about the frisson that a foreign culture provided, but many of their observations are heavily overlaid with cultural imperialism. Most of them spoke no Spanish and in Nationalist Spain followed narrowly prescribed routes. What they observed was simply fitted into their preexisting views of the world and international relations. In the collective view of Franco's foreign women, the Republican government constituted the most recent outreach of international communism as it spread worldwide. As shallow as these political analyses were, the narratives by the pro-Franco foreigners provided information and anecdotes for the use of Nationalist supporters outside Spain.

At the end of 1936 Eleanora Tennant's *Spanish Journey: Personal Experiences of the Civil War* was published in England. At home in London, Eleanora and her husband were part of Nazi Foreign Minister Joachim von Ribbentrop's social circle and had met Hitler in Berlin several times. Ernest Tennant, an English industrialist with close economic ties to Germany, was a founder of the pro-German lobby group, the Anglo-German Fellowship and, at least until 1939, a great admirer of the Nazi state (Ernest Tennant 1957, 117–118; Griffiths 1980, 233–237).

Mrs. Tennant came south armed with her own hand pump and a plentiful supply of "Flit"—"that excellent chemical"—the insect repellant with which each night she sprayed the hotel beds for bugs before she retired. As she described it, she had motored "alone and unmolested" (though seated behind a chauffeur wearing the uniform of the Falangist Party) across the Portuguese border and around the southern part of Franco's Spain (Eleanor Tennant 1936, 117–118). An Australian-born Englishwoman, Tennant possessed an unsinkable self-confidence, grounded in the certainties of a world that centered on Britain and the Empire. In the "Latin surroundings" of Spain, she was empowered by her Englishness and, where a less ebullient soul might have been hampered by a lack of Spanish, Mrs. Tennant interrogated—in English—everyone she met on her travels. They even included "Spanish Tommies"—Spanish soldiers in the Foreign Legion—among whom she was glad to report that she "never saw one single action to which any Britisher could take exception" (p. 36). After having been in Spain for "several days" she noted that she had "accumulated sufficient first-hand information to understand the main reasons for the outbreak of the war" (p. 24). It had been caused by the perfidy of Moscow and the communist followers in Republican Spain.

By contrast, in the Nationalist zone, the only part of Spain which she visited, she found that everywhere it was "business as usual." The German who set her hair in Seville was enthusiastic that bourgeois hairdos were back in style. The British manager of a factory near Huelva reported that his previously "scowling workers" had become "happy and content" since "the Glorious Uprising" (pp. 23–29). Daily, too, she heard the "most frightful stories" about the communists for the Spanish Republic. Perhaps her own colonial Australian background fostered Mrs. Tennant's interest in the relations between the Spanish metropole and her colonial people, the Moors. During the Civil War, Republican publicity against the Nationalists made much of the fact that Franco was using Moorish troops and that they were reputed to rape captured women and loot defeated villages. Mrs. Tennant would have none of this. In her words, it was a "calumny of the Reds" to suggest that "Franco was using black non-Christian troops against Spanish white Christians." Instead she stated that "scientific evidence" (though providing no indication what it might be) had "proved" that the "Moors of Africa are not a black race and have no racial connection whatever with the Abyssinians or the Negroes" (p. 118).

In a singularly British-centered analysis, Tennant concluded by approvingly quoting Dino Grandi, Mussolini's ambassador to the Non-Intervention Committee meetings in London, that only a dictator can save the day when the seeds of communism have been sewn. And she opined, telescoping the consequences of the war into her own British-centered concerns, that the Spanish Civil War would be worthwhile, even if it "washed every Spanish stone in blood," if it succeeded in opening British eyes to the dangers of communism (125).

Florence Farmborough, who broadcast regularly on Radio Salamanca for Franco on Sunday nights, also held Englishness as the ultimate yardstick against which to measure decency in the Civil War in Spain. An English teacher in Valencia of "stout Buckinghamshire stock" and a "strong royalist," Farmborough had welcomed Franco's uprising and soon afterward had moved to the Nationalist zone. Twenty years before, while a governess in Moscow, Farmborough had become a volunteer nursing assistant in the czarist army and during the Russian Army's retreat from the Eastern Front she suffered great hardship when she was separated from her nursing corps (Farmborough 1974). Because her political understanding was forged in the Bolshevik Revolution, her Spanish radio broadcasts betray a constant slippage from her commentary on Spain to her previous firsthand experiences with the "Red Guards" in Russia. By the same process, Farmborough transformed the admired Nationalists into Anglicized figures and, by contrast, transmogrified the Spanish Republicans into Russian Bolsheviks (Farmborough 1938, 17).

According to Farmborough, Spanish women's main practical contribution to Franco's victory was in knitting garments. A self-confessed nonknitter, Farmborough marveled at the energy that Spanish women expended with the knitting needles as they transformed great baskets of wool at their sides into useful articles in a soldier's wardrobe. In Franco's Spain, at least in Farmborough's broadcasts, war was "won in the van-guard with shot and shell" and in the rear guard with "work and wool" (1938, 41).

A Parisian aristocrat, the Duchesse de la Rouchefoucauld, traveled to Nationalist Spain in mid-1938. She was met at the border by monarchist friends involved with the *Seccíon Femenina,* and with a young woman as chauffeur, La Rouchefoucauld traveled around the western zone observing Nationalist social welfare activities. The narrative of her journey originally appeared in the *Revue de Paris* in October 1938 and was translated into several languages (Rouchefoucauld 1938). An enthusiastic advocate of Italian fascism and a close friend of the wife of the Italian ambassador to France, the duchess believed—quite mistakenly—that only fascism under Mussolini could "regenerate the privileges of the aristocracy" (Tabouis 1943, 385). In Nationalist Spain she discovered—equally incorrectly—that Franco was a monarchist like herself.[2] At a children's dining room run by Falangist women she was entranced as "the tiny guests and the grown ups stood with arms outstretched in Roman salute toward a large picture of Franco" (Rouchefoucauld 1938, 5).

Most of all La Rouchefoucauld was at pains to point out that female self-abnegation was the motive for women's war work in Franco's Spain. On her trip she met "hatless young girls, smart energetic and generous" but none was a feminist or a professional woman selfishly expanding her own horizons. All wished only to sacrifice themselves for others. Everywhere La Rouchefoucauld went in Franco's Spain she found the "fit proclaimed by the leadership of the Falangist women." It was the vital nexus between male egoism and female self-abnegation which were the "two levers of a healthy society." Egoism was the male lever and consisted of "action, sensual satisfaction" and "sweeping selfishness." Its complement was the "woman's lever" consisting of a "life of submission, service and sacrificial devotion" to the welfare of others (Rouchefoucauld 1938, 18).

Much more closely involved in the military prosecution of the war, two young Englishwomen, Gabriel Herbert and Pip Scott-Ellis, served in Nationalist medical units close to the front for almost the entire length of the conflict. Needless to say, they experienced the strain of war in a more immediate way than did Franco's other foreign women supporters. Gabriel Herbert provided the moving spirit for the Anglo-Spanish Mobile Medical Service. She was twenty-five years of age in 1936 and well-traveled, having frequently spent summers at her family's grand house near Portofino on the Italian coast. Her father, Aubrey Herbert, the second son of the fourth Earl of Carnavon, was a Conservative M.P. and before his death in 1923 had been drawn increasingly to Catholicism. Soon after his death, his wife and children embraced the Catholic Church (Stannard 1986, 386). Gabriel's uncle, Lord Howard of Penrith, also a Catholic convert, had been British ambassador in Madrid between 1919 and 1924.

When the civil war began, Lord Howard and a group of prominent English Catholics formed the Bishops Fund for the Relief of Spanish Distress to raise money for medical supplies to aid Franco. Gabriel became their *enlace*, the go-between, in Spain.[3] The fund was generous, furnishing an Anglo-Spanish mobile unit with eight fully equipped ambulances including portable operating tables and instrument sets. Four large trucks loaded with two hundred dismountable beds and bedding were dispatched as well as a small truck to transport staff. The Anglo-Spanish team had its own mobile X-ray unit, which sped up the treatment of head injuries and broken bones because they could be diagnosed on the spot. So well endowed was the English team that they established a depot in a secure barn south of Saragossa to store their supplies and from there Gabriel Herbert fetched by truck whatever was needed and transported it to wherever it was required. Eventually their mobile units stretched across the extended Aragon front (Alpert Interview 1982).[4]

Before the war, the hospitals and medical expertise that were available in Spain were concentrated in the large cities of Madrid and Barcelona. When the war began, a single, poorly supplied mobile unit served the whole of northern Spain. As a consequence wounded soldiers were transported enormous distances for medical attention, often traveling slung in a blanket between two swaying mules. The importance of independent transport and equipment for medical services in wartime can scarcely be overestimated. When the Nationalist Army was on the move, transport allocation was invariably scarce and chaotic. Often there would be long delays as the medical services waited for trucks to be assigned to them.

The Anglo-Spanish medical enterprise, administered independently from London, was able to function outside the ramshackle bureaucracy of the Nationalist *Sanidad and Frentes y Hospitales,* in which orders to frontline medical units passed through a labyrinth of bureaucratic channels. Often hospital teams were told to pack and move, and move again according to a plan that was incomprehensible to those at the end of the chain of command. The Anglo-Spanish team was staffed by Spaniards, and although there were a few hiccups in Spanish-to-English translation, as when "10,000 baby eels (*anguilas*) of different sizes" were ordered instead of needles (*agujas*), in general everything went smoothly. In Herbert's words, the team "worked together, played together and became friends" (Alpert Interview 1982). As a consequence, their medical interventions were highly effective. Throughout, the Anglo-Spanish Medical Service maintained harmonious relations with the Nationalist Army command, a tribute to Gabriel Herbert's administrative skills, but probably even more to the abundance of material sent from London. At the end of the war Herbert was awarded the *Medalla Militar* with merit for her work in Nationalist Spain.

Pip Scott-Ellis experienced a rather different war working in a Spanish medical team. A young woman of twenty years in 1937 and raised an Anglican, she was the middle daughter of the eighth Lord Howard de Walden and Seaford (Scott-Ellis 1995, vii–xiii). Her mother, Lady Mary Howard, was one of the select group of upper-crust English ladies who between the wars flew their own Gypsy Moth aircraft. Pip, too, when she turned eighteen, obtained a pilot's license, and at the end of the civil war, when she was employed at a canteen at Barajas Aerodrome in Madrid, spent exhilarating mornings with her hand on the joystick "ambling about the countryside" in the soaring sky above the capital (Scott-Ellis 1995, 233). She had been a debutante in London in 1936 but a year later grew weary of the social scene and determined to join her friends, the family of the Infante de Orleans, the Spanish king's first cousin, who were flyers in Franco's air force.

Pip kept a diary of her two years in Spain. It reveals her high spirits and enjoyment of life as well as documenting periods of strenuous work nursing the wounded at a series of frontline medical stations. She provides little political analysis except a perfunctory scorn for the "Reds" and an abiding irritation with the English news: "bright red and lies all through" (6 January 1938). In general, she exuded a cheerful and unexamined disdain for the lower orders which was fairly typical of her class.

Before beginning her time as a nursing assistant Pip and Consuelo, the daughter of the Marquess de Montemar, undertook some nursing training in a hospital near the Infante's country estate at Sanlúcar de Barrameda. They were taught to give injections, take blood from a vein, and identify and clean the instruments used in the operating theater. They also observed operations and were shown how to dress a wound. They made beds, washed patients, emptied pans, rolled bandages, and sterilized compresses and dressings.

In the hospital at Sanlúcar, many of the patients were, as Pip dismissively described them, "filthy smelly Moors" (14 November 1937, 11). All of them were, in her opinion, "very low class and just shout and snatch things and swear, or even worse become cheeky and make lewd remarks in Arabic" (p. 11). But, as she noted in her diary, it was "all madly interesting" and she "loved the work": even when she "disliked the people intensely," she still "liked their wounds." (p. 11).

During the Civil War, Pip divided her time between sporadic bursts of strenuous work as a nursing assistant and a highly diverting social life with the family of the Infante de Orleans. The Infante's three sons—the youngest, Ataulfo, was Pip's special friend—were flyers attached to the German Condor Legion. The extended Orleans family and their circle, including German flyers and Pip on her days off, gathered at their various houses where according to Pip, it was "great fun" and everyone was "as mad as hatters" (p. 7). Many mornings she fell into bed at 5.30 A.M. after "getting plastered" and dancing for hours to records on a phonograph (p. 17).

When it came to physical work in the hospital, however, Pip was no shrinking debutante. From October 1937 until May 1939, faced with the demands of a frontline medical service, she pitched in, and through very trying times showed that she was a hardworking nurse with a vocation for the job. When there was no one else to do it, she washed hospital linen on her knees in the river and cooked, scrubbed, and cleaned (12 March 1938, p. 53). She also learned to deal with the many "unattractive things" that nurses must face as everyday routine: pumping out stomachs and dealing with the most intimate parts of a patient's body (23 March 1938, p. 61). For example, while washing "an over-sexed head wound" who was on her ward, he had suddenly thrown off the cover and "with a wild shout produced his penis" which "left to its own devices proceeded to spray fountains in all directions." Pip "rushed for the pot" and chased after it to no avail. Finally she simply had "to grab the damn thing and hang on." She noted ruefully that she couldn't imagine how nurses could look at a man after all the things they had to do with them as patients (p. 61).

The organization of the Spanish nursing service was chaotic, and the assignment and supervision of nursing staff haphazard. The medicine practiced at the front left much to be desired. Pip was "horrified" at the "dirtiness of some of the doctors" and that often their "ideas of antisepsis were very shaky" (3 February 1938, p. 33). It "gave [her] the creeps" to see the "casual way that medical people picked up sterilised compresses with dirty fingers" (p. 33).

As well, the rhythm of work seesawed. After periods with little to do or much moving and unpacking to no discernible purpose, the hospital would be inundated with wounded, and the staff would, in her words, "work like blacks" (p. 90). In the first week of February 1938 during the Nationalist push into Teruel, wave after wave of injured arrived at the hospital, which was located six miles from the besieged town. In a single stretch of twelve hours on 5 February 1938, and in temperatures that fell well below freezing, Pip's team performed nine major operations, most on patients with horrific injuries (7 February 1938, p. 36). A week later, while on night duty, she acted as the anesthetist for an amputation, even though she had no experience of this highly skilled procedure and "was scared to death." Of the patients the medical service dealt with during these frantic days, Pip noted the depressing but perhaps predictable fact that nine out of ten died (p. 36).

To the Spaniards she met, probably the most striking thing about Pip was her independence. She always drove her own car. At great speed, she covered long distances to spend her days off with the Infante's family or to take a carload of friends at the end of a day into the nearest town for an evening in the bar getting "squiffy" and "tight as ticks" (p. 17). Her father had shipped out a new small car to Gibraltar for her arrival, and when it was stolen and wrecked in August 1938, he sent another. A young woman spinning along behind the wheel of a shining new car invariably drew comment. Just before Christmas 1937, when her oil tank sprang a leak near Béjar, she had stopped at a garage and, to the astonishment of the locals, filled up the tank and replenished the oil and water. She noted that "everyone was quite enthralled to see a young girl traveling alone and busying herself in the engine of a car. Girls here don't." (22 December 1937, p. 18). Another time, when she and Consuelo had stopped for gasoline, a crowd of boys surrounded them, claiming, she said, that because the two women were smoking cigarettes and driving a car they were in fact men in disguise (9 May 1938, p. 89).

An encounter with a Guardia Civil at Burgo de Osma near the Condor Legion's base was typical. It was early in the morning, and Pip had just dropped one of the Infante's sons at the aerodrome when one of the Guardia Civil flagged her down and asked for her pass. When she explained that she had none, he "became vastly suspicious as a young girl driving alone in the early hours of the morning is unheard of in Spain" (15 January 1938, p. 25). He assumed that she was German and with the German aviators. When she said she was English and had just driven an aviator back to the base, the Guardia assumed she was "leading a life of sin" and "was so horrified he nearly burst." He only let her go when Pip pointed out very haughtily that she was a friend of the local military commander (p. 25).

Her close family ties with the Infante placed Pip within Spanish monarchist circles. From time to time this was a handicap when there were Falangist doctors on the ward. They resented her class and her presumption that the war was being fought in order to restore the Spanish monarchy. By contrast, Spanish Falangists wished to create a new republican fascist state in Spain along the lines promoted by the Falangist movement. Pip's aristocratic friends, however, did not offer protection when her behavior seemed to challenge the bounds of respectable Spanish womanhood. The director of the Nationalist Nursing Service, Mercedes Milà, was determined to maintain the good name of Spanish nurses at the front, and in her eyes a freewheeling young foreign woman, traveling about on her own, spelled trouble. She tried unsuccessfully to stop Pip from going to the front, claiming that she was too young and irresponsible to be assigned to service in a combat zone (18 January 1938, p. 28). On several subsequent occasions Milà reprimanded Pip and Consuelo for smoking cigarettes and wearing makeup (24 March 1938, p. 61). The Duchess of Vitoria, the head of the Spanish Red Cross, also "ticked them off" in the Grand Hotel in Saragossa when she saw them smoking in uniform and threatened to "make a great row" about it in Burgos (3 May 1938, p. 84). There were official complaints, as well, that Pip had been seen drinking in bars while wearing her nurse's uniform. The Infanta sent her youngest son to tell Pip that she "disapproved of the life" that the young English-woman was leading and to urge her to leave the front immediately (19 March 1938, p. 29). At a family lunch in Saragossa Pip shocked the wife of the commander of Franco's Air Force, General Kindelán, by "making jokes about dead corpses" (10 April 1938, p. 70).

The matron at Pip's hospital in Calaceite, an older woman and a friend of the Infanta, gave Pip a stern lecture about "being correct" with the doctors: standing up when they came into the room and always addressing them with the formal "usted" rather than the informal "tu" (16 November 1938, p. 149). The older woman was shocked that Pip drank brandy and was not mollified at all when Pip explained that it was "quite usual for girls in England" (p. 150). Pip's passion for dancing—her mother had sent out a phonograph and dance records—also got her into trouble with her medical supervisors.

From a functional point of view the obsession of the Nationalist Nursing Service with propriety and proper behavior seems absurd given that the nurses were working in the harsh conditions of combat where daily they dealt with life and death in the raw. The concerns are comprehensible, however, in light of the Nationalist ideology, which placed women at the self-effacing center of a family that was strictly under male authority. Certainly Pip found extremely aggravating the constant "old-fashioned" remonstrances from "old trout" and mused that she "could not help it that she had been brought up to a lot of liberty." She claimed that "it drove [her] mad to be spied on and followed about and treated like a bloody child or a tart who must be reformed" (16 November 1938, p. 150). In any event, the criticisms of her behavior seemed to have had little effect.

In most cases, in dealing with the men around her, Pip coped with drunks and obstreperous patients with bossy aplomb. When a legionnaire escaped from her ward with "nothing on except his bandage and an overcoat" and "got sozzled and went about lifting his coat for the edification of all the girls," she "ordered him to bed with great gusto" and took away all his clothes (20 November 1938, p. 154). There were other times, though, that she had a sense of foreboding that she was a vulnerable female in a place that was profoundly, even menacingly, male. One evening at the end of 1937 Pip and four nurses drove to the movies in Monzon and, the only women in a cinema full of Italian soldiers, were harassed and "pinched" throughout the film (11 December 1938, p. 162–163).

In a more hostile atmosphere at the Municipal Council in Calaceite, where Pip had gone to round up local women to wash for the hospital, she was crammed in by soldiers who "shoved [her] about" (29 November 1938, p. 157). In a similar way, the atmosphere at the front in Tremp was menacing. The hospital was on the move, and Consuelo and Pip were stranded in town when the wardsmen they had come with went to drink in a bar. Having been warned against being seen in bars while wearing their uniforms they waited outside but, as unchaperoned females, they were immediately "surrounded by an unpleasant crowd of hostile soldiers" (9 December 1938, p. 161). In another incident, while the hospital was preparing to move from Cella, Pip and the nurses were left in a town full of soldiers who were "foul drunks." She was "scared pink" every time she went out, "especially at night" and kept at the ready the pistol that the Orleans family had given her (5 March 1938, p. 51). In the same town, as well, she was almost raped, suffering "a fate worse than death," as she called it (4 March 1938, p. 49). Four strange soldiers forced their way into Pip and Consuelo's room one afternoon when Consuelo was ill in bed. As the men became increasingly aggressive and refused to leave, Pip "suddenly realized that things were not as they should be." One soldier tried to "paw Consuelo about on the bed," and another "poked and prodded" Pip. Eventually the men left but later returned and even more aggressively insisted that they had come to sleep the night with the women. Pip was "frankly frightened." At the same time she realized that the soldiers whom they knew and who were billeted in the house were away, and even if she had been able to call them "they might well have taken sides against the women." Finally Pip convinced the intruders to leave, and the two women slept with the window shutters locked and their "bayonets" at their sides (p. 50).

These were remarkable experiences for a young woman who had come to the war straight from the social whirl of the London season. Despite her stamina and indomitable high spirits, the strenuous months at the front took their toll. As the war progressed, her possessions were stolen, including her precious radio and records. Though she suffered from painful skin ulcers and overwhelming fatigue, she remained in Spain until the end of the war. In May 1939, having celebrated Franco's victory in Madrid and been awarded a *Medalla Militar,* Pip returned to England. Five months later, when the Second World War began, she put the medical skills she had gained in Spain to good use in an Allied mobile ambulance unit in France. In this case, however, she was supporting democracy against the forces of reaction.

Conclusion

Franco's foreign women supporters came from a range of groups on the interwar right. The most numerous were monarchists. Whether it was their upper-class backgrounds, in the case of Pip Scott-Ellis and the Duchess of Rouchefoucauld, or a family history combined with committed Catholicism, as with Gabriel Herbert, or the experience of czarism defeated during the Russian civil war, which influenced Florence Farmborough, they all favored Franco. They saw him providing a bulwark against the leftist Republic and eventually restoring the monarchy in Spain. In casting Franco as the savior of Spanish royalty they were misapprised, but no more so than the other groups who shared royalist leanings in Spain between 1936 and 1939 (Blinkhorn 1990, Preston 1990, 106–107). Eleanora Tennant who, at least until the outbreak of the Second World War, admired Hitler's Germany, found equally appealing Franco's authoritarianism. Whatever the variegations in their rightist beliefs, all these women shared a vehement anticommunism. Ignorant of Spanish domestic politics, they saw the Civil War as a place in which to strike a blow against communism everywhere.

What was remarkable about these women in Nationalist Spain was not their politics but the fact that they were there at all. In the main they hailed from tolerant families that had placed few obstacles in the way of female independence. This in turn had enabled them to leave home and undertake the adventures on which they had embarked. Aristocratic and upper middle class, they were educated, well traveled, and possessed the self-confidence to face the risks that they confronted as they moved about in wartime Spain. In this sense, they were part of a long tradition of adventurous women who did not see the restrictive rules that hampered ordinary women as applying to them. Within a tradition of European women travelers, in the 1930s, their sense of autonomy and freedom to follow their political instincts and personal interests meant that they most closely resembled the cohort of New Women who had become visible between the wars.

Although dedicated to Franco's victory, the foreign women were anomalous figures once they had crossed the border, tolerated only because of their propaganda value and the support for Franco it was assumed they could generate outside Spain. Certainly, these women stood out from the Spanish women around them, and indeed in the recollections they have left, with the exception of Pip's friendship with Consuelo Montemar, there is little indication of their having much contact or fellow feeling for their Spanish sisters.

It was common for travelers in Nationalist Spain to remark upon the separation between the peace and order of the home front and the mobilized belligerency of the war zone. It was a demarcation between female/family space and male/militarized space. The ethos of the first was Catholic and female, and the second military and male. Brothels for the soldiers were part of a militarized male public space, as were medical services at the front lines. Foreign women were conspicuous in public spaces that were designated as male, occupied by soldiers pursuing the enterprises of war. The transgressiveness of female nurses functioning in this male space probably accounts for the concern of the director of Nationalist Nursing to maintain the respectability of Spanish nurses working in combat conditions.

In the western zone, as well, there were few food shortages to strain social structures. And, unlike the Republican side, the Nationalist zone was never drawn into a "total war" where front line and home front were blurred with the consequent dissolving of gender distinctions (Higgonet and Higgonet, 1987).

In the long run, and in a variety of ways, these foreign women helped to ensure Franco's victory. The propagandists, engaged in what today would be seen as public relations work, provided chapter and verse on the "horrors" of "Red Spain" and the virtues of Francoism. Probably, their writings were read by Franco's supporters abroad whose opinions had already been formed, but who used the accounts to add anecdotal evidence to their pro-Franco arguments.

The foreign women in Franco's medical units provided more practical assistance. Gabriel Herbert's Anglo-Spanish medical units made a significant improvement to the level of care that the wounded received in Northern Spain. In less well-run outfits, Pip Scott-Ellis was an energetic and committed nurse in Nationalist frontline hospitals and undoubtedly helped wherever she was stationed, though the descriptions of medical practices do not suggest great success.

The irony of the contribution by these foreign women was that in the "New Spain" that was formed under Franco's dictatorship, independent women like them were not only unwelcome but ruthlessly persecuted. In the brutal repression that followed Franco's victory, women who were known to have been active in public affairs on the Republican side were particularly targeted. Many languished long years in prison (Pamies 1985). Throughout the length and breadth of Franco's Spain a whole raft of laws were enacted to restrict the legal and social rights of Spanish women and conversely strengthen the power and authority of Spanish men (Richards 1999, 47–66).

Notes

1. In many Nationalist descriptions, militia women are violent and filthy, see Mangini 1995, 93, or Bayle 1938. Often in Falangist novels the "decent women" of Nationalist Spain—maternal, asexual and sacrificing—serve as the virtuous foil to the depraved, obscene, and violent "hyena-women" of "Red Spain." See Machtild 1991.
2. Spanish monarchists rallied to Franco because they assumed that he would restore the monarchy immediately. It took place more than forty years after the civil war ended.
3. Gabriel Herbert interview with Michael Alpert, 15 October 1982, Transcript; MS letter to Michael Alpert, 4 April 1982, Box-8: D/1 and 2 Marx Memorial Library, Clerkenwell; *Daily Sketch*, 26 November 1936; *Universe*, 30 October 1936; 18 December 1936; 2 April 1937. Public Record Office, Kew, FO 371,20544, 94–95, Lord Howard of Penrith, 20 October 1936; FO 371 20536 (27 August 1937), 229; Buchanan 1997, 119; and Fyrth 1986, 193–194.
4. Gabriel Herbert discusses the funding operation of the Anglo-Spanish Mobile Unit in Spain and her own experiences as part of a manuscript letter sent to Michael Alpert on 4 April 1982 and in a longer interview with him on 15 October 1982. See Box 801 and 2 in the Marx Memorial Library, Clerkenwell Green, London.

Part III

Interrogations: Right-Thinking, Feminisms, and the Left

14

Pauline and Other Perils:
Women in Australian Right-Wing Politics

Bronwyn Winter

On September 10, 1996, Pauline Hanson, then federal member for the Queensland electorate of Oxley, gave her first speech in the Australian parliament. Disendorsed by the (conservative) Liberal Party following her racist comments directed primarily at Indigenous Australians, Pauline Hanson had stood in the March 1996 federal elections as an independent candidate in the traditionally Labor-voting lower-middle-class/working-class electorate. In her speech,[1] Hanson lamented the plight of "mainstream Australians," who were suffering from "reverse racism" at the hands of "those who promote political correctness and those who control the various taxpayer funded 'industries' that flourish . . . servicing Aboriginals, multiculturalists and a host of other minority groups." She called for the abolition of multiculturalism and a "radical review" of immigration policy, as Australia was in danger of "being swamped by Asians . . . [who] have their own culture and religion, form ghettos and do not assimilate." The speech also attacked the "unfair" workings of Australian divorce law for "noncustodial" parents and advocated the reintroduction of conscription for men and its introduction for women. Over the following two years, "hansonism," as it quickly came to be known through Hanson and her extreme-right party, which registered in April 1997 as Pauline Hanson's One Nation, was rarely out of the media spotlight. After an ensuing period out of that spotlight, One Nation stepped onto the media main stage again in early 2001 with successes in the Western Australia and Queensland State elections. The party performed poorly, however, in the November 2001 federal election, which saw the Liberal Party reelected on a "national security" platform, following the World Trade Center attack and a fierce national debate over asylum seekers.

The meteoric rise of hansonism in a supposedly egalitarian and multicultural country came as a shock to many, if the number of academic works seeking to explain the "Hanson phenomenon" is any indicator (e.g., Adams ed. 1997, et al. 1998). It was not, however, particularly surprising in a global context in which extreme-right and religious fundamentalist movements are increasingly occupying the political terrain. Even the left had been moving steadily rightward since at least the mid-1980s if not earlier in many parts of the world, with the development of the "New Democrats" in the United States, the "Third Way" in Great Britain and Germany, ever-paler-pink socialism in France, and the apparently wholesale embrace of U.S. capitalist ideals by the former Communist bloc. Australia has undergone similar rightward political and economic shifts since what are fondly remembered as the halcyon days of the Whitlam-led Labor-left government (1972–75). Nor was the rise of hansonism surprising in a country where, despite its successes, multiculturalism often remains superficial (Castles et al. 1992), where Indigenous Australians continue to live in Third World conditions and where the history of white supremacy has long been encoded both in Australia's laws and in its extreme-right minority political formations. The fact that hansonism caught so many unawares appears to demonstrate how easily this history has been hidden.

The media hype around hansonism, the popularity of which, despite its spectacular successes, was and remains marginal, further begs the question of what other interests have been served by turning the spotlight on Hanson and away from the actions of the conservative government led by John Howard (Liberal), first elected in 1996 and reelected in 1998 and 2001. Not only has this government been able to introduce its reactionary program with relative ease, but the extremeness and ridiculousness of Hanson's pronouncements—such as that Indigenous Australians were cannibals before white settlement and that if something isn't done, we'll soon be looking at an Asian lesbian cyborg prime minister,[2]—also served to make the government's often equally racist discourse appear more "moderate" and certainly more sensible.

The Australian Political Context: Some Background

To better understand hansonism, it is worth pointing to some factors peculiar to the Australian context. In many respects, Australia resembles other Western countries and particularly English-speaking countries, in that it has a multiparty, supposedly democratic political system. Universal suffrage exists (for all persons eighteen years of age or over, excluding non-naturalized immigrants), but the structure of the electoral system along with corporate control of the media and financing of right-wing parties mean that true participatory democracy does not exist. Australia has a federal system not dissimilar to that of the United States (but with individual states perhaps enjoying less autonomy) but, along with Canada and, of course, the United Kingdom, is not yet a republic: the queen, represented by the governor-general, remains the country's head of state.

The major Australian right-wing party is the Liberal Party, comparable to the (U.S.) Republican Party or the (U.K.) Conservative Party; that is, it has nothing to do with the (to my mind erroneous) U.S. equation of "liberal" with "progressive." It is, rather, a party founded on the ideology of liberalism, Anglo model (as opposed to the French social-contract model): laissez-faire capitalism and strong individualism. The party has, since its creation in 1944, formed a parliamentary coalition with the National Party (formerly the Country Party, founded in 1920), which is a rural-based party. The rural constituency in Australia is very conservative: its dominant population is land- and equipment-rich, macho, white, and nationalistic. This is reflected in the fact that the National Party has the fewest women members of parliament, although the Country Women's Association, a "women's auxiliary" to the Country Party, was once an influential bastion of female conservatism. The Liberal-National Coalition government in power at the time of this writing is the most conservative in Australian history.

The mainstream left is made up of Australia's oldest party, the Australian Labor Party (ALP). Formed out of the trade union movement in 1891, this party has developed in similar ways and on similar bases to its British counterpart, with a few local peculiarities. One of these is the White Australia Policy, developed at the time of Federation (1901) in response to trade union protest against employer importation of cheap Asian (primarily Chinese) labor. Progressively dropped by Labor, this policy was taken up by the right and remained official Coalition policy until the 1970s. A second local peculiarity of the Labor Party is a split that occurred in the 1950s following anticommunist agitation within the party and parts of the trade union movement, backed by a powerful Catholic lobby. This split led to the formation in 1955 of the ultraright Democratic Labor Party (now defunct), which seriously undermined the Labor Party for some fifteen years.

Historically, Australia's entrenched white- and male-supremacist conservatism has been mixed with pockets of extraordinary progressiveness linked to its peculiar history as a federation of former-penal and free settler colonies, with high levels of non-northern European immigration and a significantly decimated and disadvantaged but increasingly politically active Indigenous population.[3] Some examples of progressiveness concern legislation in favor of (nonIndigenous) women. South Australia was the first place in the world to grant women the vote, and Australia was the second nation to do so (after New Zealand). Australia has also been relatively progressive concerning women's rights at work, the development of a welfare safety net, legislation punishing crimes of violence or intimidation against women, legislation recognizing lesbian and gay relationships, and the development since the 1970s of multicultural policies.

At the same time, Australia's dominant culture remains individualistic, racist, and misogynist: egalitarianism remains more of a myth than a reality (a fact pointed to in 1964 by Donald Horne in his groundbreaking *The Lucky Country*). Indigenous Australians were excluded from full citizenship until 1967, and reports of national inquiries into Indigenous health, Indigenous deaths in custody, and the practice of removing Indigenous children from their families have been damning. Racist perceptions of Indigenous people continue to lead to systematic discrimination, and discriminatory legislation, such as the Howard government's Ten Point Plan limiting indigenous access to native title,[4] or the Northern Territory's mandatory sentencing laws, continues to be adopted. The cultural celebration of male violence also continues: variations on the rape fantasy still inform advertising, pornography is freely available, so-called free prostitution is legalized, and the Australian pub culture remains a bastion of machismo. Even the "little battler" of Australian working-class culture, championed by Hanson, remains resolutely white and male, notwithstanding the fact that the majority of Australian factory workers and especially outworkers (home-based pieceworkers) are Asian-background women.[5]

Australia's rightward drift has occurred, then, within a context of a mixture of "blokey" (male) egalitarianism (a "fair go" for all) and capitalist individualism, of deep racism and vibrant albeit flawed multiculturalism, of formal equality for women and a culture of woman-hating. The rightward movement during the 1983–1996 years of Labor-right government, with a program of privatization, cutbacks to the welfare system, wage restraint and economic and fiscal liberalization, resembled that of Social Democrat parties elsewhere in the West, and paved the way for Howard's government, when elected in 1996, to move even further right than it otherwise might have been able to. Further privatizations have occurred; people on unemployment benefit are being subjected to increasingly stringent requirements (such as the infamous "work for the dole" policy); the labor market is characterized by increasing precariousness, aided by two waves of industrial relations legislation that belong more in the nineteenth century than in the twentieth or twenty-first; non-Western asylum seekers are characterized as "queue-jumping illegal immigrants" and imprisoned in detention camps; and hard-won indigenous rights are being eroded (such as through the Ten Point Plan). This creates a fertile terrain for the extreme-right to flourish.

The Coalition would not, however, have been able to apply its devastating program without another source of support: the Australian Democrats. This party, formed in 1977 by dissident progressive Liberals, occupies the political center, and it is the most woman-friendly party apart from the Australian Women's Party. The party has often had women leaders, and many Democrat women have been outspoken on a range of social justice and gender equity issues. At the same time, the Democrats' political record, as the party holding the balance of power in the Senate, is suspect: its support has enabled the Howard government to pass taxation and industrial relations legislation that further advantages the privileged and disadvantages the poor. As a result, despite their support for individuals such as current leader Natasha Stott Despoja, who has opposed her party on some of its "deals" with the Coalition, most feminists are disillusioned with the Democrats, seen as a stooge for the right.

Hanson's Politics

This, then, is the context in which hansonism flourished. Hanson exploited that context to the full, drawing both on the backlash against multiculturalism and immigration which has existed at least as long as multiculturalism itself (Lippmann 1984; Castles et al. 1992; Vasta and Castles 1996), and on a broad and long-standing base of extreme-right activism, such as the influential anticommunist and anti-Semitic think tank the League of Rights, founded in 1946, and political parties such as the Christian Democratic Party, the Shooters' Party, and Australians Against Further Immigration.

Around the time Hanson stood for election in 1996, much-publicized racist comments were also coming from dissident politicians such as Graeme Campbell, a former ALP member who, supported by the League of Rights, subsequently stood as an independent (and more recently for One Nation), and Bob Katter, a Queensland National Party member of parliament. The comments were usually also woman-hating, but these politicians' misogyny has been considered less newsworthy, so presumably less scandalous, than their racism, which has also been the case for Hanson as we shall see. Katter's notorious 1996 reference to "eco-nazis, femo-nazis and slanty-eyed ideologues," for example, met with considerable public outrage over the reference to "slanty-eyed ideologues," while there was scant concern over feminists being referred to as "nazis."[6]

Hanson has, in playing the race card that is central to One Nation's platform, drawn on national mythology in ways that are often strikingly similar to those employed by Howard. Both play heavily on the idea of "mainstream Australia" and "ordinary Australians," who are white heterosexual males with appendages called wives, and who live in suburbia in neat nuclear family groups. Howard's "ordinary Australians" are middle-class (sub)urban; Hanson's are rural, or suburban petty-bourgeois and lower-middle-class. Both use the idea of "free speech" to defend their right to express racist views against "politically correct" "censoring," and defend the rights of "mainstream" Australians (Hanson also uses the term "decent Australians") against "special interest groups" such as what Hanson calls "the Aboriginal industry" (Kalantzis and Cope 1997; see also Hanson's speeches in federal parliament, September 10, December 2, and December 10, 1996).

Hanson maintains that "to survive in peace and harmony, united and strong, we must have one people, one nation, one flag" (first parliamentary speech, 1996)—hence the name of the subsequently formed party. The entry page of One Nation's website, which until 2001 showed Hanson solemnly draped in the Australian flag (she now smiles and sports a bright pink tailored jacket), displayed the following message (also until 2001): "One Nation opposes all divisive and discriminatory policies. The contributions of all people from all countries/backgrounds are welcomed; the Party stands to ensure the rights of all citizens to freely express themselves, but not at taxpayers' expense; benefits should be because of need not race." Parliamentary interventions by Hanson, former One Nation Senator Len Harris, and New South Wales Member of the Legislative Council (Upper House) David Oldfield consistently harp on the supposed "advantages" conferred on Indigenous people, such as low-cost housing loans, native title legislation, and grants to the Aboriginal and Torres Strait Islander Commission. They also oppose both continued non–Anglo-Celt immigration and affirmative action for racialized minorities, which is said by Hanson to discriminate against "ordinary Australians." Following the United Nations' 1999 condemnation of Australia's current native title policy as discriminatory against Indigenous Australians, Senator Harris issued a press statement (August 23, 1999), in which he maintained that far from discriminating against Indigenous Australians, native title legislation discriminates against pastoralists and that the UN's criticism of Australia "can only increase the number of Australians who believe that we should pull out of the United Nations altogether." The Howard government has expressed similar views, threatening to pull out of a number of UN treaties such as the Covenant on Civil and Political Rights.

What is a "Right-Wing Woman"?

The popularity of One Nation, headed by a woman, has raised issues for feminists, who have reacted to Hanson in three main ways.[7] They have either ignored her as a trivial and ephemeral distraction, worried about the "dilemma" she posed for feminists as a right-wing, up-front, independent woman whose existence challenged global views of women's oppression and male supremacy and corresponding definitions of feminism, and/or worried about how to respond to sexist media demonization of Hanson without appearing to support her views. Other women, who may or may not identify as "feminist" but who do identify as "anti-sexist," "pro-equality," and so forth, have either used her as the point from which they distanced themselves ("Hanson is right wing, we are not"), or have used her and women like her as "proof" of the supposed unfoundedness of more radical feminist claims that the oppression of women is universal.[8] If all women are oppressed, they claim, how can we explain Hanson, a woman whose ideas are woman-hating and racist (thus also woman-hating)?

The main point of feminist agreement is, however, that Hanson is the epitome of the right-wing woman in that she espouses racist and nationalist politics, criticizes educated "elites," champions the cause of "small business" and "rural Australia," supports protectionism against globalization, and has a political style that is both populist in terms of her appeal to voters and autocratic in terms of the internal organization of her party. As concerns her persona as a woman, she supports traditional roles for women within white heterosexual social and economic structures. At the same time, she supports women's workforce participation and economic independence, presents herself as tough and independent, and eschews any of the soft, nurturing style that is associated with the "traditional" Anglo-Celtic Australian woman.

What constitutes a "right-wing woman" is not, however, as much an object of easy consensus as might be assumed. Not only do some women associated with the political right, including, on occasion, Hanson, come out with statements and policies with which feminists would not disagree, but those ostensibly on the left have been known to support (or at least fail to oppose) policies—particularly economic policies—that, while generally not specifically directed at women, are usually particularly detrimental to them. (Many ALP women have also failed to publicly dissent from their party's support for the Coalition government's post–September 11, 2001, warmongering and its tough new legislation on asylum seekers.) Part of the difficulty in accounting for this apparent contradiction is that the feminist focus is maintained on characterizing individual *politicians* as right wing or left wing along traditional party or factional lines, rather than talking about aspects of their *politics* that are right or left wing in feminist terms. While there is inevitably overlap between the two, the advantage of focusing more on the political acts and discourses of the people rather than labeling them according to their position within the party system is that we move away from either trying to classify the attributes of individuals or from subscribing unquestioningly to malestream[9] ideas of left and right, and toward establishing what right and left might mean in feminist terms. As Colette Guillaumin points out (1995, 171–175), the political, and hence feminist, distinction between right and left is not a matter of party politics, but a distinction between the cynical preservation of structures of domination ("thinking right") and the contesting of those structures to move beyond their weight and constraints ("thinking left").

This is not to suggest that malestream understandings of left and right have no validity in feminist terms. It is impossible, for example, for feminists to advocate redistribution of the world's wealth without opposing capitalism: a feminist left stance thus broadly coincides here with a malestream left stance. It *is* to suggest, however, that malestream understandings of what constitutes the political left and right in human societies do not usually include the idea that women might also count as human. Moreover, as indicated above, "traditional" malestream definitions of the left have themselves undergone considerable transformation, with a number of supposedly left-wing governments making increasing accommodations with capitalism.

Within such a context of transformation of the distinction between left and right into one between "center-right" and "reactionary to far-right," the question of what constitutes left and right in feminist terms is given scant attention, despite the growing and impressive body of literature on women's role in Australian malestream politics (e.g., Sawer and Simms 1993; Reynolds 1995; Henderson 1999). If, as Jenny Hughey from the Australian Women's Party maintains, "strong feminists are involved in all the parties,"[10] how does one define this "feminism" within the current political context and which female politicians would fit such a definition?

Discussions of why right-wing women are right-wing women is not my concern here, partly because I do not consider the reasons particularly difficult to understand. Those whose objective situation is among the class of the dominated can, for a number of reasons, collude with the dominator, in their own real or perceived self-interest: in order, for example, to attain or preserve a situation of *relative* privilege in relation to other members of their class, and/or because it is obvious to them that the left in general and feminism in particular offer danger and marginalization rather than comfort and status. Indeed, participation in right-wing movements can, paradoxically, be a source of empowerment for right wing women, affording them greater opportunities for political participation and affirmation of their social identity than they may perceive to be available among the left, as has been noted in relation to both non-Western women (Taarji 1990 on Islamist women) and Western women (Dworkin 1983; Campbell 1987), including Australian women (Sawer and Simms 1993; Reynolds 1995).

Empowerment, however, is not synonymous with feminism, even if it can be seen as one component of feminism, the latter being what Thompson (2001) calls "a system of meanings and values." Those meanings necessarily include an understanding of the ideology and political and economic structures of male domination as a fundamental element of most and possibly all human societies. In fact, feminism is not primarily "about women," and it is certainly not about different ways of being a woman or of being empowered as a woman. If it were, we would be obliged to classify Hanson as "feminist," given that she has enjoyed considerable empowerment as the leader and founder of an extreme-right political party.

Hanson's Sexual Politics

In her first parliamentary speech in 1996, Hanson identified herself as "a mother of four children, a sole parent" and as "a businesswoman running a fish-and-chip shop." She thus presented attributes that would potentially make her popular with the petty bourgeoisie (traditionally a strong source of support for extreme-right parties in the West), in particular with petty-bourgeois women. She also defends traditional sex roles: "Most definitely, I love it. I also believe in looking after the male, making sure the food is cooked and the clothes are washed and ironed. I would treat a man like a king" (quoted in Dodd 1997, 20–21). Such pronouncements endear her to rural men, and Hanson has exploited this "little woman" image. During the 1998 Queensland election campaign, for example, photographs of Hanson featured by the press included one of her in a 1950s-style checked gingham dress, preparing afternoon tea with her secretary, and another taken in rural Queensland, where she is being carried, bride style, by a middle-aged farmer with other farmers looking smilingly on.[11]

Some observers, such as Curthoys and Johnson (1998), have commented on the contradictory nature of Hanson's sexual politics. Twice divorced, Hanson has nothing good to say about her former husbands; at the same time, she vehemently opposes Australian no-fault divorce law and high levels of payment of child support by noncustodial parents, "leaving these people in destitute situations" (Hanson, Questions Without Notice in Federal Parliament, October 10, 1996). She identifies herself first as a "sole parent" but opposes welfare payments to unmarried mothers, who "continue to have children at taxpayers' expense" (Hanson media release, 1998). The fact that she is never publicly challenged on these contradictions is interesting to say the least.

She complains of media sexism ("I have got journalists out there who are determined to find out who I'm going out with. It wouldn't happen if I was a man"),[12] but at the same time she is openly misogynist, claiming that women are backstabbing and jealous, while men are better friends (Dodd 1997, 20). She also follows a masculinist line in trivializing feminist protests against male violence: at a public meeting during the 1998 Queensland election campaign, Hanson's response to the issue of wife bashing was to crack jokes about nagging wives.[13]

More recently, Hanson was featured in both *Australian Style* magazine and the Sunday press as preparing for a "stylish" comeback into the political limelight. The November 21, 1999 story in the *Sun Herald* shows a suitably sleeked full-length fashion-model-type photograph of her: her short hair is blow-wave straightened, and she sports an elegant but casual pantsuit along with an affectedly casual pose. She would not, in fact, look altogether out of place in a business and professional lesbian club (which is as much if not more a comment about the fashion industry's construction of lesbian chic, as lesbianism becomes coopted from a political movement into a lifestyle choice and even simply a fashion statement, than it is about Hanson herself).[14] Since the *Australian Style* story, however, Hanson has reverted to her more "traditional" look, but it is evident that, while other female politicians are, with few exceptions, tailoring their suits, vowels and policies to the male political elite's image of tamed and groomed femaleness, Hanson frequently flouts the requisite jacket-and-pearls look, preferring to tailor her image to the idea that her actual or sought-after constituency has of femininity: a politician who has not lost her ability to attract men. For example, following the February 2001 Western Australian and Queensland elections, Hanson arrived at the tally room wearing a long and gaudy party dress, considered inappropriate in such a setting.[15]

Moreover, although she plays the "gender" card when it is useful, defending women's reproductive and employment rights, Hanson distances herself from anything remotely suggestive of affirmative action for women. Thus, when Stott Despoja, then deputy leader of the Democrats, told the press in 1998 that she would like to see a woman for the first President of a future Australian Republic as this would be symbolic of Australia's national commitment to sex equality, Hanson issued a press release stating: "Stott Despoja must understand that first and foremost what makes us equal is that we are all human beings [...] I am offended by women like Natasha Stott Despoja who's [sic] words and actions belittle and patronise women by promoting them purely based on gender not merit." This "merit" argument is also favored by most if not all of the women, and their male colleagues, on the mainstream right (as well as by many men on the mainstream left), who have opposed quotas for female candidates for election because preselection should be based on "merit." A number of female politicians from the malestream left have dismissed this argument as spurious, since "merit" is defined by the men who hold the power, and some have wryly observed that in any case if "merit" were really the issue, most of those men would not be where they are (Reynolds 1995, 131–132).

Hanson surrounds herself with men in the One Nation hierarchy: advisers David Oldfield and David Etteridge have been referred to as her "minders," her "protectors," the "brains behind Hanson," and so on, and Oldfield reportedly saw himself as Hanson's "knight in shining armour" (interview with *Who Weekly,* cited by Ellison and Deutchmann 1997, 148). These comments give the impression that Hanson is some kind of puppet for the male-dominated extreme right, her popularity being manipulated by the "real" (male) movers and shakers. This assumption is not, however, borne out by the facts: Hanson has shown that she will not be crossed, nor is she content to be a dependent figurehead. She has had a number of well-publicized disagreements with male advisers whom she has fired (Pasquarelli 1998)—as well as a couple with women (notably her former "authorized" biographer and her former secretary) although women remain prominent in the party's hierarchy, unlike most other extreme-right splinter parties in Australia. Hanson is also on record as saying that "democratic" functioning is a euphemism for "mob rule."[16] Hardly the behavior of a puppet.

Marian Simms has noted that Hanson's politics, combined with her mixture of tough masculinist individualism and cultivation of "feminine" imagery, along with her peculiarly charismatic leadership style, "blow[s] the soft, maternal model of female politics out of the water" (Simms 1996, quoted in Dodd 1997). Simms's comment can, however, appear somewhat puzzling, and certainly anachronistic, if one considers the political style of many white Western right-wing women of the post-Thatcher years. While it is true that aspects of Hanson's particular persona and politics set her apart from many women on the Australian right, they also have much in common, including blowing "out of the water" the "maternal model" that was once prevalent in the large and active women's auxiliaries to conservative parties (Sawer and Simms 1993, esp. pp. 193 ff.). But even here, one may well ask whether the "maternal model" corresponded to the women's behavior or to men's expectations concerning this behavior.

Women in the Mainstream Right

A number of similarities exist between Hanson and Liberal Party women, particularly as concerns their individualism and male-identified political style: aggressive and disciplined rather than "nurturing." Unlike Hanson, however, many of these women identify strongly as women politicians, are members of women's fora and lobby groups within their own party, and support legislation that ranges from workplace equality measures to legislation for reproductive rights and against (some forms of) male violence.

Senator Amanda Vanstone, who until 2001 was minister for justice (subsequently minister for family and community services with responsibility for the Office for the Status of Women), is one such politician. She is involved with the Liberal Party Women's Council and Liberal Women's Network. Her Justice Department was responsible for tougher legislation on trafficking in women

(Criminal Code Amendment [Slavery and Sexual Servitude] Act, 1999), as well as for two reports recommending improved measures for combating domestic violence (1998) and femicide (1999), and for Model Criminal Code proposals for sexual offences (1999).

These measures are not without their problems. Those against trafficking in women distinguish between "forced" and "free" prostitution, and only concern cases "where a person is engaged to provide sexual services because of force or threats [or deception] and is not free to cease or depart" (Justice Department Media Release, August 11, 1999). The target is the international sex trade, where pimps acting as "immigration" agents lure women from Southeast Asia to Australia, promising them work or marriage. The women, who have often paid fees for the "services" of such agents, arrive to find themselves penniless, often virtually imprisoned, with no legal status in Australia and their passports confiscated (D. Hughes et al. 1999).

As appalling as this situation is, and as laudable as is the legislation designed to combat it, the assumption that there is such a thing as free prostitution, which can be positively contrasted to these extreme forms of trafficking, remains problematic, as does the notion of freely given consent on which it is based. Within a relationship of domination, consent is never freely given. Indeed, it has often been noted by feminists that it is precisely through this consensual (or social-contract) model that domination operates within liberalism (Pateman 1988; Mathieu 1991). Radical feminists have argued that as sexuality is a, or even the, primary site of male domination, the sexual servicing of men is not a "job" like any other and there is no such thing as "free" prostitution (Jeffreys 1997).

Other measures put in place by Vanstone's Justice Department include the establishment of a Women in Law Enforcement Strategy. A July 9, 1998, media release from Vanstone's Department concerning this strategy is headed "Feminine WILES put to work." The misogynist connotations of this are so obvious as not to need comment, not to mention the double-edged nature, in feminist terms, of campaigns to have more women enter institutions such as the police force. On the one hand, it is desirable to move more women (preferably those who are supportive of other women) into the police force to ensure that women making complaints and bringing charges concerning male violence and harassment in particular are treated with fairness and respect. On the other hand, however, given that the police officer's role is primarily to uphold "law and order" as these are interpreted within male-supremacist societies, moving more women into the police force is as likely to divert these women from feminism as it is to divert the police force from its masculinist mission.

It is worth noting in passing that the logic of such pushes for "mainstreaming" and "gender equity" relies on the undiscussed assumption that the best thing for women, and for society, is to incorporate greater numbers of women into all existing institutions. It is rarely if ever asked whether (a) the presence of greater numbers of women in formerly male-dominated areas has significantly improved women's status or simply devalued the work done in such areas (secretarial work and primary school teaching are both striking examples of the latter case) or (b) whether the continued existence of all institutions (such as the police force, the army, and the church) in their current forms, or at all, is socially useful or desirable. This is worrying for the broader advancement of feminist concerns, as it is demonstrable that the feminist issue in relation to many of these institutions is not moving women *into* them, but rather, moving men *out*, that is, dismantling the institution altogether.

In any case, whatever the merits or otherwise of her actions as justice minister, Vanstone is politically committed to the ideology of capitalist individualism. In her first parliamentary speech in 1985, she supported disposing of permanent employment in all but the highest echelons of the Public Service, criticized government encouragement of "dependency" among welfare recipients, affirmed her "passionate belief in capitalism . . . with its corner-stone of individualism" as "it is the system best equipped to cope with human frailty" for reasons that she did not make clear, and defended unequal distribution of wealth on the spurious grounds of "merit."[17]

A Liberal Party woman more clearly identified with feminist principles and well thought of by many feminist organizations and individuals, Marlene Goldsmith, former member of the Legislative Council (NSW), has been outspoken in her condemnation of violence against women, but has taken a less "feminist" stance on other issues. She has in particular attacked a supposed "trendy elitism" in the ALP, attacks that closely resemble the hansonist line on the "new class elites" (Goldsmith 1996). These elites are never defined with any clarity by those who refer to them, but the term would appear to refer to left-leaning professionals and intellectuals who have supposedly frozen out "ordinary people" from political participation. Terms like "chardonnay socialist" have become a common put-down.

Finally, Liberal Party women, for all their "gender-equity" credentials, almost all uphold so-called traditional family values, support militarism, push a law-and-order line, and many belong to parliamentary Christian groups. The right-wing allegiances of these women rather beg the question of whether the difference between extreme-right politics and "mainstream" right politics is, at least as concerns their masculinism, truly qualitative or simply a matter of degree.

While feminists can easily be outspoken in their objections to Hanson, it is less easy for them to voice objections to Liberal Party women who have openly supported feminist voices on some issues. These women are actual or potential allies for feminists seeking to provide services to women and/or to lobby public and private institutions. Feminist organizations often cannot afford to make enemies of Liberal Party women, particularly when the Coalition is in government, if they want to retain access to government funding and be included in information loops.

This uneasy alliance between some feminists and some right-wing women politicians is also, however, somewhat of a trap, and not only because government support or funding becomes a means of "taming" feminist organizations, pressuring them to be less outspokenly radical or critical of the government. The presence of "pro-equality" women in parliament also gives their parties a certain "street cred" with women—particularly middle-class women—who are concerned about issues such as women's representation in the public sphere, workplace equality, and male violence. The Liberal Party can thus portray itself as "women friendly" while it continues to push a woman-hating agenda in welfare, education, industrial relations, fiscal policy, and the rights of Indigenous Australians and other ethnic minorities. Indeed, a public tribunal on women's human rights abuses in Australia, organized in Melbourne on May 21, 1999 by the Women's Rights Action Network of Australia, demonstrated that women's rights, particularly those of Indigenous and other racialized women, have a very low priority for the Howard government.[18]

For all the fuss that was made about Hanson, then, she and her party are the least of Australian women's problems. Or rather, they have been problematic as a deflector, not only from the reactionary program embarked upon, virtually unhampered, by the Coalition, but also from consideration of what politics feminists might be supporting when they are supporting "antisexist" women from other political parties. Moreover, the almost total lack of attention paid by Hanson's opponents (including feminists) to Hanson's own agenda for women demonstrates how low a political priority women's rights really are. Had Hanson not been blatantly racist, it is very doubtful that she would have stirred up much political passion; certainly her traditionalist and misogynist ideas on women alone would not have generated it.

Conclusion

A distinction can and must be made between "feminist" politics and "gender equity" politics, as the latter bear only a very superficial resemblance to feminism. Hanson opposes sexism, but her politics could not be considered "feminist" by any stretch of the imagination. Vanstone opposes the more extreme manifestations of male violence against women, and supports women's full participation in public life, but her support of capitalism and individualism are decidedly *anti*feminist. Both Vanstone and Hanson, like others on the malestream right, prefer spurious "merit"-based arguments to affirmative action. Women on the malestream right of politics can thus, genuinely or cynically, embrace some "feminist" arguments, albeit in diluted form, while at the same time pushing a strongly masculinist agenda.

Even women on the malestream left can embrace a limited and individualistic approach to "feminism." While detailed discussion of ALP women falls outside the parameters of this chapter, it is worth noting that many of them, including those who are outspokenly feminist, "think right" in a number of ways. First, they frequently offer limited interpretations of feminism as being something "very personal" and generally confined to issues of workplace equity and "balancing family and work" (Senator Kate Lundy, 1998)—even though they place these interpretations firmly within a broader social justice framework, unlike their Liberal colleagues. Second, they do not always address issues such as who will provide the increased child care they lobby for so women can more easily enter political life, nor how much these (overwhelmingly female) providers of child care (and no doubt other domestic labor) will get paid. Which means they have not fully addressed the issues of socioeconomic class (and its links with racialization), gendered work, or "traditional" sex roles.

Feminism is not only about gender equity in the workplace nor how many women there are in parliament; nor is it about "women's empowerment." Important as such empowerment is, it is only meaningful in feminist terms if linked with putting an end to male supremacy. Indeed, it is arguable that women's empowerment is as much an effect of ending male supremacy as it is a contributor to it, and we have seen that women can also find "empowerment" within male-supremacist structures.

Finally, whatever the good intentions of women in politics, even some of those on the malestream "right," it must be remembered that the main aim of the political elite is not and never has been to serve "the people" and even less to serve the *female* people, but to preserve its own power (Le Dœuff 1995).

Certainly, feminists, as people who live in this society and have to deal with its institutions, which includes suffering the consequences of the decisions and actions of those who run them, need to find ways of participating in those institutions so as to limit their potential to damage women and even, ideally, so as to contribute to some degree of women's empowerment in the feminist sense of the word. This, apart from supporting "left-wing" women's entry into parliament, can occasionally mean making peculiar strategic alliances, such as, in the Australian case, feminist overtures to Goldsmith or Vanstone.

But let us not confuse strategic alliances along the way to our goals with the goals themselves, for we may find—and indeed, already are finding—that along the way these goals not only are becoming much more modest, but also lie increasingly to the right. And on that malestream right, Hanson is only the highly visible tip of a very large iceberg. Which begs the question: are the politics of more "progressive" right-wing women really less "perilous" for feminists than those of Pauline Hanson?

Notes

1. See http://www.onenation.com.au/
2. http://www.onenation.com.au/
3. Twenty-three percent of the Australian population are born overseas, and 27 percent more have at least one parent born overseas. In 1996 2.1 percent of the population was Indigenous (Australian Bureau of Statistics, http://www.abs.gov.au/).
4. Native title gives Indigenous Australians certain rights over culturally significant sites in rural areas. The Ten Point Plan deems that where the rights of the native title holder are inconsistent with those of a pastoralist leasing Crown land, the former will be permanently extinguished. See http://www.aph.gov.au/senate/committee/ntlf_ctte/report_16/f06diss.pdf.
5. In 1997, the Textile, Clothing and Footwear Union estimated the number of home-based outworkers at three hundred thousand, mostly migrants and women, "paid as little as [AUS]$2 an hour." (http://www.actu.asn.au/national/media/media97/970529joint.htm). (Australia's total population is about 20 million). See also Alcorso 1991.
6. *Sydney Morning Herald,* February 15, 1996 and the *Australian,* February 27, 1996.
7. These reactions have appeared mainly through feminist discussion at conferences and similar fora. Some feminist scholarly perspectives are also given in Ellison and Deutchmann 1997, Curthoys and Johnson 1998, and Winter 1998.
8. See, for example, Rosey Golds, "'Women's issues' wearing thin," *Sydney Morning Herald,* September 12, 1997.
9. The term, an amalgamation of the terms "male" and "mainstream," was coined by Mary O'Brien (1981). I use it here in a different way to refer to the masculinist conception of politics, where the left/right distinction is according to the extent to which parties subscribe to or oppose the ideology of capitalist individualism.
10. http://www.isis.aust.com/awp.hughey.htm, 1998.
11. *Sydney Morning Herald,* June 30, 1998, p. 1, and June 12, 1998 p. 4, respectively.
12. Quoted in the *Sydney Morning Herald,* September 26, 1997.
13. Australian Broadcasting Commission's *Four Corners* current affairs television program, August 10, 1998.

14 . Interestingly, Hanson does not oppose homosexuality, and even had a policy of extending property rights to gay partners (Kingston 1999, 188), although One Nation's website contains homophobic material.

15. Jennifer Hewett, "How the Woman in the Party Frock Changed the Ground Rules," *Sydney Morning Herald*, February12, 2001.

16. The *7.30 Report,* ABC Television, August 5, 1998.

17. http://www.aph.gov.au/senate/senators/homepages/web/sfs-7E4.htm

18. http://www.nwjc.org.au/wrana/

15

Playing "Femball": Conservative Women's Organizations and Political Representation in the United States

Ronnee Schreiber

In 1979, Beverly LaHaye mobilized a small group of conservative women and organized them into the Concerned Women for America (CWA). Twenty-three years later, the CWA is a national women's organization that claims five hundred thousand members.[1] In 1991, another group of conservative women challenged feminist organizations and offered its support for the nomination of Judge Clarence Thomas to the U.S. Supreme Court. That ad hoc group is now institutionalized as the Independent Women's Forum (IWF). Both of these prominent organizations present a substantial threat to the feminist movement.[2] Like feminists, they are well organized, politically active, and seek access to government institutions, political parties, and national media. And, like feminists, they claim to represent women's interests. As these organizations vie with feminists over what women need, they publicly contest definitions of women's interests and influence political debates and policy outcomes.

Though a sizable volume of literature exists on conservative politics in the United States (Diamond 1995; Guth et al. 1995; Moen 1992; Hertzke 1988; Conover and Gray 1983; Crawford 1980), comparatively little of it addresses the specific participation of women and women's organizations (for exceptions see Klatch 1987; Marshall 1995; Blee 1991). Furthermore, most research on national women's organizations (Ferree and Martin 1995; Costain 1988; Gelb and Palley 1987) puts feminist or liberal women's organizations at the center of its analyses, offering a narrow assessment of women's policy activism. Although some scholars have examined conservative women's efforts to oppose the Equal Rights Amendment (Mansbridge 1986) and abortion (Ginsburg 1989; Luker 1984), few address the role of conservative women organized as a countermovement[3] to challenge the myriad goals of the feminist movement (see Marshall 1995, for an exception). My analysis of the CWA and the IWF fills this empirical gap.

As organizations competing with feminists over the right to make representational claims about women, the CWA and IWF must engage in activities that position them as the more credible (as compared with feminists) arbiters of women's interests. As women opposed to the goals of feminist organizations,[4] conservative women leaders would seem justified in establishing *women's* groups to oppose feminist activism. But the IWF speaks critically of politics based on a group's identity. It generally considers appeals to group-based claims as antithetical to individual self-sufficiency and progress.[5] And although evangelical

Protestant women like those of the CWA have a history of activism based on their identities as women, mothers, and/or evangelical Protestants (Ginsburg 1989; Luker 1984), their organizing into a professional, well-staffed national women's organization belies their call for women to prioritize their traditional roles as stay-at-home mothers and wives. In addition, both organizations repeatedly criticize feminists for making identity-based representational claims as and for women. So why have these women organized into national *women's* organizations? And how do being *women's* organizations influence their organizational goals and strategies?

Using information from interviews with leaders of both organizations (including their presidents, board members, and legislative staff),[6] textual analyses and participant observation,[7] this chapter explores the extent to which conservative women's organizations rely on the relationship between gender identity and representation to further their goals.[8] I argue that being *countermovement women's* organizations influences the representational strategies of these two organizations. In particular, I show that, consistent with other countermovement actors, both of these organizations adopt the successful strategies of their opponents, in this case, feminists (Zald and Useem 1987). Specifically, as countermovement women's organizations rivaling feminists over who legitimately represents women, the CWA and IWF co-opt feminist strategies of acting collectively as women and positioning women in leadership roles to contest feminist claims to speak as and for women. As such, I find that *gender identity* is salient to these organizations and influences their representational strategies. While gender identity does matter to these organizations, as *countermovement women's* organizations they also encounter competing influences that mediate the extent to, and the form in which, gender identity is invoked (Meyer and Staggenborg 1996; Zald and Useem 1987). Although these groups adopt the feminist strategy of invoking gender identity, they must appeal to their conservative constituencies and allies and bridge women to conservative causes (Meyer and Staggenborg 1996; Marshall 1995; Zald and Useem 1987). As I show, the need as countermovement women's organizations to engage in feminist strategies *and* appeal to conservative constituencies often conflicts and results in a number of paradoxes.

Finally, while both of these organizations decidedly oppose the contemporary feminist movement, each embodies a specific worldview consistent with Klatch's distinction among conservative women (1987), as discussed in the following section. Thus, I also attend to how variations in their conservative ideologies affect their efforts.

The Organizations

While the feminist movement in the United States is disparate and reflected in a range of local and national efforts, parts of it have also become institutionalized into interest groups (Ferree and Martin 1995). It is frequently these national organizations (e.g., the National Organization for Women [NOW], the Feminist Majority Foundation [FMF], and the National Abortion and Reproductive Rights Action League [NARAL]) who, in the minds of the news media (Huddy 1997), Congress, and the public, encapsulate feminist political activity. The CWA and the IWF envision themselves as antidotes to these national feminist organizations.

Like feminists, however, conservative women are not monolithic. Klatch categorizes them as either "social conservatives" or "laissez-faire conservatives," each representing a different worldview with regard to gender, religion, economics, and the role of government (1987). "Social conservatives" claim to be deeply religious,[9] see the "traditional family"[10] as the center of society, and root social problems in the moral realm. "Laissez-faire" conservatives point to the economic realm as the source of problems and emphasize individuality and the desire for freedom from government intrusion.

Klatch also argues that socially conservative women tend to be gender identified, while laissez-faire conservative women do not recognize their "collective interests as women" (1987, 10) and are not necessarily antifeminist. While the organizations I have chosen generally represent women from these perspectives, with the CWA being composed of socially conservative women and the IWF of laissez-faire conservatives, I find that the laissez-faire conservatives of the IWF also express the need to act collectively as women. Indeed, this group of laissez-faire conservatives does believe that feminism is, at least, partly to blame for many social and economic problems. As I show, its reasons for turning to collective action are mostly strategic, but it cites gender identity as an important factor in its potential for success. Despite some variations from Klatch's ideal types, then, these two organizations represent the range of institutionalized conservative women activists in the United States.

The strong growth of the CWA in the 1970s and early 1980s coincided with the politicization of the Christian Right (Green et al. 1996). Originally located in San Diego, California, the organization started locally to oppose the Equal Rights Amendment (ERA) and legalized abortion. In 1985, CWA relocated to Washington, D.C., establishing a national office and a national presence. LaHaye, a white, middle-class woman, has close ties to the broader Christian Right movement (her husband, Tim LaHaye, was on the Moral Majority's first board of directors). Given her ability to mobilize women through churches, mass mailings, and radio, she has successfully made a name for herself and for CWA.

Today CWA has a professionally staffed office in Washington, D.C., members in all fifty states, and claims to be the largest women's organization in the United States.[11] Locally, its mostly white female membership[12] gather in prayer chapters (about five hundred throughout the United States) to take action on CWA's political agenda. Through advocacy on its issues, the CWA works in coalition with such conservative organizations as the Christian Coalition, the Family Research Council, and several antiabortion groups.

Its multi-issue, socially conservative policy agenda includes opposition to homosexuality, legalized abortion, pornography, and the United Nations, and support for prayer in schools and "religious liberty." While CWA often speaks broadly to "women's issues," it occasionally specifies that its policies particularly affect poor women and women of color. This is evident in the case of welfare reform, which it supports, and the funding of international family planning programs, which it opposes (Schreiber 2000).

By comparison, the IWF is a much younger and smaller organization,[13] but one that has garnered considerable attention and clout since its founding. Established in 1992, it grew out of a network of women who worked for President George Bush's administration. These conservative women leaders are well connected to, or are in themselves, key policy and opinion makers.[14] Resembling more of a think tank than a grass-roots organization, it was founded to take on the "old feminist establishment" (Independent Women's Forum 1996). In the laissez-faire conservative tradition (Klatch 1987), it describes itself as an organization that promotes "common sense" and provides "a voice for American women who believe in individual freedom and personal responsibility" (Independent Women's Forum 1996). Unlike the CWA, it does not have a grass-roots membership but does employ professional staff, most of whom are white women.[15]

The IWF delights in caricaturing feminists and "debunking" feminist policy claims. It has collaborated with other conservative organizations, including the American Enterprise Institute and the Center for Equal Opportunity. Its policy program, which reflects its laissez-faire ideology and explicit desire to challenge feminists, includes opposition to pay equity policies, support for college-age women seeking an alternative to "rigid feminist orthodoxy,"[16] and advocating for gender segregation in basic military training. Like CWA, it frequently references "women" in universal terms, but there are times when the organization specifies that its advocacy will help poor women and women and men of color. For example, it claims that tax breaks for businesses that offer flexible work hours will help working-class women (Schreiber 2000).

Countermovements, Gender Identity, and Political Representation

Countermovement Strategies

As organizations explicitly formed to challenge the feminist movement, I consider the CWA and the IWF to be "countermovement" organizations. Scholarship that regards countermovements as dynamic and interactive (Meyer and Staggenborg 1996; Marshall 1995; Lo 1982) offers a valuable framework for assessing the goals and strategies of these two groups. This literature argues against the conceptualization of countermovement organizations as purely reactionary and static (Marshall 1995) and focuses instead on countermovement organizations' engagement and interaction with both opponents and supporters (Meyer and Staggenborg 1996). In this way, scholars draw attention to how these relationships affect organizational actions (Lo 1982). Thus, to best understand the CWA and IWF, I consider that they operate in a political context rife with competing values and audiences and show how both groups negotiate this tension through their representational strategies.

Gender Identity and Political Activism

In this chapter I ask: when and how do these conservative women's organizations see their identities as *women's* groups to be central to their political actions? That is, I am interested in their attempts to engage in identity politics, in politics based on their sense of what it means to be female. For *interest groups* like the CWA and IWF, engaging in identity politics also means making claims on behalf of women; that is, it means *representing* them.

The strategy of invoking gender identity to make representational claims is not without its critics. Judith Butler (1992) argues that identity categories are never merely descriptive but always normative, and as such exclusionary. She cautions that when "the category of women is invoked as describing the constituency for which feminism speaks, an internal debate invariably begins over what the descriptive content of that term will be" (15).

Indeed, women of color, poor and working-class women, and lesbians have longed criticized national women's organizations for their inattention to diversity and for deploying the category "woman" to make universal claims without regard to the differences that exist among women (see e.g., Phelan 1993; Mohanty 1991; Collins 1990; Lefkowitz and Withorn 1986). Identity politics, these critics contend, runs the risk of assuming all women have a "true essence—that which is most irreducible, unchanging, and therefore constitutive of a given person or thing" (Fuss 1989, 2); that is, that such politics is "essentialist."

There are scholars, however, who want to retain some version of identity politics, but call for more careful attention to its effects, purposes, and processes (Phelan 1993; Spivak 1993; Fuss 1989). Spivak's ideas have often been consolidated under the phrase "strategic use of essentialism" (Spivak 1993, ix). Spivak calls for deconstructing identity categories, but adds that deconstruction should be a *critique*, not the rejection of identity politics that relies on potentially essentializing categories. She clarifies that "[a] strategy suits a situation; a strategy is not a theory" (4) and thus argues for attention to how particular identity categories are deployed in specific political situations.

As I show, Spivak's emphasis on the *strategic* use of essentialism provides important insights that help explain why the CWA and IWF have opted to engage in some level of identity politics, even though they criticize feminists for doing the same. Both organizations, but especially the IWF, invoke gender identity critically and self-consciously to contest feminist political activism. Nonetheless, these conservative women's organizations can suffer from the same essentializing tendencies as feminists when they make claims as and for women. For example, rarely does either organization talk about racial or class differences among women in general, or within its own membership. However, as I discuss, its strategic use of gender identity provides them legitimacy to contest feminists claims to representing women's interests.

Gender Identity and Political Representation

To articulate the *forms* in which gender identity is invoked by these countermovement women's organizations, I employ the concepts of "descriptive" and "substantive" representation. Pitkin argues that descriptive representation depends on a "representative's characteristics, on what he is or is like.... The representative thus 'stands for' others" (1967, 61). By contrast, substantive representation is the notion that representatives need not share an identity with those they represent; instead representation is based on the content of a person's actions or what the representative "acts for" regardless of who s/he is (Pitkin 1967, 118). While Pitkin distinguishes between these conceptualizations, some scholars argue that there can be a direct relationship between the two and that "acting for" can follow from "standing for" (Thomas 1994; Dodson and Carroll 1991). That is, that a person who shares experiences or social locations with another is more likely to understand that person's interests and act accordingly. As I demonstrate, the degree to which any or all of these representational philosophies shape the CWA's and IWF's political strategies is influenced by their status as countermovement women's organizations.

Standing for Women: Descriptive Representation as an Organizational Strategy

Playing "Femball"

The success of a political movement can illustrate the value of collective action to opponents (Marshall 1995; Zald and Useem 1987). For both organizations, feminists have demonstrated not only the success of collective action, but the success of organizing *as* women to achieve political goals. The CWA and IWF follow feminists' lead and argue that to successfully challenge feminists, they, too, must make claims *as* women.

Anita Blair, vice president of the IWF, acknowledged this strategic use of gender identity (Spivak 1993) to counteract feminism with the ironic use of a sports metaphor: "We strongly believed and believe today that women are not a political interest group," but "in this credentialist age ... there's a game going on, and the other side fielded a team and we didn't" (interview by author, October 30, 1998, Arlington, Va.). She argues that feminists are playing "femball," and in order for the IWF to compete, it has to act according to the terms established by the team that got there first—feminists. The IWF's Sally Satel summarized this sentiment most succinctly: "I see IWF as largely a reactive group. If it weren't for the feminists, it wouldn't exist" (interview by author, February 17 1999, Washington, D.C.).

Like the IWF, the CWA was born to compete with feminists generally, and the National Organization for Women specifically. Seriah Rein, CWA's New Jersey area representative, argued, "It is in the public's interest to maintain our identity as a women's organization and as a counterpoint to what NOW is doing specifically" (interview by author, August 6, 1998, Paramus N.J.). Similarly, CWA's Kenda Bartlett related:

> They hear the Patricia Irelands, the Eleanor Smeals, the Kate Michelmans, all of them saying we represent women in America, what American women think. And these women are saying this is not what I believe and not what I think ... so they have looked for a place where they can get information that states their point of view, and they have found that in CWA (Phone interview by author with Bartlett, November 4 1998).[17]

As countermovement women's organizations formed to challenge feminism, making representative claims as women is critical for these groups. It enables them to directly confront feminists while establishing themselves as legitimate representatives of women's interests. And, as *women's* organizations, they are not only able to fight feminists on their terms, but they may be better suited than male-led conservative organizations to appeal to other women who see their lives being represented by women like themselves. CWA founder Beverly LaHaye puts it this way: "We women need heroines. We want to see living examples of Christian women who stand against the immoral, godless, feminist teaching" (1993, 80).

A Media Voice for Women

Mass media are important outlets for movements and countermovements—they enable organizations to reach members, potential participants, and policy makers. But the media are also favorite targets of disdain for many conservatives, with critics claiming that liberals have a stronghold on this institution. Not surprisingly, then, the CWA and the IWF contend that conservative women's organizations are dismissed by the media (LaHaye 1993). Like their conservative counterparts, these conservative women's organizations seek media access to get publicity and enable "balanced" reporting; but they also interact with the media *as* women "to challenge feminist organizations and the representation of women's identities and interests."[18]

For example, Anita Blair says this of IWF's founding as a woman's organization:

> I think it was a reaction to particularly the media surrounding the Clarence Thomas/Anita Hill and the Year of the Woman. At that time you couldn't pick up a newspaper or listen to a radio or television program without hearing women think this or women think that. And invariably, it was a left-wing women's perspective. And most of us . . . felt that it was not at all a woman's perspective, because we were women and we had a different take on these things. (Interview by author, October 30 1998, Arlington, Va.)

Indeed, one of the IWF's first projects was to publish a *Media Directory of Women Experts* that lists three hundred "knowledgeable women who can provide *balanced* commentary on timely subjects ranging from 'Aviation' to 'Workplace Issues.' As IWF board member, Wendy Gramm, noted:

> I always think it's great to have women as spokesmen. . . . Even though we believe that we are not crazy about having hyphenated Americans. . . . But on the other hand we have found that for our organization that it has been helpful to have a woman going up there and saying something about this issue or that . . . people may be more receptive if they hear it from a woman. (Phone interview by author, January 20 1999)

Gramm, herself a "hyphenated American" (Asian-American), sharply illustrates the tension felt by the IWF because of its decision to strategically invoke gender identity (Spivak 1993). Since attributions based on gender or race conflict with laissez-faire conservative ideology, the organization's leaders profess discomfort with making identity-based claims. In a move that seems contradictory, however, the IWF does invoke gender identity by making claims as women in the media.

To attract media attention, the CWA created a more public role for its former president, Carmen Pate. Several staff told me that the CWA decided to move Pate into the role of spokesperson to get a woman's face in the media to represent them. "We are trying hard now with Carmen . . . to present that to the media, because we are not getting the media coverage that NOW gets. And we've got to stop that. We have five hundred thousand members, NOW has sixty to seventy thousand, and they get all the attention," bemoaned CWA Board member Jan Roberto (interview by author, September 25, 1998, Alexandria, Va.).

The CWA's Rosaline Bush said that she and her organization "feel that women need spokesmen. We do not believe that NOW speaks for us" (interview by author, October 18 1998, Washington, D.C.). Indeed, the IWF's Gramm's and the CWA's Bush's use of the term "spokesmen" here points to the invocation of conservative ideology for these groups, even though they are making claims about the need for women to be active in the public sphere. For them, choosing the term "spokeswomen" or spokesperson would be a nod to feminists who have long called for gender-sensitive and inclusive language (Spender 1985).

The CWA and IWF recognize that having women publicly speak for them gives them the attention and legitimacy to challenge feminists and represent women's interests. And because they are women challenging other women's political views, the media are eager to give them access; controversy generates interest and viewership (Huddy 1997).

Women as Policy Activists

Like the media, policy-making entities are important targets, as they are also institutions through which women's identities and interests get constructed and defined. Both organizations articulate that having women spokespeople and constituents lends legitimacy to the policies they advocate. It is more difficult for conservatives to be attacked as "antiwoman" if women are making the political claims. The CWA and the IWF are well aware of the salience of gender identity in this context. When asked by a *Washington Post* reporter why "antifeminists" should form a women's organization, IWF's executive director Barbara Ledeen said: "You can't have white guys saying you don't need affirmative action. We feel we have credibility to say 'not all women think the way you may expect' (Rosenfeld 1995).

And, in discussing the impact of women lobbying against abortion a special assistant to CWA's founder La Haye recited thoughts similar to Ledeen's: "Whereas if the answer is coming from a woman, it is likely to carry more credibility . . . coming from the mouth of a woman it would carry more weight" (phone interview with Arrington by author, October 14, 1998).

In addition, the CWA's former lobbyist argued that because men feel they will be attacked by feminists and, perhaps the "liberal" media, women make better spokespeople on conservative issues:

> Sometimes it takes women to stand up and stomp their feet and say enough . . . The Equal Rights Amendment was a perfect opportunity for that to happen; because that was so much perceived as a woman's fight and a woman's battle. Men were so scared to speak out, they still are . . . But we are able to walk into a [congressional] office and say we represent five hundred thousand women in this country. That rings a bell. (Interview with Laurel MacLeod by author, August 18 1998, Washington, D.C.)

Indeed, CWA does make claims on behalf of its large grass-roots constituency of women. Kenda Bartlett, a CWA staff member discussed this effect: "When our lobbyists go to Washington, D.C., or our volunteers go [to Capitol Hill], and they say they represent the largest women's public policy organization in the United States, that has clout (phone interview by author, November 4 1998).

Given the (false) stereotype of feminist women as man haters, it might benefit feminist organizations to get public support from men for their policy concerns. The CWA and IWF however, rely on just the opposite approach to gain legitimacy as representatives for their issues. For these conservative women's organizations, who advocate for policies that many feminists and liberals see as "antiwoman," having women speak should give them broader appeal among conservative constituencies and allies and policy makers and the public.

A Distinct Woman's Perspective?

Since both organizations consider the differences between men and women to be natural, one would expect organizational beliefs that reflect these values, with claims that women's organizations are necessary because women have different needs and viewpoints than men. This perspective, for example, has motivated some women to engage in political activism because of what they consider to be their unique experiences and interests as mothers (Jetter, Orleck, and Taylor 1997). That is, that substantive will follow from descriptive representation. While this generally holds true for the CWA, it is not the case for the IWF. Why this difference?

Despite their similarities in opinion about gender differences, the CWA and the IWF do represent different constituencies. As noted, the CWA's base is composed mostly of "social conservatives" who favor "traditional" gender roles (Klatch 1987). The IWF's looser network of associates is more activated by its libertarian or "laissez-faire" (Klatch 1987) views on economic and government policies. The need to appeal to, and mobilize, their differing conservative constituencies mediates the extent to which these organizations see the correlation between descriptive and substantive representation, or more specifically gender identity and women's interests, as relevant to their political strategies.

The CWA believes that women's unique perspectives qualify them to make group-based political claims. One CWA staffer summed it up this way: "I think that the true woman, mother, family member's voice, needs to be heard more than it is . . . we definitely view the family as why we're doing what we're doing, but with the woman's vantage point" (interview with B. Franceski by author, October 29, 1998, Washington, D.C.).

Both organizations believe that having women speak for them gives them credibility to represent women and challenge feminists. It is entirely different, however, to say that women's messages are different from men's because of their biological differences and differing social locations as wives and mothers. While each organization favors a "messenger" who is female, only the CWA claims that its identity as a women's organization also hinges on women's differences from men. While the IWF does not disagree that women are different from men, it proclaims that the only differences that justify its forming into a woman's organizations are the differences among women, not between women and men. As IWF's Anita Blair told me: "We just simply wanted to show, to coin a phrase, that gender is not determinism. You know, your sex does not dictate your political views. So the IWF in particular wanted to present another voice. We wanted to be a voice for women who had different views" (interview by author, October 30, 1998, Arlington, Va.).

In fact, using gender as a primary organizing principle clearly created tensions for the organization. One IWF associate noted this about the organization's leaders: "They come from a philosophical background that leads them to believe that they are interested in what the argument is, not who the deliverer of the argument is. So . . . the challenge was finding people to actually run the organization, and in a sense *limit* themselves (name withheld, interview by author, 1999; emphasis added).

Because of the IWF's strong belief in individualism and distaste for identity politics, it has to justify its being a women's organization. As noted, it does so in highly strategic terms, conceding to feminists the relative value of acting as women. Nonetheless, the IWF considers gender-based identity activism to be "limiting" in that it has the potential to exclude men and laissez-faire conservative women who do not see their interests as collectively defined and determined. For the IWF, descriptive representation is often invoked, but not necessarily as a direct correlate with substantive representation. While this may seem paradoxical, it exemplifies a striking tension produced by its being a countermovement women's organization.

Conservative Ideology Trumps Gender

While gender identity matters to the CWA and the IWF, there are times when both repudiate its significance. Given findings that women in elected office prioritize women's interests (Swers 1998; Thomas 1994; Dodson and Carroll 1991) I expected that the CWA and IWF would want to increase the number of women in political office to heighten attention to women's issues. Neither organization, however, devotes resources to increasing the number of women in public office.

Given the IWF's criticism of the relationship between identity and interests in other contexts, its views about women in public office are not that surprising. But the CWA also denies that women elected officials would be more likely than men to bring different *policy* concerns to a legislative body's agenda. It argues for supporting candidates and elected officials based on issues, not identity. There are several possible explanations for this position.

First, the push to increase more women in office appears to be too similar to affirmative action—a policy that the CWA and many other conservative organizations oppose.[19] The CWA's Seriah Rein noted:

> I don't think you need to have cancer to be able to articulate how to prevent it and how to deal with it and how to treat it. I don't believe in quotas period. I know some men who can more effectively express the concerns of women than a lot of women I know. . . . I don't think you should have a certain percentage of women for the sake of having women, I think that is the big disservice we did with blacks in affirmative action. . . . I feel the same way about women being represented in Congress. (Interview by author, August 6 1998, Paramus, N.J.)

Second, empirical studies of women elected officials suggest that women tend to be more liberal than their male counterparts within the same party (Thomas 1994; Dodson and Carroll 1991). Given these findings, the CWA may not be in any hurry to call for the election of more women to elected office. There are already many men in public office who support its policy agenda.

Nonetheless, while the CWA does not embrace the idea of increasing women in office, its former lobbyist Laurel MacLeod did acknowledge that some women elected officials may have more credibility on its issues than men (1998). Thus, the CWA may seek out like-minded women in office to speak on behalf of its issues at key times during a legislative contest. As MacLeod confided: "If you had more women in Congress like Linda Smith and Helen Chenoweth, who are pro-life and are willing to go down and speak out, and on some issues really give courage to the men, I would see that as an enormous and very positive change" (interview by author, August 18 1998, Washington, D.C.).

It is somewhat surprising that these organizations do not push for more women in political office. The "impact on women in public office" literature does find that a range of women bring "women's traditional areas of concern"[20] to the policy-making process (Dodson and Carroll 1991). Since the particulars of these "traditional areas of concern" were not defined by researchers, it is unclear exactly what policy *positions* elected women would take on them. Thus conservative women's organizations might benefit from conservative women's election to office. That they have chosen *not* to actively encourage and support the election of more women to public office suggests the need as countermovement women's organizations to appeal to and mobilize their conservative allies, at the risk of not co-opting a successful feminist strategy.

Conclusions

Both organizations consider gender identity to be an organizational resource. My research suggests that factors associated with being countermovement women's organizations help determine the form in which, and the extent to which, gender identity is invoked. The CWA holds a more essentialist view of women's identities and interests and promotes these beliefs not only by positioning women in key leadership positions, but by (mostly) advocating for a woman's perspective that is distinct from men's. In so doing, it signifies women as different from men. Consistent with its socially conservative ideology and desire to contest feminist representational claims, the CWA positions itself as an organization that speaks to the "true" nature of women's interests.

The IWF is more self-consciously essentialist (Spivak 1993) in its deployment of the category "woman" and mostly invokes gender identity to raise the question of *which* women's interests are getting represented. In its case, identity politics, and more specifically the use of descriptive representation, is a reactive gesture, one meant to counter feminist political actions. It emanates not from the belief that women are different from men and thus have particular interests, but on the need as a countermovement women's organization to "risk" essentialism to achieve the political goal of proving feminists to be wrong in their claims about women's interests.

Both organizations also reify the problem of relying on descriptive and descriptive-substantive representation. As many feminists have argued (J. Butler 1992; Mohanty 1991; Collins 1990), assuming a correlation between identity and interests elides differences among those within a group. When conservative women's organizations make representational claims as women, whether to counter feminists or speak to women's "true" nature, they suggest a homogeneity of interests and experiences that may not exist even among conservative women. And although the IWF critiques its own use of gender identity, this does not nullify the power that it has as a national organization to promote particular narratives about women's interests.

My research also points to questions for future studies. Through engagement with identity politics, both feminist and conservative women battle over whose stories about women are most representative. Given that these narratives about women's lives have very real policy implications, the battle over their authenticity is quite valid. But there is another critical aspect to these competing narratives: considering the "consequences of . . . stories in terms of power and change" (Phelan 1993, 773). That is, what meanings do these differing accounts of women's lives have? In this spirit, future research could investigate if and why conservative women's organizations may (or may not) be more effective and successful than feminists. What impact might the CWA and IWF have on the policies for which they advocate? Does speaking as women really help them achieve their goals? Are their stories about women more credible and plausible than those offered by feminists? Given that the media do give them access and that these organizations have close ties to powerful members of Congress and the new Bush Administration, we should expect that they will indeed be taken seriously as policy advocates for women.

Invoking gender identity enables the CWA and IWF to establish themselves as legitimate representatives of women's interests. Thus, the CWA's and IWF's activism poses a challenge to feminists as they strive to sway policy makers, mobilize members and influence the media and public. Their acting as and for women, however, also reinforces the feminist contention that women's issues and interests are relevant to politics.

Notes

1. According to the CWA, this figure represents the number of people who have contributed money to the organization within the past twenty-four months.
2. The feminist movement in the United States is far-reaching and includes national organizations, community groups, direct service providers, campus-based groups, and list servers (Brownmiller 1999; Blee 1998; Echols 1989; C. Cohen, Jones, and Tronto 1997; Ferree and Martin 1995; Martin 1990). When the CWA and IWF talk about the feminist movement, however, they are mostly referring to nationally organized interest groups, especially the National Organization for Women (NOW), the Planned Parenthood Federation of America (PPFA), the American Association of University Women (AAUW), and the Feminist Majority Foundation (FMF). Both the IWF and CWA consider such feminist groups to be their opponents and name these feminist organizations as proxies for the entire feminist movement. To be consistent with the organizations under study, when I talk about the "feminist movement" or "feminists" in this chapter, I, too, am referring to these institutionalized political actors unless otherwise stated.
3. "Countermovement" organizations "make contrary claims simultaneously to those of the original movement" (Meyer and Staggenborg 1996, 1631). The original movement in this case is the feminist movement.
4. For example, the CWA opposes legalized abortion and rights for gays and lesbians. The IWF opposes gender-integrated basic training in the military and government funding of day care.
5. While this is generally true of the IWF, it sometimes advocates for policies that call for attention to gender-based differences. For example, it argues against gender-integrated military training because of women's physical differences from men and the potential for sexual tension.
6. All of the women interviewed for this study are white.
7. I examined organizational periodicals from 1993 to 1998 and website pages from 1997 to 2000. The CWA puts out the monthly *Family Voice*, and the IWF publishes

quarterly the *Women's Quarterly* and *Ex Femina*. In addition, I attended two national CWA conventions—September 19–21, 1996, at the Sheraton Washington Hotel in Washington, D.C., and September 24–27, 1998, at the Radisson Plaza Hotel in Alexandria, Va. I also attended an IWF conference entitled "Scared Sick?" at the National Press Club in Washington, D.C., on February 17, 1999. Finally, I was an invited participant at the "Core Connections: Women, Religion, and Public Policy" symposium, held October 8–9, 1999, at the John F. Kennedy School of Government at Harvard University; associates from both organizations were participants.

8. This research was supported by the American Association of University Women (AAUW) Educational Foundation.

9. Most of the members of the CWA identify as evangelical or fundamentalist Protestants (Guth, et al. 1995).

10. I employ this phrase to reflect the CWA's use of it. It is important to note, however, that while the CWA invokes the term "traditional family" to refer to a heterosexual unit comprising married individuals likely to have children, its use of the phrase belies the social and cultural constructions that have helped create the fiction of static and ahistorical understandings of both "traditional" and "family" (see Shorter 1977 for more discussion).

11. On its website, www.now.org, NOW also claims to have half a million members; CWA argues that NOW actually has fewer than one hundred thousand.

12. While CWA does not keep data on the demographics of its membership, I was told that most members are white (no information on class could be given). My experiences at its national conferences confirm that most of the organization's activists are white women.

13. The IWF does not have members, but distributes about sixteen thousand copies of its quarterly magazine. This figure consists of paid subscribers and those who receive them gratis.

14. For example, board member Wendy Gramm is married to U.S. Senator Phil Gramm (R-Tex.), and board president Ricky Silberman worked for U.S. Supreme Court Justice Clarence Thomas when he directed the Equal Employment Opportunity Commission. I note these connections not to downplay the success and political agency of these conservative women, but to note some of their political contacts and situate them within the conservative movement.

15. At the time I conducted my interviews, all but one of the staff members was white. Like the CWA, the IWF does not keep data on the racial and class composition of its associates.

16. Descriptions of their issues can be found at "www.iwf.org/issues/".

17. The women Bartlett is referring to are Patricia Ireland, the former president of NOW; Eleanor Smeals, a founder of the FMF; and Kate Michelman, the executive director of NARAL.

18. While both organizations criticize the media for lack of representation, their claims are not necessarily well founded. For example, the organization Fairness and Accuracy in Reporting (FAIR) cites that in 1995 "the *New York Times* published six opinion pieces by IWF leaders, the *Wall Street Journal* published five, the *Washington Post* three. . . . [D]uring the same period those same papers chose to publish no commentary on any subject by anyone from NOW . . . or the Feminist Majority Foundation" (Flanders 1996).

19. In addition to the IWF, these organizations include the Center for Equal Opportunity, the American Enterprise Institute, and the Campaign for a Color-Blind America.

20. I use the term "traditional areas of concern" here to mirror the language used by Dodson and Carroll (1991). They use the term "traditional" to reflect national public opinion among women in the United States over the past few decades, and thus the meaning of "traditional" here is limited in its historical and cultural manifestations.

16

Islamisms and Feminisms in Egypt: Three Generations of Women's Perspectives

Azza Karam

Islamism is a quintessentially political ideology and movement, dedicated to bringing about an Islamic regime that will rule by shari'a (Islamic law), and thereby to Islamizing the entire society.[1] It has to be clearly distinguished from mainstream Islamic/Muslim religion and indeed, even from so-called Islamic fundamentalist movements, many of which have no political ambitions. Islamism emerged in the 1980s with the international demise of other political ideologies (e.g. communism and socialism), the continuance of illegitimate and authoritarian regimes in the Middle East, and the dominance of American-style global capitalism. In its espousal of economic justice for the poorest members of a society, Islamism bespeaks elements of socialism, but its insistence on Islamic religion as the "only solution" (to all political, social, and economic problems), belies a clear right-wing tendency, similar to the Christian Right in the United States Islamism is the most credible political ideology of opposition in much of the Middle East—particularly in a context where much of the existing opposition is seen as ineffective and mediocre. Yet only recently have the voices of its women advocates come to light. The predominant response dismisses the female advocates of Islamisms as sufferers from a severe case of "false consciousness" or as devotees of political and social programs that are incomplete or flawed.

I carried out research on Islamist women, especially in Egypt, from 1990 to 1998. In this chapter I share some of my findings and maintain that the moderate Islamist movement (i.e., the Muslim Brotherhood) includes a small but important cadre of women who are not simply mainstream female activists but *feminists.*

In the following pages, I elaborate why I refer to these women as "feminists," and I analyze the works of Islamist women activists representing three different generations: Zaynab Al-Ghazali (born 1971), Safinaz Qazim (born 1939), and Heba Ra'uf (born 1965) These Islamist feminists express their viewpoints on feminism or *Qadiyyat al-Mar'a* ("the woman's issue"), Islamisms, and the state. I trace continuities and changes in their ideas and actions, and I highlight developments regarding Islamist feminisms.

All three women come from middle-class backgrounds and have been politically active since their teens: joining demonstrations, giving talks, organizing protests, and, above all, writing. The material for this chapter comes from an analysis of their written works, their life histories, and my own and others' interviews with them.

Feminism

These women devote themselves to writing, advising, and campaigning, ostensibly in the name of all Muslims, but also on specific issues related to women. Since these women are aware of women's oppression and are actively seeking to combat it, I consider them feminists. I define feminism as the awareness of women's inequality and subordination in society, and the concomitant attempt to change this situation for a more egalitarian and just society. Each of these women realizes that women are oppressed in today's world, and each in her own way fights against this oppression in the name of a proper Islamic society and state. They reject the usage of the term "feminist" to describe themselves not because they do not conform to the definition above—for they do—but because it is a Western term (i.e., in the language of an oppressive and colonial West) and because it connotes, to them, lesbianism and promiscuity, neither of which they endorse.[2] Also, these women's rejection of the term reflects a historical legacy that equates advocates of women's rights with imperialist tendencies.

The term "feminist" has no direct equivalent in Arabic. A translation of the term *nisa'iyya/niswiyya*, is equivalent to womanist, which is different from feminist. Those Arab women who use the English term "feminist" therefore sound foreign, and those who use the Arabic equivalent are uncomfortable with its exclusivist implications. Also, many women activists in the Arab world would rather redefine feminism in terms of its objectives of creating a more just society for both women and men.

Nevertheless, referring to Islamist women (and even secular ones) as feminists is not without contention. However, feminisms have already become an important feature of any polity, whether or not they are thus named. By referring to some activists as feminists, I am highlighting the common ground among different Egyptian women's political agendas. Otherwise this common ground would be lost in a polarized political space where the major actors and decision makers are still largely conservative men.

Muslim communities and countries in the Middle East and elsewhere actually boast a wide variety of feminist activism. Elsewhere I have elaborated on these (Karam 1998), but for my purposes here it will suffice to mention three main strands of feminist discourse among these groups: Islamist, religious, and secular. Together, they form a continuum of discourse, but they differ according to the methods advocated. Islamist feminism, itself encompassing a wide variety of beliefs and practices, maintains that the most effective means of combatting women's oppression and inequality is the exclusive use of existing Islamic sources (the Qur'an, the Prophet's sayings and doings, and the scholarly interpretations of religious texts). Religious feminists argue that all forms of religious resources are important in the fight against injustice, as long as they are amenable to being interpreted in an enlightened fashion, and coherent with international conventions. Secular feminists will not tolerate any reference to religion, believing such sources to be inherently oppressive to women, and potentially divisive for the formation of a unified woman's movement.

These groups also differ in their relationships with existing state structures in the Middle East. Islamist women, for example, see most of the ruling regimes as illegitimate, and thus stand in political opposition to them. Religious and secular feminists feel that states should play an active role in the process of women's empowerment and emancipation, and may cooperate selectively at times with them. Attitudes toward difference and inclusion also differ. Islamist feminists believe that to be one of them requires clear religious, political, and social commitments. Either you are one of them, or you are *not*, and hence potentially an enemy. Ironically, secular feminists share the same views. Nawal El-Saadawi, a physician and novelist, is a secular feminist who has been long touted in the Western world as Egypt's most famous feminist, followed by Aida Seif al-dawla, Gehan AbuZeid, and Iman Baybars. Religious feminists, on the other hand, are more inclusive of diversity—in fact, their entire credo is based on flexibility and an absence of restrictive or exclusive strategies. Theirs is the closest to a "live and let live" strategy, and they boast intellectuals such as Leila Ahmed, Mona Abusenna, and novelists Salwa Bakr and Noha Radwan.

The Background

Egyptian women have traditionally been extremely active politically, socially, and economically. Many are proud to boast of more than a century of clearly defined feminist activism. Feminism started to emerge in the context of colonialism (Egypt was first colonized by the French in the mid-1800s and then by the British from 1882 till 1923 nominally, and 1952 actually). British colonial rulers used the "sorry state of Egyptian women" as one of the yardsticks for the nation's overall underdevelopment, and as a justification for why Egyptians needed to be "civilized/colonized." Old guard Egyptians resisted the first rumblings on women's rights, since they could confirm colonial attitudes. Still today, advocates of women's rights must contend with accusations of cultural inauthenticity, "Westernization," and "immorality"—which potentially detract from the task at hand, and can make life more difficult for committed activists. At a time of Western cultural and political hegemony, most feminists are caught between two fires: resenting colonial hegemony on the one hand, while advocating for women's rights on the other.

Egyptian women obtained the right to vote in the mid-1950s after the 1952 revolution, during the socialist regime of President Gamal Abdel Nasser. Presently, women constitute more than 50 percent of the population but fewer than 5 percent of the parliamentary deputies.

Rural women have always toiled in the fields. Women constitute more than 50 percent of the labor force, excluding the informal sector where they dominate. Egyptian women, while moderately pleased with the legislation that guarantees equal wages and various benefits, criticize aspects of it such as the lack of citizenship rights for their children (especially for those married to non-Egyptian men).

Nevertheless, Egyptian women from all social classes are at least half of the students in today's universities. Egypt has at least two women ministers of state, women ambassadors, and an impressive cadre of intellectuals, novelists, academics, artists, affluent businesswomen, and innumerable civil society activists.

Zaynab Al-Ghazali

> It is true that I am over seventy [years of age] but my call has not been defeated. My
> voice will continue to ring till the last day of my life. I am still able to practice the
> Da'wa[3] through giving lessons to some of the Muslim sisters and attending Islamic
> conferences, and I pray to Allah to grant me success and help me to accomplish my
> desires to elevate Islam and Muslims
>
> —Al-Hashimi, *The Ideal Muslimah*

Zaynab Al-Ghazali's reputation as "a soldier of God" is almost legendary among
women and men Islamists. When the Nasser regime cracked down heavily on
the Muslim Brotherhood and almost decimated the Islamic movement in the
1950s and 1960s, Al-Ghazali almost single-handedly rebuilt support for it (both
in Egypt and abroad), and looked after the families of the jailed and dead.

Al-Ghazali's actively established the groundwork for an Islamist movement
in Egypt. Though she started her political life in a religious-cum-secular feminist
group in the 1920s, Al-Ghazali soon took to proselytizing for a politicized Islamic
consciousness. She set up the Muslim Women's Association (MWA) at the age of
eighteen, in 1936. Nasser continually harassed and eventually banned the MWA
and imprisoned and tortured her; her prison memoirs document the atrocities.
She has written innumerable articles and lectured extensively in Pakistan, the
United States, and Saudi Arabia and exerts a formidable influence on both men
and women Islamists in all parts of the Muslim world. Al-Ghazali's basic tenets
on Muslim women are a secular feminist's nightmare. She rejects a separate
"women's issue" within Islam and maintains that Islam's perception of men and
women is as a nature that has divided into two, and neither is complete without
the other. Al-Ghazali argues that "a good Muslim girl" has a responsibility toward
God and parents, who are holy and sacred and to whom she owes obedience. A
girl should accept, obey, and be passive until she must act as a religious beacon for
the rest of the community.

Al-Ghazali states that women have been led away from their "nature":

> Woman's role in society is to be a mother, to be a wife.... What has happened since we
> have left the circle of natural disposition to the circle of invention? For a few limited
> pennies we have sold our motherhood and then we ask about the role of women in
> society? What kind of a society is this where the home that forms the seed of the
> society has been ruined by tearing women between home and the workplace. (1985, 4)

Al-Ghazali sees this terrible state of affairs as a result of a Western conspiracy.
She warns:

> The West that has lied and fraudulently claimed that they have liberated women,
> will be faced with the natural end of the circle of time when things return to their
> natural order. Then they will know that they have destroyed both home and work
> the day they betrayed the world and called for the necessity of women being rented
> in order to obtain her food and drink from the fruits of her own labor, so she
> became a human distortion and an available commodity for the lust of the wolves.
> So do not be fooled by her being a Prime Minister. Women's skill in the rearing of
> her sons and preparing them for their leading and productive roles in society is far
> more valuable and useful. (1985, 4).

Like most Islamists, Al-Ghazali fails to distinguish between different Western influences when talking about "the forces of evil" and the "external threat" to Islam. She argues that Zionists are the external force dooming the Muslim world; they have "ordered Muslims to become 'hippies' and Muslim women to bare their bodies [as] singers and dancers" (Al-Ghazali 1983, 24).

Al-Ghazali continually emphasizes that women's main and indeed only role, "firstly and secondly and thirdly," is to be a good wife and mother who brings up the next generation of Muslim children.

Women's role during conflicts is a continuation of their roles as mothers and wives. They should fire up the male fighters. For example, Afghani women could contribute to the jihad[4] against the Russian occupation by "injecting the *mujahedin* (fighters) with enthusiasm which can renew the souls of *jihad* for *jihad*" (Al-Ghazali 1988b, 27). Although she refers to the Muslim woman *combatants* during the early years of Islam, contemporary Muslim women should "give hope with tender words." "Honest motherhood" is about as active as they need be. What kinds of roles did Al-Ghazali envisage for unmarried or childless women? Judging by her example (she is childless), childless women should become full-time soldiers of God.

Al-Ghazali literally holds women responsible for the sorry state of Islamic culture and society. In an article addressed to women, Al-Ghazali pontificates: "Yes my lady you are responsible for our dependency on those non-Muslims who call for disbelief, immorality and chaos. . . . You adorn yourself and rebel against our religion and all our inheritances. . . . Yes my lady you are responsible for the decline of Islamic culture" (quoted in Al-Hashimi 1990, 115). Because women are unable or unwilling to put all their energies into being good wives and good mothers, the family and home have suffered, and with it Islamic society. Women are, therefore, quite formidable and powerful figures, and their duties as wives and mothers are of paramount importance. "God in His infinite wisdom has created woman's natural disposition in such a way that she specializes in making a man happy and comfortable, so he [the man] can improve his productivity and do his duty wisely and observantly by her" (quoted in Al-Hashimi 1990, 115).

Why would a woman want to carry the double burden of family and work simultaneously? "My daughter, what have you got from the calls for equality, and what have you got for deviating from your disposition? . . . The disposition of women ordains [you] to live in order to build. . . . To build men . . . to build great women who build men to become a great *umma* [nation]" (quoted in Al-Hashimi 1990, 115). Women are indirect builders (but builders nevertheless) of the Muslim nation. Dismissing ideas about inequality, Al-Ghazali says that women are equal to men when it comes to faith and belief. God does not distinguish the efforts of the two sexes. So what more equality does the Muslim woman want? Al-Ghazali asks.

The irony lies not so much in what Al-Ghazali preaches, but in her own lifestyle. She "pledged to Allah on the day I established the Group (MWA) that I would never submit my life to anybody beside Him" (Al-Ghazali 1995, 14). Moreover, she describes her marriage as "only a contingent worldly event, but brotherhood in Allah is everlasting: it does not elapse nor can it be measured in the world and all that is therein" (1995, 169). She clearly implies that spreading the Islamic *Da'wa* or faith is more important than marriage. Is hers a very special case? Was she the only Muslim woman allowed to actively proselytize in the name of her faith?

Al-Ghazali divorced her first husband because she felt he was preventing her from being an Islamist activist (Ahmed 1992, 200). Since obtaining a divorce is extremely difficult for most women, her act is nothing short of amazing. Amazing, too, is her ability to separate her actions from her theory. She writes, "A woman asking her husband for divorce is a crime that deserves punishment,[5] for is there anything more terrible than a woman threatening the nest of her marriage and her motherhood?!" (1989, 48). Yet she openly admits she asked her first husband for divorce, and she stipulated to her second husband that he must not interfere in her Islamist activism. Thus, it is obvious that Al-Ghazali applies double standards: one to herself and another to other Muslim women. Her own essentially public role and her private life contradict all that she is preaching. Nevertheless, she remains a powerful figure.

Over time Al-Ghazali's position has changed significantly. In the early 1980s, Al-Ghazali began to talk of "choice" and acknowledge that women should determine how they wish to participate in society. She said,

> There is a [baseless] attempt to curtail Muslim women's roles in life. A Muslim woman can work on two levels: she can bring up her children in the spirit of Islam, and she must explain to them that their land in Palestine and Afghanistan is unjustly taken and God's orders are delayed, and that their inescapable duty is to change these corrupt circumstances in the Islamic world. The second level is that she herself joins in this *jihad*. It is up to the Muslim [woman] to balance it out and arrive at the most positive outcome. (Al-Ghazali 1985, 38)

Like her male Islamist colleagues (such as Qutb, Sheikh Mohammad Al-Ghazali, and Yusuf Al-Qaradawi), Zaynab Al-Ghazali argues that as long as Islamic law is absent, Muslims are in some state of war. In such a situation, women have an important and active role to play, which they must determine for themselves. Yet Al-Ghazali denies any inequality exists between men and women's roles; women's work in the name of Islam is a duty. These seeming contradictions underlie much of what Al-Ghazali has to say about women.

The subtle alteration in her discourse may well coincide with an increasing sense of urgency felt by the Islamists to reach their political goals more quickly. Al-Ghazali may have realized that the younger generation, less influenced by her, and saturated with certain Western influences, had to be involved on its own terms. Moreover, some of the secular activists of the time had proven that they could also succeed in attracting a growing number of members. The secular feminism of the 1980s and 1990s (e.g., that characterized by novelist and physician Nawal al-Sa'dawi) was gaining in momentum.

Safinaz Qazim

> I wish we had no feminism here [in Egypt] at all.
> —Safinaz Qazim, in an interview, October 1994

Qazim is rarely mentioned in the literature on women Islamists in Egypt. Though she does not have the influence and consequent "grandeur" of Al-Ghazali, Qazim remains a figure to be reckoned with. In her early fifties, she

learned from and was guided by Al-Ghazali, and is the link between her generation and the Islamists of the 1990s.

In our first meeting, I was struck by the fact that her bookshelf boasted a
picture of Khalid Al-Islambuli, Sadat's assassin. Qazim sat under that picture,
on what was obviously her favorite chair, to hold forth about Islamism and feminism. Since Sadat imprisoned her during his self-declared "purge" of all
oppositionists in September 1981, she views Al-Islambuli as a "liberator, who
freed me from [state] oppression and tyranny."

Qazim's impact is not as strong as that of her mentor because Al-Ghazali's
linkages with Hasan Al-Banna, the founder of the Muslim Brotherhood, have
lent her some of the latter's allure and legitimacy. Qazim claims no such historic
link to the Muslim Brotherhood. Moreover, as the first publicly active woman
Islamist, Al-Ghazali's reputation remains unrivaled. Al-Ghazali's Islamic education was more extensive than that of Qazim. The latter's education and training
was in journalism and the arts, and her Islamic knowledge is derived from her
extensive readings and studying of Islam. Many books have been written about
Al-Ghazali, but no one has yet written about Qazim.

Safinaz Qazim was highly impressed with Malcolm X, whom she was influenced by when she studied art in the United States in the 1960s. On her return to
Cairo, she campaigned vigorously for an Islamic society. Declining to join any
one group, Qazim levels her criticism and proposals for alternatives principally
through her pen.

Nevertheless, Qazim's viewpoints are interesting precisely because of what
differentiates her from Al-Ghazali. Qazim speaks as a Muslim woman who lived
in the West for a few years in the turbulent 1960s and came to Islam as a result of
contact with the Western world. As a Muslim, Arab, middle-class woman intellectual she faced negative Western reactions to all these aspects of her identity.

She levels her heaviest criticisms against all aspects of Muslim society which
she perceives as being "ape imitations of the West" (Qazim 1986, 21). She criticizes the dichotomy which she believes the West tries to impose, to discredit and
eliminate cultural authenticity and religion.

> In the face of Europe stands the "canceled" world with its cultures and beliefs,
> wherein all its achievements have been reduced to completing the tools necessary
> to imitate Europe—most important of which are "Westernization" and "Secu-
> larization." ... This so that the "canceled" world can come forward with its
> accreditation papers to be accepted within "Modernity": And in this canceled
> world, wars take place which end up in secular dictatorships which force their
> masses to take religion lightly and eliminate it from their worlds, if not forcing
> them in some instances to atheism. All this while whipping these countries into
> obedience so that they become dutiful "monkeys" obliged to imitate "Europe."
> (Qazim 1986, 21)

Unlike Al-Ghazali, Qazim alludes to her prison torment only in the context of
comparisons with life in general. She sees her prison experience as a testing of
her faith, and as a metaphor for the state of political and moral corruption the
country is in. "Prison for me is the emergency laws, and the exceptional laws that
allow the minister of interior to arrest and imprison a citizen without declaring
any reason!" (1986, 27). Qazim decries state power that treats people not as citizens, but rather as "hostages or captives."

She sees other civil institutions (such as human rights and civil liberties associations) as being no better. Qazim contends that these institutions include among their members people of "intense backwardness and ugliness [of character], and have a residue of suspicious and primitive behavior which abuses freedom and human rights" (1986, 28).

Qazim, like many Islamists, believes that both state and secular institutions are a failure, which is why she calls for an "Islamic solution" to all problems. The Islamic solution is attractive precisely because it is new and untried, in contrast to other avenues followed by the state and by secular organizations and found to be ineffective, corrupt, and hypocritical. Islamists maintain that one government shortcoming is its nonadherence to correct Islam and its adoption of secularism in some form or another. Since they construct secularism as a morally bereft and destructive ideology, they view all secular institutions as hopeless, corrupt failures.

Qazim, unlike Al-Ghazali, openly admits that women have been and are oppressed, as evidenced by women's ignorance of religion and of their rights and obligations within it. Were they knowledgeable, she argues, unhappiness caused by fighting with family, with society, and with culture would decrease, and women would be valued, respected, and stronger. She maintains that this oppression has little to do with their sex and more with general tyranny. Thus, she refuses to acknowledge it as simply a matter of women's oppression.

> There has been oppression against women, but that is a result of ignorance (*jahiliyya*) and barbarism (*hamajiyya*). These are pre-Islamic legacies. It is very important to make a distinction between our heritage (*irth*) and what actually takes place. It is not the oppression of man to woman, but the oppression of someone who does not fear God to a fellow human being. (Interview by author, October 1994)

She insists that "there are issues which are far more serious than women's oppression or inability to obtain her rights, like the prohibition against believing in the one God" (interview by author, October 1994). Here she refers to the impact of Western hegemony, which she perceives as being idolatry.

Qazim's opinions on feminism, or any so-called Western-inspired movement to secure women's rights, are predictable. Feminism arose from the excess repression and liberalization that Western societies underwent.

> I am one of [feminism's] most ardent enemies. There is a general principle within Islam that there must be justice. It follows that as a Muslim I can play and take a role in my society. I have no case that is "woman's"; rather, I have a case of a victim of injustice. It could be described that as a Muslim who *happens* to be a woman, I deal with a victim of injustice who also *happens* to be a woman. This is a fundamental difference with a feminist. A feminist works from the conviction and basis that she is aiding those of her sex. (Interview by author, October 1994)

Qazim's emphasis on justice is closely tied to her ideas on respect between members of the family and society at large, as well as between the state and citizens.

Qazim believes that feminism misrepresents and harms women. Feminism is divisive: "[it] ultimately leads to a fight between two camps: men and women." Feminism is as bad as, if not worse than, Zionism, and she equates the two with a "women's nationalism." Both, she says, claim a certain space as exclusively their own, at the expense of another segment of society (Qazim 1994a, 45). In an interview published in *Al-Ahram Weekly*, she says "I am all for women's liberation . . . a woman's commitment to shari'a is the highest degree of liberation a woman can achieve. It is true that many of the rights which shari'a grants to women are violated, but it is also true that women should strive to gain those rights. Women should seek those rights as human beings (2–8 March, 1995, 3). "Feminism chains women," she says, to a certain erroneous idea and alienates them from their "humanity."

Moreover, Qazim argues that God prefers women because of their child-bearing functions. Men, on the other hand, are preferred over women because of their physical strengths and their concomitant capacity to be financial providers. Hence, in this functional preference lies the equality between the sexes. "The basis in Islam is the equality between man and woman despite the admission of the difference between them. Difference does not mean inequality. . . . One should not desire the attributes of the other. For Allah is just. And ultimately there is balance" (Qazim 1994b: 103).

Regarding female circumcision, Qazim said it was too horrible to even begin to imagine. She opined that such practices are a residue of pre-Islamic times, and should therefore be gradually eradicated (interview with author, November 1995). She has never considered subjecting her daughter to this practice. Qazim comments that "it is ironical that the continuous attempts to associate female genital mutilation with Islam are made by Western countries where women had to suffer from the chastity belt for hundreds of years" (interview with Dina Ezzat, *Al-Ahram Weekly*, July 1994).

Qazim believes that some commandments in the Qur'an, such as those relating to the *hijab*, or the veil, or to husbands' rights to beat their errant wives are simply to be accepted without questioning. She says that "if God, in His holy book, says that the man can beat a woman for disobeying His orders, then a woman has to accept God's will" (*Al-Ahram Weekly*, July 1994). As for the veil, Qazim argues that it is an unquestionable Islamic injunction and thus, "primarily a matter of obedience." Also, the *hijab* forces men to deal with the veiled woman on an equal footing, because they will be attracted by the mental rather than the physical attributes of women. [6]

Qazim maintains that the veil enables women to have a pronounced and as open a public appearance as they wish and allows them all the rights accorded them by Islam. According to Qazim, Islam gives women many rights as long as they are obedient to God. Obedience to Allah's laws—as opposed to man-made ones—is a reaffirmation of cultural authenticity, and of unique identities as Muslims in a heathen world.

It is interesting to note that Qazim, like Al-Ghazali, divorced her husband. Neither of these women seems to be oppressed, weak, or ignorant of her rights. Both of these women *exercise* their rights and obtain the desired results. And therein lies the most crucial aspects of these two Islamist women's activism: strength of character, self-confidence, knowledge of religion and determination, and explicit views and goals for the future.

Heba Ra'uf

Heba Ra'uf is in her early thirties, a wife and mother of two, and a teaching assistant in the political science department at Cairo University. Having received a relatively exclusive Western (German and English) preuniversity education, Ra'uf exemplifies why Muslim women recourse to Islamism and why they find it to be empowering. Reflecting on her experience in a preuniversity German school, Ra'uf exclaims:

> Nobody has to explain to me what it means to be preached to, what missionarism is, or what it is like to have one's own culture ridiculed and demeaned by another! At school they [the foreign teachers] were adept at making us feel inferior. Though there was a chapel for Christian students to pray there once a week, they refused to give us a room to pray for our five prayers a day! Although other students were allowed to wear whatever they liked, I was not allowed to put on the proper *tarha* (head scarf), instead I was restricted in the way I covered my hair. . . . If you did not have a boyfriend you were very strange, in fact, something must be wrong with you and your customs that forbid this. They tried to impress upon us that they were the civilized Westerners, and that those of us who tried to be good Muslims were very strange. (Interview with author, May 1993)

Thus Islam allowed Ra'uf to reinstate her identity in the face of such disregard and enabled her to work through her anger and resentment. However, some of this anger springs from misunderstandings and misconceptions of Western society. For example, many Islamists perceive the open and "shameless" quest for homosexuality[7] to be normalized in Western cultures, and they see this as an indicator of the levels of moral degradation that the West has come to, and of what will happen to them if we espouse the same cultural and social beliefs that they do.

Misperceptions about the Western Other abound in Heba's Islamist ideas: "The top school curriculum setters in France are homosexuals!" Apparently, there is a fear that open homosexuality will lead to the spread of it, whereas containment (occurring discreetly) and public disdain will reduce the rate of spreading. "I don't want this openness, I am against homosexuality, let them practice it inside their homes!" (interview with author, October 1995).

Another perception of the Western Other has to do with ideas that the West purportedly has on motherhood. The West supposedly discredits and sees motherhood as unnecessary: "Twenty years from now, motherhood in the West will be a matter of adoption, and adoption under the guise of a do-gooder charitable goal [said in a very sarcastic manner]. Why is there a negative birth rate in France? Because motherhood is becoming unnecessary!" (interview with author, November 1994).

Armed with her negative experiences and misconceptions, Ra'uf explains that she felt she had to make a choice. Entering the university, Ra'uf realized she was going to choose how she would live the rest of her life. Either she would "give in" and become Western oriented, or she would seek an alternative authenticity from her own cultural background—Islam. She chose the latter. Ra'uf sought a means to assert both her independence vis-à-vis unwelcome patterns of self-definition and simultaneously identify with a legitimate self-affirmative mission. Full of her memories of oppressive Westernism, she opted for some form of vindication against Westernism in all its forms that provided her with a sanctified sense of value and purpose.

Ra'uf, who was tutored by the two giants of Islamist activism, Zaynab Al-Ghazali and Safinaz Qazim, represents the younger generation of Egyptian Islamist women activists and leaders. However, she does not share identical points of departure or even conclusions. Ra'uf's discourse differs significantly from that of her male and female colleagues who address women as, at best, part and parcel of a larger struggle and, at worst, of secondary importance.

Many Islamist men and women activists deny outright there is a "woman's issue" since, it is argued, Islam refers to the issues of *bani Adam,* or the human race. Ra'uf, while supporting the larger struggle, nevertheless clearly and yet subtly gives women's issues some centrality in a number of ways.

First, Ra'uf's respect for traditional authoritative Islamic texts allows room for a reading that offers refreshing and novel interpretations on women's roles. Ra'uf confidently argued and subsequently *proved*, that according to highly valued Islamic scholarship, women are allowed to occupy the highest public functions *as long as they are qualified*. Distinctions therefore should not be based on gender, but on qualifications. Ra'uf effectively backed up the claim that qualified women were entitled to occupy such positions as heads of states or judges. This is an extremely contentious point, however, especially among the ranks of the Muslim Brotherhood itself. By adopting this stance, while simultaneously rendering herself a leader of many of the younger Islamist women, Ra'uf combines courage with shrewd political maneuvering.

Second, Ra'uf's public stance, whether with younger female Islamist conscripts or via her work as an editor of the woman's page in *Al-Sha'b*,[8] highlights her relatively liberal stance. According to her, "women become more influential in traditional societies in transition characterized by a lack of a stable base. The weighing scale should be God, for if affairs are left to men only they will be despots, and if left only to women, they will be malignant (interview by author, November 1994). Ra'uf laughs at mosque preachers who talk only about women's duties and obligations and ignore politics. This kind of proselytizing is unproductive because it separates women's issues from broader political participation.[9]

Third, Ra'uf's standpoint on women, a cornerstone of her overall Islamist advocation, is relatively innovative. In an interview with the *Middle East Report*, she argues that women's liberation in Muslim societies "necessitates a revival of Islamic thought and a renewal within Islamic jurisprudence." Moreover, in the same article she claims that she is not aiming at reconstructing Islamic law (as opposed to deconstructing it), but "actually defending Islam from stagnation and bias" (Interview with Heba Ra'uf Ezzat 1994, 25–26).

Ra'uf adamantly refuses to recognize the legitimacy of feminism, claiming it is divisive and individualistic. Feminism is "not necessary," since Islam is not only a way of life but a "very political existence." Moreover, feminism is but a vestige of the West that does not apply to Islamic cultures. Besides, Ra'uf argues,

Feminism aims only at women, has one ever heard of "masculinism"?! In order to address the whole issue of women's oppression, one must address the whole society. It is both men and women who have to be targeted, especially since we must aim to change the traditional way of thinking of the whole fabric of society. (Interview with author, September 1994)

Effectively, Ra'uf maintains that an Islamic liberation movement targets men and women together and aims to change the existing mentalities that result in gender oppression.

On The Family

Relativism, a theoretical ill resulting from Western influence, means, according to Heba, that calamities like homosexuality become normal and acceptable to the rest of society:

> That is my problem with postmodernism—there is no room for religion at all because there is this denial of absolutes. There have to be certain absolutes in our society, otherwise everything becomes relative, and anything permissible, and, even worse, you become the idiot who is being pigheaded, and the person in the wrong. Islam is a combination of the absolute with the relative. (Interview with author, November 1994)

Ra'uf ties relativism to the loss of extended families, the lack of importance accredited to the family, and the growth of individualism, another negative heritage of Westernism. She claims that Westernism and certain Islamic traditions emphasize the family as a purely functional social unit. Both ignore the vital political role that the family has. "Instead of elevating the role of the family to regard it to be as important as any public activism, the family was denigrated as a 'private' matter."[10]

Ra'uf argues that alternatively, Islamic political theory considers the family as an essential political unit and the basis of society. In her schema, the proper Muslim family becomes the means to women's liberation.

Ra'uf argues that political authority should be vested in the family, not the state. The state, a religiously corrupt regime, is ill equipped to handle all the responsibilities expected of it. Further, Westernization has defiled the government's policies, resulting in the spreading of destructive Western values of individualism, which have contributed to the breakdown of Islamic family values. It was precisely these values of solidarity and mutual respect, protection, and status for family members, which offered women protection. Their absence is one of the reasons behind women's oppression.

Ra'uf's central argument is that the family unit is a microprocess of the state, with the same procedures for management and articulation. In undemocratic societies the family is particularly important because it is the one public/private institution that the state *cannot* ban. "No state can ever forbid people to have families."[11] Thus, the family effectively becomes the main bulwark of freedom for all its members against state oppression. Inherent in this argument is that the family also becomes the guarantor of its members' freedoms.

Ra'uf's second theme is that the dichotomy between public and private (a vestige of some Western feminist and anthropological theories) is a falsehood, since the private—the family—is a microcosm of the larger public arena in which power is exercised. Ra'uf thus effectively appropriates the feminist dictum of "the personal is the political," and adds the dimension of the family: the personal (woman) is the public (family) is the political (state). Further, she contends that just as *shura* (consultation) should be realized in the running of the state, so it should also take place in the running of the family. As Ra'uf states, "Islam considers family as the starting point for any real Islamic society. The same values [as these operating in the macropublic arena] should dominate."[12]

Ra'uf argues that women should be actively involved in the running, manage-ment, and defense of their Islamic nation (*umma*). "Military service should become obligatory for women as well as for men," she states, since the Muslim nation is effectively in a state of war. Ra'uf claims that "raising children is a very important political function," and thus:

> Family is not an obstacle; it can be turned into an obstacle. Women who stay at home bringing up children, protect that unit [the family] in society; giving their children certain probably positive values. Then these women can go and perform other public and equally important roles. No one has twenty-four hours [a day] to devote to only one sphere.[13]

Although Ra'uf's statement directly contradicts Al-Ghazali's earlier affirmations, she obviously idealizes the family, notably with regard to its liberating potential for women. She ignores the fact that much of the oppression and violence women suffer is a result of the internalization of certain harmful social norms and their practice *within* families. Practices such as female circumcision, for example, are carried out at the behest of mothers on their own daughters. Though the state plays a role in institutionalizing oppressive patriarchal struc-tures, to idealize the family in opposition to the state is to perpetrate the same dichotomy of thought that Ra'uf criticizes—"We must stop thinking and seeing things in dichotomies."[14]

But one must keep in mind that Ra'uf's is primarily a political message against the existing state structure, and an attempt to formulate Islamic women's liber-ation. Taking the family as the central unit of analysis and action, Ra'uf appeals to generally acceptable values, while simultaneously cloaking a woman-centered appeal. It is not feasible for her to be forthright, since she risks direct confronta-tion with her male colleagues and with current Islamist treatises. Hers is the innovative but veiled language of the minority within the Islamist current. Nevertheless, it remains significant that she attempts to develop this minority discourse from the podium of a majority force, the wide popular social base that the Muslim Brotherhood occupies in present-day Egypt.

Ra'uf describes her goal as changing the dominant paradigm "from within." She respects the traditional sources, while simultaneously seeking their reinter-pretation and innovation. Similarly, she strategically places herself within the dominant Islamist trend, but actively works to promote her version of what women should be doing. Ra'uf presents a personal political example, legitimized by a tactically placed religious discourse.

Though Ra'uf continues to amass support for her opinions, especially from women student circles, the consistency and effectiveness of her views remain questionable. Ra'uf's own self-definition as an "Islamist" fluctuates depending on her audience. Within the space of a few weeks she described herself as an "Islamist" in a personal interview, then retracted and negated the term, then described herself as one. If she is prepared to compromise on her self-definition, will she do the same with her opinions on the necessity to reinterpret and innovate on issues relating to women? Her current standpoint is motivated by political ambition. When faced with the exigencies of *realpolitik,* her advocacy of "an Islamic women's liberation movement" may end up as nothing more than what Egyptians would call *ahlam al-siba,* "dreams of youth."

Significantly, Ra'uf has gradually but definitively shifted away from the patriarchal emphasis of Al-Ghazali and Qazim's main arguments. Though much of her discourse carries within it the vestiges of anti-Westernism, and especially antifeminism, she nevertheless elaborates and emphasizes women's roles. She maintains that there is no such thing as a separate women's issue, but she develops an elaborate structure that serves to protect and enhance women's sociopolitical roles and rights, and that of the family. By intentionally breaking the barrier between public and private, Ra'uf has quite cleverly created a way out of the glorification of motherhood as women's only role. She thus implies that *motherhood and the family are political roles.* By stating it in such a way she is deconstructing and reconstructing Muslim women's roles. It can be correctly argued, however, that Ra'uf's advocacy for the role of political mothers is merely what Al-Ghazali has typified for a long time. However, Al-Ghazali has herself occupied political motherhood while preaching domesticity and an indirect political role as the primary role for other women. Ra'uf on the other hand has theorized the role, lives it, and sees it as part and parcel of any woman's involvement within Islamism. Moreover, if the family is the political arena and the constituent of a state, then sisters are also capable of playing an important guiding political role as members of this family-state.[15]

Ra'uf has sought a relatively more liberating discourse of empowerment from within an Islamist hegemonic paradigm, effectively creating a subnarrative to the grander narratives of Islam. In arguing for women's liberation from within that hegemonic paradigm, she has attempted to make a break, which is in apparent contradiction to her argument that women do not need a separate issue. By emphasizing the family, Ra'uf is seeking to bridge "the gap" between men and women and argue for a collective (Muslim) enterprise, in contrast to Western individualistic and divisive feminism.

Men and women Islamists consistently uphold the dichotomy in analysis and presentation: good/bad, Muslim/Western (or non-Muslim), legitimate/non-legitimate, public/private, man/woman. By constantly maintaining these binarisms, Islamists are using their own forms of reflexivity, which is part and parcel of their own discursive strategies and disciplinary power. To be with them is to be good, Muslim, legitimate, public, and male; to be against them is bad, Western, illegitimate, private, and female.

By employing such divisive binarisms as a means (intentional or otherwise) of disciplinary power, Islamists accomplish two things. First, they are continually strengthening their power base by delineating who and what they are against. And second, they are co-opting all the "womanpower" they need to carry out what is effectively an Islamic revolution. This latter aspect of co-opting womanpower, however, is done with a built-in safety mechanism: the justification *to legitimately exclude them later on.* For not only has the domestic sphere become glorified, but motherhood is now the ultimate political occupation which only women can excel at. Ra'uf's thesis of women's liberation via the family thus sanctions the bases that Islamists, once in power, can then tell their women members to continue their jihad and *da'wa within* the politicized family. So women are not told to "go back to the homes," because in a sense they never left the home.

By Way of Conclusion

One cannot be an Islamist woman activist without wearing the veil, which is taken as acceptance of and devotion to Islamism. I have yet to meet an unveiled Islamist feminist. But Islamist feminists do not all wear the same form of *hijab*. On the contrary, in the case of Al-Ghazali, Qazim, and Ra'uf, it seems that the more they advocate women's rights, the more stringent the form of veil. Al-Ghazali, for example, often satisfies herself with a simpler *hijab*, while Ra'uf wears the *khimar*.[16]

Similarly, Islamist feminists do not all wear their ideas in the same fashion. Although Al-Ghazali champions some ideal of womanhood, hers nevertheless remains a traditional visualization of women as obedient wives, wonderful mothers, and great soldiers of God. The contradictions between her own public and assertive role and the private obedient role that she advocates for Muslim girls and women delegitimizes much of what she says. Nevertheless, Al-Ghazali remains an Islamist pioneer, one who has tutored and mothered generations of Islamist men and women. As Ra'uf herself once said, "She is our mother and teacher." Also important to keep in mind is that Al-Ghazali's ideas on women did not remain static throughout her career. In fact, her conceptualization of women's roles witnessed a gradual shift in the 1980s in response to the exigencies of the political enterprise and the demand for a broader power base, which necessitated a more active participation of women in Islamist movements.

The Islamist discourse of the 1970s was capable of reaching and mobilizing Qazim, who, though sympathetic with the Muslim Brotherhood's ideology, remained unattached to any party or group. Qazim wholeheartedly shares Al-Ghazali's belief that Islamism is the only way forward for all Muslim societies. Moreover, both women share the view, albeit formulated differently, that the current Egyptian state is totally subservient to, or influenced by, corrupt Western ideologies. Both decry the savagery of the state in their own way, as well as emphasize its total delegitimation as a structure of authority.

As far as feminism is concerned, Qazim's ideas are far more elaborate, and hence critically targeted, than Al-Ghazali's. The reasons for this lie in the fact that feminism—and especially a secularized and Westernized version of it— became more problematic at the same time that Islamism itself became a dominant feature of Egyptian political life, during the mid-1970s and 1980s. Furthermore, with both a literary background and a spell in the United States, Qazim was far more exposed to the Western feminist rhetoric dominant at the time (e.g., on issues such as the right to abortion, to premarital sexual relations, gay rights and homosexuality), which she took to represent all feminisms. The latter meant that while she was more prepared than Al-Ghazali to recognize and admit the oppression of women, she was more vehement and clearer in her opposition to the manner in which "feminism" is propagated. Where she goes further than any other Egyptian feminist is in her visualization of feminism as a sister to Zionist ideology, and part of a grander "Euro-Ameri-Zionism."

Ra'uf constitutes a continuity with Al-Ghazali and Qazim insofar as she herself is a disciple of Muslim Brotherhood thought who believes that Islam is the only solution and sees the power of the state as repressive and illegitimate. Ra'uf, Al-Ghazali, and Qazim are all in the same continuum insofar as they share and perpetrate the dichotomous visualization of Islamist thinking, with all its resulting exclusion of the ideas of the Other. All three women are popular leaders with their own set of disciples, furthering Islamism by using and developing their disciplinary power and remaining firmly under—and benefiting from—Islamist hegemony in Egyptian society.

Where Ra'uf breaks with her former mentors—male and women activists—is in her use of these dichotomizing strategies and hegemonic framework to argue for a more openly feminist stance. And here feminism is used in the sense in which I defined it earlier on: as an awareness of women's oppression because of their gender, and the willingness to directly undermine this oppression and create an egalitarian society. Ra'uf seemingly argues for an authoritative family to replace the state, and a political mother within that family-state structure as the authority. By so advocating, Ra'uf is simultaneously calling for a mechanism that would protect women, while paving the road for women to become leaders within it.

Effectively, when looking at Islamist feminism we began with "natural dispositions," moved to the dictatorship of society and state by Euro-Ameri-Zionism, and ended up with family states and political mothers. Contemporary politics indicates that political motherhood will emerge as a triumphal norm adaptable to and possibly adopted by many other feminists across the board. The essence of this position is that it builds a bridge between what is sacred and what is practical for many women of today. As such, it has the potential to build bridges between the different forms of women's convictions, allowing for their belief in the sanctity of motherhood while entitling them to public participation and, indeed, politicizing all these "traditional" roles and rendering one and all a moral and political obligation. Thus, the irony would be that whatever the fate of Islamist politics in Egypt and the rest of the Arab world, political motherhood may survive as the strongest legacy yet—of Islamism.

Notes

1. The contents of this article are elaborated in Karam 1998.
2. Islam, like the other monotheistic faiths, does not condone homosexuality. Islamists in turn, including the women activists among them, reject homosexuality as an aberration of what God ordained. It is important to note, however, that most feminists in Egypt (as in many parts of the Muslim world) rarely come out openly in support of homosexuality; the whole issue remains largely shrouded in taboo.
3. *Da'wa* can be broadly translated as the call of Islam, or the call to Islam; it also means invitation.
4. Literally *jihad* means struggle. Originally, *jihad* was seen to refer to the spiritual struggle that all believers must undergo to purify their souls. In later years, the term was used to denote "holy war" or struggles against nonbelievers, enemies of Islam, or illegitimate rulers.
5. In this case she advocates the Qur'anic stipulation of the husband beating the disobedient wife, which she elaborates in her article.
6. On the complex arguments on the veil, see Karam 1996.
7. The Arabic word for homosexuality is *shudhudh*, which means deviance.
8. *Al-Sha'b* is a weekly opposition newspaper published by an alliance of the Muslim

Brotherhood Party and the Labour Party, a relatively old socialist agenda turned sympathetic to the right.

9. Statement made during the International Conference on Populations and Development (ICPD), September 1994.
10. Ra'uf elaborated on this during a talk given at the International Conference on Population and Development (ICPD), which was held in Cairo in September 1994. Ra'uf shared a panel with a high-ranking member of the Islamist-dominated Labour Party, an indication of her own status in and among the movement.
11. Statement made by Ra'uf during ICPD, September 1994.
12. ICPD, September 1994.
13. ICPD, September 1994.
14. Statement made during ICPD, September 1994.
15. This last statement is my own elaboration.
16. Whereas the *hijab* is diverse, it consists mostly of a scarf around the face, which covers the hair and the neck and may extend to cover the bosom as well. The rest of the dress can vary—from a long shirt over loose trousers (or even tight jeans) to skirts that start at just below the knee or go all the way to completely cover the legs. A *khimar*, however, is not as diverse and is stricter: the scarf, which covers the hair and neck, extends sometimes to just above the knees, and the dress is almost always loose and flowing down to the feet. Also unlike the varied colorful nature of the *hijab*, the *khimar* tends to be gray, blue, or brown.

part IV.

Righted Bodies:
Discipline, Excess,
Pleasure

17

Confronting Double Patriarchy: Islamist Women in Turkey

Burçak Keskin

Turkish politics has witnessed a clash between secularism and Islam, which is identified with the struggle of modernity vis-à-vis "traditional backwardness,"[1] since the foundation of the Republic in 1923.[2] The founding elite—the Kemalists[3]—equated modernity with European manners, and traditionalism with the Ottoman past and Islamic values. Women's bodies became the crucial site manifesting the conflict between Kemalist secularism and Islamist activism because women in Republican Turkey, like their counterparts in other nation-state building processes (Chatterjee 1993, Yuval-Davis and Anthias 1989), were identified as the major signifiers of new national values.[4]

In this paper, I explore women's agency in Turkish Islamic revivalism with close attention to the *new veiling movement* of the 1980s. My argument is threefold. First, I maintain that Islamist women's veiled presence in the public sphere challenges the legitimacy of the secular Republican regime and hence receives a severe opposition rather than a warm "sisterhood" welcome from the secular women groups. Second, I argue that some women within Islamic circles are deliberately (re)defining their identity with reference to Islamic sources and thus threatening the Islamist elite's patriarchal domination. Last, I conclude that the combination of these two distinct forms of confrontation, which I term "double patriarchy," constrains Islamist women's chances for political equality.

To explore these arguments, I first locate the Islamist women's movement in the spectrum of Turkish women's activism. I then discuss how the Islamist woman's identity is simultaneously defined vis-à-vis the Kemalist image of the *new Turkish woman* and the Islamist construct of *traditional woman*. Last, I focus on particular events, illustrating how the Islamist women's identity claims are curtailed "doubly" by the patriarchal Islamist elite and also by the secular—and more specifically, the Kemalist—women.

Mapping Out the Women's Movement Terrain in Turkey

Women and Nation-State Building

Feminist activism in Turkey dates back to the 1870s when urban women in the Ottoman Empire began to publish journals demanding women's equal access to the political and economic sphere.[5] In the following years, women actively participated in public affairs, especially during the First World War (1914–1918) and the War of Independence (1919–1923). They mobilized rallies, worked as nurses, and served as soldiers carrying ammunition to the front. After the establishment of the Republic in 1923, the Kemalists felt the necessity to assimilate women's activism into the secular nationalist rhetoric. Ömer Çaha argues that such assimilation not only provided the Kemalists with a vanguard in launching their radical secularization reforms, but also co-opted a strong rival with the capacity to mobilize resources autonomous from the state (1996, 115–116). This interpretation, I shall argue, is insightful but limited, because it underestimates nationalism's approach to womanhood.

Floya Anthias and Nira Yuval-Davis are among the first to point out the political significance of women's maternal duties. Women's role as the fundamental caregiver for younger generations, they argue, transforms the mother-child relationship into an essential venue for the perpetuation of cultural identity (1989, 7). National liberation movements, in turn, define their struggle as being waged to protect the *mother*land or women's honor. Women thus mark the boundaries of national differences. In a similar vein, Partha Chatterjee argues that nationalism in the colonial world separated the cultural domain into two spheres: the material sphere, in which the colonial state prevailed, and the spiritual sphere, which belonged to the colonized. Women, due to their close association with traditions, resided in the latter and constituted the central *objects* of national liberation struggles, because the anticolonial movements aimed at "cultivat[ing] the material techniques of modern Western civilization while retaining and strengthening the distinctive spiritual essence of the national culture" (1993, 120).

Valentine Moghadam asserts in her study of the Middle Eastern societies that "women's emancipation type of revolutions" demand that women take active roles in the break with the "backward" ancien régime. "The family type of revolutions," on the other hand, underline women's domestic roles and make them into passive actors in public life (1993, 94–95). Deniz Kandiyoti (1992, 240–248) analogously argues that women's emancipation may be endorsed as indigenous and legitimate by secular nationalisms or denounced as alien and impious by Islamic movements or state-supported fundamentalisms. With these arguments in mind, I now turn to the discussion of how the Kemalists utilized the "women's question" to mobilize support for themselves.

Kemalism and Turkish Women

In establishing a nation-state over the ashes of the Ottoman Empire, the Kemalists adopted Ernest Renan's magic formula: "to remember and to forget certain parts of the history." They wanted the new nation to *remember* the sufferings of the Ottoman military and political decline. Associating the decline with the Ottoman sultanate and its theocratic rule, they demanded that the new nation *forget* that the modernization and "secularization" efforts dated back to the late eighteenth century. They instead argued that the Ottoman past was Islamic, traditional, and hence backward. The Kemalists further claimed that Turks had a more egalitarian society before they accepted Islam, and they promised to bring modernity to the nation by reviving the pre-Islamic Turkish tenets. Given their precarious political power, they could not ban Islamic practices officially but only discouraged its public representations, especially in the very visible target of the woman's veil. The celebrations on national holidays were, for instance, marked by the physical exercises of unveiled young women. In the 1930s, the Kemalist women's organizations launched antiveiling campaigns in which they distributed overcoats and urged veiled women to wear these instead of the traditional *çarşaf*[6] (Çaha 1996, 130). The unveiled woman's body soon became the symbol of women's emancipation.

Kemalist reforms demanded Turkish women join their male peers in elevating Turkey to "the level of contemporary civilizations"[7] and in eradicating the Ottoman legacy in the society. The adoption of a slightly modified version of the Swiss Civil Code in 1926 was an outright manifestation of these objectives. The code thoroughly redefined gender relations and provided the wife with equal footing to the husband in the family affairs. Similarly, coeducational schools were opened in 1924 not only to create a skilled female labor force but also to break away from the Islamic principles that legally justified women's seclusion in the Ottoman Empire.[8] The introduction of universal suffrage in 1934 further endorsed a sexually mixed public realm that challenged the Ottoman notion of public.

The Kemalist reforms conceptualized a "yeni Türk kadını" (new Turkish woman)[9] with a Westernized, modern, secular appearance and a highly visible public participation. She was not only the *signifier* of the break with the Ottoman past but also the *transmitter* of the new national culture. Though this identity was periodically challenged in the following years—especially after 1980—it nevertheless continued to be the reference point in mapping out the landscape of Turkish women's activism.

Diversification of the Turkish Women's Movement

The Turkish political spectrum was centered on the Kemalist principles,[10] but the rapid industrialization and subsequent migration to the cities resulted in political polarization and fragmentation. Various Marxist and socialist groups emerged in the mid-1960s and argued that Turkey should be elevated from the Kemalist bourgeois to a socialist/communist level. Depending on their ideological commitments, these groups occupied the left of the center. Islamism and ultranationalism, on the other hand, characterized the right of center. These groups distinguished themselves by their conservative agendas based, respectively, on religious values and a racially-defined Turkish identity.

The political fragmentation affected women's movements as well. The leftist activism generated numerous women's groups that basically celebrated a blend of Kemalist principles with Marxist ideals. When the 1980 military coup d'état crushed the leftist opposition, these women had the chance to establish autonomous organizations and to question the way Marxism and socialism treat women. Some of them kept their previous ideological allegiances and called themselves "socialist feminists." Others, calling themselves "independent feminists," decided to organize autonomously from the state and the surviving leftist organizations, claiming to tackle women's problems from the standpoint of women (Sirman 1989).

The Islamist women occupied another pole in this fragmented sphere with the intention to combine Islamic communitarian values with modern technology. The secularists often labeled them as "rightists," or, even worse, as "reactionaries" who wanted to bring back the decadent Ottoman rule. The

Islamist women had to negotiate their social roles within their own communities as well. Before dwelling upon the Islamist women's struggles, it is necessary to focus briefly on the movement's historical trajectory and predominant action frames.

The Islamist Women's Movement in Modern Turkey

Delineating the Boundaries of the Movement

There is no one Islamist women's movement in Turkey. While some women are organized under the auspices of the pro-Islamic parties,[11] others work at women's organizations or magazines or participate in religious brotherhoods that have varying degrees of contact with the pro-Islamist parties. Still others have no or minimum connection to formal organizations. One should therefore approach the Islamist women's movement "as a network of groups and organizations prepared to mobilize for protest actions to promote (or to resist) social change; and, [of] individuals who attend protest activities or contribute resources without necessarily being attached to the [specific] movement groups or organizations" (Rucht 1996, 186).

There is also a great degree of divergence among the Islamist women on crucial social issues such as the composition of a proper Islamic life or the nature and extent of their relations with secular groups. Islamist women's identity claims therefore swing between submissive assertions such as "the Islamist woman should stay at home and look after her children"[12] and moderate statements such as "the Islamist woman should reconcile her everyday social practices with her Islamic duties and responsibilities."[13] Though the Islamist women diverge on women's social and political agency, one can argue that they all agree on one point—the necessity to change the political system in line with Islamic principles of governance (Göle 1997, 96) which would win them equal footing in educational, economic, and political spheres.

A Brief Historical Trajectory of the Islamist Women's Movement

After the Second World War, Turkey witnessed rapid industrialization accompanied by rural-to-urban migration. The urbanization brought about new social problems as the migrants suffered from social and cultural uprootedness. Some migrants turned to leftist or ultranationalist groups and others to the political parties that supported Islamic values. The social unrest in urban centers during the 1970s culminated in street fights, especially between radical left and ultranationalist groups. On September 12, 1980, the Turkish military intervened to assume political power, claiming that they did so to avoid a possible civil war. Crushing leftist—and the ultranationalist activism, the military regime unintentionally led to the emergence of "alternative publics" such as Kurds, Islamists, and feminists. These groups questioned the artificial homogeneity of Turkish national identity and struggled relentlessly for greater representation in the public sphere (Alankuş-Kural 1997, 7).

Faced with these challenges, the military realized the need to redefine the Kemalist principles. The new blueprint, known as *Türk-Islam Sentezi* (Turkish-Islamic Synthesis), aimed to co-opt Islam into the nationalist rhetoric. Its proponents asserted that the Turkish nation—best characterized by family, mosque, and military—declined as a result of excessive mimicry of Western ways of life. To resurrect the nation, the state, they argued, should take an active role in formal education. Islam was redefined as the essence of national culture, and mandatory religion courses were introduced at all levels of primary and high school education (Toprak 1990, 10–12).

It is crucial to note here that the military did not intend to islamize the society but to utilize Islam for the interests of the state.[14] The Turkish-Islamic Synthesis in the end failed to reestablish the secular Kemalist hegemony but strengthened the Sunni groups at the expense of other Muslim minorities—especially the Alevis[15]—and ethnic communities (Yavuz 1998, 140–148). Though the military tried to reverse the concessions given to the Islamist Sunni groups, they could not do so before the Islamic Other of the Kemalism mobilized enormous support among urban dwellers. Bearded men in loose Islamic attire appeared for the first time in the streets and later were elected to the, parliament where they minimally concealed their Islamist stand, often by donning a modern suit. There was also a tremendous increase in the number of veiled students attending universities, which had always been thought of as "the castles of [Turkish] modernity" (Göle 1996, 84).

The first conflict over veiling was reported in 1968 when Hatice Babacan, a female student in Ankara University Divinity School, was dismissed for wearing a head scarf to school. A group of students protested the decision, but state authorities did not give in to their demands to allow veiling at school. Similar incidents were reported throughout the 1970s, but it was only a decade later that the veiled students came to be considered an important threat to Republican values.

In 1982, the Higher Education Council[16] decided to ban the veil at university campuses. The increasing protests forced the council to allow the wearing of *türban*—a scarf that covers the hair but not the chest. However, the Islamist women refused to don the *türban*, claiming it was not in accordance with Islamic principles.[17] Six years later in 1988, the council reissued the ban on veiling, but the parliament passed a law that allowed "the covering of head and body on the basis of religious faith."[18] A few months later, however, the Constitutional Court[19] amended the law, ruling that the veil was a *political symbol* rather than a require-ment of a *religious faith* (Abadan-Unat 1998, 297–298; Özdalga 1998, 41–46). The decision was met with further demonstrations across the country.

The veiling issue once more became a hot topic in the mid-1990s, when the pro-Islamic Welfare Party participated in the coalition government as a senior partner. The opposition between the Islamists and secularists reached its zenith when Merve Kavakçı, an elected member of the Virtue Party, came to the parlia-ment to be sworn in with her veil on. Vehement public protests followed, and about a year later Kavakçı lost her parliamentary seat because of a technicality[20] (Göçek 2000).

The major distinguishing feature of the veiling protests in the post-1980 period was that most, if not all, of the public participants were women in contrast to the male Islamist protesters of a decade earlier.[21] Veiled women became more visible and militant than ever before, organizing sit-ins, participating in demon-strations, and even starting death-fasts against the ban on veiling. They were the invisible hands behind the electoral victory of the Welfare Party in 1994 as well.

The party had 1 million registered women members, constituting one third of its total number of registered members. Though the women did not hold any official position in the local or central party organizations at that time, they worked relentlessly during the electoral campaign. In the 1998 national elections, the Virtue Party, the heir of the Welfare Party, fielded two unveiled women, as well as Kavakçı and another veiled woman, as candidates. It now has three unveiled women on its central committee. Secularists frequently argued that the Virtue Party's unveiled M.P.s and members serve as tokens to demonstrate that it is not a threat to Turkish democracy. Though I agree with this assessment, I find it more fruitful to pose the question in terms of women's agency within the party. Women are indeed more fully involved in Islamic parties than their secularist counterparts, but their political demands, as will be argued later, are silenced or dismissed to a large extent. It is thus necessary to take into account the *quality* as well as the *quantity* of women's political participation in assessing the scope of Islamist women's activism.

Islamist women's identity claims are expressed not only in the pro-Islamic party programs but also in the journals in which Islamist women are published. Though the women do not own these publications, they nevertheless write almost all of the articles in them. The most well-known journals are *Kadın ve Aile* (Woman and family), *Bizim Aile* (Our family), *Mektup* (The letter) and *Kadın Kimliği* (Women's identity). *Kadın ve Aile,* which is affiliated with the Nakşibendi brotherhood, has the highest circulation and also maintains an Internet version (http://www.aitco.com/islam/kadin-aile). *Bizim Aile,* on the other hand, is published by the women of the Nurcu brotherhood (Acar 1991, 283). *Mektup,* which is also associated with the Nakşibendis, promotes the most radical view. *Kadın Kimliği,* on the other hand, conveys moderate and commercialized messages, with articles on veiled women's weight problems and makeup concerns outweighing the sections devoted to political activism.

A small number of Islamist women work as columnists or reporters for the leading Islamist newspapers, such as *Zaman* (Time), *Akit* (Contract), and *Milli Gazete* (National newspaper), and for journals such as *Aksiyon* (Action), *Köprü* (Bridge), *Islam, Icmal* (Epitome), *Öğüt* (Advice). As will be elaborated latter, these women have to comply with the publication's general approach to women's issues. Their supervisors usually expect them to write features on issues concerning family and the children, and their "hard" news reporting is limited to accounts of the women-only meetings organized by the Islamist groups (*Pazartesi* March 1999, 10–11). Despite these restrictions, the Islamist women have been able to make their way through the Islamist media and to document their own experiences on what it means to be a veiled woman in Republican Turkey, a perspective that is consciously and systematically overlooked in the secularist media.

The New Islamist Woman Identity in Turkey: Modern but not Necessarily Secular

Islamist women's writings reveal that the *Islamist woman* identity is constructed in opposition to two images—a "positive," secularist image of the *new Turkish woman* and a "negative," Islamist construct of the "gelenekçi kadın" (*traditional woman*).

The *Islamist woman* first distinguishes herself from the "modern" unveiled "new Turkish woman" who acts in accordance with secular norms of conduct.

Idealizing the Islamic golden age, the *Islamist woman* then acquires a unique selfhood drawing from the piety and obedience of the Prophet's daughter, Fatimah, and from the outspokenness of his favorite wife, Aisah. For the *Islamist woman*, the veil symbolizes the connection to early women of Islam rather than the submission to patriarchy or another form of *human* power.

The *Islamist woman* identity is then complemented with a negation—what Islamist women are not. Cihan Aktaş, a prominent Islamist women writer, calls this unique Other to veiled women the *traditional woman*. The *traditional woman* is the one who "passively subjects herself to the requirements of common sense. She is so immature that she cannot recognize the difference between the traditions of her society and the divine rules of Islam" (1988, 81; translation mine). For Aktaş, the *traditional woman* does not know how to veil herself appropriately. She holds some religious beliefs, but she is not able to comprehend the world through the lenses of Islam (1988, 81–83). The religious traditionalism of the *traditional woman*, Aktaş argues, does not prevent the infiltration of Western amorality into the society. It is only *aydın müslüman kadın* (the enlightened Muslim woman)[22] who can and does struggle for the well-being of the Islamic community (1988, 91–118). The *enlightened Muslim woman* represents "the intelligent, brave, chaste, productive and virtuous woman" who tries to lead her life through a complete submission to Islam, often challenging traditional interpretations of Islam that minimize women's participation and instead presenting the "genuine" message of God which encourages women's activism (121–155). The construct of the enlightened Muslim woman reinstates that not every veiled women is an Islamist woman. It helps differentiate between the modern and the traditional veiled women, promoting the enlightenment of the latter with modern Islamist values. Ernest Gellner (1992) elaborates such a differentiation in his study of contemporary Islamist movements. He states:

> Contrary to what outsiders generally suppose the typical Muslim woman in a Muslim city doesn't wear the veil because her grandmother did so, but because her grandmother did not: her grandmother in her village was far too busy in the fields, and she frequented the shrine without a veil, and left the veil for her *betters*. The granddaughter is celebrating the fact that she has joined *the grandmother's betters*, rather than her loyalty to her grandmother (16).

The construction of Islamist woman's identity then involves a struggle against both the secularist *modern*ism and the traditional religiosity: Islamist woman takes issue with the new Turkish woman, who relegates Islam to the private sphere, on the one hand, and with the traditional woman, who does not have a comprehensive understanding of Islamic manners, on the other.

The Islamist woman suffers from the difficulty of reconciling her public roles with her communal responsibilities. She is, above all, expected to be a wife, a mother, and a homemaker with explicit tasks of maintaining harmony in the family and raising the young in accordance with Islamic principles. Though she is expected to take an active role in jihad,[23] her ultimate jihad involves protecting her family from the "dangerous" and "evil" forces of the Kemalist Westernization (Acar 1991, 282–295). In other words, a *mujahidde*[24] may participate in public demonstrations as long as these do not override her primary duties. Her career is also shaped by the needs of her family and community. She is encouraged to specialize in certain fields such as gynecology, so that "she may help her sisters who are not admitted to the state hospitals because of their veils" (Aktaş 1991, 124–130). The range of patriarchal restrictions over Islamist women's public existence can be better illustrated if we explore their struggle with the Islamist elite for political equality.

Confronting the Islamist Patriarchal Elite

Islamist women's political participation has been a highly contentious issue in Islamist circles. It is commonly accepted that Islamist women should assist their male peers in gaining votes. The patriarchal Islamist elites accept women's right to vote, but they prefer that Islamist women not run for elections. Islam, they assert, does not impose restrictions on women's right to govern, but the existing political norms in Turkey do not allow the Islamist women to fully express their religious identity. They thus conclude that it is better for women to wait and support the Islamist men until the latter come to power and reestablish the "golden age" (Demir 1998, 126–130).

The Islamist women, however, are not willing to easily give up the struggle for equal political representation. Commenting on the Welfare Party's man-only election lists in 1994, Silam Haşim, an Islamist woman writer, asks:

> If you are pushing women into the streets to convey your ideology, why do you reify the impediments on their way to the Parliament? If you claim to solve the veiling problem as such, I doubt your sincerity. If women had not dedicated themselves to this struggle [against the ban on veil] so much, you would never attempt to deal with the veiling issue. You should be consistent. If you take women into the streets, you should take them to the Parliament as well. (cited in Demir 1998, 134; translation mine)

Haşim's demands were condemned by a woman member of the patriarchal Islamist elite, Seyhan Coşkun, who responded stating:

> If my Muslim brothers do not protect my interests as a woman and I have to elect someone of my sex to speak for me, I say nothing but good heavens! For Muslim men are the guardians of Muslim women as much as Muslim women are for them, I do not need to become a member of the Parliament. Muslim men will be successful, because they have their wives assisting them. Muslim women may not be actually involved in politics but they influence, and even direct, the decision makers! (Cited in Demir 1998, 131, translation mine)

After the 1994 election, the chairperson of the Welfare Party's Women Commission resigned from her post, arguing that women deserved more power in the party (Yavuz 1998, 522). Those women who chose to stay in the party and struggle with the Islamic patriarchy from within the movement were given four candidates in the 1998 elections.

The 1994 election was not the only instance when women were silenced within the Islamist movement. A similar confrontation occurred in 1988 between the women and the patriarchal elite when a group of women began to publish a woman's page in the mainstream Islamist daily *Zaman*. On this page, the writers argued that women's subordinate status in Islam was not inherent in the Qu'ran but due to the male prejudices prevalent in Muslim societies. In one such article, Mualla Gülnaz wrote:

> Patriarchal oppression is a phenomenon ... existing along with capitalism or socialist oppression. Our history and culture are influenced by this oppression to a larger extent. ... It is just *a* big lie that women are not devalued in this region. ... I am not aware that our history and culture refer to a golden age when egalitarian rules predominated. (Cited and translated by Göle 1996, 123)

Such articles challenging the patriarchal interpretations of the Islamic texts met with severe criticisms from the male columnists of the same newspaper, and the women lost their jobs before the end of the year (Y. Arat 1998).

The silencing of Islamist women's voices was crystal clear in the case of Merve Kavakçı. The Virtue Party declared a few hours before Kavakçı's veiled appearance at the parliamentary oath-taking ceremony that if she were not allowed to take her oath with her veil on, they would not take sides on the issue as a political party (*Hürriyet* April 30, 1999). Some male Islamist writers, especially those in *Akit* and *Milli Gazete*, criticized the party administration for not backing up Kavakçı against the secularist ostracism. It may be argued that the party did not explicitly support Kavakçı not only because of its patriarchal attitudes toward women's political participation but also to avoid being closed down. Still, in the last instance, the party elite felt vindicated about their previous assertions about Islamist women's political participation that "veiled women cannot yet participate fully in the current political system and should wait until an Islamist, just order is established."

The analysis above argued that Islamist women have to fight against the secularist ostracism and also the Islamist patriarchy. In the rest of the paper, I turn to the secularist women's responses to their veiled *sisters'* struggle for an "equal but different" voice in the public sphere.

Can We Be Sisters? Islamist Women Encounter Secularist Women

When the Higher Education Council permitted students to wear *türban*, Kemalist woman professors protested the decision and refused to teach. Similar attitudes appeared in Kemalist women's publications. Based on her analysis of the Islamic sources, Bahriye Üçok[25] argued that the new veiling is not a religious but a political expression of one's worldview. Another renowned Kemalist women's studies professor, Necla Arat, asserted that veiled women are "a group of people who could not—and do not want to—break with the backwardness of the past. They want to sustain the female image prescribed by traditional ideology and hence to abolish the women's rights granted in the early Republican period" (1997, 77; translation mine). Necla Arat's assessment echoes Renan's formula stated earlier in this chapter that Kemalist women advocate *forgetting* the Islamic/Ottoman traditions and *remembering* instead the early years of the Republic.

The titles of secular women's works also give clues as to how they perceive their Islamist counterparts. The best example is Gürgün Özsoyeller's *Türkiye'de İki Kadın Dinamiği: Şeriatçı-Çağdaş* (Two types of women's activism in Turkey: Islamist versus contemporary)[26] (1995), where the reader is provided with the main thesis by just looking at its title: the Turkish women will *either* be modern *or* submit to the oppressive religion. A similar juxtaposition is present in Nihan Akgökçe's article entitled "*Kadın ve Aile* Dergisi Müslüman mı; Modern mi?" ("Is the *Kadın ve Aile* an Islamic or a modern journal?") (1994). Though Akgökçe's assessment is not as biased as Özsoyeller's elaboration,[27] her title nevertheless implies the same secularist argument that it is impossible to reconcile religious identity with "the modern."

Secularist women's vehement reaction to Merve Kavakçı also illustrates their perceptions of their Islamist counterparts. Organizing anti-Kavakçı demonstrations across the country, the Kemalist women groups claimed that Kavakçı had no right to veil in the parliament because religious practice is a private matter whereas serving as a M.P. is a public duty. For them, Kavakçı had to take off her veil if she wanted perpetuation of democracy in Turkey. A large independent feminist association, Ka-Der (the Association for Sponsoring the Women Candidates in the Elections), on the other hand, did not make any public statements regarding the Kavakçı affair. In my interviews with its members (July 1999), I found out that a group of members supported Kavakçı's choice to observe her religion as a woman and her right to veil. However, they were outnumbered by those who found Kavakçı's action as a threat to secularism and women's rights. It is necessary to note here that Ka-Der always had an ambiguous stand on the issue of having veiled members. Since its foundation, the association members publicly evaded the question of whether they would accept veiled women's membership or participation in the association's activities.

In summary, both Kemalist and feminist women excluded their veiled sisters from the public realm in the person of Kavakçı. Their prejudice about the symbolic meaning of women's veil for Turkish secularism reinforced further polarization among the women's groups and weakened the possibilities for an issues-based women's coalition. Favoring secular nationalism over struggle for women's emancipation from all kinds of patriarchy, Kemalist and feminist women ended up helping the Islamist elite to further silence Islamist women's demands for greater political participation.

Epilogue

In the post-1980 period, some of the third-generation Republican women entered the public realm with their veils on and advocated their version of an "equal but different" womanhood in their publications. They demanded full participation in social life despite the secularist restrictions of the state and the communitarian limitations put forth by the patriarchal Islamist elite. In their struggle, they were not supported by their secular sisters, leaving them with "double patriarchy" rooted in Islamist conservatism and secularist bias of Turkish feminisms.

Martin Riesebrodt argues in his study of contemporary fundamentalisms that "the more the women have their own autonomous and autocephalous institutions within the fundamentalist movements, the better the chances are there that they will build permanent, stable organizations and train a new generation of female activists" working toward emancipation from religious patriarchy (1993a, 259). Lacking both autonomy from the Islamist patriarchal elite and support from other women's groups at large, the Islamist women in Turkey are trying hard to convey their claims for an alternative womanhood. The recent public discussion on the Kavakçı affair and its negative outcome signify a battle lost by the Islamist women against double patriarchy. Nevertheless, the Islamist women continue their involvement in party politics, engage in demonstrations, and write about their experiences within the limits of the current political discourse. Secularist women have mobilized even further in opposition, in reaction, and rarely, in support of their sisters.[28] If the Islamist women can find allies, especially among other women groups, they will not only be able to redefine their social position but also eventually shatter the patriarchal social practices in contemporary Turkey both from within and from outside.

Notes

I would like to thank to Müge Göçek, Cihan Tugal, and the editors for their comments on the earlier versions of this chapter.

1. I am aware that the terms "backward," "traditional," "advanced," "modern" are not only socially constructed but also politically loaded. I do not believe in the superiority of any value system, be it a "Western" or "non-Western" culture. In this chapter, I use these terms in quotation marks and sometimes italicize them in order to illustrate the Turkish nationalist discourses around religion, history, and social development.
2. This is not to say that this is the only power struggle at the macrolevel. Another major conflict in contemporary Turkish politics revolves around Kurdish ethnicity versus Turkish nationalism. For the purposes of this chapter, I will dwell upon only the struggle between Islamic revivalism and Kemalist nationalism.
3. Kemalism in this chapter refers to the ideological rhetoric as well as the praxis of Westernization reforms employed by the Republican founding elite. It is named after Mustafa Kemal Atatürk, the founder of the Turkish Republic. Atatürk's followers and the founding elite are both called Kemalists.
4. This is not to say that women have only been *objects* in contemporary Turkish politics. On the contrary, they continually negotiate their identity claims with the elite of their particular social group as well as with the elite of the predominant discourse of the time.
5. Serpil Çakır (1994) traces the Ottoman women's activism through a comprehensive analysis of women's magazines published in the late nineteenth and early twentieth centuries. The Ottoman women nevertheless did not enjoy as high a degree of freedom as their Republican counterparts. Though they received support from the Westernists of their time, they did not have extensive support from the ruling elite. Despite their relentless efforts, the Ottoman women were depicted as "passive subjects behind the lattice" in the Republican discourse. The lattice metaphor was frequently used in early Republican novels in order to stress the "backwardness of religion."
6. *Çarşaf* is a type of veiling that covers the body and the face completely with the exception of the eyes.
7. This phrase is first used by Atatürk at a public speech and has been the motto of the transformation project. The "contemporary civilizations" refer to the capitalist, secular, European democracies.
8. It is important to avoid a biased approach to Islam. No less than any religion, Islam prescribes certain limitations with respect to the conduct between the sexes. Such prescriptions vary among religions as well as among different practices and interpretations within one religion. Claiming that Ottoman women were prohibited from public affairs because of Islamic practices ignores women's activism in the Ottoman Empire.
9. The term "yeni Türk kadını" is introduced by Ziya Gökalp in his book *The Principles*

of Turkism. Gökalp is known as an important scholar who inspired the formulation of Turkish nationalism in the early Republican period.

10. There are six fundamental principles that define the essentials of the Kemalist project: populism, etatism, republicanism, nationalism, reformism, and secularism.

11. Religious political parties are constitutionally prohibited in Turkey. However, several parties are regarded as formal instruments of Islamist activism throughout the Republican history. Three of them are regarded as heirs to the same orientation: Milli Selamet Partisi (National Salvation Party) of the 1970s, Refah Partisi (Welfare Party) from 1980 to 1997, and Fazilet Partisi (Virtue Party) after 1997.

12. See the Islamist women's journal *Mektup* (The Letter) for such arguments.

13. An example of such a reconciliation is the expectation that the Islamist woman can work outside and engage in public activities as long as she does not ignore her maternal responsibilities. I elaborate this argument later in the discussion of the Islamist women's jihad. There are also groups of Islamist women who demand to be treated as " exact equals" to their male counterparts. Being called "Islamist feminists," these women gain support especially among university students. I focus on their demands later in my discussion of women writers in the Islamist daily *Zaman.*

14. This strategy raises questions about the principle of secularism and, I would argue, it is the main reason behind the crisis of secularism in contemporary Turkey. A vivid example is the official celebration of religious holidays. On those holidays, state offices are closed, and politicians make public statements emphasizing national unity. Another example is state supervision of the content of *hutbe* (the Friday speech delivered at mosques). These practices should not lead the reader to think that Turkey is not a secular country. In contrast to some other states in the region, Turkey does not have an official religion. These hybrid practices once more show us that secularism has a unique connotation in each country depending on the country's specific political structure.

15. Alevis constitute the second largest religious community in Turkey. Their practice of Islam bears similarities to Shiism. Some people even call them "Anatolian Shiites."

16. The Higher Educational Council supervises university education in Turkey.

17. There is not a clear-cut definition of proper veiling in the Qur'an, and different practices are observed in Islamic societies. Some assert that a proper veil should conceal all curvatures of women's body, whereas others argue that concealing women's hair is adequate. These interpretations draw upon traditions and customs of societies rather than religious texts.

18. At the time, Anavatan Partisi (Motherland Party) had the majority in the parliament. It is claimed that the leader of the party, Turgut Özal, had close relations with the religious brotherhoods, especially with the Nakşibendis.

19. The Constitutional Court is the supreme judicial institution that supervises the procedural appropriateness of all legislation.

20. Merve Kavakçı holds U.S. citizenship because of her marriage to a U.S. citizen. In such cases, Turkish law requires that the individual appeal to the Turkish authorities for double citizenship. If the person fails to do so, her/his file is sent to the appropriate Turkish court for expulsion from Turkish citizenship. Kavakçı lost her Turkish citizenship because she had not informed the authorities about her citizenship status.

21. Following Ilyasoglu (1998), I will refer to all veiling protests in the post-1980 period as the "new veiling movement" in the rest of the paper.

22. Aktaş presents a typology of womanhood in her book (1988) in which the enlightened Muslim woman corresponds to the ideal of the Islamist woman I try to delineate here.

23. Jihad means conquest for the world of Islam. It is waged at two fronts: one spiritual, in the believer's own conscience, and one social, in society at large. Here, it refers to the latter front—conveying Islamic principles to other individuals.

24. *Mujahidde* refers to a female participant in *jihad.*

25. Bahriye Üçok was a well-known Kemalist scholar who was assassinated in 1990. Her assassination was attributed to the Islamist groups that she criticized in her articles.

26. The word "çağdaş" means "belonging to the age, contemporary." It also has the connotation of "being modern."

27. It is important to note that Akgökçe is a secular feminist and writes regularly in *Pazartesi*, the feminist journal discussed in footnote 28 below. Özsoyeller is, on the other hand, a Kemalist professor.

28. The correspondence between the feminists and Islamist women in the feminist journal *Pazartesi* (Monday) provides an exception to this pattern. *Pazartesi*, a prominent feminist journal with the highest circulation, covered the Islamist women's struggles for equality more extensively than all other feminist journals and the mainstream secularist media. For a comprehensive analysis of relations between the Islamist women and independent feminists, see Keskin 1999.

18

Queering *Hindutva*: Unruly Bodies and Pleasures in Sadhavi Rithambara's Performances

Bishnupriya Ghosh

The emergence of Hindu right-wing female icons in India such as Rithambara has sparked furious debate in progressive circles on the relationship between activism, female icons, and empowerment. Each of the major organizations in the Sangh Parivar (the Hindu nationalist coalition)[1] flaunts a women's wing: the RSS has the Samiti; the VHP, the Durga Vahini; and the BJP, the Mahila Morcha. Trained as a Samiti member, Sadhavi Rithambara became one of the sensational VHP (and later, BJP) women performers/acolytes instrumental in mobilizing support for the Ramjanmabhumi[2] cause. For many feminist theorists the spectacle of the female orator/activist is important, curious, even painful for several reasons. For one—as Amrita Basu (1993) suggests—there is the salient fact of women's increased participation, and seemingly greater prominence, in contemporary Hindu nationalist mobilizations. For another, these women's exercise of violence has put into question earlier arguments about links between women and pacifism, and specifically, in the South Asian context, the Gandhian equation of femininity with nurture, spiritual strength, and nonviolence.

My concerns here start with this latter issue. I argue that the sexualized and violent speech of the central Hindu nationalist female public performers (not to be confused with the female ideologues) is necessitated by their role in the Ramjanmabhumi movement as instigators of affect and emotion, and as progenitors of nonrational collective identifications. These women performers are undoubtedly integral to Hindu nationalist mobilization as public spectacles, rather than key decision makers who bring women's concerns to the table. They lack political clout in defining male *Hindutva* or Hindu rule (Pant 1997; Larocque 1997; A. Basu 1998), but serve dual, if contradictory, purposes: they homogenize *Hindutva* and make its platform palatable to a broader political spectrum, thereby expanding its upper-caste urban base; and they enable women to inhabit the public spheres of work and politics as citizens.

My focus is not on women's issues and agendas, but on the performative spaces occupied by female performers and the possible effects of such discursivity, with Rithambara as the case study. I thus separate *Hindutva* discourse's pedagogical intent from its performative effect, a departure from earlier analyses such as Pant's (1997) indictment of Rithambara's protofascist agendas. I argue that the internal contradictions, mixed and fragmented metaphors, images and stories in Rithambara's speeches may be rehearsed confusion put to savvy political ends, yet the performative space provides listeners occasions for consuming queer pleasures deeply apposite to the pedagogic heteronormative gender ideologies of *Hindutva*.

Sadhavi Rithambara: Public Spectacle, Political Functions, and Queer Resistance

In any analysis of the performative and affective dimension to the Hindu feminine that emerges in the *Hindutva* discourses, the spectacular Sadhavi Rithambara, legendary for her violent, sexual, shrill, and rage-filled pre-1992 performances (Mukhia 1995; Kakar 1995), provides a compelling example. A young woman from a rural, lower-class, lower-caste background, Rithambara entered Hindu nationalism through the Samiti, but rose to public prominence via the VHP. By May 1991, she was campaigning for the BJP's electoral bid; as we shall see, her mobility within Hindu nationalism speaks to the mobility of her symbolic registers. Critics concerned with the psychological, rather than political, effect of *Hindutva*'s female public performers have focused on Rithambara as the most memorable figure of the erotic *sadhavi* (ascetic) phenomenon. Mukhia (1995, 1365) notes the contradictory pull of Rithambara's chosen title against her given name: a *sadhavi*, or renouncer of worldly desires, who gains moral ascendancy to comment on worldly affairs and to denounce whom she pleases, including male comrades; and *rithambara*, the celestial nymph in Hindu mythology who uses her physical beauty to seduce ascetics. "Sadhavi Rithambara" is thus a simultaneous sexing and desexing, a liminality that prefigures the contradictions of her performances.

One hears comparatively little about Rithambara in the post-Ramjanmabhumi years, following the destruction of the Babri mosque in 1992. Her zenith as a public figure was at the height of *Hindutva* consciousness-raising and mobilization, not in its aftermath, which was preoccupied with the more onerous tasks of building coalitions in government or making policy. It is in those early years of mobilization that we witness Hindu nationalist discourse's highly libidinized symbolic strategies geared toward harnessing political will.

Basu (1995, 159) notes that Rithambara's and Uma Bharati's meteoric rise during the Ramjanmabhumi movement falsely projected the BJP as a grass-roots movement. Neither of these performers was economically dependent on or politically linked to powerful male figures (fathers, brothers, husbands). The Ramjanmabhumi campaign provided their first activist opportunities, and they proved particularly adept at drawing men to it.[3] Rithambara's infamous exhortations to violence galvanized Hindu men and women to demonstrate and riot, culminating in the destruction of the Babri mosque. Reportedly fifty-five thousand women were among the two hundred thousand people gathered there, fulfilling specific roles including protecting men from police blows. Rithambara's performances from October 30, 1990—the first BJP *rath yatra* (chariot procession) to Ayodhya—until December 6, 1992 are the subject of this chapter because these were the hell-raising speeches that sparked anti-Muslim violence.

The Rithambara performances of these tumultuous years are filled with deliberately vague, highly selective sketches from Hindu mythography, necessary for garnering national consensus on a Hindu nation yet to be aligned with state power. The political suturing—weaving together various classes, castes, regions, on the one hand, and various mythographies of different Sangh Parivar groups on the other—may well be the central achievement of these women leaders (A. Basu 1998, 177, 161). Striking instances of such melding may be found in Rithambara's adroit role playing. On one memorable occasion, she adopted the persona of the Sikh hero Bhagat Singh's mother, thereby implicitly expounding a Hindu-Sikh historical alliance that excludes Muslims. This persona adoption obfuscates the fact that Bhagat Singh died in anti-British struggle from which the RSS was absent; only later did the RSS claim anti-British activity among its valiant historical engagements. Rithambara's historical referential vagueness serves the political/electoral aspirations of the BJP by symbolically welding discrepant electorates (Hindu and Sikh) together.

I read Rithambara's performances as dutifully working for *Hindutva* while simultaneously revealing a covert rage against the Hindu nationalist male cadre. I contend that while female Hindu nationalist performers like Uma Bharati, Vijayraje Scindia, and Sadhavi Rithambara undoubtedly subscribe to hetero-normative domesticated Hindu femininity against virile homosocial masculinity, in that process they occupy deeply ambivalent social spaces. Any analysis of Sadhavi Rithambara's flamboyant speeches will show her recurrent evocation of "queer" bodies of rage, lust, defecation, and secretion used to stimulate and enrage her predominantly male audiences in their call to arms.

This writing of national political subjectivity in these particular gendered terms has roots in several modern encounters in the region. The sexed body has always been a fecund site for regulating and delimiting political communities. Although coming to different conclusions, Chatterjee (1990) and Sarkar (1997) have cataloged the history of the Hindu woman's body, its secular ritualizations, its control, the disciplining of its desires, and its indispensability to formations of South Asian nationalist discourses in mid- and late-nineteenth-century cultural revivalisms. Hence my preoccupation with the sexed and gendered body as metaphor, image, and performance in Rithambara's discourses. Here, one finds, in the Foucauldian sense, the queered feminine body of excesses and pleasures, thus the obverse of the disciplined, domesticated, and normative female body.

Before turning to the discourse analysis that is the heart of this chapter, I delineate the theoretical landscape of my reading. First, I pause on formulations of "queer" that are pertinent here, subsequently outlining how I read the "queer body." Then, I define context-specific designations of normative sexuality that enable us to demarcate the "queer" in Rithambara's performances.

Consuming Unruly Bodies: Border Trouble in the *Hindutva* Regime

In the 1980s and 1990s, "Western" theoretical models were increasing criticized as inadequate to explore postcolonial contexts (Ghosh 1998)—more so in the case of the native than the settler postcolonies. I am well aware that my deployment of queer theory—discussions of queer as non-normative, as resistance, as excessive, as performative—may be regarded as one such spurious application. Yet I argue that at the historical juncture of India's globalization (following trade liberalizations and media privatization), which is roughly commensurate with the *Hindutva* movement's growth, "queer" emerges as a visible "outside"/contaminated "inside" to the movement's promulgation of a disciplined Hindu national body politic and citizenry. Elsewhere[4] I discuss the visibilization of queer sexuality (see also John 1998, 372) in Hindu nationalist discourse similarly to Alexander's (1997) exegesis on sexual legislation in the Bahamas. Alexander demonstrates how the government's enthusiastic embrace of tourism in the Bahamas as a rational mode of survival simultaneously generated fears of a permeable cultural border, now policed by evoking the diseased bodies of sexual Others. Likewise, in the Hindu nationalist hysteria over Deepa Mehta's "lesbian" film *Fire*, legal and other modern discourses politicize and make visible certain "unruly" bodies—sexual outlaws who are nonproductive citizens such as the "sodomite," the "prostitute," the "lesbian" (Alexander 1997, 68). These figures' existence both normalizes heteropatriarchy and reinforces cultural borders in the age of multinational capital. The *Hindutva* movement's dependence on a visual consumer culture—audiences who watch television, buy calendar art and posters, and enjoy spectacles (light and sound carnivals) drawn from Hindu myth—engenders a similar anxiety of cultural permeability. Indian convulsions over the Beauty Queen Pageant in November 1996, the debates over sexual speech in Hindi film songs and satellite televisual transmissions such as *Baywatch*, and the legal contest over the film *Bandit Queen*, reflect a growing unease over the increasing intrusion of sex and sexuality into the public sphere.

What I have been suggesting is that visible sexualized and gendered "unruly" bodies—"queer" bodies—have become essential to unifying a Hindu cultural ethos in the age of globalization. Bacchetta (1999) makes a similar point, tracing *Hindutva's* genealogies of "queer" and queerphobic bodies, practices, and lifestyles, as well as queerphobic scholarly writing on Hindu nationalism. Bacchetta encapsulates "dual operations" of colonially and heteronormatively informed productions of Otherness in Hindu nationalism along two vectors: "xenophobic queerphobia," which positions "queer" outside the Hindu nation; and "queerphobic xenophobia" wherein queerdom is metaphorically extended to all Hindu nationalism's Others regardless of their sexual identity (143–144). Bacchetta notes her use of "queer" as a transient theoretical measure, in the absence of a single term that captures queer practices, lifestyles, and identities in the Indian context. She then archives existing terminologies of queerness, both classical and current, in the subcontinent, thus taking seriously the problem of effacing "local," contextual-historical understandings of terms within a "dominant" (for the term "queer," read "Western") formulation (145).

Similarly, I deploy "queer" as a transient measure, although my emphasis differs: I focus on queer pleasures and their possibilities. I use "queer" as a descriptive term for non-normative or unruly bodies and the desires of those bodies, with the understanding that the "norm" is "locally" comprehended (through *Hindutva's* patrilineal normativity, which I outline below). Moreover, I feel that under cultural and political flows in the era of globalization, the current Hindu nationalist understanding of "queer," accessed through media originating in the West, retains its Western usage and values. This ("Western") kind of queerness is precisely the complex of practices that the Hindu right loves to, even needs to, hate: the Other whose forms and norms require constant reiteration in the larger project of delimiting a body politic. Bodies and pleasures that Hindu nationalists ideologically constitute as "queer" or unruly are therefore central to *Hindutva*—hence, their repetition in Hindu nationalist performances.

The sexual body and the sexual gaze have always been rabidly policed along racialized religious lines in Hindu nationalist mythographies. Indeed, cultural controversies that talk endlessly about sex[5] in an attempt to preserve the sacred space of the normative Hindu female body are contrived attempts at stimulating nonrational affective Hindu nationalist solidarity, particularly when the national consensus on _Hindutva_ agendas seems beleaguered. For example, in 1997 the Hindu nationalist group Shiv Sena stormed artist M. F. Husain's studio alleging that he, known for his unconventional projects, had painted naked images of Saraswati (Hindu goddess of learning) and Draupadi (heroine of the Hindu epic _Mahabharata_). Most interesting here is the Hindu nationalist discourse that categorized this as a cultural crime. As a member of the national elite that Hindu nationalists target as stooges of the West, but also (not accidentally) as a Muslim, Husain was accused of visually raping Hindu-Indian womanhood.[6] Here were the necessary Others to the Hindu nation: the Muslim who must be disciplined within the nation-space, and the Westernized Indian as the contaminated Other who must be expelled. The incident sheds light on how women's bodies and the sexual gaze that fixes on them become essential ingredients in the structuring of Hindu nationalist cultural norms. Thus it is no surprise that it is the visible queer body of excesses, of deviant pleasures and errogenous zones, that emerges in full splendor and occupies center stage in Rithambara's performances.

My focus is not on queer actors Othered in _Hindutva_ discourses, but rather on Rithambara's evocation of an "unruly" body politic—a Hindu nation whose territorial organization perpetually disintegrates and exceeds any symbolic bordering. Because this unruly body politic is apposite to the disciplined gendered territory of the Hindu nation avidly visualized and mapped in Rithambara's speeches, I designate it as "queer." My discussion below of Rithambara's use of a specific modality of the Hindu feminine will exemplify the local norm against which this queered unruly body must be understood.

Finally, a word on the politics of my queering Rithambara's performances. I am interested in the multiple pleasures and possibilities of Rithambara's multifaceted performances for her listeners in the private and public spheres, thus the multiple modes of consuming the disciplined and unruly bodies she posits. This reading creates a context for locating the possible queer pleasures of even the most ardent of Hindu nationalist followers. Arguably, it is the queer unruly body that provides the most affective (libidinal) dimension to Rithambara's performances. It follows, then, that the more aroused one is by these performances, the stronger one's queer attachments (unconscious as they may be).

Rithambara's evocation of unruly bodies leads us to the sites where her speeches are consumed. Certainly, in _Hindutva_'s affective impact, the importance of Rithambara lies in her notoriety and popular acclaim (A. Basu 1998, 169–170). But, there is also the question of technology and the private consumption of these public performances. In her assessment of the phenomenon of female public visibility versus the austere reserve of the Hindu nationalist women's local organizing, Sarkar (1997) observes that cheap visual and audio technologies enabled the rapid dissemination of Hindu consciousness. Sarkar analyzes a well-known cassette of Rithambara's speeches, tracking how her original 1990 open air speech/performance was replicated, remastered, and distributed to sustain the immediacy of Hindu militancy.[7] Sarkar notes that the "live performance" dimension sutures the private listener to the greater original audience, whose presence is implied through feedback effects. Indeed the very fact of remastered performances, with the added glamor of government bans on such cassettes, carries the possibilities of Rithambara's performances into the private sphere—to be played in homes and courtyards and neighborhoods where they offer women a very different erotic charge from the heteronormative roles Hindu nationalism otherwise asks them to play.

Undoubtedly, cassette distribution has been most instrumental in politicizing housebound women in ways closest to Mahatma Gandhi's movements. To trace the dissemination of Rithambara's cassettes today, and to catalog how she is remembered in publications such as *Jagriti* (the Samiti's bulletin), would be a worthy follow-up to this research. But here, I raise the possibility that alongside Rithambara's cassette's dissemination of identity there might be other secret pleasures for women who listen(ed), privately: the delights of queer bodies evoked in recalling the motherland's sacral geography, the cathartic effect of Rithambara's license to denounce, and her performance of women's rage and helplessness in the postindependence polity.

Below, I will dissect one of Rithmbara's typical speeches delivered in Hyderabad in April 1991. But before launching into a closer look at the bodies that emerge and disintegrate in that speech, I pause briefly on some historical aspects of the RSS and Samiti's gendered and sexed imaginaries (as central elements of Rithambara's symbolic register), to situate the local norm against which I pit the queer bodies of Rithambara's performances.

The Pedagogic Feminine: The RSS, the Samiti, the BJP, and Rithambara

While decrying the commodification of women's bodies and souls on the global market, Rithambara unquestionably sells the heteronormative regulations of masculinist Hindu nationalism. She promotes gendered and sexed imaginaries that reappropriate nineteenth-century Hindu revivalist iconography (Bacchetta 1996). Further, from the early Hindu revivalists of the colonial era to the contemporary politicized *Hindutva*, women's bodies—which seemingly escaped the transformative effects of colonialism—have always functioned as imaginative loci for the (re)constitution both of the Hindu nation and its particular forms of heteropatriarchal political economies. As Sarkar (1997) demonstrated, in both earlier and contemporary forms of Hindu cultural nationalism, woman was at once personified as inspirational nation-space, a sacral geography, and idealized as the active progenitor of the Hindu race and culture. This second, more secular function was prescribed by religious duty/practice. The RSS depicts the goddess figure occupying the entire geographic "national" space of the subcontinent (the grounding mythography of *akhand Bharat*, or undivided India), positing the female body as "pure" uncontaminated space/ethos. But the Samiti trains muscular female bodies for the eugenic project of producing children and protecting one's chastity (a virtue guaranteeing the patrilineal line and its property transfers). These RSS and Samiti mythographies (the parent bodies of the Sangh Parivar) provide the cultural registers for *Hindutva*'s pedagogies of the feminine, and in Rithambara's discourse they find a new telling.

One of the key symbolic elements of the RSS-Samiti perceptual grid is the figure of the mother-goddess (Bacchetta 1994, 1) as the motherland or national body. Since this figure assumes centrality in Rithambara's speeches (Pant 1997), most of my comments here unpack this figuration. Bacchetta (1996, and chap. 3 of this volume) cautions that the RSS and the Samiti have divergent conceptions of the feminine, though they both posit the figure of *Bharatmata* (the idealized sacral motherland). The RSS promotes normative, domesticated, chaste femininity, a passive territorialized mother/nation in need of protection from virile sons, splitting off the fierce combative characteristics of warrior-goddesses in Samiti literature and locating those attributes in the heroic male subject (Bacchetta 1996, 150). The RSS's women subjects range widely, they are constructed predominantly mothers, with Sita as the idealized wife for the Hindu male; the male cadre necessarily see performers such as Rithambara as rarities. The Samiti, however, exalts a pantheon of independent women (nevertheless bound to Hindu males as a collectivity), claiming heritage from the Vedic period when women occupied high positions of scholarship and prowess.

For Rithambara, the idealized sacral body of the motherland is always the nostalgic dream, the unity from which the secular nation is sundered; thus the recurrent image of the fallen nation of zones and partitions, the dismembered body politic. As Menon and Bhasin (1998) and Butalia (1999) have demonstrated in their histories of India's 1948 Partition, the fate of the fallen and communally divided nation was historically played out on the bodies of real women through rape. Prior to this, the Samiti, founded in 1936, posited potential rape as a motive for its own creation. Already, this offers a protofeminist take on the male RSS cadre's capacities, for women must learn to protect themselves in the absence of male support. The Samiti itself allows some women to move beyond traditional gender roles, while pedagogically advocating motherhood and domesticity.

Clearly, Rithambara, working with an eye to BJP electoral politics—particularly the party's platform of "family values" (Bacchetta 1999b, 150)—works with the notion of the domestic, normative feminine, since one of her intentions is to call her *brothers* to arms (in 1991 speeches). Moreover, given the need to link the Hindu nation into a territorial unit (the war over the Babri mosque is, of course, a war of territory), she tries to stabilize this feminized territory while keeping its libidinal charge through the cry of revenge for desacralizing the mother's body. Hence, we see a plethora of enumerations in her speeches: exact places (such as the Delhi Boat Club), leaders (e.g., Shahabuddin), numbers (Hindu and Muslim populations), territories (Kashmir, Delhi, Jammu), and so on. These elements of specificity add the borders of the contemporary scene around the mythologized sacral body of the mother, *Bharatmata*, organized as a patrilineal polity to be reclaimed from the invaders/intruders. Because Rithambara is so invested in establishing this heteronormative feminine as the local norm, excesses that accrue to this body are "queered." The excesses are many, as we shall see, ranging from fragmentation and dissolving to defecating, eating, drinking, fighting/killing, buggering, and sucking. At such pitched moments in her crescendos, which Pant (1997) likens to the "rhymed cadence" of a Hindu sermon or trance-inducing music of night vigils, some characteristics of the Samiti's fierce feminine surface to generate an erotic and aggressive charge. Hence I see her partially self-conscious performance of affect as actually running counter to—even transgressing—the very parameters of femininity and national and territorial integrity that she so painstakingly envisions for her audiences.

Unruly Bodies: Zones, Fragments, Pleasures/Displeasures

In attempting to produce a unitary national territory and ethos, Rithambara skill-fully weaves together a loose selection of Hindu myths, stories, rumors, historical incidents, and common lore into a register that speaks to everyone and remains deliberately vague in its cultural genealogies. This is particularly true of the 1991 speech examined here, delivered before a VHP rally. Rithambara spoke in melodic couplets, starting with an invocation of gods and heroes: Sita and Hanuman from the epic *Ramayan* and its author, the sage Valmiki; Shiva and Krishna of two dominant Hindu traditions; Hindu historical figure Swami Dayananda and Sikh figure Guru Gobind Singh (deliberately posited as anti-Muslim allies); Buddha and Mahavira (the founders of two other major South Asian religions); and the Hindu nationalist personified figure of Mother India. The logic of the placement of these names in relation to each other ostentatiously confuses the mythic and the historical, imparting mythic status to human figures and historical truth to myths. For instance, Swami Dayanada is referred to as a "sage" alongside Sage Valmiki of mythic fame, thereby elevating the former's position. By the same token, Buddha, whom Buddhists regard as both founder and a manifestation of God, is swiftly reduced to a historical figure when coupled with the martial hero Guru Gobind Singh. Much more can be said about Rithambara's evocations of gods and heroes, but for my purposes here I will focus only on the Mother India/goddess figure in the 1991 speech.

Rithambara begins and ends the hero invocations in this speech with the image of Mother India, the sacral *Bharatmata* resplendent in RSS discourses where the phallic saffron flag flies over the maternal body-politic that signifies the nation's territory (Bacchetta 1996, 147). At several climactic moments, she circuitously repeats this rising flag imagery. The mounting crescendo itself performs a phallic rise, drawing to a resounding close various stories and para-bles in a speech that begins with fairly prosaic secular references to the storming of the Delhi Boat Club.

The sacral force of the goddess assumes spatial form in the geographic demarcation of a motherland. Here, Rithambara draws from Hindu myths in which sacral land is demarcated by the sixteen places where parts of Sati's (the god Shiva's beloved) dismembered body fell. (Sati is reborn as a series of goddesses). Each of these places are *pithastans* or pilgrimage sites for Hindus, whose devout traversing of these locations spatially *re-member* Sati's body (Bacchetta 2000, 267). In her Hyderabad speech, in keeping with re-membering, Rithambara calls the virile Hindu sons of contemporary India to restore the mutilated maternal body. This geographic staging of national unification also restores the original idealized Hindu civilizational ethos (enshrined, say the proponents of *Hindutva*, in the great epics) which are split by the modern secu-larist discourses of difference, with Muslim Pakistan as the reminder (and future threat) of disintegration. The first staging of this "united India" (Hindustan) occurred as early as 1980, with the VHP *Ekmatayajna*, a sacrificial ceremony publicizing India (and Pakistan) as ideally the land of Hindus. In the years to come, the RSS disseminated maps featuring an undivided India, and equated the Hindu woman's body to the "temple" violated by the Babri Masjid, the sixteenth Muslim mosque built by the emperor Babar (Bacchetta 2000). The first disintegration of the unitary feminine body surfaces with Rithambara's evocation of dismembered arms, also recalling the mother-goddess whose power lies in her eight arms: "What do we have? An India with its arms cut off."[8] More painful is the attempted division of Hindus via the government's Mandal Commission recommendations for increasing the seats reserved for Other Backward Classes (in government educational institutions and employment), thereby dividing the "Hindu community,"—a catalyst for the 1990 *rath yatra*. Rithambara repeatedly cautions against "fragmentation" by "reservations," "experiments in Hindu-Muslim unity" that dismember the Hindu body—a dissection "carried out on the Hindu chest as if he is a frog, rabbit, or cat." Here Hindus are represented as vulnerable animals, in contrast to Muslims as donkeys or dogs, or virulent mosquitos or flies, figures perhaps related to RSS discourses on miscegenation (Bacchetta 1994b, 2, 154).

Here the spatial slides into an organic metaphor of good (Hindu generative) and bad (Muslim biological) reproduction, as Rithambara hypothesizes Muslims' capacity to outpopulate Hindus:

> Try to feel the unhappiness and pain of the Hindu who became a refugee in his own country. The Hindu was dishonoured in Kashmir because he was a minority. But there is a conspiracy to make him a minority in the whole country. The state tells us Hindus to have only two or three children. After a while, they will say do not have even one. But what about those who have six wives, have thirty or thirty-five children and breed like mosquitos and flies?
>
> Why should there be two sets of laws in this country? Why should we be treated like stepchildren? I submit to you that when the Hindu in Kashmir became a minority he came to Jammu. From Jammu he came to Delhi. But you Hindus are on the run all over India, where will you go? Drown in the Indian Ocean or jump from the peaks of the Himalayas? (Kakar 1995, 208)

Here is a careful welding together of diseased breeding and the spread of contagion over space, drawing on RSS discourses. Furthermore, in RSS and Samiti mythographies, the eternal Hindu nation has a bad seed, a stepchild, in the Muslim; this essentalized conception is inverted—the Hindus are stepchildren now—in the present fallen nation (with the secular state as arbiter). Such essentialized, highly metaphorical content is swiftly concretized through Rithambara's insistence on spatializing the Hindu nation. In this instance, the spatial is conceived of as geopolitical and electoral space—the language of "refugees," state policy, and "minority" formations woven into purview of contemporary Indian territory (Kashmir to Jammu, to Delhi, and then to the southern tip of the subcontinent). This is an excellent example of how existent (*Hindutva*) symbolic registers are carefully woven into Rithambara's pitch for electoral power.

The mutilated sacral land and its ethos double elsewhere in the speech as the healthy or sick body politic, the metaphors of fluids compounding the spatial imagery with the organic:

> Wherever I go, I say, "Muslims, live and prosper among us. Live like milk and sugar. If two kilos of sugar are dissolved in a quintal of milk, the milk becomes sweet!" But what can be done if our Muslim brother is not behaving like sugar in milk? Is it our fault if he seems bent on being a lemon in milk. He wants the milk to curdle. He is behaving like lemon in milk by following people like Shahabuddin and Abdullah

Bukhari. I say to him, Come to your senses. The value of milk increases after it
becomes sour. It becomes cheese. But the world knows the fate of the lemon. It is
cut, squeezed dry and then thrown on the garbage heap. Now you have to decide
whether you will act as sugar or like lemon in milk. (Kakar 1995, 205)

Here, Rithambara deploys a well-known lemon-milk-sugar parable already
rewritten by the RSS, mobilizing it to signify Muslim selfishness (lemon) and
Hindu selflessness (milk/cow) to sell the Hindu nationalist claim that Hinduism
is the only tolerant ethos that will allow others to live peacefully, if only the others
will not disrupt that harmony. Rithambara reiterates Hindu generosity elabo-
rately at two other points in the speech: the Namdev parable (a dog steals
Namdev's bread, so Namdev chases the dog—not to regain his bread but rather
to give the dog his butter, too); and the preceding claim equating Hinduism with
creation and Islam with destruction (204). In the homespun milk-sugar-lemon
parable, Rithambara tangentially references various other groups' assimilation
into "Hindu" India. For example, the sugar image evokes the reputed Parsi lore of
entering India, begging for asylum, promising to dissolve among Hindus like
sugar in milk, thereby sweetening the body politic but not occupying space or
insisting on cultural difference. The point is, of course, that Muslims have not
assimilated and therefore must be expelled from the body politic ("cut" and
"thrown" away), which has the ability to restore itself: the milk becomes cheese
when mixed with lemon. Here Muslims as lemon juice are responsible for added
value (if one were to closely follow the logic of this parable), but this is not picked
up, making this one of those vaguely worked-out affective stories Rithambara
uses and discards to rouse and empower. Her gift also lies in the quick ability to
move from the figurative dimension to the real, for suddenly the lemon becomes
two actual Muslim fundamentalist leaders targeted by name (Shahabuddin and
Abdullah Bukhari). And the organic metaphor is laced with sexual connotations:
curdled milk connoting semen in street slang, implying the Muslim male's defilement of the feminized Hindu body politic, bringing both sickness and shame.

Indeed Rithambara deploys both the organic and the spatial to conjoin two
different Hindu mythic geographies: the current Hindu possible and idealized
body politic, imagined as the project of *Ramrajya*, and the essentialized sacral
geography of *Bharatmata*. The pilgrimages of Hindus to the sixteen sites of Sati's
body are conflated with the mass pilgrimage to Ayodhya, the kingdom of Ram.
To reclaim Ram's birthplace would literally entail weeding out signs of defilement (the Babri Masjid) from the Hindu landscape. Here it is Ram's followers
and devotees who will re-member the idealized sacral geography of the motherland. Rithambara claims Ram, the warrior-king (and sometimes the lovable
warlike toddler, Ram Lala), to be every ideal citizen whose consciousness leads to
political action: "Ram is the representation of national consciousness.... He is
the life of fishermen, cobblers, and washermen"[9] (203). He is also the national
ethos, the active male principle inspired by the memory of a feminine sacral
ground. Rithambara emphasizes the sacred nature of this national consciousness repeatedly, reminding us that the fight over Ram's birthplace is morally, not
materially driven (as over a "piece of land or cloth"). It is the good fight for a
whole civilizational ethos. In her quick sutures of various carefully selected
aspects of Hindu mythography, Rithambara's logic remains ambivalent. At times,
the national ethos is Ram, whose manifestation in a thousand warriors will save

the fallen motherland; at others, it is Mother India as civilizational ethos that is lost in the secular national memory. What remains more stable in this scenario, however, is the gendering of these roles: the feminine is to be rescued by the virile son, with the censure of the effeminacy of Mahatma Gandhi's followers reputed for "pacifying" Indian Muslims. The postindependence rule of these Gandhians is mythified in Rithambara's account as the fallen times, rule of hermaphrodites recorded in the *Ramayan* before Ram's return from exile (211)—a form of "queerphobic xenophobia," in Bacchetta's (1999b, 155) schemata, where Hindu nationalists ascribe secularists and non-Hindus queer identity.

In the above analysis I have identified two kinds of fragmentation and zoning of the idealized motherland: the first, modern history as loss and division, depicted through images of mutilation and defilement; and the second, the libidinal figure of the son divided from a harmonious dyad with the maternal body and striving to reclaim her in a fallen world. In a consequent Akbar-Birbal narrative, Rithambara evokes a third kind of fragmentation, zoning the body politic in the gendered terms of the restorative feminine space (of the "home") in contrast to the strife-filled masculine "world" (Chatterjee 1989). Popular as children's fare in modern India, the Akbar-Birbal folktales feature the great Mughal emperor, Akbar, and his wise Hindu minister, Birbal, and present a harmonious and witty interpretation of Mughal rule. Rithambara reinterprets the good faith of these tales, caustically deploying one of them to not only prove Birbal's intellectual superiority (typical in these stories, which have always functioned as mechanisms for grappling with Muslim political ascendancy) but also Akbar's animal-like stupidity and helplessness. In short: Akbar and Birbal embark on a journey when Birbal prostrates himself before the holy *tulsi* plant (revered in Hinduism for spiritual and medicinal properties) and the more prosaic nettle, claiming the *tulsi* and nettle to be his "mother" and "father," respectively. Akbar derides him for this, and true to Rithambara's earlier claim of Muslim destructiveness, pulls the plants out jokingly; but the nettle infects him, and he starts itching (like a donkey or a dog, we are told) and begs Birbal to help him. At this juncture, the sage minister prescribes a remedy: "Go ask forgiveness of my mother *tulsi*. Then rub the paste made out of her leaves on your body and my father will pardon you" (207).

A recurrent claim emerges in this speech: the notion of an organic citizenship—nonsectarian, naturalized if not sacralized—that is Hindu, but also feminine. Women as healers, domestic preservers of *tulsi* plants, and the possessors of indigenous medical knowledge, are ecologically linked to the "natural" landscapes of the body politic. Men appear along with history, in the fallen time of necessity and division. In the spatial metaphors, zoning and fragmentation represent the transformative hurt of history. Women personify lost unity and as restorative agents have the power to transmute this fallen time and place to a remembered myth. And in the organic metaphors, the milk or *tulsi* (indigenous gifts of the mother's body/land) that will "cure" the sick body politic bears out the Hindu nationalist modalities of the normative feminine, where women are "outside" of the decayed realm of politics—or indeed the intact "home" against the fallen world. Thus *Hindutva* "champions" women as bastions of Hindu living traditions that should now form—sustain, nurture, make possible—a politically instrumental national ethos. One of the logics of Rithambara's tirade, then, radically places women as commentators on the political world, whose outside-inside-ness precisely offers sustenance. Many have noted the rage against the state by these women performers of the Ramjanmabhumi mobilization: for instance, Amrita Basu (1998) notes that Rithambara is as critical of M. K. Gandhi as she is of BJP leader V. P. Singh. For her, the paternalistic state and the market are as destructive to the Hindu polity as are Muslims (175). Thus Rithambara's male audiences are situated as the last recourse to crisis, emerging out of painful necessity, while women remain abiding "natural" resources, inspiration and critics of the body politic.

Men are thus both protectors and signifiers of failed plenitude; women must be saved, on the one hand, but also have self-regenerative capabilities, on the other. Such logic contributes to the deep ambivalence of Rithambara's speeches, a confusion that gives her certain license for rage, pleasure, excess. Consider Rithambara's further detailing of the *Ramayan* in the same speech. The organic body with restorative powers is also the forest of the *Ramayan* where asylum and sustenance may be found: "How will the sage Valmiki look after Sita? How will Ram eat Shabri's berries?" (Kakar 1995, 203). Both Valmiki, a hunter belonging to a low caste, and Shabri, an untouchable who fed Ram berries during his exile, are reminders to all Hindus of the need to stay undivided along caste lines. But this is also where links between the idealized motherland and the ideal body politic fall apart. The forest is irrevocably the pastoral "outside" to Ram's rightful kingdom, the very *Ramrajya* that the designers of *Hindutva* seek to establish; but the forest is also the place of harmony where upper and lower castes coexist and where Sita finds shelter. Characteristically, these confusions are brought to fruitful political ends: merely a vague reference is made to Ram's good relations with the lower castes despite his aristocratic lineage, but no attention is paid to other RSS anti–Other Backward Caste discourses. In some RSS mythographies, the *vanavasis* (forest dwellers) as tribals (categorized as Other Backward Castes in modern Indian political discourse) are read as indigenous to the national body; but they are culturally unmarked until uplifted into Hindu civilization by Brahmins (Bacchetta 1994b, 204). Then they are seen as lower-caste peoples within the Hindu nationalist civilization and its body politic, *Ramrajya*.

Even more interesting is just who is being nurtured and why. In the chaotic hysterical motherland, daughters drink from the breast as do sons; they are the limbs that come to the service of the frail mother (Pant 1997); their thighs are branded by red-hot rods and must be avenged (Kakar 1995, 208). The idealized maternal body slung in a harmonious dyad with male infant/citizen disintegrates. In its place appears the body organized into zones of pleasure and displeasure— limbs, arms, penises, thighs, breasts, anuses, and mouths fill the sacral landscape. In direct reference to the extensive RSS literature on Muslim oppositional stances to Hinduism, at the raucously vulgar end to Rithambara's speech (which elicited much laughter), she zones Hindus and Muslims as sites for consuming or defecation: "Whatever the Hindu does, it is the Muslim's religion to do its opposite. I said, 'If you want to do everything contrary to the Hindu, then the Hindu eats with his mouth; you should do the opposite in this matter too!'" (213). Here Rithambara authoritatively inserts herself into the verbal phallic adage, in keeping with Hindu traditions of oral transmission in which the speaker/ composer always inserts his or her person into the narration as "I said." This part of the speech exemplifies the highly sexual and transgendered nature of Rithambara's performances: she adopts the privileges of male speech (sexual aggression, intimate vulgarities, suggestive insinuation), assumes a male familiarity with the men in the audience; has a phallic vision of herself as a male actor, seeing her voice rise like a saffron flag, in the very act of visualizing the idealized motherland for male consumption; and she is obsessed with male virility and women's (as mothers and citizens) anger/aggression (though historically rationalized as righteous). These bigendered elements become transgressive in a speech aimed at a careful orientation of gender roles along active (male)/passive (female) axes, a matrix necessary to stabilize the symbolic territory of the Hindu nation.

Unfailingly Rithambara transmutes herself from her feminine position as potential-victim-turned-desexed-renouncer-of-worldly-desires to a virile, if disembodied, political actor whose rage decimates the sorry remains of the current period and who provides the courage for the re-membering of the motherland (Mukhia 1995, 1365). Alongside the male who is the intended audience of Rithambara's call, brandishing swords, producing and drinking milk, emerge the daughters of *Hindutva*—irrevocably in the public sphere because of the inadequacy of male protection. They are warriors by default.

Pedagogically Rithambara's manifestos slavishly replicate the normative gender imaginaries (the domestic feminine and the hypervirile masculine) of the RSS, albeit with an eye to concrete electoral politics. But in the process of performing, within the rhythms, patterns, and flows of each speech (most of which, at least in the early years of *Hindutva*, are structured in a similar fashion to the one analyzed here), she assumes a hysterical and enraged persona whose unstable contours, sometimes derived from Samiti gender representations, challenge any systematic representation of gendered binaries. Hence she is the male gazer infatuated with the lost maternal body; she embodies the national ethos and civilizational memory; she is the female citizen who has removed herself from the sexed male scopic drive; she is the raucous male buddy who freely insults the Muslim as a common enemy; she is artist, cartographer, and mouthpiece for a revolution; and she is the virile daughter craving the queer pleasures of re-membering her mutilated mother.

A Queer Performer Speaks of Queer Bodies for Possibly Queer Consumption?

In my discussion of the 1991 Hyderabad speech, I have tried to establish two nodes of queerness in Rithambara's discourse. First, her evocation of the queer unruly body in attempting to establish Hindu normativity: the idealized, maternal, heteropatriarchally sanctioned (domesticated) feminine body she initially invoked in rage-filled performances disintegrates in verbal excesses extensively dwelling on body functions (semen-producing or milk-curdling Muslims, and the berry-eating milk-drinking Hindu male infant); on anomalies (the political world of hermaphrodites who testify to the current wrong ordering of things); and, most centrally, on the sexualized fallen and attacked female sacral body—the temple, and the pilgrimage site. Tales of fragmentation (cutting, expelling, mutilating), insertion (rapes or infections), insides and outsides, combat the nostalgic evocations of a unitary, re-membered ethos and land. Bleeding and dripping body parts, the body charged with lust or rage, operate against Bharatmata's disciplined, gendered, normative body/body politic. Thus inevitably, and indeed paradoxically, it is this unruly body zoned for pleasure and pain that becomes the imaginative landscape for Hindus to wage holy war in the early 1990s. Second, I have suggested that both Rithambara, as bigendered performer, as well as her audiences might well elicit queer pleasures from consuming the queer bodies, landscapes, and pleasures of her discourse in both live and remastered performances. This queer comes into being because of the radical disjuncture between Rithambara's pedagogic intent and her performance of *Hindutva* agendas.

It should be clear by now that my deployment of queer implies queering as a life-enhancing strategy—as Boyarin put it in a City University of New York conference (1999) on religion, sexuality, and citizenship—that subverts and releases the disciplinary mechanisms of the normative. Here both Rithambara's production of the embattled non-normative body, and her listeners' possibly queer pleasures in consuming it become political acts of pleasure—personal resistance, rather than mass mobilization. Despite much feminist criticism on the postmodern politics of pleasure (often perceived as temporary excursions into a political field, rather than sustained engagement), I would insist that the project of queering *Hindutva* might have lasting value. Desacralizing and queering the Hindu body and landscape can foreground the contrived nature of the "pure" heteronormative feminine, linking it more directly to state power and capital. And, more important, it can provide a discursive context for new avenues of consuming Rithambara, a realm of the queer possible for listeners in whose memory Rithambara's performances still loom urgent and inspirational.

Notes

1. The RSS (Rashtriya Swayamsevak Sangh) is a social movement, the VHP (Vishwa Hindu Parishad or World Hindu Council) is the RSS's churchlike network, and the BJP (Bharatiya Janata Party) is its political party, which has held state power in India since 1998.
2. Ramjanmabhumi refers to the Hindu nationalist call (from the mid-1980s) to destroy the Babri Masjid, a sixteenth-century mosque, and to resurrect a temple marking the birthplace of the Hindu god Ram in its place.
3. Coalition of South Asian Women (COSAW) *Bulletin* (1993).
4. Ghosh 2002.
5. John and Nair (1999, 1) note that the call to sexual abstinence in nation-building meant, in the Foucauldian sense, that "sexual desire be talked about endlessly."
6. On RSS constructions of hypersexed Muslim males and Westernized Indian's alliances with the "porno-West" (reversing Anne McClintock's [1995] "porno-tropics"), see Bacchetta (1999b, 152).
7. Sarkar (1997) insists technology dangerously effaces itself thereby re-creating reality-effects.
8. Kakar (1995), 207. All further citations from the Hyderabad speech will be from Kakar's translation.
9. Kakar notes fishermen, cobblers, and washermen are lower castes, thus signifying Rithambara's crafted rhetoric of inclusion.

19

Right-Wing Women, Sexuality, and Politics in Chile during the Pinochet Dictatorship, 1973–1990

Margaret Power

[Feminism] fails to consider the differences [between a man and a woman] that derive from her nature and that were imposed on her in order to fulfill her mission, which is to preserve the species.... [F]eminism has gone beyond the acceptable limits and pushed women to the extreme of [demanding] the right to abortion [and] sexual freedom, which deny woman her principal right: to possess and act according to her true, genuine and special essence, that which confers upon her her unique feminine identity.

—Sara Navas, *La Nación*, 4 July 1987

They [leftist feminists in Chile] want to integrate the feminine with the masculine in circumstances that would impose on women the same life as that of a man. This would violate a woman's right to be different [from a man]. Just as socialism has failed in economic matters, its initiatives in this area of society are doomed to generate serious harm. [Feminists] respect neither human nature, in this case that of the woman, nor what is natural to society.

—María Fernanda Otero, *El Mercurio*, 3 July 1990

Sara Navas, a lawyer, actively opposed the democratically elected Popular Unity (UP) government of Salvador Allende (1970–1973). She welcomed the military coup led by General Augusto Pinochet that overthrew Allende in September 1973. Navas held several important positions under Pinochet and served as Chile's representative to the Inter-American Commission on Women of the Organization of American States from 1986 to 1988 (interview, 5 November 1993).[1] María Fernanda Otero has a long history of antileftist activism. When she was a young girl, Otero supported the opposition to Allende. During the Pinochet regime, she joined Renovación Nacional (National Renewal), one of two rightist pro-Pinochet parties (interview, 15 October 1994).

As Navas's and Oteros's statements illustrate, both women exalted in conventional gender ideas that conflated womanhood with heterosexual motherhood. They felt reassured and comforted, not oppressed or constrained, by normative conceptions about femininity. Like many rightist women in Chile, they rejected what they perceived to be feminists' attempts to eliminate gendered distinctions between women and men. They understood feminism as an attack on their identity as women and their biologically determined destiny to be wives and mothers.

Indeed, many feminists do argue that notions of femininity and masculinity reflect social beliefs, not biologically determined attributes. As Judith Butler notes,

"What we take to be an internal essence of gender is manufactured through a sustained set of acts, posited through the gendered stylization of the body" (1999, xv).

The beliefs that women should have the right to control their own bodies, to experience sexual pleasure, to determine the number of children they have, and to choose their sexual partner(s) are basic tenets for most feminists. When women do not enjoy these rights, many feminists hold men or patriarchal society responsible. Yet clearly not all women share these values, a reality that many feminists do not understand. Indeed, many feminists find it hard to accept that other interpretations of womanhood exist and that the women who hold them operate to implement their ideas. Many rightist women in Chile repudiate feminist notions of emancipation and proudly proclaim an essentialist, unchangeable notion of womanhood and manhood. Their attitudes toward sexuality flow from their ideas about what it means to be a woman, and a man, and explain, in part, their support for the military dictatorship.

For many people the idea that right-wing women hold conservative ideas about sexuality seems so obvious that it scarcely needs discussion. I certainly held this assumption before I began this study. Yet what I did not understand, and what other scholars have ignored, is why and how rightist women in Chile linked their ideas about women and sexuality to their support for the dictatorship of General Augusto Pinochet (1973–1990).

This chapter explores rightist Chilean women's construction of womanhood and sexuality during the Pinochet dictatorship. It makes three central arguments. First, for these women there was an organic and "natural" connection between sexuality and what it meant to be a woman. To them womanhood was synonymous with motherhood, and motherhood signified heterosexuality and marriage. Their conceptions about gender and sexuality not only affirmed their identities as mothers and morally superior women, they also informed and reflected their ideas about society and politics. Second, their attitudes toward sexuality both predated the dictatorship and influenced the military regime's willingness and ability to proclaim its own ideas on this subject. In other words, far from acting as an agent of sexual repression, in the eyes of right-wing women the dictatorship promulgated their fundamental beliefs. Third, understanding rightist Chilean women's thoughts on sexuality is central to explaining why they supported the military regime; many did so because it preached ideas about gender and sexuality that closely matched their own. For them, the Pinochet regime represented both morality and the correct way of living, not brutality and repression as it does to so many people.

In their discussions of women in Hitler's Germany, Mussolini's Italy, and Franco's Spain, Claudia Koonz, Victoria de Grazia, and Aurora Morcillo, respectively, analyze women's relationship to these fascist governments. I find both parallels and divergences with Chile. According to Koonz, many German women rejected the "new freedoms" for women that had emerged in the 1920s because these freedoms "unsettled the majority of women, for whom new opportunities meant loss of protection." As a result, they, like their conservative counterparts in Chile, supported "authoritarian rule" because it "would, they hoped, impose order and health on the nation and tie fathers to their families" (Koonz 1987, 12–13). Thus, many Chilean women supported the curfew imposed by the dictatorship because it meant that their husbands would be home with them and their children, not out drinking with friends or fooling around with other women. In Chile, unlike fascist Italy, where "the fascist state denied women any role in decisions regarding childbearing," women supporting the dictatorship played an active role in promoting pro-natalist policies. A key difference was that women in Italy, according to de Grazia, "were presumed to be antagonists of the state, acting solely on family interests without regard for the nation's needs" (De Grazia 1992, 5). The Chilean military regime knew it could count on its devoted group of female followers who saw themselves as key defenders of both their family and their nation. While Catholic Spain and Catholic Chile shared many similar perspectives on women's role as mothers and their centrality to the family, in the 1950s "the Francoist Catholic version of femininity stressed women's asexuality, exalting either virginity or motherhood (Morcillo 2000, 4–5). Although women in Chile promoted virginity and motherhood, they did not emphasize asexuality. In fact, they acknowledged a woman's right to her sexuality, as long as it was expressed in the confines of marriage.

Much of the literature on women during the Pinochet years focuses on women who were victimized by or who opposed the dictatorship. These accounts expose the brutality of the military regime, highlight the particular ways in which it oppressed women, and reveal the multiplicity of forms and contexts in which women resisted the dictatorship. A common theme that emerges from this literature is that Pinochet maintained power primarily through rampant repression. Jean Franco argues that "the military government of Pinochet ... violently disciplined society to make way for the economic miracle" (1999, 116). Maxine Molyneux (2000, 62) writes that "the new society (created by the military) would restore authority through a return to a patriarchal order founded on a retraditionalized, privatized family. Women would be disciplined and their rights curtailed." While these texts accurately analyze both the generalized and gendered policies of brutality practiced by the armed forces, they inherently suggest that the military lacked a social base and, as a result, relied primarily on force and brutality to sustain its rule. This perspective ignores the significant number of Chileans who welcomed the military coup and depicts Chilean women as an undifferentiated group. Many women suffered from the dictatorship, a sizable sector fought against it, while others were fanatically devoted to it. Far from feeling disciplined by military rule, this latter group of women felt affirmed by it.

The Military Dictatorship

The armed forces ruled Chile through a combination of repressive tactics directed against the regime's opponents and policies that ensured the support of their backers. Women were the Pinochet regime's most visible and enthusiastic supporters. During the Allende years, right-wing and Christian Democratic women organized the first large, public demonstration against his government and spearheaded resistance to it.[2] In the March 1973 congressional elections, the last ones held before the military coup, 60 percent of women voted against UP candidates, while only 50 percent of men did. Many scholars and nonscholars alike generally believe, albeit erroneously, that only upper- and middle-class women opposed the UP government, thus making class the decisive factor in explaining why women rejected the Allende government. Yet women of all classes, to varying degrees, voted and demonstrated against the leftist government. Upper-class women opposed Allende because the government's goal of redistributing the nation's wealth more equitably, through land reform and nationalization, directly threatened their economic interests and status. However, large numbers of Chilean women from all classes held the Allende government responsible for the severe shortages of goods and the general level of chaos and disorder that they experienced.[3] The anxiety they felt at not having the food they needed to sustain their families and the insecurity the political situation produced in them caused many women to look to military rule as the solution to their problems.

To build on women's successful activism against Allende and convert it into effective support for military rule, the dictatorship sponsored two women's organizations, both headed by Lucía Hiriart, Pinochet's wife. The Secretaría Nacional de la Mujer (SNM) offered seminars and educational programs to middle- and upper-class women who supported the regime. The lectures given to them by military officers and government officials provided these women with the ideological tools they needed to defend the dictatorship. The Centros de Madres (Mothers' Centers, CEMA), the other organization, worked directly with poor women in their neighborhoods. The Mothers' Centers offered women classes in sewing, hygiene, and crafts, as well as the possibility of receiving medical and legal services. Middle- and upper-class women, many of them members of the SNM, led the local Mothers' Centers and brought the ideas and attitudes they had learned in their seminars directly to the lower-class women with whom they worked. Thousands of women joined these organizations and thousands more attended their programs or worked in the Mothers' Centers. In 1980 the SNM had a membership of more than 10,000, and 230,000 women belonged to Mothers' Centers (Bunster 1988; Chuchryk 1991, 160).

In 1988 the military regime held a plebiscite on its rule. The majority voted against the dictatorship, thus forcing Pinochet to call for presidential elections in 1989. The opposition to Pinochet won the election. In 1990 Christian Democrat Patricio Alywin, the candidate of the democratic opposition, assumed the presidency, and the Pinochet dictatorship effectively ended.

Motherhood: Self-Realization and the Defense of Family and Patriotic Values

For right-wing women, motherhood was both a woman's destiny and her identity. Right-wing women considered maternity so natural that any woman who rejected or failed to achieve motherhood was, they believed, denying her true nature and doomed to lead a miserable and frustrated life. So powerful was their belief that some rightist women imbued maternity with a force that transcended women's active participation in it. For example, an article in *Amiga* (Friend), the journal of the SNM, counsels women to breastfeed their babies. It describes women's development from childhood to adulthood as, essentially, the biological process of preparing them to be mothers. "From the first years of a woman's life, her body begins to prepare the marvelous task which nature has assigned her, and that is maternity." This biological imperative is so powerful that, in some instances, it is the active agent, while women are merely the passive receptacles in which it takes place. As the article in *Amiga* continues, "Her body ... provides her with the organs that function actively during her pregnancy and, later, during breastfeeding. One of these organs is the mammary gland which, during the period of nursing, becomes active, constantly producing milk, even during the time she is asleep" (*Amiga*, February 1978, 3). This quote suggests a vision of pregnancy and nursing in which the body's natural mechanisms trump the women's own consciousness.

Motherhood was a woman's patriotic duty, a central way for her to participate in the nation. This understanding of motherhood, as a biological necessity, a precondition for a woman's personal realization, and her responsibility as a citizen, blunted the distinction between the private and the public. The military government sought to "nationalize" women in order to put them at the service of the state (Morcillo 2000, 69). Women needed to both produce children to populate the nation and provide loyal supporters to the Pinochet regime who were vigilant to the dangers of communism.

Carmen Grez is an upper-middle-class woman who participated in the anti-Allende women's movement, banging her empty pots and pans to signal her displeasure with the UP government.[4] She also served as the head of a Mothers' Center during the UP years (interview, 6 June 1994). In recognition of her important contributions to the anti-Allende movement, Pinochet named her director of the SNM, a post she held from 1973 to 1981. As the leader of the conservative women's organization, she articulated rightist women's (and the military's) ideas about gender and organized other women to adopt these concepts (*Amiga*, October 1976).[5] A speech she gave in 1978 at the closing ceremony of the SNM illustrates the connections she believed existed among motherhood, the family, and politics:

> The Secretariat's most important job is to make sure that Chilean women understand, in all its ramifications, the responsibility that falls upon them to form future generations of Chileans. Their children must love the fatherland and be willing and able to defend it against all dangers. Their children must grow up to be healthy and strong, in a family that inculcates in them moral, social, and cultural values. (*El Cronista*, 8 April)

Clearly, Grez understood the family as a site where women should pair the social and biological reproduction of their children to simultaneously accomplish two goals: their development into citizens of a rightist regime and the construction of the nation as a heterosexual family unit writ large.

Right-Wing Women's Ideas about Sexuality and Politics

Rightist women's ideas about sexuality flowed from their views about womanhood. A woman had the right to enjoy sexual relations, but only with her husband. These women actively opposed sexual relations that took place outside of marriage. Furthermore, these women linked women's sexuality to motherhood, a practice that María Elena Valenzuela labels "sexuality-maternity." "Through procreation women redeem the earthly character of their sexual impulses, converting them into the values of dedication, spirit of sacrifice, and selflessness toward their children" (Valenzuela 1995, 164). While their attitudes toward sexuality (regardless of their practices) are fairly common in a Catholic society, what distinguished these women's beliefs was the way in which they moved across scales, from family to nation, and linked them with politics.

For many right-wing women, "proper" sexuality became a weapon in the battle against communism. During the UP years, many pro-Pinochet women demonstrated against Allende because they believed that the lack of goods and social chaos during his government undermined the nuclear family and threatened their role as mothers. Under Pinochet, these women continued to uphold the family and motherhood as central to the defense of a moral society and a strong nation.

Right-wing women participated in the military's efforts to legitimize and institutionalize the regime through a redefinition of the enemy. Although they continued to evoke what they termed the horrors of the Allende years, after 1980 they focused much of their ire on what they considered communist-inspired attacks on the family: pornography, birth control, abortion, divorce, and *feminism*. These women seldom included homosexuality in their list until the 1990s.

The emergence of feminist ideas and organizations during the Pinochet regime challenged rightist women. Since men had dominated the leftist parties, the repression meted out by the dictatorship primarily targeted them. Many women became politically active in their defense and in the struggle for democracy, justice, and basic survival. The absence of leftist men afforded anti-Pinochet women more political independence and gave them more space to develop their own opinions. As a result, many of them were more receptive to feminism than they had been in the past. Activists in this movement tied their demands for women's liberation to opposition to the dictatorship. Their slogan, "Democracy in the country and in the home," neatly linked both their antidictatorial and feminist beliefs (Frohman and Valdés, 1995). In one 1983 publication, "The Feminist Manifesto," the Movimiento Femenista group "called for the decriminalization of abortion, and adultery and changes to divorce legislation," a demand that undoubtedly antagonized rightist women (Matear 1997, 87).

Pro-Pinochet women opposed the demands of the feminist movement in order to undermine these women's criticisms of the Pinochet dictatorship; moreover, the values of the feminist movement directly challenged their fundamental beliefs about "natural" femininity. Pro-Pinochet women parried the opposition women's critique of the dictatorship by cloaking the general and his regime in the cloth of morality. Emphasizing "moral" issues that reflected their conservative values, these women showed their faith in the superiority of their beliefs and sought to project themselves as morally better than the women who opposed Pinochet. They continued to frame their struggle as a defense of motherhood, the family, the nation, and morality, and against (as they defined them) the antifamily, antinational, and immoral positions of communists and the new enemy, feminists.

Women were not the only ones to articulate the connections between the family, society, and nation. In 1979 Pinochet derided communists' supposed attack on society and the family in a speech he prepared for the sixth anniversary meeting of the SNM (*Amiga*, November 1979, 4). In it, he decried the "global presence of a massive campaign that aims to destroy the family." He stated that the family, and by this he meant the male-dominated, heterosexual family, was "the sure source of the correct moral and psychological formation of man." According to Pinochet, the sinister, but unspecified, forces of communism were attempting to weaken Western civilization by attacking the family. "Do not forget that the dissolution of the family ... has invariably been one of communism's preferred tactics to penetrate the West." Although the goals and methods of "those who follow Marx and Lenin" remain the same, their tactics have changed. "Drugs, pornography and delinquency are part of this sinister arsenal ... that appear in our world today. They are part of the enemies' of order, justice, liberty, and faith desperate attempt to take over a vacillating and weakened humanity."[6] To foil these nefarious plans, Pinochet pledged his government's opposition to any attempt to "induce limits to people's procreation." He extolled motherhood, pointing out that the country needed to "experience a significant population growth, since the human element is the nation's most basic resource" (*Amiga*, November 1979, 5–6; Pieper 2000, 159).

Reproductive Issues

Although the population of Chile was predominantly Catholic, many Chileans supported the use of contraceptives and the right to an abortion in the late 1960s and the 1970s.[7] During the 1960s "eighteen of twenty Chilean bishops ... permitted couples to use contraceptive devices."[8] The UP government headed by Salvador Allende, a medical doctor, attempted to democratize the health care system. Government officials supported "sex education as a crucial element within family planning programs" and "declared family planning and access to contraceptive techniques the basic right of women and men" (Pieper 2000, 123, 139–140). Allende called for the legalization of abortion (which failed to pass the opposition-controlled Congress), and his government did not prosecute doctors who performed abortions (Pieper 2000, 139; Jiles Moreno 1992, 160).

In 1979, the military government formally proclaimed its position on reproduction with ODEPLAN's (Office of National Planning) announcement of the "Chilean Government's Policy on Population."[9] The new program favored population growth and opposed birth control, abortion, and sterilization. Many of the dictatorship's key civilian advisors were conservative Catholics who opposed birth control for religious reasons. Padre Hasbun, a priest who had called on Catholics to actively struggle against Allende and now encouraged them to support Pinochet, urged women to adopt the image of the Virgin Mary, "the incarnation of purity" as their model (Valenzuela 1995, 76–84). These right-wing counselors undoubtedly affected the military regime's position on reproductive issues. A second factor also influenced the dictatorship's new policy: its hope to "win[] the sympathy of the Catholic Church, which opposed modern methods of birth control," and thereby soften the church's criticism of the military's massive abuse of human rights (Jiles Moreno 1992, 187). Despite the regime's efforts, women continued to have abortions, and the birthrate did not increase. According to Benjamín Viel, a proponent of birth control and longtime head of the Chilean Association for the Protection of the Family, "[from 1980] onwards, the birthrate has not declined and the number of abortions [carried out annually] fluctuated between 30,000 and 35,000" (*La Nación*, 16 September 1990).

Although the military never directly accused "the communists" of supporting abortion in order to destroy the family, it did link them to attacks on the family. In March 1980 *Amiga* interviewed Jovino Novoa, one of Pinochet's main advisors, about his government's thinking on family-related issues. He emphasized that the government believes that "the family nucleus is the base of society. Therefore, the state ... must ensure that families are constituted harmoniously." When asked if he believed that the family was under attack, he replied, "The family is being attacked by political systems and doctrines that prevail in some parts of the world. The family is being attacked by pornography, for example."

Novoa affirmed the government's commitment to combat pornography, along with other "symptoms of decomposition" through "sports, cultural activities … and by strengthening [Chile's] national and patriotic values." He also called upon the Mothers' Centers to attack pornography, although he did not specify by what means (*Amiga*, March 1980, 7–10).

In 1981 Amelia Allende (no direct relation to Salvador Allende), the leader of the SNM, took up the battle cry.

> Divorce, abortion, and pornography … are all attacks directed against the family. … If love and respect are lost, then the family also loses its unity and those who most benefit from this are the Marxists. They try to foment misunderstanding within the family in order to weaken this vital nucleus of society. This is a typical practice of Marxists, as is their promotion of feminist struggles, whose only goals are to divide and destroy. (*La Nación*, 26 July)

In the 1980s the SNM and Mothers' Center's actively took up the issue of reproduction. Lucía Hiriart, whose husband General Pinochet commanded the Chilean military as it imprisoned, tortured, and murdered tens of thousands of Chileans, summarized many conservative women's perspective on abortion. At a press conference commemorating the eighteenth anniversary of the Mothers' Centers she said, "Abortion is the most serious crime that can be committed" (*La Tercera de la Hora*, 6 November 1991). Carmen Grez, who had been the leader of the SNM for eight years, clearly indicated both her profound opposition to abortion and the feelings of racial superiority that defined much of Chile's white elite. When asked if she would support an abortion if her fifteen-year-old daughter were raped, she replied, "No. Not even if she was raped by a Black man. I could never justify an abortion" (*El Mercurio*, 19 April 1981).

The SNM promoted this under-no-circumstances antiabortion view. *Amiga* published an article entitled "From the Very Instant of Conception" that argued against abortion even if the mother's life is in danger. "When a mother's life is in danger, the child is not the cause of the danger; rather it is the mother's sickness [that is the problem]." The article urged doctors to treat the mother and to avoid an abortion. Even more powerful than the text itself is the graphic that accompanies the article. The graphic consists of four pictures of a fetus, portrayed as a fully conscious and suffering (boy) child, being "murdered" by different abortive methods (*Amiga*, May 1981, 15–16). Male subjectivity permeated these women's portrayal of abortion. The (male) medical professional—the authority— disconnected the fetus from the mother, and the graphic assumed that the fetus was male.

In opposition to abortion, or any "unnatural" method of birth control, the women of the SNM and the Mothers' Centers proposed the Billings Method, "a natural method of birth control" (*Amiga*, October 1980, 20). Australian Doctors Evelyn and John Billings developed this method to offer Catholics an alternative to the birth control pill. The Billings Method encourages a woman to determine when she is likely to conceive by noting changes in her cervical mucus.[10] The arguments the Mothers' Centers and the SNM advanced as to why women should prefer the Billings Method are significant. Instead of chastising women who use birth control on religious or moral grounds, they contend that natural birth control benefits women. They advocated it, in part, because it, unlike "artificial birth control," does not "produce adverse effects in the human body" (*Amiga*, October 1980, 20–21).

The Catholic Church promoted this "natural method" of birth control during the 1980s. In 1981 the Mother's Centers national office announced its full support for the Billings Method and its plan to provide information to women in the centers about it.

> Natural methods of family planning offer the couple much more than just the possibility of having or not having a child: they also engender communication, dialogue, and mutual understanding. They teach respect for life, emphasize family values, and, to top it off, do not cost any money, since they don't require the use of artifacts or medicines that can damage a woman's body.
>
> Furthermore, the natural methods of family planning agree with the principles proposed by the Supreme Government in its statement of policy on population. (CEMA Chile, 40)

Several aspects of this appeal are important. First, it is devoid of the moralistic overtones and the appeals to motherhood that characterized so much of what the Mother's Centers published. In fact, it approaches the woman as a woman, not a mother, who has needs and desires of her own that must be considered. Second, it promotes an honest discussion between the couple about their sex life, a topic that was still fairly taboo in Chilean public life at the time. It suggests that a woman's use of the Billings Method will improve her married life and relationship with her husband. Third, it pitches the appeal to women in language that suggests that a woman has the right to both a good sex life and a relationship based on equality with her husband.

When I first read this text, I was puzzled because it differed markedly from almost anything else I had read in any other SNM or Mother's Centers publications. Why this sudden concern for a woman-*qua*-woman's needs, when all other references to woman conflated her identity with that of the mother (in service to the family) or the volunteer (in service to the state)? Several thoughts occurred to me. First, it probably pleased the military regime to find a church policy with which it could agree, since tension over the military's abuse of human rights marked much of the state's relationship with the church. Second, the dictatorship cut back on the state's support for birth control for women. The Billings Method, which cost nothing, offered women a free alternative method of birth control. Third, the Mother's Centers and the regime realized that in order to win women over to the Billings Method they needed to heighten its appeal to women. Thus, they promoted it by saying to women that with the Billings Method they could have it all: the number of kids they wanted, a good relationship with their husbands, and the knowledge that they have fulfilled their responsibility to the state, all at no monetary cost. Fourth, it reflected many right-wing women's ideas about proper sexuality. Sex was fine, as long as it took place within marriage.[11] However, the Billings Method had two major drawbacks: first, it depended on a woman's ability to accurately and methodically measure her cervical mucus. Even for middle- and upper-class women who had the time, space, and energy to gauge the physical changes their bodies go through, this method demanded discipline and consistency. For poor and working-class women, whose lives and circumstances were more demanding, it was even more of a challenge. Second, the success of the method depended upon the male partner's willingness to respect and trust the woman's assessment and wishes. In Chile, as elsewhere, such an attitude could not be guaranteed, and therefore the Billings Method could not be relied upon to guarantee women control over reproduction.

Homosexuality: Why the Silence?

Remarkably, in the 1980s right-wing women did not list homosexuality as one of the dangers confronting the family. How to interpret their silence on this issue (Foucault 1980, 11–12)? On one level, so prevalent was the heterosexual norm in Chile during the 1970s and the 1980s that right-wing women apparently believed they did not need to include homosexuality in their list. However, these women's silence in no way indicates tolerance, let alone acceptance, of homosexuality. Rather, their silence on the issue merely suggests that because a public movement in support of gay rights did not exist in Chile at that time, these women did not feel compelled to speak out against it. The absence of commentary reflects the privilege experienced by many heterosexuals who choose to ignore those expressions of sexuality that they fear or hate. Yet, even though they did not publicly articulate it as such, their entire perspective on sexuality reflected their denial of homosexuality. The links these women made between sexuality, marriage, and procreation obviously excluded homosexuals who could not marry and would have found it difficult, if not impossible, to conceive children at that time, in that society. In other words, these right-wing women predicated their stance of "proper" sexuality on a rejection of nonheterosexual sexuality.

Few homosexual men or lesbian women were "out" in Chilean society during this period. Neither the demand for lesbian rights nor even an open recognition of lesbians' existence was part of the Chilean women's movement's agenda for much of the 1980s. A lesbian organization, Ayuquelén, which means to feel/be good in Mapuche, the primary indigenous language, formed in 1984. But it was not a public organization and primarily offered personal support to the small group of lesbians who composed it (*El Canelo*, May 1994, 10–13). The Movement for Lesbian and Homosexual Liberation (Movilización por la liberación lesbica y homosexual, MOVILH), a public gay rights organization, did not develop in Chile until 1991, after the Pinochet dictatorship ended (Marco Ruiz, interview, 13 March 1994).

To return to my question, why did right-wing women ignore homosexuality? Right-wing women responded to what they believed threatened that which they held most dear: their identity as morally superior mothers who defended their families, their nation, and their beloved general against the dangers of communism and, increasingly, feminism. Because it was so invisible, and because the emerging feminist movement did not prioritize the demand for lesbian or gay rights, homosexuality was not an issue that they felt compelled to deal with. They constructed gender, and based on that, sexuality, according to their belief that women were supposed to be mothers and men were supposed to be fathers, and relationships were supposed to be with members of the opposite sex, in the context of marriage. They ignored homosexuality because they could, not because they liked it. In the 1990s, after a homosexual movement emerged in Chile that demanded an end to sexual oppression and challenged binary gender roles, right-wing women began to attack homosexuality and defend heterosexuality (Baldez 2002).

"The Chilean Woman is not a Feminist, She's Feminine"
(Amiga, October 1980, 3)

By and large, right-wing Chilean women rejected feminism because they disagreed with its vision of womanhood. Right-wing women simply did not think that men oppressed them. Their enemy was communism, not the patriarchy or male supremacy. They saw themselves as courageous heroines who had boldly defied the Marxist government of Salvador Allende and, in so doing, saved Chile from the communists and their families from destruction.

Perhaps more fundamentally, these women rejected feminism because they embraced their identities as mothers and wives. They had a limited notion of feminism and mistakenly believed that feminism attempts to make women into men and denies women the right to be mothers. While many feminists do question the gendered division of labor that makes them the person with primary responsibility for taking care of children, feminism certainly supports motherhood. However, a difference would be this: feminists believe that women have the option to choose motherhood; right-wing Chilean women assume that biology has made that choice for them.

Despite their general opposition to feminism as an ideology, rightist women selectively appropriated some of its ideas and issues. For example, many rightist women spoke out against on-the-job discrimination against women and called for equal pay for women and men. However, even when they supported some feminist demands, they made clear that they disapproved of its basic beliefs. Gabriela Campusano, Miss Chile 1980, articulates this somewhat ambiguous relationship to feminism. Since she was not a political activist, her response reflects the extent to which conservative ideas permeated much of Chilean society, particularly younger women. Also, the fact that she was crowned Miss Chile indicates that the military regime approved of her attitudes and believed that she would do a good job at representing Chile internationally. When a reporter asked her, "What do you think about women's struggle to conquer their rights?" she responded,

> Women must evolve and become modern and have the same rights as men do in many things. Women should achieve all that they wish to, without forgetting what they really are: women. Women are in this world to have children, set up a home and, although many people may not like it, depend on men. I wouldn't like to feel that I am better than my future husband, because we women are fragile. It's nice to feel as if someone is protecting us. (*Hoy*, 21 March 1980, 49)

Like many conservative women Miss Chile 1980 holds contradictory ideas. She both accepts some feminist demands and asserts conservative ideas about gender. She supports the idea that women should have equal rights and claims to oppose any limitations placed on them, yet she also argues that men should retain the dominant position in relationships. Her statement echoes the same illusory, even hollow, promises of the Billings Method: women can have it all, at no cost and without any struggle, and men will cooperate.

Conclusion

Two ideas have dominated most discussions of right-wing women in Chile: first, they supported the dictatorship to defend their economic interests, and second, the Chilean armed forces, the quintessential bastion of male supremacy, imposed their vision of gender roles on a reluctant population that was too scared to challenge them. This chapter offers a different perspective. It argues that the dictatorship reflected many women's fundamental ideas of correct gender relations and that the regime's statements and policies on these issues strengthened many conservative women's adherence to the military. In fact, the military's proclamation of its support for motherhood and the family, a view that dovetailed with that held by many right-wing women, served to strengthen the loyalty these women felt for the dictatorship, not diminish it. In their eyes, the Pinochet regime represented morality and courage in opposition to the anti-family forces of Marxism that threatened them. For many conservative women, the military's repressive policies against those it defined as its political opponents represented justified repression against those whom threatened the fabric of their family life and nation. These people, whom right-wing women typically referred to as Marxists or communists, were the enemy. They represented immorality and danger, and if they had to be eliminated in order to preserve the family and motherhood, then so be it.

These women's ideas about gender defined their attitudes toward sexuality and explain, in part, their identification with the dictatorship. As this chapter makes clear, right-wing women supported the military regime not only because it was anticommunist, but also because it was antifeminist. Rightist women disliked and rejected feminism because it called for more open approaches to gender and sexuality. These women's ideas on sexuality—their opposition to abortion and pornography, their advocacy of marriage and procreation—were not side issues to them. They were central to their identities and their politics and fueled much of their enthusiasm for the dictatorship. Right-wing women in Chile happily backed a government that equated sexuality with marriage and procreation. They did not aspire to be sexually liberated; they were content to live in a society that frowned on an open exploration of sexuality. They advocated heterosexual relations and marriage as both the proper and the most fulfilling expression of a woman's sexuality.

The end of the dictatorship in 1990 ushered in a period of more open debate on sexual issues. Leftist representatives have repeatedly attempted to legalize abortion, the day-after pill, and divorce, but a conservative bloc of rightist and Christian Democratic officials have not allowed their legislation to pass. Gay and lesbian rights activists have challenged the dominant heterosexual norm through public demonstrations and media appearances, although entrenched ideas about sexual orientation prevail. According to one recent study, two thirds of Chileans reject the idea that a homosexual couple should be able to adopt a child (*La Ter-*

cera de la Hora, 5 May 2000).

Ideas about heterosexual relationships and sexuality have changed to some extent. Based on her study of sexual attitudes, Chilean sociologist Teresa Valdés concludes that 77 percent of women have sexual relations with men before marriage and many women envision the possibility that their marriage will fail (*Santiago Times,* santiagotimes.chip.mic.cl, 19 March 2000). Yet, according to a recent study, Chileans still find it very difficult to discuss sex and many women fake orgasms (*La Nación,* 22 November 1999). Perhaps the most disturbing reflection of social attitudes toward gender and sexuality is that Joaquín Lavín, presidential candidate in the 2000 elections, received the majority of women's votes. Lavín is a member of both the extreme right *Unión Independiente Democrática* (Independent Democratic Union) and the conservative and elitist Catholic organization Opus Dei.[12]

Notes

I would like to thank Paola Bacchetta, Lisa Baldez, Deborah Cohen, Sandy McGee Deutsch, Benjamin Evans, Elisa Fernández, Dagmar Herzog, Jane Juffer, Melinda Power, Issam El Naqa, and Annie Statton for their helpful comments on earlier drafts of this chapter.

1. I tape-recorded and translated all the interviews, which were conducted in Santiago, Chile.
2. In December 1971 opposition women marched against Allende and banged empty pots and pans to symbolize their belief that his government's policies left them without food.
3. The majority of working-class women in all Santiago neighborhoods except two cast their ballots for the opposition in the March 1973 parliamentary elections. See Power 2002.
4. After the successful December 1971 march against Allende (see n. 2), the opposition used the empty pot to symbolize rejection of the socialist government.
5. Between September 1975 and August 1976 the SNM organized courses in which more than forty-eight thousand women studied "patriotic and family values."
6. Pinochet's accusation that Marxists were behind the promotion of pornography in Chile is ludicrous, as are his charges that they wish to destroy the family. Internationally, and in Chile, pornography is a multibillion dollar business that is securely in the hands of capitalists.
7. "In 1976, after nearly three years of military rule, 91% of the population of Santiago 'favored family planning' and supported the use of 'artificial' methods of birth control over 'natural' ones." In addition, according to a Gallup Poll, 74 percent advocated the legalization of abortion. See Jiles Moreno 1992, 188.
8. Both the Catholic Church and many Catholic doctors in Chile supported birth control in order to prevent abortions and because they agreed with the prodevelopment discourse that identified smaller families with progress and modernity. See Pieper 2000, 24–26, 57.
9. ODEPLAN was the government office that designed the economic policies implemented by the military regime. Many of its leading staff members had studied in the department of economics at the University of Chicago, hence their sobriquet, the Chicago Boys.
10. According to the Billingses (2002), "virtually every fertile woman observes, or can be trained to observe, the secretion of a particular pattern of mucus coming from the cervix around the time of fertility."
11. For Catholic women who believed that sexual relations serve procreative purposes,

the Billings Method could be used to discourage sexual intercourse except on those days when they were likely to become pregnant. The Billings Method allowed those women who did not want to become pregnant to enjoy sexual relations more securely.

12. The party is pro-Pinochet and the more conservative of the two right-wing parties. In January 2000 Lavín ran against Ricardo Lagos, the socialist candidate for president. He lost, but a majority of women voted for him, in part because he projected himself as a loving and responsible patriarch who takes care of his wife and seven children. Opus Dei is an extremely reactionary Catholic organization that gained prominence in Franco's Spain.

Works Cited

Abadan-Unat, N. 1990. "Islam ve Kadın" (Islam and woman). *Cumhuriyet*, 23–29 September.
———. 1998. "Türkiye'de Kadın Hareketleri ve Küreselleşme" (The Turkish women's movement and globalization). In *Aydınlanmanın Kadınları* (The women of the Enlightenment), ed. N. Arat. Istanbul: Cumhuriyet Yayınları.
Abadan-Unat, N. and O. Tokgöz. 1994. "Turkish Women as Agents of Social Change in a Pluralist Democracy." In *Women and Politics Worldwide*, ed. B. S. Nelson and N. Chuodhery. New Haven, Conn.: Yale University Press.
Acar, F. 1991. "Women in the Ideology of Islamic Revivalism in Turkey: Three Islamic Women's Journals. " In *Islam in Turkey: Religion in a Secular State*, ed. R. Tapper, 280–301. London: I. B. Tauris
Adams, Philip. 1997. *The Retreat from Tolerance*. Sydney: ABC Books.
Addis Saba, Marina. 1998. *Partigiane: Tutte le donne della Resistenza*. Milan: Mursia.
———, ed. 1988. *La Corporazione delle Donne: Ricerche e studi sui modelli femminili nel ventennio fascista*. Florence: Vallecchi.
Ahmed, L. 1992. *Women and Gender in Islam*. New Haven, Conn.: Yale University Press.
Akgökçe, N. 1994. "*Kadın ve Aile* Dergisi Müslüman mı, Modern mi?" (Is *Kadın ve Aile* Islamıst or modern?). In *Türkiye'de Kadın Olmak* (Being a woman in Turkey), ed. N. Arat, 177–194. Istanbul: Say Yayınları.
Aktaş, Cihan. 1988. *Sistem İçindeki Kadın* (The woman within the system). Istanbul: Beyan Yayınları.
———. 1989–90. *Tanzimat'tan Günümüze Kılık Kıyafet ve İktidar* (Clothing and state power from Tanzimat to today). 2 vols. Istanbul: Nehir Yayınları.
———. 1991. *Tesettür ve Toplum: Başörtülü Öğrencilerin Toplumsal Kökenleri Üzerine Bir İnceleme* (Veiling and society: A study on the veiled students' social background). Istanbul: Nehir Yayınları.
Alarcón, Norma. 1997. "The Theoretical Subject(s) of *This Bridge Called My Back* and Anglo-American Feminism." In *The Second Wave*, ed. Linda Nicholson. New York: Routledge.
Alcorso, Caroline. 1991. "Non-English Speaking Background Immigrant Women in the Workforce: Report for the Office of Multicultural Affairs." Wollongong, New South Wales: Centre for Multicultural Studies, University of Wollongong.
Alexander, Jacqui. 1997. "Erotic Autonomy as a Politics of Decolonization: An Anatomy of State Practice in the Bahamas Tourist Economy." In *Feminist Genealogies, Colonial Legacies, Democratic Futures*, ed. Jacqui Alexander and Chandra Mohanty. New York: Routledge.
Al-Ghazali, Harb. n.d. *Istiqlal al mar'a fi al islam* (The independence of women in Islam). Cairo: Dar Al Mustaqbal Al 'Arab.
Al-Ghazali, Zaynab. 1979. "*Al Jam'iyyat al nisa'iyya*" (Feminist organizations). In *Al Da'wa* 42 (November 1979).
———. 1981. "Veiling *Infitah* with Muslim Ethic: Egypt's Contemporary Islamic Movement." *Social Problems* 28, 4: 465–485.
———. 1985. "Dawr Al-Mar'a fi Bina' Al-Mujtama" (The role of woman in the building of society). Paper presented at the Conference of Muslim Women, Lahore, November.
———. 1986. Ayyam min hayati (Days of my life). Cairo: Dar Al Shuruq.
———. 1988a. "Dawr Al-Mar'a Al-Muslima" (The role of the Muslim woman). *Al-Umma* (October).

————. 1988b. *"Ibnati Hadhihi Al-Sutur Elayki"* (My daughter these lines are for you). *Lewa' Al-Islam* 11 December.

————. 1995. *Return of the Pharaoh: Memoir in Nasir's Prison.* Translated by Mokrane Guezzou. London: The Islamic Foundation.

Al-Hashimi, Muhammad Ali. 1990. *The Ideal Muslimah.* n.p.

Alivizatos, Nickos. 1981. "Emergency's Regime and Political Rights." In *Greece in the '40s: A Nation in Crisis*, ed. John O. Iatrides. Hanover, N.H.: University Press of New England.

Allen, Ann Taylor. 1991. *Feminism and Motherhood in Germany, 1800–1914.* New Brunswick, N.J.: Rutgers University Press.

Allen, John. 1999. "Spatial Assemblages of Power: From Domination to Empowerment." In *Human Geography Today*, eds. Doreen Massey, John Allen, Philip Sarre. Cambridge, UK: Polity Press.

Al-Masri, Sana'. 1989. *Khalf al-Higab: Mawqif Al-Jama'at al-Islamiyya min Qadiyyat al-Mar'a* (Behind the veil: The position of Islamist groups on the woman's issue). Cairo: Sina.

Al-Nasr, Mahmud Saif. 1985. "Shaikh Sha'rawi wa imra'a a' Khati'a" (Shaikh Sha'rawi and a sinful woman). *Al Ahali*, 3 July, 8.

Al-Qaradawi, Yusuf. 1991. *Fatawi Mu'asira li Al-Mar'a wa Al-Usra Al-Muslima* (Contemporary Fatwa for the muslim woman and family). Cairo and Oman: Dar Al-Ira' and Dar Al-Dia'a.

Al-Sha'rawi, Muhammad. 1992. *Al-Mar'a Al-Muslima* (The Muslim woman). Cairo: Maktabet Zahran.

Alter, Joseph. 1992. *The Wrestler's Body: Identity and Ideology in North India.* Berkeley: University of California Press.

Althusser, Louis. 1984. "Ideology and Ideological State Apparatuses." In *Essays on Ideology*, 1–60. London: Verso.

Alves, Branca Moreira. 1980. *Ideologia & feminismo: A luta da mulher pelo voto no Brasil.* Petrópolis, Brazil: Vozes.

Andersen, Walter, and Shridar Damle. 1987. *The Brotherhood in Saffron: Rashtriya Swayamsevak Sangh and Hindu Revivalism.* New Delhi: Vistaar Publications.

Anderson, Benedict. 1983. *Imagined Communities: Reflections on the Origin and Spread of Nationalism.* London: Verso.

Andrews, George Reid. 1991. *Blacks and Whites in São Paulo, Brazil, 1888–1988.* Madison: University of Wisconsin Press, 1991.

Arat, N. 1997. *Susmayan Yazılar* (Writings that will never choose silence). Istanbul: Bilgi.

Arat, Yesim. 1990. "Islamic Fundamentalism and Women in Turkey." *Muslim World* 80, 1 (January): 17–23.

————. 1998. "Feminists, Islamists, and Political Change in Turkey." *Political Psychology* 19 (1): 117–131.

————. 1999. *Political Islam in Turkey and Women's Organizations*, Istanbul: TESEV Yayınları.

Arendt, Hannah. 1975. *The Human Condition.* Chicago: University of Chicago Press.

Arendt, Hans-Jürgen, Sabine Hering, and Leonie Wagner, eds. 1995. *Nationalsozialistische Frauenpolitik vor 1933. Dokumentation.* Frankfurt am Main: dipa-Verlag.

Avdela, Efi, and Aggelika Psarra. 1985. *O Feminismos stin Ellada tou Mesopolemou.* Athens: Gnosi.

Ayata, S. 1996. "Patronage, Party and the State: The Politicization of Islam in Turkey." *Middle East Journal* 50, 1: 40–56.

Ayata, S. and A. Güneş-Ayata. 1998. "Religious Communities, Secularism, and Security in Turkey." In *New Frontiers in Middle East Security*, ed. L. G. Martin. New York: St. Martin's Press.

Bacchetta, Paola. 1994a. "'All Our Goddesses Are Armed': Religion, Resistance, and Revenge in the Life of Militant Hindu Nationalist Women." In *Against All Odds: Essays on Women, Religion, and Development from India and Pakistan*, eds. Kamala Bhasin, Ritu Menon, and Nighat Said Khan, 132–156. New Delhi: Kali for Women.

————. 1994b. "Communal Property/Sexual Property: On Representations of Muslim Women in a Hindu Nationalist Discourse." In *Forging Identities: Gender, Communities, and the State*, ed. Zoya Hasan. Boulder, Colo.: Westview.

————. 1996. "Hindu Nationalist Women as Ideologists: Rashtriya Swayamsevak Sangh, Rashtra Sevika Samiti, and Their Respective Projects for a Hindu Nation." In *Embodied Violence: Communalizing Women's Sexuality in South Asia*, eds. Kumari Jayawardena and Malathi de Alwis. New Delhi: Kali For Women.

————. 1999a. "Militant Hindu Nationalist Women Re-Imagine Themselves: Notes on Mechanisms of Expansion/Adjustment." *Journal of Women's History* 10, 4 (winter): 125–147.

————. 1999b. "When the (Hindu) Nation Exiles Its Queers." *Social Text* 17, 4 (winter): 141–166.

————. 2000. "Sacred Space and Conflict in India: The Babri Masjid Affair." *Growth and Change* 31, 2 (spring): 255–284.

Bacchetta, P. 2002. "Hindu Nationwide Women: On the Use of the Feminine Symbolic to (Temporarily) Displace Male Authority." In Laurie L. Patton (ed.) *Jewels of Authority: Women and Textual Tradition in Hindu India*. (London and New York: Oxford University Press)

Baker, P. 1984. "The Domestication of Politics: Women and American Political Society, 1780–1920." *American Historical Review* 89, 3.

Bald, Suresht R. 2000. "The Politics of Gandhi's 'Feminism': Constructing 'Sitas' for Swaraj." In *Women, States, and Nationalism: At Home in the Nation?* ed. Sita Ranchod-Nilsson and Mary Ann Tétreault, 81–97. New York: Routledge.

Baldez, Lisa. 2002. *Why Women Protest: Women's Movements in Chile*. New York: Cambridge University Press, 2002.

Ballesteros Gaibrois, Manuel. n.d. "La letra 'Y': Su historia y presente." Madrid: Sección Femenina, F.E.T. y de las J.O.N.S.

Balletbo, Ana. 1982. "La mujer bajo la dictadura." *Sistema* 49.

Bamat, Thomas, and Jean-Paul Wiest, eds. 1999. *Popular Catholicism in a World Church: Seven Case Studies in Inculturation*. Maryknoll, N.Y.: Orbis Books.

Bard, Christine, ed. 1999. *Un siècle d'antiféminisme*. Paris, Fayard.

Barkun, Michael. 1994. *Religion and the Racist Right: The Origins of the Christian Identity Movement*. Chapel Hill: University of North Carolina Press.

Barrachina, Marie-Aline, 1991. "Ideal de la Mujer Falangista. Ideal Falangista de la mujer." In *Las Mujeres y la Guerra Civil Española*, III Jornadas de estudio monográficos. Salamanca, octubre 1989, 211–217. Madrid: Ministerio de Cultura.

Basu, Amrita. 1993. "Feminism Inverted: The Real Women and Gendered Imagery of Hindu Nationalism." *Bulletin of Concerned Asian Scholars* 25, 4 (October–December): 25–37.

————. 1997. "Hindu Women's Activism in India and the Questions It Raises." In *Women and the Hindu Right*, ed. Tanika Sarkar and Butalia Urvashi, 167–184. New York: Routledge.

————. 1998. "Appropriating Gender." In *Appropriating Gender: Women's Activism and Politicized Religion in South Asia*, ed. Patricia Jefferey and Amrita Basu. New York: Routledge.

Basu, Tapan. 1994. *Khaki Flags and Saffron Shorts: A Critique of the Hindu Right*. New Delhi: Orient Longman.

Bayle, Constantino. 1938. "La Cárcel de mujeres en Madrid." *Razon y Fe*, 113: 435–450.

Becker, Marjorie. 1995. *Setting the Virgin on Fire: Lázaro Cárdenas, Michoacán Peasants, and the Redemption of the Mexican Revolution*. Berkeley: University of California Press.

Bellonci, Goffredo. 1929. "Il palazzone." *L'Italia Letteraria*, 23 June, p. 8.

Bennett, David. 1988. *The Party of Fear: From Nativist Movements to the New Right in American History*. Chapel Hill: University of North Carolina.

Berktay, F. 1992. "Looking From the Otherside: Is Cultural Relativism a Way Out?" In *Doing Things Differently*, ed. J. De Groot and M. Maynard. New York: MacMillan.

Besse, Susan K. 1996. *Restructuring Patriarchy: The Modernization of Gender Inequality in Brazil, 1914–1940.* Chapel Hill: University of North Carolina Press.

Bihr, Alain. 1998. *Le spectre de l'extrême droite. Les Français dans le miroir du Front national.* Paris: Les Éditions de l'Atelier.

Billings, John, and Evelyn Billings. 2000. Foreword to *Studies on Human Reproduction,* by James B. Brown. http://www.billings-centre.ab.ca/bc_his.htm. April.

Birenbaum, Guy. 1992. *Le Front national en politique.* Paris: Balland.

Blee, Kathleen. 1991. *Women of the Klan.* University of California Press.

———. 1993. "Evidence, Empathy, and Ethics: Lessons from Oral Histories of the Klan." *Journal of American History* 80, 2 (September).

———. 1997. "Motherhood in the Radical Right." In *The Politics of Motherhood: Activist Voices from Left to Right,* ed. Alexis Jetter, Annelise Orleck, and Diana Taylor. Hanover, N.H.: University Press of New England.

———. 1998. *No Middle Ground: Women and Radical Protest.* New York: New York University Press.

———. 2000. "White on White: Interviewing Women in U.S. White Supremacist Groups." In *Race-ing Research: Methodological and Ethical Dilemmas in Field Research,* ed. France Winddance Twine and Jonathan Warren. New York: New York University Press.

———. 2001. *Inside Organized Racism: Women and Men in the Racist Movement.* University of California Press.

Blinkhorn, Martin. 1990. "Conservatism, Traditionalism, and Fascism in Spain." In *Fascists and Conservatives: The Radical Right and the Establishment in Twentieth-Century Europe,* 118–137. London: Unwin Hyman.

Blom, Ida. 1995. "International Trends. Feminism and Nationalism in the Early Twentieth Century: A Cross-Cultural Perspective." *Journal of Women's History* 7, 4: 82–94.

Boak, Helen. 1990. "Women in Weimar Politics." *European History Quarterly* 20: 369–399.

Bock, Gisela. 1984. *When Biology Became Destiny: Women in Weimar and Nazi Germany.* New York: Monthly Review Press.

———. 1996. "Equality and Difference in National Socialism Racism." In *Feminism and History,* ed. J. W. Scott. Oxford: Oxford University Press.

Bolter, Flora. 2000. "Les femmes du MNR et du Front national." *Prochoix* 15 (September–October 2000).

Boris, E. 1993. "The Power of Motherhood: Black and White Activist Women Redefine the 'Political.' "In *Mothers of a New World,* ed. S. Koven and S. Michel. New York: Routledge.

Bosi Maramotti, Giovanna. 1982. "Margherita Sarfatti: Appunti per una storia della letteratura femminile nel periodo fascista." In *Il pensiero reazionario: La politica e la cultura dei fascismi,* ed. Bruno Bandini, 101–112. Ravenna: Longo.

Boyarin, Daniel. 1999. Panel on "Historical Contexts: Sex, Regulation, and Religious Traditions." Presentation at "Whose Millennium? Religion, Sexuality, and the Values of Citizenship." City University of New York, 13 April.

Boylan, Kristina A. 2000. "Mexican Catholic Women's Activism." Ph.D. diss., Oxford University.

Brewer, J. D. 1984. *Mosley's Men: The British Union of Fascists in the West Midlands.* Hampshire, U.K.: Gower.

Bridenthal, Renate. 1993. "Organized Rural Women and the Conservative Mobilization of the German Countryside in the Weimar Republic." In *Between Reform, Reaction, and Resistance: Studies in the History of German Conservatism from 1789 to 1945,* ed. Larry E. Jones and James Retallack, 375–405. Oxford, U.K.: Berg.

Bridenthal, Renate, and Claudia Koonz. 1977. *Becoming Visible: Women in European History.* Boston: Houghton Mifflin.

Brink, E. 1990. "Man-Made Women: Gender, Class and the Ideology of the Volksmoeder." In *Women and Gender in Southern Africa to 1945,* ed. C. Walker. Capetown, South Africa: David Philip.

Brown, Lyle C. 1964. "Mexican Church-State Relations, 1933–1940." *Journal of Church and State* 6, 2 (spring).

Brownmiller, S. 1999. *In Our Time: A Memoir of a Revolution.* New York: Dial Press.

Broxson, Elmer R. 1972. "Plínio Salgado and Brazilian Integralism, 1932–1938." Ph.D. diss., Catholic University.

Buchanan, Tom. 1997. *Britain and the Spanish Civil War.* Cambridge: Cambridge University Press.

Bunster, Ximena. 1988. "Watch Out for the Little Nazi Man That All of Us Have Inside: The Mobilization and Demobilization of Women in Militarized Chile." *Women Studies International Forum* 11, 5.

Butalia, Urvashi and Rita Menon. 1998. *The Other Side of Violence: Voices from the Partition of India.* New Delhi: Penguin Press.

Butler, Judith. 1990, 1999. *Gender Trouble. Feminism and the Subversion of Identity.* New York: Routledge.

———. 1992. "Contingent Foundations: Feminism and the Question of Postmodernism." In *Feminists Theorize the Political,* ed. Judith Butler and J. Scott, 3–21. New York: Routledge.

Butler, Kim D. 1998. *Freedoms Given, Freedoms Won: AfroBrazilians in Post Abolition São Paulo and Salvador.* New Brunswick, N.J.: Rutgers University Press.

Çaha, Ömer. 1996. *Sivil Kadın: Türkiye'de Sivil Toplum ve Kadın* (Civic woman: Civil society and women in Turkey). Ankara, Turkey: Vadi Yayınları.

Çakır, R. 1994. *Ne Şeriat, Ne Demokrasi: Refah Partisi'ni Anlamak* (Neither Islamic law nor democracy: To understand the Welfare Party). Istanbul: Metis Yayınları.

Çakır, S. 1994. *Osmanlı Kadın Hareketi* (Ottoman women's movement). Istanbul: Metis Yayınları.

Cameron, Dolly. 1934. "Reception at Sulgrave Club for Eminent Italian Writer and Critic. *Washington Times,* 17 April, 14.

Campbell, Beatrix. 1987. *The Iron Ladies: Why Do Women Vote Tory?* London: Virago.

Cannistraro, Philip V., and Brian Sullivan. 1993. *Il Duce's Other Woman: The Untold Story of Margherita Sarfatti, Mussolini's Jewish Mistress, and How She Helped Him Come to Power.* New York: William Morrow.

Castles, Stephen, Mary Kalantzis, Bill Cope, and Michael Morrissey. 1992. *Mistaken Identity: Multiculturalism and the Demise of Nationalism in Australia.* 3rd ed. Sydney: Pluto Press.

Cecchi, Alberto. 1926. "*Dux* di Margherita Sarfatti." *Critica Fascista* (1 July): 243–245.

CEMA Chile. n.d. *Ocho años de labor femenina a lo largo y ancho del país.* Santiago: Editora Nacional Gabriela Mistral.

Chalmers, David M. 1981. *Hooded Americanism: The History of the Ku Klux Klan.* Durham, N.C.: Duke University Press.

Charles, Nickie, and Helen Hintjens. 1998. "Gender, Ethnicity, and Cultural Identity: Women's 'Places.'" In *Gender, Ethnicity, and Political Ideologies,* ed. Nickie Charles and Helen Hintjens. New York: Routledge.

Chatterjee, Partha. 1989. "Nationalist Resolution of the Woman Question." In *Recasting Women: Essays in Colonial History,* ed. Kumkum Sangari and Suresh Vaid, 233–254. New Delhi: Kali for Women.

———. 1993. *The Nation and Its Fragments: Colonial and Post-Colonial Histories.* Princeton, N.J.: Princeton University Press.

Childers, Thomas. 1983. *The Nazi Voter: The Social Foundations of Fascism in Germany, 1919–1933.* Chapel Hill: University of North Carolina Press.

Chuchryk, Patricia. 1991. "Feminist Anti-Authoritarian Politics: The Role of Women's Organizations in the Chilean Transition to Democracy." In *The Women's Movement in Latin America: Feminism and the Transition to Democracy,* ed. Jane S. Jaquette. Boulder, Colo.: Westview Press.

Clark, B. 1989. "History of the Roman-Dutch Law of Marriage from a Socio-Economic Perspective." In *Essays on the History of Law,* ed. D. P. Visser. Cape Town: Juta.

Cochran, Floyd. 1993. "Sisterhood of Hate." Privately published and circulated through the Web.

Cohen, C., K. Jones, and J. Tronto, eds. 1997. *Women Transforming Politics*. New York: New York University Press.

Cohen, Philip. 1996. "Nationalism and Suffrage: Gender Struggle in Nation-Building America." *Signs: Journal of Women in Culture and Society* 21, 3: 707–727.

Collins, Patricia Hill. 1990. *Black Feminist Thought: Knowledge, Consciousness, and the Politics of Empowerment*. New York: Routledge.

Comer, James. 1923. "A Tribute and a Challenge to American Women." In *Papers Read at First Annual Meeting [of the Ku Klux Klan]*. n.p.

Comité Diocesano de la JCFM de Guadalajara. n.d. *JCFM*. Guadalajara, Mexico: Comité Diocesano de Guadalajara.

Committee on South Asian Women. 1991. *Bulletin* 8, 3–4. Issue on "Women and the Hindu Right." September.

Concerned Women for America. 1995. *Welcome to Concerned Women for America*. Membership packet. Washington, D.C.: Concerned Women for America.

Conclusiones aprobadas en la Segunda Asamblea General de la UFCM. 1935. *Boletin Eclesiástico de la Diocesis de Guadalajara (BEG)* 4, 4 (1 April).

Conover, P. J., and V. Gray. 1983. *Feminism and the New Right: Conflict over the American Family*. New York: Praeger.

"Consultas.: 1937. *Christus* 2, (17 April).

Coppola, Vincent. *Dragons of God: A Journey through Far-Right America*. 1996. Atlanta: Longstreet Press.

Costain, A. N. 1988. "Representing Women: The Transition from Social Movement to Interest Group." In *Women, Power and Policy: Toward the Year 2000*, ed. Ellen Boneparth and Emily Stoper. New York: Pergamon Press.

Crawford, A. 1980. *Thunder on the Right: The "New Right" and the Politics of Resentment*. New York: Pantheon.

Crew, David. 1998. *Germans on Welfare: From Weimar to Hitler*. Oxford: Oxford University Press.

Cronin, M. ed. 1996. *The Failure of British Fascism: The Far Right and the Fight for Political Recognition*. London: Macmillan.

Crummett, María de los Angeles. 1977. "El Poder Feminino: The Mobilization of Women against Socialism in Chile." *Latin American Perspectives* (fall): 106–121.

Cullen, Stephen. 1987. "The British Union of Fascists: Ideology, Membership, and Meetings, 1932–1940." Master's thesis. Nuffield College, Oxford University.

———. 1996. "Four Women for Mosley: Women in the BUF 1932–1940." *Oral History* 24, 1 (spring).

Curthoys, Ann. 1993. "Identity Crisis: Colonialism, Nationalism, and Gender in Australian History." *Gender and History* 5, 2.

Curthoys, Ann, and Carol Johnson. 1998. "Articulating the Future and the Past: Gender, Race, and Globalisation in One Nation Discourse." *Hecate* 24, 2: 97–114.

Cutrufelli, Maria Rosa et al. 1994. *Piccole italiane: Un raggiro durato vent'anni*. Milan: Anabasi.

d'Appollonia, Ariane Chebel. 1988. *L'extrême droite en France. De Maurras á Le Pen*. Brussels: Éditions Complexe.

Darrow, Margaret. 1996. "French Volunteer Nursing and the Myth of War Experience in World War One." *American Historical Review* 101, 1 (February): 80–106.

Davis, Nathaniel. 1985. *The Last Two Years of Salvador Allende*. Ithaca, N.Y.: Cornell University Press.

De Felice, Renzo. 1965. *Mussolini il rivoluzionario 1883–1920*. Turin: Einaudi.

de Grazia, Victoria. 1982. "Il fascino del priapo: Margherita Sarfatti biografa del Duce." *Memoria* 4 (June).

———. 1992. *How Fascism Rules Women. Italy 1922–1945*. Berkeley: University of California Press.

De Grand, Alexander. 1976. "Women under Italian Fascism." *The Historical Journal*. 19 (4).

De Groot, Joanna. "The Dialectics of Gender: Women, Men and Political Discourses in Iran c. 1890–1930." *Gender and History* 5.

Deleuze, Gilles and Féliz Guattari. 1972. *L'Anti-Oedipe.* Paris: Minuit.

DellaPergola, Sergio. 1987. "Demographic Trends of Latin American Jewry." In *The Jewish Presence in Latin America*, ed. Judith Laikin Elkin and Gilbert W. Merkx. Boston: Allen and Unwin, 1987.

de Méndez, Margarita G. 1980. "Síntesis Histórica de la UFCM." *AF*, special issue (September).

Del Valle, Matilde. 1940. "Delegación Central de Obreras: La conciencia de responsabilidad," *AF* 5, 20 (September).

Del Valle, Sofía, interviews with Alicia Olivera de Bonfil, Mexico City, 3 Nov. 1972 and 14 Feb. 1973 (INAH/PHO/4/11).

Demir, H. 1998. *Islamci Kadinin Aynadaki Sureti* (Islamist woman's reflection in the Mirror). Istanbul: Bilgi Yayınları.

Derrida, Jacques. 1967. *De la grammatologie.* Paris: Minuit.

Deutsch, Sandra McGee. 1999. *Las Derechas: The Extreme Right in Argentina, Brazil, and Chile, 1890–1939.* Stanford, Calif.: Stanford University Press.

Diamond, S. 1995. *Roads to Dominion: Right-Wing Movements and Political Power in the United States.* New York: Guilford.

Di Febo, Giuliana. 1987. *La Santa de la Raza: Un culto barroco en la españa franquista.* Barcelona: Icaria.

Di Febo, Juliana. 1991. "*El Monje Guerrero*: Identidad de género en los modelos franquistas durante la guerra civil." In *Las Mujeres y la Guerra Civil Española*, III Jornadas de estudio monográficos. Salamanca, octubre 1989, 202–210. Madrid: Ministerio de Cultura.

"Dirigentes–Como Formarlas," *Christus*, 2, 20 (July 1937).

Dobratz, Betty A., and Stephanie L. Shanks-Meile 1997. "*White Power, White Pride!*": The White Separatist Movement in the United States." New York: Twayne Publishers.

Dodd, Helen J. 1997. *Pauline: The Hanson Phenomenon.* Brisbane, Australia: Boolarong Press.

Dodson, D., and S. Carroll. 1991. *Reshaping the Agenda: Women in State Legislatures.* New Brunswick, N.J.: Center for the American Woman and Politics.

Dodson, D., S. Carroll, R. Mandel, K. Kleeman, R. Schreiber, and D. Liebowitz. 1995. *Voices, Views, Votes: The Impact of Women in the 103rd Congress.* New Brunswick, N.J.: Center for the American Woman and Politics.

Dombrowski, Ann Nicole. 1999. *Women and War in the Twentieth Century: Enlisted with or without Consent.* New York: Garland.

Dreifuss, René Armand. 1987. *1964: A conquista do estado. Açao Política, poder e golpe de classe.* Translated by Ayeska Branca de Oliveira Farias, Ceres Ribeiro Pires de Freitas, Else Ribeiro Pires Vieira, and Glória Maria de Mello Carvalho. Petrópolis, Brazil: Vozes.

Driver, Felix, and David Gilbert. 1998. "Heart of Empire? Landscape, Space and Performance in Imperial London." In *Environment and Planning D: Society and Space*, vol. 16, pp. 11–28.

Driver, Nellie. n.d. *From the Shadows of Exile.* Unpublished autobiography. J. B. Priestly Library, University of Bradford.

Dulles, John W. F. 1970. *Unrest in Brazil: Political Military Crises 1955–1964.* Austin: University of Texas Press.

Durakbaşa, A. 1998. "Kemalism as an Identity Politics." In *Deconstructing the Images of "The Turkish Woman,"* ed. Z. Arat. New York: St. Martin's Press.

———. 1994. "Women in the British Union of Fascists." In *This Working-Day World*, ed. S. Oldfield. London: Taylor Francis.

———. 1995. "Women and the British Extreme Right." In *The Far Right in Western and Eastern Europe*, eds. Luciano Cheles, Ronnie Ferguson, and Michalina Vaughan. 2nd edition. New York: Longman.

———. 1998. *Women and Fascism.* London: Routledge.

Durham, Martin. 1992. "Gender and the British Union of Fascists." *Journal of Contemporary History*. 27.

du Toit, Marijke. 1992. "'Dangerous Motherhood": Maternity Care and the Gendered Construction of Afrikaner Identity, 1904–1939." In *Lara Marks and Hilary Marland, Women and Children First, International Maternal and Infant Welfare, 1870–1945*, ed. Valerie Fildes. Routledge: London.

———. 1996. "Women, Welfare, and the Nurturing of Afrikaner Nationalism: A Social History of the Afrikaanse Christelike Vroue Vereniging, c. 1870–1939." Ph.D. diss., University of Cape Town.

Dworkin, Andrea. 1978. *Right-Wing Women*. New York: Perigee Books.

———. 1983. *Right-Wing Women: The Politics of Domesticated Females*. London: Women's Press.

Echols, Alison. 1989. *Daring to Be Bad: Radical Feminism in America 1967–1975*. Minneapolis: University of Minnesota Press.

Elam, Norah. 1935. "Fascism, Women and Democracy." *Fascist Quarterly* 1, 3 (July).

Ellison, Anne, with Iva Deutchmann. 1997. "Men Only: Pauline Hanson and Australia's Far Right." In *Pauline Hanson: One Nation and Australian Politics*, ed. Bligh Grant, 141–150. Armidale, Australia: University of New South Wales Press.

Enciclopedia Treccani. 1936. Vol. 30, p. 870. Rome: Treccani.

Enders, Victoria L. 1990. "Problematic Portraits: The Ambiguous Historical Role of the *Sección Femenina* of the Falange." In *Constructing Spanish Womanhood: Female Identity in Modern Spain*, ed. Victoria L. Enders and Pamela Radcliff, 375–397. Albany, N.Y.: SUNY Press.

———. 1992. "Nationalism and Feminism: The *Sección Femenina* of the Falange." *History of European Ideas* 15, 4–6 (August): 673–690.

Enders, Victoria L. and Pamela Radcliff. 1999. "General Introduction: Contesting Identities/Contesting Categories." In *Constructing Spanish Womanhood: Female Identity in Modern Spain*, ed. Victoria L. Enders and Pamela Radcliff. Albany, N.Y.: SUNY Press.

Episcopado Mexicano. 1935. "Carta Pastoral Colectiva ... sobre la doctrina educativa de la Iglesia," 21 November 1935. *Christus* 1, 1 (1 December).

Eraslan, S. 2000. "Refahlı Kadın Deneyimi" (The experience of the women of the Welfare Party). In *Osmanlı'dan Cumhuriyet'e Kadının Tarihi Dönüşümü*, ed. Y. Ramazanoğlu. Istanbul: Pınar Yayınları.

Evans, Richard J. 1976. *The Feminist Movement in Germany 1894–1933*. London: Sage.

Falter, Jürgen, Thomas Lindenberger, and Siegfried Schumann. 1986. *Wahlen und Abstimmungen in der Weimarer Republik: Materialien zum Wahlverhalten 1919–1933*. Munich: C. H. Beck.

Farmborough, Florence. 1938. *Life and People in National Spain*. London: Sheed and Ward.

———. 1974. *Nurse at the Russian Front. A Diary 1914–18*. London: Constable.

Farr, Barbara Storm. 1987. *The Development and Impact of Right-Wing Politics in Britain 1903–1932*. New York: Garland.

Fazilet Partisi. 1999. *Genel Merkez Hanımlar Komisyonu 1998–1999 Yılı Faaliyet Bülteni* (The Virtue Party, Central Committee Ladies' Commissions, annual activity bulletin 1998–1999). Ankara, Turkey: Fazilet Partisi.

Ferree, M. M., and P. Y. Martin. 1995. *Feminist Organizations: Harvest of the New Women's Movement*. Philadelphia: Temple University Press.

Flanders, L. 1996. Conservative Women Are Right for Media Mainstream. *Extra!* March/April, 1–3. Florence: La Fenice.

Foucault, Michel. 1980. *The History of Sexuality*, Vol. 1. New York: Vintage Books.

Fowler-Salamini, Heather, and Mary Kay Vaughan. 1994. *Women of the Mexican Countryside, 1880–1990*. Tucson: University of Arizona Press.

Franco, Jean. 1999. *Critical Passions*, Durham, N.C.: Duke University Press.

Fredericka, Queen. 1971. *Metron Katanoiseos*. Athens: Vivliometafrastiki.

Friedan, Betty. 1963. *The Feminine Mystique*. New York: Faber and Faber.

Fritzsche, Peter. 2001. "The Case of Modern Memory." *Journal of Modern History* 73 (March).

Frohmann, Alicia, and Teresa Valdés. 1995. "Democracy in the Country and in the Home. The Women's Movement in Chile." In *The Challenge of Local Feminisms: Women's Movement in Global Perspective*, ed. Amrita Basu (Boulder: Westview Press).

Front National. 1990–1991. *Le guide du militant, Les dossiers tricolores de National Hebdo*, no. 3, Winter.

———. 1993. *300 mesures pour la renaissance de la France*. Paris: Éditions nationales.

Führer, Karl Christian. 1990. "Für das Wirtschaftsleben 'mehr oder weniger wertlose Personen.' Zur Lage von Invaliden- und Kleinrentnern in den Inflationsjahren 1918–1924." *Archiv für Sozialgeschichte* 30: 144–80.

Furchtgott-Roth, D., and C. Stolba. 1999. *Women's Figures: An Illustrated Guide to the Economic Progress of Women in America*. Washington, D.C.: AEI Press.

Fuss, D. 1989. *Essentially Speaking*. New York: Routledge.

Fussell, Paul. 1980. *Abroad: British Literary Travelling Between the Wars*. Oxford: Oxford University Press.

Fyrth, Jim. 1986. *The Signal Was Spain: The Aid Spain Movement in Britain 1936–39*. London: Lawrence and Wishart.

Fyrth, Jim, and Sally Alexander. 1991. *Women's Voices in the Spanish Civil War*. London: Lawrence and Wishart.

Gabrielli, Patrizia. 1999. *Fenicotteri in volo: Donne comuniste nel ventennio fascista*. Rome: Carocci.

Gaitskell, Deborah and Elaine Unterhalter. 1989. "Mothers of the Nation: A Comparative Analysis of Nation, Race and Motherhood in Afrikaner Nationalism and the African National Congress." In *Woman-Nation-State*, ed. N. Yuval-Davis and S. Anthisa. London: MacMillan.

Galindo Mendoza, Alfredo, M.Sp.S. 1945. *Apuntes geográficos y estadísticos de la Iglesia Católica en México*. Mexico City: Administración de la Revista 'La Cruz.'

Gallego Méndez, María Teresa. 1983. *Mujer, Falange y franquismo*. Madrid: Taurus.

Gallucci, Carole C. 1995. "Alba de Céspedes's There's No Turning Back: Challenging the New Woman's Future." In *Mothers of Invention: Women, Italian Fascism, and Culture*, ed. Robin Pickering-Iazzi, 200–219. Minneapolis: University of Minnesota Press.

Gallucci, Carole C. and Ellen Nerenberg, eds. 1999. "The Body and the Letter: Sibilla Aleramo in the Interwar Years." *Forum Italicum* 33, 2 (fall): 363–391.

———. 2000. *Writing beyond Fascism: Cultural Resistance in the Life and Works of Alba de Céspedes*. Teaneck, N.J.: Fairleigh Dickinson University Press.

Gandhi, M. K. 1927. *An Autobiography or The Story of My Experiments with Truth*. Translated from Gujarati by Mahadev Desai. Ahmedabad, Gujarat, India: Navajivan Publishing House.

Garibi Rivera, José. 1936. "Primera Carta Pastoral," 12 April 1936. *Christus*, 1, 7 (June).

Gelb, J., and Palley Marian Lief. 1987. *Women and Public Policies*. Princeton, N.J.: Princeton University Press.

Gellner, Ernest. 1983. *Nations and Nationalism*. London: Basil Blackwell.

———. 1992. *Postmodernism, Reason, and Religion*. New York: Kegan and Paul.

Geraldini, Arnaldo. 1961. "Si è spenta Margherita Sarfatti, biografa del Duce" *Corriere della Sera*, 31 October.

Ghosh, Bishnupriya. 1998. "The Post-Colonial Bazaar." *Postmodern Cultures*. Online October.

———. 2001. "Among Ashes: The Political Promise of the *Fire* Controversy." Unpublished manuscript.

Giddens, A. 1991. *Modernity and Self-Identity*. Stanford, Calif.: Stanford University Press.

Giel, Lawrence A. 1967. "*George R. Dale—Crusader for Free Speech and a Free Press*." Ph.D. Diss., Muncie, Ind.: Ball State University.

Gilman, Sander L. 1990. *Jewish Self-Hatred: Anti-Semitism and the Hidden Language of the Jews*. Baltimore: Johns Hopkins University Press.

Ginsburg, F. 1989. *Contested Lives: The Abortion Debate in an American Community.* Berkeley: University of California Press.

Göçek, F. M. 2000. "To Veil or Not to Veil? The Contested Location of Gender in Contemporary Turkey." *interventions* 1, 4: 521–535.

Gökalp, Ziya. 1972. *Türkçülüğün Esaslari* (The principles of Turkism). Istanbul: Milli Eğitim Basımevi.

Goldsmith, Marlene. 1996. *Political Incorrectness: Defying the Thought Police.* Sydney: Hodder and Stoughton.

Göle, Nilufer. 1996. *Forbidden Modern.* Ann Arbor: University of Michigan Press.

———. 1997. "The Quest for the Islamic Self within the Context of Modernity." In *Rethinking Modernity and Turkish Identity in Turkey,* ed. S. Bozdogan and R. Kasaba, 95–112. Seattle: University of Washington Press.

Golwalkar, M. S. 1939. *We or Our Nationhood Defined.* Nagpur, India: Bharat Prakashan.

———. 1996. *Bunch of Thoughts.* Bangalore, India: Sahitya Sindhu Prakashana.

Gordon, Linda. 1987. "Review Essay: Nazi Feminists?" *Feminist Review* 27: 97–106.

Goribar de Cortina, Refugio. 1938. "La UFCM y su Ayuda al Seminario," *AF* 4, 2 (February).

Goribar de Cortina, Refugio. 1987. "Balance del Año." *AF* 3.

Gottlieb, Julie V. 1999. "Women and Fascism in the East End." *Jewish Culture and History* 1, 2.

———. 2000a. *Feminine Fascism: Women in Britain's Fascist Movement 1923–1945.* London: I. B. Tauris.

———. 2000b. Suffragette Experience through the Filter of Fascism." In *A Suffrage Reader,* ed. Claire Eustance, Joan Ryan, and Laura Ugolini. London: Cassell.

Graff, F. N. 1924. "A Tribute to the Women of the Ku Klux Klan." *Dawn,* 26 January 1924.

Graham, Helen. 1996. "Women and Social Change." In *Spanish Cultural Studies: An Introduction,* ed. Helen Graham and Jo Labanyi, 99–116. Oxford: Oxford University Press.

Gramsci, Antonio. 1971. *Letteratura e vita nazionale.* Rome: Riuniti.

Grand Dragon. 1923. "A Tribute and Challenge to American Women." In *Papers Read at the First Annual Meeting of the Knights of the Ku Klux Klan.*

Grathwol, Robert P. 1980. *Stresemann and the DNVP: Reconciliation or Revenge in German Foreign Policy.* Lawrence: Regents Press of Kansas Press.

Green, J. C., J. L. Guth, C. E. Smidt, and L. A. Kellstedt. 1996. *Religion and the Culture Wars: Dispatches from the Front.* Lanham, Md.: Rowman and Littlefield.

Griffiths, Richard. 1980. *Fellow Travellers of the Right. British Enthusiasts for Nazi Germany, 1933–99.* London: Constable.

———. 1998. *Patriotism Perverted: Captain Ramsay, the Right Club, and British Anti-Semitism 1939–40.* London: Constable.

Grossmann, Atina. 1991. "Feminist Debates about Women and National Socialism." *Gender and History* 3, 3: 350–358.

Guenena, Nemat. 1986. "The Jihad: An Islamic Alternative in Egypt." *Cairo Papers in Social Science* 9, 2 (summer).

Guillaumin, Colette. 1995. *Racism, Sexism, Power, and Ideology.* New York: Routledge.

Güneş-Ayata, A. 1995. "Women's Participation in Politics in Turkey." In *Women in Modern Turkish Society,* ed. Ş. Tekeli. London and New Jersey: Zed Books.

———. 1998. "Laiklik, Güç ve Katılım Sçgeninde Kadın ve Siyaset" (Women and politics in the triangle of participation, power and secularism). In *75 Yılda Kadınlar ve Erkekler,* ed. A. Berktay Hacımirzaoğlu. Istanbul: Tarih Vakfı Yayınları.

Guth, J. L., J. C. Green, L. A. Kellstedt, and C. E. Smidt. 1995. "Onward Christian Soldiers: Religious Activist Groups in American Politics." In *Interest Group Politics,* ed. A. J. Cigler and B. A. Loomis, 55–76. Washington, D.C.: Congressional Quarterly Press.

Hackett, Amy. 1976. "The Politics of Feminism in Wilhelmine Germany, 1890–1918." Ph.D., diss. Columbia University.

Haddad Yazbeck, Y., and J. Esposito, eds. 1997. *Islam, Gender, and Social Change.* New York: Oxford University Press.

Hahner, June E. 1990. *Emancipating the Female Sex: The Struggle for Women's Rights in Brazil, 1850–1940.* Durham, N.C.: Duke University Press.

Halberstam, Judith. 1998. *Female Masculinity.* Durham, N.C.: Duke University Press.

Hansen, Thomas Blom. 1999. *The Saffron Wave: Democracy and Nationalism in Modern India.* Princeton, N.J.: Princeton University Press.

Hanson, Randall S. 1994. "The Day of Ideals: Catholic Social Action in the Age of the Mexican Revolution, 1867–1929." Ph.D. diss. Indiana University–Bloomington.

———. 1997. "Mujeres Militantes: Las Damas Católicas and the Mobilization of Women in Revolutionary Mexico, 1912–1929." Paper presented at the Conference on Latin American History, New York, January.

Hardisty, J. 1999. *Mobilizing Resentment: Conservative Resurgence from the John Birch Society to the Promise Keepers.* Boston: Beacon Press.

Harrowitz, Nancy. 1996. "Margherita Sarfatti and the Culture of Fascism." *Il Veltro* 40, 1–2 (January-April): 143–148.

Heinsohn, Kirsten. 2000. "Im Dienste der deutschen Volksgemeinschaft: Die 'Frauenfrage' und konservative Parteien vor und nach dem Ersten Weltkrieg." In *Nation, Politik und Geschlecht: Frauenbewegungen und Nationalismus in der Moderne,* ed. Ute Planert, 215–233. Frankfurt am Main: Campus Verlag.

Henderson, Anne. 1999. *Getting Even: Women M.P.s, on Life, Power and Politics.* Sydney: HarperCollins.

Heper, M. 1981. "Islam, Polity and Society in Turkey: A Middle Eastern Perspective." *Middle East Journal* 35, 3: 345–363.

Hertzke, A. D. 1988. *Representing God in Washington.* Knoxville: University of Tennessee Press.

Hertzman, Lewis. 1963. *DNVP: Right-Wing Opposition in the Weimar Republic, 1918–1924.* Lincoln: University of Nebraska Press.

Higgonet, Margaret, and Patrice Higgonet. 1987. "Double Helix." In *Behind the Lines: Gender and the Two World Wars,* ed. Margaret Randolph Higgonet, 31–47. New Haven, Conn.: Yale University Press.

Hiller von Gaertringen, Friedrich Freiherr. 1960. "Die Deutschnationale Volkspartei." In *Das Ende der Parteien 1933,* ed. Erich Matthias and Rudolf Morsey, 543–652. Düsseldorf: Droste.

Hobsbawm, Eric. 1990. *Nations and Nationalism since 1780.* New York: Cambridge University Press.

Hobsbawm, Eric, and Terence Ranger, eds. 1993. *The Invention of Tradition.* New York: Cambridge University Press.

Hofmeyr, I. 1987. "Building a Nation from Words: Afrikaans Language, Literature, and Ethnic Identity, 1902–1924." In *The Politics of Race, Class, and Nationalism in Twentieth-Century South Africa,* ed. S. Marks and S. Trapido. London: Longman.

Holzbach, Heidrun. 1981. *Das "System Hugenberg." Die Organisation bürgerlicher Sammlungspolitik vor dem Aufstieg der NSDAP.* Stuttgart: Deutsche Verlags-Anstalt.

Hong, Young-Sun. 1998. *Welfare, Modernity, and the Weimar State, 1919–1933.* Princeton, N.J.: Princeton University Press.

hooks, bell. 1981. *Ain't I a Woman: Black Women and Feminism.* Boston: South End Press.

Horne, Donald. 1964. *The Lucky Country.* Ringwood, Victoria, Australia: Penguin Books.

Huddy, L. 1997. "Feminists and Feminism in the News." In *Women, Media, and Politics,* ed. P. Norris, 183–204. New York: Oxford University Press.

Hughes, Donna M., Laura Joy Sporcic, Nadine Z. Mendelsohn, Vanessa Chirgwin. 1999. *The Factbook on Global Sexual Exploitation.* Kingston: University of Rhode Island, Coalition Against Trafficking in Women.

Hughes, Michael. 1988. *Paying for the German Inflation.* Chapel Hill: University of North Carolina Press.

Ilıcak, N. 1998. "Dame de Sion'dan Fazilet Partisi'ne" (From Dame de Sion to the Virtue Party). In *Kadınlar Olmadan Asla,* ed. Z. Göğüş. Istanbul: Sabah Kitapları.

Ilyasoglu, A. 1998. "Islamist Women in Turkey: Their Identity and Self-Image." In *Decon-*

structing the Images of "The Turkish Woman," ed. Z. Arat, 241–262. New York: St. Martin's Press.

Independent Women's Forum. 1996. *Who Are We? The Future.* Recruitment pamphlet. Washington, D.C.: Independent Women's Forum.

"Instrucción Pastoral del Comité Ejecutivo Episcopal ... sobre la conducta que deben observar acerca de la enseñanza," *Christus* 2, 19 (June 1937).

"Interview with Heba Raouf Ezzat." 1994. *Middle East Report* (MERIP).

Jayawardena, Kumari. 1986. *Feminism and Nationalism in the Third World.* London: Zed.

Jeansonne, Glen. 1996. *Women of the Far Right: The Mothers' Movement and World War II.* Chicago: University of Chicago Press.

Jeffery, Patricia and Amrita Basu, eds. 1998. *Appropriating Gender: Women's Activism and Politicized Religion in South Asia.* New York: Routledge.

Jeffreys, Sheila. 1997. *The Idea of Prostitution.* Melbourne: Spinifex.

Jetter, A., A. Orleck, and D. Taylor. 1997. *The Politics of Motherhood.* Hanover, N.H.: University Press of New England.

Jiles Moreno, Ximena. 1992. *De la miel a los implantes. Historia de las políticas de regulación de la fecundidad en Chile.* Santiago: Corporación de Salud y Políticas Sociales.

John, Mary and Janaki Nair. 1999. "Sexuality in Modern India: Critical Concerns." *Journal on Communication for Development* 3, 1 (April): 4–8.

John, Mary. 1998. "Globalisation, Sexuality, and the Visual Field: Issues and Non-Issues for Cultural Critique." In *A Question of Silence: The Sexual Economies of Modern India,* ed. Mary John and Janaki Nair. New Delhi: Kali for Women.

Joseph, Sherry. 1998. "The Law and Homosexuality in India." CEHAT. International Conference on Preventing Violence, Caring for Survivors. November 28–30, 1–5.

Kadıoğlu, A. 1994. "Women's Subordination in Turkey: Is Islam Really the Villain?" *Middle East Journal* 48, 4, 654–660.

Kakar, Sudhir. 1995. *The Colours of Violence.* New York: Viking, Penguin.

Kalantzis, Mary and Bill Cope. 1997. "An Opportunity to Change the Culture." In *The Retreat from Tolerance,* ed. Philip Adams, 57–85. Sydney: ABC Books.

Kandiyoti, D. 1989. "Women in the Turkish State: Political Actors or Symbolic Pawns?" In *Women, Nation, State,* ed. N. Yuval-Davis and F. Anthias. London: MacMillan.

————. 1992. "Women, Islam, and the State: A Comparative Approach." In *Comparing Muslim Societies: Knowledge and the State in a World Civilization,* ed. J.R. Cole, 238–60. Ann Arbor: University of Michigan Press.

Kaplan, Caren. 1994. "The Politics of Location as Transnational Feminist Critical Practice. In *Scattered Hegemonies: Postmodernity and Transnational Feminist Practices,* ed. Inderpal Grewal and Caren Kaplan. Minneapolis: University of Minnesota Press.

Kaplan, Temma. 1982. "Female Consciousness and Collective Action: The Case of Barcelona, 1910–1918." *Signs: Journal of Women in Culture and Society* 7, 3.

Kapur, Ratna. 1999. "Postcolonial Erotic Disruptions: Legal Narratives of Culture, Sex, and Nation in India." University Seminars, Columbia University, October.

Karam, Azza M. 1995. "Feminismo o islamismo en Egipto: en busca de nuevos paradimas' (Feminism and Islamism in Egypt: In Search of new paradigms). In *Papeles: Cuestiones Internacionales de Paz, Ecologia y Desarrollo,* no. 55. Madrid: Centro de Investigación para la Paz.

————. 1996. "Challenging Static Symbolism: Women and 'The Veil.'" *Thamyris: Mythmaking From Past to Present,* 3,2 (autumn). *Special Issue: Gender in the Middle East—Transnational Connections and Contestations.*

————. 1998. *Women, Islamisms, and the State: Contemporary Feminisms in Egypt,* London: Macmillan.

Katrak, Ketu. 1992. "Indian Nationalism, Gandhian 'Satyagraha,' and Representations of Female Sexuality." In *Nationalisms and Sexualities,* eds. Andrew Parker and Mary Russo, 395–407. New York: Routledge.

Kaviraj, Sudipta. 1997. "Filth and the Public Sphere: Concepts and Practices about Space in Calcutta." *Public Culture* 10, 1: 83–113.

Keddie, Nickie. R. 1991. Introduction to *Women in Middle Eastern History*, ed. N. R. Keddie and B. Baron. New Haven, Conn.: Yale University Press.

Keene, Judith. 1988. *Last Mile to Huesca: An Australian Nurse in the Spanish Civil War.* Sydney: University of New South Wales Press.

———. 1998. *"Nor More Than Brothers and Sisters:* Women in Frontline Combat in the Spanish Civil War." In *Modern Europe: Histories and Identities,* ed. Peter Monteath and Frederic Zuckerman. Adelaide: Australian Humanities Press.

———. 2001. *Fighting for Franco: International Volunteers in Nationalist Spain during the Spanish Civil War 1936 to 1939.* London: Continuum.

Kelkar, Lakshmibai. 1988. *Pathadarshini Shriramakatha.* Nagpur, India: Sevika Prakashan.

———. n.d. *Stri-Ek Urja Kendra. Strivishayak Vicharon ka Sankalan.* Nagpur, India: Sevika Prakashan.

Keskin, Burcak. 1999. "The Dilemma of Women's Activism in Turkey: To Be (Modern) or Not to Be?" M.A. thesis, University of Chicago.

Kessler-Harris, A. 1993. "Women and Welfare: Public Interventions in Private Lives." *Radical Historical Review* 56.

Kingston, Margo. 1999. *Off the Rails: The Pauline Hanson Trip.* Sydney: Allen and Unwin.

Kishwar, Madhu. 1985a. "Gandhi on Women," Parts 1 and 2. *Economic and Political Weekly* 20, 40: 1691–1702.

———. 1985b. "Gandhi on Women," Part 3. *Economic and Political Weekly* 20, 41: 1753–1758.

Klatch, Rebecca. 1987. *Women of the New Right.* Philadelphia: Temple University Press.

Knight, Alan. 1990. "Revolutionary Project, Recalcitrant People: Mexico, 1910–1940." In *The Revolutionary Process in Mexico: Essays on Political and Social Change, 1880–1940,* ed. Jaime E. Rodríguez. Los Angeles and Irvine: UCLA Latin American Center Publications and Mexicano/Chicano Program.

Koonz, Claudia. 1976. "Conflicting Allegiances: Political Ideology and Women Legislators in Weimar Germany." *Signs: Journal of Women in Culture and Society* 1: 663–683.

———. 1987. *Mothers in the Fatherland: Women, the Family, and Nazi Politics.* New York: St. Martin's Press.

Kothar, Raini. 1970. *Politics in India.* New Delhi: Orient Longman.

Koven, Seth and Sonya Michel. 1990. "Womanly Duties: Maternalist Politics and the Origins of Welfare States in France, Germany, Great Britain, and the United States, 1880–1920." *American Historical Review* 95, 4.

———. 1993. *Mothers of a New World: Maternalist Politics and the Origins of Welfare States.* New York: Routledge.

Krüger, Hanna. 1936. *Die unbequeme Frau. Käthe Schirmacher im Kampf um die Freiheit der Frau und die Freiheit der Nation 1865–1930.* Berlin: Hans Gott-Verlag.

Kruger, L. 1991. "Gender, Community and Identity: Women and Afrikaner Nationalism in the Volksmoeder Discourse of Die Boerevrou, 1919–1931." M.A. thesis, University of Cape Town.

Küçükkurt, M., N. Güz, and C. Anık. 1996. "The Role of Gender in Political News and Commentary in Turkish Newspapers: The Case of Tansu Çiller." In *Gender and Media,* ed. N. Dakovic, D. Derman, and K. Ross. Ankara, Turkey: Med-Campus Project Publication.

Kushner T. and K. Lunn. 1989. *Traditions of Intolerance.* Manchester: Manchester University Press, 1989.

———, eds. 1990. *The Politics of Marginality.* London: Frank Cass.

Lafaye, Jacques. 1976. *Quetzalcoatl and Guadalupe: The Formation of Mexican National Consciousness, 1531–1813.* Chicago: University of Chicago Press.

LaHaye, B. 1993. *The Desires of a Woman's Heart.* Wheaton, Ill.: Tyndale House.

Lakoff, R. 1976. *Language and Women's Place.* New York: Octagon Books.

Lange, Silvia. 1998. *Protestantische Frauen auf dem Weg in den Nationalsozialismus: Guida Diehls Neulandbewegung 1916–1935.* Stuttgart: Metzler.

Lannon, Frances. 1991. "Women and Images of Women in the Spanish Civil War." In *Transactions of the Royal Historical Society* 1: 213–228.

Larocque, Brendan. 1997. "Rhetoric and Reality in *Hindutva*: A Reply to Niraj Pant's "Facilitating Genocide." *Ghadar* 1, 2 (26 November 1997): 1–5.

La Rouchefoucauld. 1938. *Spanish Women.* New York: Peninsular News Service.

La UFCM en Ocotlán. 1940. *AF* 5, 21 (1 October).

La Unión de Damas Católicas Mexicanas [UDCM] en el XX Aniversario de su Fundación: 12 de septiembre de 1912. 1933. *AF* 1, 1 (January).

Laurens, Corran. 1995. "'La Femme au Turban': les Femmes tondues." In *The Liberation of France. Image and Event*, ed. H. R. Kedward and Nancy Wood. Oxford: Berg Publishers.

Lavrin. Asunción. 1995. *Women, Feminism, and Social Change in Argentina, Chile, and Uruguay, 1890–1940.* Lincoln: University of Nebraska Press.

Leck, Ralph M. 2000. "Conservative Empowerment and the Gender of Nazism: Paradigms of Power and Complicity in German Women's History." *Journal of Women's History* 12, 2: 147–169.

Le Dœuff, Michèle. 1995. "Problèmes d'investiture. (De la parité, etc.)" *Nouvelles Questions Féministes* 16, 2: 5–80.

Lefkowitz, R., and A. Withorn. 1986. *For Crying Out Loud.* New York: Pilgrim Press.

Legarreta, Dorothy. 1984. *The Guernica Generation: Basque Refugee Children of the Spanish Civil War.* Las Vegas: University of Nevada Press.

Leo XIII. 1891. *Rerum Novarum* (http://www.ewtn.com, "Document Library").

Leopold, John A. 1977. *Alfred Hugenberg: The Radical Nationalist Campaign against the Weimar Republic.* New Haven, Conn.: Yale University Press.

Lerner, Victoria. 1979. *La educación socialista.* Mexico City: El Colegio de México.

Lesselier, Claudie, and Fiametta Venner, eds. 1988. "The Women's Movement and the Extreme Right in France." In *The Nature of the Right: A Feminist Analysis of Order Patterns*, ed. Gill Seidel, 173–185. Amsterdam: John Benjamin Publishers.

———. 1997. *L'extrême droite et les femmes. Enjeux et actualité.* Villeurbanne, France: Éditions Golias.

Lesser, Jeffrey. 1995. *Welcoming the Undesirables: Brazil and the Jewish Question.* Berkeley: University of California Press.

Levine, Robert M. 1968. "Brazil's Jews during the Vargas Era and After." *Luso-Brazilian Review* 5 (June).

———. 1970. *The Vargas Regime: The Critical Years, 1934–1938.* New York: Columbia University Press.

Lewis, D. S. 1987. *Illusions of Grandeur: Mosley, Fascism, and British Society 1931–81.* Manchester: Manchester University Press.

Liebe, Werner. 1956. *Die Deutschnationale Volkspartei, 1918–1924, Beiträge zur Geschichte des Parlamentarismus und der politischen Parteien, 8.* Düsseldorf: Droste.

Linehan, T. P. 1996. *East London for Mosley: The British Union of Fascists in East London and South West Essex 1922–40.* London: Frank Cass.

Lippmann, Lorna. 1984. *Racist propaganda and the immigration debate.* Richmond, Victoria, Australia: Clearing House on Migration Issues.

Lipset, S. M., and E. Raab. 1970. *The Politics of Unreason: Right-Wing Extremism in America, 1790–1970.* New York: Harper and Row.

Lo, C. Y. 1982. "Countermovements and Conservative Movements in the Contemporary U.S." *Annual Review of Sociology* 8:107–134.

Luker, K. 1984. *Abortion and the Politics of Motherhood.* Berkeley: University of California Press.

Lundy, Kate. 1998. "Finding My Feminism." In *Talking Up: Young Women's Take on Feminism*, ed. Rosamund Else-Mitchell and Naomi Flutter, 43–52. Melbourne: Spinifex.

Macciocchi, Maria-Antoinetta. 1969. "Female Sexuality in Fascist Ideology." *Feminist Review* 1: 67–82.

Machtild, Abert. 1991. "*La Bestia y el Angel*. Imágenes de las mujeres en la novela falangista de la Guerra Civil." In *Las Mujeres y la Guerra Civil Española Española*, III Jornadas de estudio monográficos. Salamanca, octubre 1989, 371–377. Madrid, Ministerio de Cultura.

Macías, Anna. 1982. *Against All Odds: The Feminist Movement in Mexico to 1940*. Westport, Conn.: Greenwood Press.

Macleod, Arlene Elowe. 1991. *Accomodating Protest: Working Women, the New Veiling, and Change in Cairo*. New York: Columbia University Press.

Maffei, Eduardo. 1984. *A batalha da Praça da Sé*. Rio de Janeiro: Philobiblion.

Mangini, Shirley. 1995. *Memories of Resistance: Women's Voices from the Spanish Civil War*. New Haven, Conn.: Yale University Press.

Manne, Robert, ed. 1998. *Two Nations: The Causes and Effects of the Rise of the One Nation Party in Australia*. Melbourne: Bookman Press.

Mansbridge, Jane. 1986. *Why We Lost the ERA*. Chicago: University of Chicago Press.

Mardin, Ş. 1969. *Din ve Ideoloji* (Religion and ideology). Ankara, Turkey: Ankara Üniversitesi SBF Yayınları.

———. 1973. "Center-Periphery Relations: A Key to Turkish Politics?" *Daedalus* 102, 1, 169–90.

———. 1977. "Religion in Modern Turkey." *International Social Science Journal* 29, 2: 279–297.

———. 1981. "Religion and Secularism in Turkey." In *Atatürk, Founder of a Modern State*, ed. A. Kazancıgil and E. Özbudun. London: C. Hurst and Company.

———. 1983. "Religion and Politics in Modern Turkey." In *Islam in the Political Process*, ed. J. Piscatori. Cambridge: Cambridge University Press.

———. 1989a. "Culture and Religion towards the Year 2000." In Turkish Political Science Association, *Turkey in the Year 2000*, Ankara, Turkey: Sevinç Matbaası.

———. 1989b. *Religion and Social Change in Modern Turkey*. Albany: SUNY Press.

Marinetti, F. T. 1924. *Futurismo e fascismo*. Foligno: Campitelli.

Marpicati, Arturo. 1933. "*Dux* di Margherita Sarfatti." *Saggi di letteratura*. Florence:

Marshall, S. 1995. "Confrontation and Co-optation in Antifeminist Organizations." In *Feminist Organizations*, ed. M. M. Ferree and P. Y. Martin, 323–338. Philadelphia: Temple University Press.

Martin, Angela, and Sandra Kreist. 1998. "Encountering Mary: Ritualization and Place Contagion in Modernity." In *Places Through the Body*, ed. Steve Pile and Heidi Nast. New York: Routledge.

Martin, Patricia Yancey. "Rethinking Feminist Organizations." *Gender and Society*. 4 (2 June).

Martin Gaete, Carmen. 1987. *Usos amorosos de la posguerra española*. Barcelona: Editorial Anagrama.

Massey, Doreen. 1993. *Space, Place, and Gender*. Minneapolis: University of Minnesota Press.

Matear, Ann. 1997. "Desde la Protesta a la Propuesta: The Institutionalization of the Women's Movement in Chile." In *Gender Politics in Latin America*, ed. Elizabeth Dore New York: Monthly Review Press.

Mathieu, Nicole-Claude. 1991. "Quand céder n'est pas consentir." In *L'Anatomie politique: Catégorisations et idéologies du sexe*. Paris: côté-femmes éditions.

Mayer, Nonna. 1999. *Ces Français qui votent FN*. Paris: Flammarion.

Mazower, Mark. 1993. *Inside Hitler's Greece*. New Haven, Conn.: Yale University Press.

Mazumdar, Sucheta. 1991. "For Rama and Hindutva: Women and Right-Wing Mobilization." *COSAW Bulletin* (September): 2–8.

McClintock, Anne. 1995. *Imperial Leather: Race, Gender, and Sexuality in the Colonial Contest*. New York: Routledge.

McLean, Nancy. 1994. *Behind the Mask of Chivalry: The Making of the Second Ku Klux Klan*. New York: Oxford University Press.

McSweeney, William. 1980. *Roman Catholicism: The Search for Relevance*. New York: St. Martin's Press.

Meeker, M. M. 1990. "The New Muslim Intellectuals in the Republic of Turkey." In *Islam in Modern Turkey*, ed. R. L. Tapper. London: I. B. Tauris.

———. 1994. "The Muslim Intellectual and His Audience: A New Configuration of

Writer and Reader among Believers in the Republic of Turkey." In *Cultural Transitions in the Middle East*, ed. Ş. Mardin. Leiden: E. J. Brill.

Meldini, Piero, ed. 1975. *Sposa e madre esemplare: Ideologia e politica della donna e della famiglia durante il fascismo*. Florence: Guaraldi.

Melucci, Alberto. 1998. "The Process of Collective Identity." In H. Johnston and B. Klandermans (eds.) *Social Movements and Culture*. Minneapolis: University of Minnesota Press.

Menon, Ritu and Kamala Bhasin. 1999. *Borders and Boundaries: Women in India's Partition*. New Delhi: Kali for Women.

Mernissi, Fatima. 1987. *Beyond the Veil: Male-Female Dynamics in Modern Muslim Society*. Revised ed. London: Al Saqi Books.

———. 1991. *The Veil and the Male Elite: An Interpretation of Women's Rights in Islam*. Old Tapan, N.J.: Addison-Wesley Publications.

Mexican Constitution. "Mexicano: Esta es tu Constitución." 1968. Mexico: Cámara de Diputados del H. Congreso de la Unión, XLVII Legislatura.

Meyer, D. S., and S. Staggenborg. 1996. "Movements, Countermovements, and the Structure of Political Opportunity." *American Journal of Sociology* 101, 6 (May): 1628–1660.

Meyer, Jean. 1973–1974. *La cristiada*. 3 vols. Mexico City: Siglo XXI.

Miller, Barbara Ann. 1981. "The Role of Women in the Mexican Cristero Rebellion: A New Chapter." Ph.D. diss., University of Notre Dame.

Miller, Hope Ridings. 1934. "Aristocracy Responding to Large Family Drive, Announces Italian Woman Leader Visiting Here." *Washington Post*, 17 April.

Millett, Kate. 1989. *Sexual Politics*. London: Virago.

Mink, Gwendolyn. 1990. "The Lady and the Tramp: Gender, Race, and the Origins of the American Welfare State." In *Women, the State, and Welfare*, ed. Linda Gordon. Madison: University of Wisconsin Press.

Moen, M. 1992. *The Transformation of the Christian Right*. Tuscaloosa: University of Alabama Press.

Moghadam, Valentine. 1993. *Modernizing Women: Gender and Social Change in the Middle East*. Boulder, Colo.: Lynne Riener.

Mohanty, C. T. 1991. "Under Western Eyes: Feminist Scholarship and Colonial Discourses." In *Third World Women and the Politics of Feminism*, ed. C. T. Mohanty, A. Russo, and L. Torres, 51–80. Bloomington: Indiana University Press.

Molyneux, Maxine. 2000. "Twentieth-Century State Formations in Latin America." In *Hidden Histories of Gender and the State in Latin America*, ed. Elizabeth Dore and Maxine Molyneux. Durham, N.C.: Duke University Press.

Mondello, Elisabetta. 1987. *La nuova italiana: La donna nella stampa e nella cultura del ventennio*. Rome: Riuniti.

Moodie, Dunbar T. 1975. *The Rise of Afrikanerdom. Power, Apartheid, and the Afrikaner Civil Religion*. Berkeley: University of California Press.

Morcillo, Aurora. 2000. *True Catholic Womanhood: Gender Ideology in Franco's Spain*. DeKalb: Northern Illinois University Press.

Mosley, Nicholas. 1983. *Beyond the Pale*. London: Secker and Warburg.

Mosley, Oswald. 1932. *The Greater Britain*. London: B.U.F. Publications.

———. 1933. *Fascism in Britain*. London: B.U.F. Publications.

———. 1940. *The British Peace and How to Get It*. London: B.U.F. Publications.

———. 1968. *My Life*. London: Thomas Nelson and Sons.

Mosse, George. 1985. *Nationalism and Sexuality: Middle Class Morality and Sexual Norms in Modern Europe*. Madison: University of Wisconsin Press.

———. 1990. *Fallen Soldiers*. Oxford: Oxford University Press.

Mossuz-Lavau, Janine. 1998. "Résistantes face au Front national." In *Femmes, le mauvais genre*. Special Issue of *Le Monde diplomatique, Manières de voir*, no. 44, March–April.

Mostert, Dirk. 1940. *Gedenkboek van die Ossewaens op die Pad van Suid-Afrika*. Cape Town: Nasionale Pers.

Muel-Dreyfus, Francine. 1996. *Vichy ou l'éternel féminin*. Paris: Éditions du Seuil.

Mukhia, Harbans. 1995. "The Transmutation of Identities." *Economic and Political Weekly of India* (June 10): 1365–1368.

Muncy, R. 1991. *Creating a Female Dominion in American Reform, 1890–1915.* New York: Oxford University Press.

Mussolini, Benito. 1993. *Opera omnia,* eds. Edoardo Susmel and Duilio Susmel. 44 vols.

Nachmani, Amikan. 1993. "Miror Images: The Civil Wars in China and Greece." *Journal of Hellenic Diaspora* 19, 1: 71–112.

Nader, L. 1989. *Orientalism, Occidentalism, and the Control of Women.* Leiden: E. J. Brill.

Najmabadi, A. 1991. "Hazards of Modernity and Morality: Women, State, and Ideology in Contemporary Iran." In *Women, Islam, and the State,* ed. Deniz Kandiyoti. Hong Kong: MacMillan.

Nandy, Ashish. 1983. *The Intimate Enemy.* Delhi: Oxford University Press.

———. 1990. "The Politics of Secularism and the Recovery of Religious Tolerance." In *Mirrors of Violence,* ed. Veena Das. Delhi: Oxford University Press.

Nast, Heidi J. 1988. "Unsexy Geographies." In *Gender, Place, and Culture* 5, 2.

Negrete, Martaelena. 1988. *Relaciones entre la Iglesia y el estado mexicano, 1930–1940.* Mexico City: El Colegio de México y la Universidad Iberoamericana.

Nora, Pierre. 1996–1998. "Generation." In *Realms of Memory: Rethinking the French Past,* ed. Pierre Nora. 3 vols. New York: Columbia University Press.

Nozzoli, Anna. 1988. "Margherita Sarfatti Organizzatrice di Cultura: 'Il Popolo d'Italia.'" In *La Corporazione delle Donne: Ricerche e studi sui modelli femminili nel ventennio fascista,* ed. Marina Addis Saba. Florence: Vallecchi.

O'Brien, Mary. 1981. *The Politics of Reproduction.* London: Routledge and Kegan Paul.

Olson, E. A. 1985. "Muslim Identity and Secularism in Contemporary Turkey: The Head-scarf Dispute." *Anthropological Quarterly* 58, 4: 161–172.

O'Meara, D. 1983. *Volkskapitalisme: Class, Capital, and Ideology in the Development of Afrikaner Nationlalism, 1934 to 1948.* Braamfontein, South Africa: Ravan Press.

Öncü, A. 1994. "Packaging Islam: Cultural Politics in the Landscape of Turkish Commercial Television." *New Perspectives on Turkey* 10 (spring): 13–36.

Opitz, Günter. 1969. *Der Christlich-soziale Volksdienst. Versuch einer protestantischen Partei in der Weimarer Republik.* Düsseldorf: Droste.

Orban, Clara. 1995. "Women, Futurism, and Fascism." In *Mothers of Invention: Women, Italian Fascism, and Culture,* ed. Robin Pickering-Iazzi. Minneapolis: University of Minnesota Press.

Orfali, Birgitta. 1990a. *L'adhesion au Front national. De la minorité active au mouvement social.* Paris: Kimé, 1990.

———. 1990b. "Le FN ou le parti-famille," *Esprit,* October.

Orozco y Jiménez, Francisco. 1930a. Circular 15–30, "A los Sres. Sacerdotes del Arzobispado," 28 April.

———. Circular 16–30. 1930b. "A los Sres. Curas y Rectores de las Iglesias de esta Ciudad." *BEG,* 1, 4 (1 June).

Özdalga, E. 1998. *The Veiling Issue, Official Secularism, and Popular Islam in Modern Turkey.* Richmond, Surrey, U.K.: NIAS-Curzon.

Özsoyeller, G. 1995. *Turkiye'de Iki Kadin Dinamigi: Seriatci-Cagdas* (The two types of women's activism in Turkey: Islamist versus modern). Istanbul: Ortam.

Palacio, Sara. 1981. "El punto de vista de la *Sección Femenina*: 'La historia nos ha traicionado.' Entrevista con Lula de Lara." *Tiempo de Historia* 7, 83 (October).

Pamies, Tomasa. 1985. *Cárcel de mujeres (1939–1945).* Barcelona: Sirocco Books.

Pant, Niraj. 1997. "Facilitating Genocide: Women as Fascist Educators in the *Hindutva* Movement." *Ghadar* 1, 1 (May): 1–7.

Panzini, Alfredo. 1929. "Un romanzo di Margherita Sarfatti." *Il Corriere della Sera.* 26 May, 3.

Parsons, Wilfrid. 1936. *Mexican Martyrdom.* New York: Macmillan.

Pasquarelli, John. 1998. *The Pauline Hanson Story, by the Man Who Knows.* Frenchs Forest, New South Wales: New Holland.

Passerini, Louisa. 1987. *Fascism in Popular Memory: The Cultural Experience of the Turin*

Working Class. Translated by R. Lumley and J. Bloomfield. Cambridge: Cambridge University Press.

Passmore, Kevin. 1999. "Planting the Tricolor in the Citadel of Communism: Women's Social Action in the Croix de feu and Parti social français." *Journal of Modern History* 71, 4 (December): 814–851.

Patel, Sujata. 1988. "Construction and Reconstruction of Women in Gandhi." In *Economic and Political Weekly*, 20 February: 377–387.

Pateman, Carole. 1988. *The Sexual Contract*. Cambridge, UK: Polity Press.

———. 1989. *The Disorder of Women: Democracy, Feminism, and Political Theory*. Cambridge, UK: Polity Press.

Payne, Stanley G. 1961. *Falange: A History of Spanish Fascism*. Stanford, Calif.: Stanford University Press.

———. 1995. *A History of Fascism, 1914–1945*. Madison: University of Wisconsin Press.

———. 1999. *Fascism in Spain, 1923–1977*. Madison: University of Wisconsin Press.

Peñalosa de Del Río, Carmen. 1940. "La Granja de Santa Rosa." *AF* 5, 20 (September).

Perrineau, Pascal. 1997. *Le symptôme Le Pen. Radiographie des électeurs du Front national.* Paris: Fayard.

Phelan, S. 1993. "(Be)Coming Out: Lesbian Identity and Politics." *Signs: Journal of Women in Culture and Society* 18, 4 (summer): 765–790.

Piat, Yann. 1991. *Seule tout en haut à droite*. Paris: Fixot.

Pickering-Iazzi, Robin. 1997. *Politics of the Visible: Writing Women, Culture, and Fascism*. Minneapolis: University of Minnesota Press.

———, ed. 1995. *Mothers of Invention: Women, Italian Fascism, and Culture*. Minneapolis: University of Minnesota Press.

Pieper, Jadwiga E. 2000. "From Contested Duties to Disputed Rights. The Social Politics of Fertility Regulation in Chile, 1964–1989." Ph.D. diss., Rutgers University.

Pieroni Bortolotti, Franca. 1978. *Femminismo e Partiti Politici in Italia 1919–1926*. Rome: Riuniti.

Pile, Steve. 1996. *The Body and the City*. London: Routledge.

Pinkus, Karen. 1995. *Bodily Regimes: Italian Advertising under Fascism*. Minneapolis: University of Minnesota Press.

Pitkin, H. F. 1967. *The Concept of Representation*. Berkeley: University of California Press.

Pius XI. 1930. "Sección Pontífica: Carta Encíclica . . . Sobre la Cristiana Educación de la Juventud," [*Divini Illus Magistri*]. Rome, 31 December 1929, *BEG*, 1, 3 (1 May).

———. 1931. *Quadregesimo Anno.* (Available at www.ewtn.com, "Document Library.)

———. 1937a. "Nos es muy conocido" [*Firmissiam Constantiam*], in *Christus* 2, 18 (May).

———. 1937b. "Sobre el comunismo ateo" [*Divini Redemptoris*]. (19 March 1937) in *Christus* 2, 18 (May).

Postma, W. 1918. *Die Boervrou—Moeder van haar Volk*. Bloemfontein, South Africa: Nasionale Pers.

Power, Margaret. 2002. *Right-Wing Women in Chile: Feminine Power and the Struggle against Allende, 1964–1973*. University Park: Pennsylvania State University Press.

Preston, Paul. 1990. *The Politics of Revenge. Fascism and the Military in Twentieth-Century Spain*. London: Unwin Hyman.

Primo de Rivera, Pilar. 1983. *Recuerdos de una vida*. Madrid: Ediciones Dyrsa.

Prini, Orazia Belsito. 1934. *Figure del tempo mussoliniano: Margherita Sarfatti*. Piacenza, Italy: Tipografia de "La Scure."

Qazim, Safinaz. 1982. *Fi Al-Sufur wa Al-Hijab* (On non-veiling and veiling). Cairo: Maktabet Wahba.

———. 1984. "Al Ra'ida Nabawiyya Musa wa In'ash dhakkirat al umma" (The pioneer Nabawiyya Musa and the reviving of the nation's memory). *Majallat al hilal*, January.

———. 1986. "An Al-Sijn wa Al-Hurriyya" (On prison and freedom). Cairo: Al-Zahra' li Al-'Elam Al-Arabi.

———. 1993. "Al-Mar'a Al-Muslimma wa Al-Tahaddiyyat" (The Muslim woman and the challenges). *Zahrat Al-Khaleej*, 4 December.

————. 1994a. "Al-Feminism: Harakat Al-Getto Al-Nissa'iyya." (Feminism: The ghetto feminist movement). *Al-Mussawar* 24 June.

————. 1994b. "Badihiyat Tama Nisyaniha." (Forgotten basics). *Zahrat Al-Khaleej*, 12 March.

————. 1994c. "Madha Ya'ni an Takouni Mar'a Muslima?" (What does it mean to you to be a Muslim woman?). *Zahrat Al-Khaleej*, 29 January.

Quataert, Jean H. 1979. *Reluctant Feminists in German Social Democracy, 1885–1917.* Princeton, N.J.: Princeton University Press.

Qutb, Mohammad. 1991. *Tahrir Al-Mar'a* (The liberation of woman). Cairo: Maktabet Al-Sunna.

Qutb, Sayyid. 1991. *Milestones.* 3rd ed. Delhi-6: Markazi Maktaba Islami.

Raby, David L. 1974. *Educación y revolución social en Mexico, 1921–1940.* Mexico City: Sep-Setentas.

Ras l'front. 1998. *Radiographie du FN.* Paris.

Reagin, Nancy. 1995. *A German Women's Movement: Class and Gender in Hanover, 1880–1933.* Chapel Hill: University of North Carolina Press.

Reich, Peter Lester. 1995. *Mexico's Hidden Revolution: The Catholic Church in Law and Politics Since 1929.* Notre Dame, Ind.: University of Notre Dame Press.

Renan, E. 1969. "What Is a Nation?" In *Renan: Selected Works,* ed. H. Peyre. Paris: Presses Universitaires de France.

Reynolds, Margaret. 1995. *The Last Bastion: Labor Women Working towards Equality in the Parliaments of Australia.* Sydney: Business and Professional Publishing.

Richards, Michael. 1999. *A Time of Silence: Civil War and the Culture of Repression in Franco's Spain 1936–1945.* Cambridge: Cambridge University Press.

Richter, Heinz. 1986. *British Intervention in Greece. From Varkiza to Civil War. February 1945 to August 1946.* London: Merlin Press.

Riesebrodt, Martin. 1993a. "Fundamentalism and the Political Mobilization of Women." In *The Political Dimensions of Religion,* ed. S. Arjomand. Albany: SUNY Press.

————. 1993b. *Pious Passion: The Emergence of Modern Fundamentalism in the United States and Iran.* Berkeley: University of California Press.

Roberts, Mary Louise. 1994. *Civilization without Sexes: Reconstructing Gender in Postwar France, 1917–1927.* Chicago: University of Chicago Press.

Romero de Solís, José Miguel. 1994. *El Aguijon del Espíritu: Historia contemporánea de la Iglesia en Mexico, 1895–1990.* Mexico City: IMDOSOC.

Rosenfeld, M. 1995. "Feminist Fatales: This Conservative Women's Group has Traditionalists Seething." *Washington Post,* 30 November, D1.

Ross, Loretta. 1995. "White Supremacy in the 1990s." In *Eyes Right! Challenging the Right Wing Backlash,* ed. Chip Berlet. Boston: South End Press.

Rothmann, M. E. 1976. *My Beskeie Deel.'n Outobiografiese Vertelling.* Cape Town, Tafelberg.

Roura, Assumpta. 1998. *Mujeres para después de una guerra. Informes sobre moralidad y prostitución en la postguerra española.* Barcelona, Spain: Flor del Viento Ediciones.

RSS. 1984. *Sri Balasaheb Answers Questions.* Bangalore, India: Sahitya Sindhu.

Rucht, D. 1996. "The Impact of National Contexts on Social Movement Structures: A Cross-Movement and Cross-National Comparison." In *Comparative Perspectives on Social Movements,* ed. Doug McAdam, 185–204. Cambridge: Cambridge University Press.

Ruddick, Sara. 1989. *Maternal Thinking: Toward a Politics of Peace.* New York: Ballantine Books.

Ruinas, Stanis. 1930. *Scrittrici e scribacchine d'oggi.* Rome: Accademia.

Ruíz y Flores, Leopoldo. 1935. "Carta Abierta al Sr. Presidente de la República," 5 November 1934. *BEG* 6, 1 (1 January).

Rupp, Leila. 1977. "Mothers of the Volk: The Image of Women in Nazi Ideology." *Signs: Journal of Women in Culture and Society* 3, 2: 362–379.

————. 1997. *Worlds of Women: The Making of an International Women's Movement.* Princeton, N.J.: Princeton University Press.

Saktanber, Ayse. 1994. "Becoming the Other as a Muslim in Turkey: Turkish Women vs. Islamist Women." *New Perspectives of Turkey* 11, 99–134.

———. 1996. "Women, Islamism and Politics in Turkey: A Critical Perspective," *Middle East Policy* 5, 3 (September): 170–173.

———. 1997. "Formation of a Middle Class Ethos and Its Quotidian: Revitalizing Islam in Urban Turkey." In *Space, Culture, and Power*, ed. A. Öncü and P. Weylan. London: Zed Books.

Salgado, Plínio. 1935. *Despertemos a naçao!* Rio de Janeiro: Livraria Jose Olympio.

Samiti (Rashtra Sevika). 1988. *Preface to Rashtra Sevika Samiti*. Nagpur, India: Sevika Prakashan.

———. 1989. *Lakshmibai Kelkar ki Jivani*. Nagpur, India: Sevika Prakashan.

———. 1990. *Pratah: Smaraniya Mabilaen* Nagpur, India: Sevika Prakashan.

Sanbay, A. 1985. "Türkiye'de Siyasal Modernleşme ve Islam" (Political modernization and Islam in Turkey). *Toplum ve Bilim* 29–30 (spring–summer): 45–64.

Saracinelli, M., and N. Totti. 1983. *L'Italia del duce: L'informazione, la scuola, il costume*. Rimini: Panozzo.

Sarfatti, Margherita Grassini. 1913. "Perchè le donne han bisogno del voto." *La Difesa delle Lavoratrici*, 16 November.

———. 1914. "Le nuove leggi sull'ordinamento della famiglia." *La Difesa delle Lavoratrici*, 8 March.

———. 1925. *The Life of Benito Mussolini*. London: Butterworth.

———. 1926. *Dux*. Milan: Mondadori.

———. 1929. *Il palazzone*. Milan: Mondadori.

———. 1933. "Women under Fascism." *New York Herald Tribune Sunday Magazine*, 12 November.

———. 1937. *L'America, ricerca della felicità*. Milan: Mondadori.

———. 1945. "Mussolini: Como lo conocí." *Crítica* (18 June–3 July).

———. 1955. *Acqua passata*. Rocca San Casciano: Cappelli.

Sarkar, Tanika. 1991. "The Woman as Communal Subject: Rashtrasevika Samiti and Ramjanmabhoomi Movement." *Economic and Political Weekly* 26, 35: 2057.

———. 1996. "Heroic Women, Mother Goddesses: Family and Organization in Hindutva Politics." In *Women and the Hindu Right: A Collection of Essays*, ed. Tanika Sarkar and Urvashi Butalia. Delhi: Kali for Women.

Satel, S. 1999. "Scared Sick? Unfounded Fear and Its Effect on Health and Science Policies." *Ex Femina*, May, 1.

Sawer, Marian and Marian Simms. [1986] 1993. *A Woman's Place: Women and Politics in Australia*. 2nd ed. Sydney: Allen and Unwin.

Schaser, Angelika. 2000. *Helene Lange und Gertrud Bäumer: Eine politische Lebensgemeinschaft*. Cologne: Boehlau Verlag.

Scheck, Raffael. 1997. "German Conservatism and Female Political Activism in the Early Weimar Republic." *German History* 15: 34–55.

———. 1999. "Women against Versailles: Maternalism and Nationalism of Female Bourgeois Politicians in the Early Weimar Republic." *German Studies Review* 22: 21–42.

———. 2000. "Zwischen Volksgemeinschaft und Frauenrechten: Das Verhältnis rechtsbürgerlicher Politikerinnen zur NSDAP 1930–33." In *Nation, Politik und Geschlecht. Frauenbewegungen und Nationalismus in der Moderne*, ed. Ute Planert. 234–52. Frankfurt am Main: Campus.

Schreiber, Ronnee. 2000. "'But Perhaps We Speak for You': Antifeminist Women's Organizations and the Representation of Political Interests." Ph.D. diss., Rutgers University.

Scott, James. 1990. *Domination and the Arts of Resistance*. New Haven, Colo.: Yale University Press.

Scott, Joan Wallach. 1996. *Only Paradoxes to Offer. French Feminists and the Rights of Man*. Harvard University Press.

Scott-Ellis, Priscilla. 1995. *The Chances of Death*. Edited by Raymond Carr. Wilby, Norwich: Michael Russell.

Sección Femenina, F.E.T. y de los J.O.N.S. n.d. *Consejos Nacionales. Crónica de los Consejos: Años 1937, 1938 y 1939.*

———. n.d. *Consejos Nacionales. Misión y organización de la S.F. (Sección Femenina).* Madrid.

Sen, Samita. 1993. "Motherhood and Mothercraft: Gender and Nationalism in Bengal." *Gender and History* 5, 2: 231–243.

Sexto Censo General de la Nación, 6 de marzo de 1940: Resumen General. 1942. Mexico, Talleres Gráficos de la Nación.

Sheth, Pravin. 1998. *Political Development in Gujarat.* Ahmedabad, India: Karnavati Publications.

Shorter, E. 1977. *The Making of the Modern Family.* New York: Basic Books.

Simöes, Solange de Deus. 1985. *Pátria e família: As mulheres no golpe de 1964.* Petrópolis, Brazil: Vozes.

Sinha, Mrinalini. 1997. *Colonial Masculinity.* New Delhi: Kali For Women.

Sirman, N. 1989. "Feminism in Turkey: A Short History." *New Perspectives on Turkey* 3, 1: 1–34.

Skidelsky, Robert. 1975. *Oswald Mosley.* London: Macmillan.

Skidmore, Thomas E. 1985. "Historical Perspectives." In *Race, Class, and Power in Brazil*, ed. Pierre Michel Fontaine. Los Angeles: UCLA, Center for Afro-American Studies.

Slaughter, Jane. 1997. *Women and the Italian Resistance.* Denver: Arden Press.

Smith, Niel, and Cindy Katz. 1993. "Grounding Metaphore: Towards a Spatialized Politics." In *Place and the Politics of Identity*, ed. M. Keith and S. Pile, 67–83. London: Routledge.

Sombra, Luiz Henrique, and Luiz Felipe Hirtz Guerra, comps. 1998. *Imagens do Sigma.* Rio de Janeiro: Arquivo Público do Estado do Rio de Janeiro.

Sontag, Susan. 1980. "Fascinating Fascism." In *Under the Sign of Saturn.* New York: Farrar Straus Giroux.

Spackman, Barbara. 1996. *Fascist Virilities: Rhetoric, Ideology, and Social Fantasy.* Minneapolis: University of Minnesota Press.

Spender, D. 1985. *Man Made Language.* London: Routledge and Kegan Paul.

Spivak, Gayatri Chakraverty. 1988. In *Other Worlds: Essays in Cultural Politics.* New York: Routledge.

———. 1993. *Outside in the Teaching Machine.* New York: Routledge.

———. 1994. "Can the Subaltern Speak?" In *Colonial Discourse and Postcolonial Theory: A Reader*, ed. Patrick Williams, Laura Chrisman. New York: Columbia University Press.

Stacey, Judith, and Barry Thorne. 1993. "The Missing Feminist Revolution in Sociology." In *American Feminist Thought at Century's End: A Reader*, ed. Linda S. Kauffman. Oxford: Blackwell.

Stanley, Susie C. 1996. *Feminist Pillar of Fire: The Life of Alma White.* Cleveland: Pilgrim Press.

Stannard, Martin. 1986. *Evelyn Waugh. The Early Years.* London: Dent.

Starling, Heloisa Maria Murgel. 1986. *Os senhores das gerais: Os novos inconfidentes e o golpe de 1964.* Petrópolis, Brazil: Vozes.

Stephenson, Jill. 1975. *Women in Nazi Germany.* London: Croom Helm.

Stone, Marla. 1998. *The Patron State: Culture and Politics in Fascist Italy.* Princeton, N.J.: Princeton University Press.

Striesow, Jan. 1981. *Die Deutschnationale Volkspartei und die Völkisch-Radikalen 1918–1922.* Frankfurt am Main: Haag+Herchen.

Sunar, I., and B. Toprak. 1983. "Islam in Politics: The Case of Turkey." *Government and Opposition* 18, 4.

Swers, M. 1998. "Are Women More Likely to Vote for Women's Issue Bills Than Their Male Colleagues?" *Legislative Studies Quarterly* 23, 3 (August).

T. C. Başbakanlık Kadının Statüsü ve Sorunları Genel Müdürlüğü. 1998. *Cumhuriyet'in 75. Yılında Türkiye'de Kadının Durumu* (In the 75th year of the Republic. The status of women in Turkey). Ankara: Takav Matbaacılık Yayıncılık A.Ş.

Taarji, Hinde. 1990. *Les voilées de l'islam.* Paris: Balland.

Tabouis, Geneviève. 1943. *Ils l'ont appelé Cassandre*. Paris: Editions de la Maison Française.

Talash, G. 1996. *Siyaset Çıkmazında Kadın* (Women in the quandary of politics). Istanbul: Ümit Yayıncılık.

Tekeli, Ş. 1986. "Emergence of the New Feminist Movement in Turkey." In *The New Women's Movement*, ed. D. Dahlerup. Beverly Hills: Sage.

Tennant, Eleanora. 1936. *Spanish Journey: Personal Experiences of the Civil War*. London: Eyre and Spottiswoode.

Tennant, Ernest W. D. 1957. *True Account*. London: Max Parrish.

Tevanian, Pierre, and Sylvie Tissot. 1998. *Mots à maux. Dictionnaire de la lepénisation des esprits*. Paris: Editions Dagorno.

Thalman, Rita. 1982. *Être femme sous le IIIème Reich*. Paris: Laffont.

Thomas, S. 1994. *How Women Legislate*. New York: Oxford University Press.

Thompson, Denise. 2001. *Radical Feminism Today*. London: Sage.

Thurlow, R. 1998. *Fascism in Britain: A History 1918–1985*. London: I. B. Tauris.

Todorov, Tsvetan. 1984. *Mikhail Bakhtin: The Dialogical Principle*. Minneapolis: University of Minnesota Press.

Tonelli, Luigi. 1929. "Margherita Sarfatti." In *Alla ricerca della personalità*, 249–256. Catania.

Toprak, B. 1981. *Islam and Political Development in Turkey*. Leiden: E. J. Brill.

———. 1994. "Women and Fundamentalism: The Case of Turkey." In *Identity, Politics, and Women: Cultural Reassertions and Feminisms in International Perspective*, ed. V. M. Moghadam. San Francisco: Westview Press.

Torres Septien, Valentina. 1992. "La UNPF: La lucha por la enseñanza de la religión en las escuelas particulares." In *La ciudad y el campo en la historia de México*, Vol. 2, ed. Ricardo Sanchez. Mexico City: UNAM/IIH.

Trindade, Hélgio. 1974. *Integralismo (O fascismo brasileiro na década de 30)*. Sao Paulo: Difel.

Trippe, Christian F. 1995. *Konservative Verfassungspolitik 1918–1923. Die DNVP als Opposition in Reich und Ländern*. Düsseldorf: Droste.

Tromp, Sebastián, SJ. 1937. "Editorial: De los principios de la AC propuestos a los Obispos Mexicanos en la Encíclica *Firmissiam Constantiam*. *Christus* 2, 21 (August).

Tsaldari, Lina. 1967. *Ethikai Koinonikai, Politikai Prospatheiai*, Vol. A. Athens: Autoedition.

Tuñón, Julia. 1999. *Women in Mexico: A Past Unveiled*. Austin: University of Texas Press.

Turan, I. 1991. "Islam and Nationalism as Political Ideology." In *Islam in Modern Turkey: Religion, Politics, and Literature in a Secular State*, ed. R. L. Tapper, 40–56. New York: St. Martin's Press.

Urso, Simona. 1994. "La formazione di Margherita Sarfatti e l'adesione al fascismo." *Studi storici* 35, 1 (January–March): 153–81.

Valenzuela, María Elena. 1995. "The Evolving Roles of Women Under Military Rule." In *The Struggle for Democracy in Chile*, ed. Paul W. Drake and Iván Jaksíc. Lincoln: University of Nebraska Press.

Van Rensberg, A.P. 1966. *Moeders van ons Volk*. Johannesburg: Afrikaanse Pers Boekhandel.

Varikas, Eleni. 1993. "Gender and National Identity in *fin de siecle* Greece." *Gender and History* 5, 2.

Vasta, Ellie, and Stephen Castles, eds. 1996. *The Teeth Are Smiling: The Persistence of Racism in Multicultural Australia*. St. Leonards, New South Wales: Allen and Unwin.

Vaughan, Mary Kay. 1997. *Cultural Politics in Revolution: Teachers, Peasants, and Schools in Mexico, 1930–1940*. Tucson: University of Arizona Press.

Veccia, Theresa R. 1997. "'My Duty as a Woman': Gender Ideology, Work, and Working-Class Women's Lives in Sao Paulo, Brazil, 1900–1950." In *The Gendered Worlds of Latin American Women Workers. From Household and Factory to the Union Hall and Ballot Box*, ed. John D. French and Daniel James. Durham, N.C.: Duke University Press.

Vellianitis, Spyridon. 1934. *I koinoniki pronoia en Elladi kata to etos 1933*. Athens: Vlastos.

Venner, Fiammetta. 1997. "Une autre manière d'être féministe? Le militantisme féminine d'extrême droite." In *Les femmes et l'extrême droite*, ed. Claude Lesselier and Fiammetta Venner. Reprint *French Politics and Society* 11, 2, (spring 1993).

——. 1999. "L'extrême droite et l'antiféminisme." In *Un siècle d'antiféminisme*, ed. Christine Bard. Paris, Fayard.

Vera, Rodrigo. 1998. "Derechos humanos y democracia, los futuros puntos del conflicto Iglesia-Estado." *Proceso* 1134 (26 July).

Vervenioti, Tasoula. 1994. *I gynaika tis antistasis. I eisodos ton gynaikon stin politiki.* Athens: Odysseas.

——. 2000. "The Adventure of Women's Suffrage in Greece." In *When the War Was Over: Women, War, and Peace in Europe, 1940–1956*, ed. Claire Douchen and Irene Bandhauer-Schoffmann. Leicester University Press.

von Saldern, Adelheid. 1994. "Victims or Perpetrators? Controversies about the Role of Women in the Nazi State." In *Nazism and German Society*, ed. D. F. Crew. London: Routledge.

Walker, Dennis Paul. 1976. "Alfred Hugenberg and the Deutschnationale Volkspartei." Ph.D. diss., Cambridge University.

Walter, Tony, and Grace Davie. 1998. "The Religiosity of Women in the Modern West." *British Journal of Sociology* 49, 4 (December).

Walzer, Anke. 1991. *Käthe Schirmacher. Eine deutsche Frauenrechtlerin auf dem Wege vom Liberalismus zum konservativen Nationalismus.* Pfaffenweiler: Centaurus-Verlagsgesellschaft.

Ware, Vron. 1996. "Island Racism: Gender, Place, and White Power." *Feminist Review* 54 (Autumn).

Waylen, G. 1996. "Analysing Women in the Politics of the Third World." In *Women and Politics in the Third World*, ed. H. Afshar. London and New York: Routledge.

Webber, G. C. 1984. "Patterns of Membership and Support for the British Union of Fascists." *Journal of Contemporary History* 19, 4 (October).

Weigand, Kate. 1992. "The Red Menace, the Feminine Mystique, and the Ohio Un-American Activities Commission: Gender and Anti-Communism in Ohio, 1951–1954." *Journal of Women's History* 3, 3.

Weinstein, Barbara. 1997. "Unskilled Worker, Skilled Housewife: Constructing the Working-Class Women in Sao Paulo, Brazil." In *The Gendered Worlds of Latin American Women Workers. From Household and Factory to the Union Hall and Ballot Box*, ed. John D. French and Daniel James. Durham, N.C.: Duke University Press.

Weiß, Hermann, and Paul Hoser, eds. 1989. *Die Deutschnationalen und die Zerstörung der Weimarer Republik. Aus dem Tagebuch von Reinhold Quaatz 1928–1933.* Munich: Oldenbourg.

Welch, S. 1985. "Are Women More Liberal Than Men in the U.S. Congress?" *Legislative Studies Quarterly.*

West, Guida and Rhoda Lois Blumberg. 1990. "Reconstructing Social Protest from a Feminist Perspective." In *Women and Social Protest*, ed. Guida West and Rhoda Lois Blumberg. New York: Oxford University Press.

Whitner, Laurens. 1982. *American Intervention in Greece, 1943–1949.* New York: Columbia University Press.

Wilford, Rick. 1998. "Women, Ethnicity and Nationalism: Surveying the Ground." In *Women, Ethnicity, and Nationalism*, ed. Rick Wilford and Robert Miller. New York: Routledge.

Winter, Bronwyn. 1998. "Pauline Hanson and the 'Dilemmas' of Right-Wing Women for Feminism." In *Selected Papers from the 7th Australian Women's Studies Association Conference*, ed. Chilla Bulbeck, 192–204. Adelaide: University of South Australia.

Yaraman, A. 1999. *Türkiye'de Kadınların Siyasal Temsili* (Political representation of women in Turkey). Istanbul: Bağlam Yayınları.

Yasmal, Colette. 1991. "Les cadres du Front national: les habits neufs de l'extrême droite." In *SOFFRES. L'État de l'opinion 1991*, ed. Olivier Duhamel and Jérôme Jaffé. Paris: Editions du Seuil

————. [1989] 1996. "Sociologie des élites du FN, 1979–1986." In *Le Front national à découvert*, ed. Nonna Mayer and Pascal Perrineau. Paris: Presses de la Fondation Nationale des Sciences Politiques.

Yavuz, M. H. 1998. *Islamic Political Identity in Turkey: Movements, Agents, and Processes.* Ph.D. diss., University of Wisconsin-Madison.

Yuval-Davis, Nira. 1997. *Gender and Nation.* London: Sage.

————. 1998. "Beyond Differences: Women, Empowerment and Coalition Politics." In *Gender, Ethnicity, and Political Ideologies,* ed. Nickie Charles, Helen Hintjens, 168–189. New York: Routledge.

Yuval-Davis, Nira and Floya Anthias. 1989. *Woman, Nation, State.* London: Macmillan.

Zakaria, Fouad. 1988. :The Standpoint of Contemporary Muslim Fundamentalists." In *Women of the Arab World: The Coming Challenge—Papers of the Arab Women's Solidarity Association Conference,* ed. Nahid Toubia, trans. (Nahed El Gamal). London: Zed Books.

————. 1989. *Al-Sahwa Al-Deeniya fi Mizan Al-Aql* (The religious revival in the balance of the mind). Cairo: Dar al-Fikr.

Zald, M. N., and B. Useem. 1987. "Movement and Countermovement Interaction: Mobilization, Tactics and State Involvement." In *Social Movements in an Organizational Society,* ed. M. N. Zald and J. D. McCarthy, 247–271. New Brunswick, N.J.: Transaction Books.

Zaman. http://www.zaman.com.tr.

Žižek, Slavoj. 1999. "The Spectre of Ideology." In *Mapping Ideology.* London: Verso.

Zuccotti, Susan. 1996. *The Italians and the Holocaust: Persecution, Rescue and Survival.* Lincoln: University of Nebraska Press.

Zuhur, Sherifa. *Revealing Reveiling: Islamist Gender Ideology in Contemporary Egypt.* Albany, N.Y.: SUNY Press.

Contributors

Paola Bacchetta is Associate Professor of Women's Studies at the University of California, Berkeley. . She is the author of a book of Hindu nationalism entitled *RSS and the Nation: Gendered Discourse/Gendered Practice* (forthcoming) and author of numerous articles on gender, sexuality, feminisms, social movements, political conflict, and Hindu Nationalism.

Kathleen M. Blee is Professor of Sociology at the University of Pittsburgh. Her most recent books are *Inside Organized Racism: Women in the Hate Movement* (2002) and, coedited with France Winddance Twine, *Feminism and Antiracism: International Struggles for Justice* (2001).

Kristina A. Boylan recently completed her doctorate in Modern Latin American History at the University of Oxford. She lives and teaches in Washington, D.C.

Sandra McGee Deutsch is a Professor of History at the University of Texas–El Paso. She is the author of *Las Derechas: The Extreme Right in Argentina, Brazil, and Chile, 1890–1939* (1999).

Marijke du Toit obtained her doctoral degree at the University of Cape Town and lectures in Historical Studies at the University of Natal, South Africa.

Victoria L. Enders teaches in the Honors and Women's Studies Programs at Northern Arizona University, Flagstaff. She coedited with Pamela Radcliffe the anthology *Constructing Spanish Womanhood: Female Identity in Modern Spain* (1999).

Carole C. Gallucci is Assistant Professor of Italian at the College of William and Mary. She is coeditor of *Writing beyond Fascism: Cultural Resistance in the Life and Works of Alba de Céspedes* (2000). She is working on a book on Italian women intellectuals during Fascism.

Julie V. Gottlieb is a Lecturer in Modern History at the University of Manchester (UK), and the author of *Feminine Fascism: Women in Britain's Fascist Movement, 1923–1945* (2000).

Bishnupriya Ghosh teaches in the English Department at the University of California, Davis. She has published essays, coedited an anthology, *Interventions* (1997), and completed a book manuscript in postcolonial literature, film, gender, and sexuality studies.

Azza Karam is an Egyptian national and the Director of the Women's Department at the World Conference on Religion and Peace in New York. She has worked since the 1980s in the Middle East and Europe on gender, development, human rights, democratization, conflict, and political Islam. Her books include *Islamisms and the*

State (1998); *Women in Parliament: Beyond Numbers* (1998); and *Transnational Political Islam* (forthcoming).

Judith Keene is the Director of the European Studies Centre at the University of Sydney where she teaches Contemporary European History. Her most recent work is *Fighting for Franco: International Volunteers in Nationalist Spain during the Spanish Civil War 1936 to 1939* (2001).

Burçak Keskin is a doctoral student in Sociology at the University of Michigan, Ann Arbor. Her interests are historical sociology, sociology of culture, nationalism, social change, and gender.

Claudie Lesselier teaches history and is a feminist activist in Paris. She is the author of numerous articles about the right in France and co-edited with F. Venner, *L'extrême droite contre les femmes, enjeux et actualité*. Villeurbanne, France: Edtions Golias, 1997.

Margaret Power is Assistant Professor of History at the Illinois Institute of Technology. She is the author of *Right-Wing Women in Chile: Feminine Power and the Struggle against Allende, 1964–1973* (2002).

Ayse Saktanber is Associate Professor of Sociology in the Department of Sociology and the Gender and Women's Studies Program at the Middle East Technical University, Ankara. She is the author of *Living Islam: Women, Religion and Politicisation of Culture in Turkey* (2002) and the coeditor of *Fragments of Culture: The Everyday of Modern Turkey* (2002).

Raffael Scheck is Associate Professor of History at Colby College. He has published a book on Admiral Tirpitz and German right-wing politics and articles on women in the Weimar Republic and Hitler's Swiss funding.

Ronnee Schreiber is an Assistant Professor of Political Science at San Diego State University. She studies women in American political institutions and women's activism on public policy issues. She is currently working on a book manuscript about national conservative women's organizations and has published work on national feminist organizations and women in the U.S. Congress.

Tasoula Vervenioti is a historian and free-lance researcher who lives in Athens, Greece. She is the author of *I gynaika tis Antistasis: I eisodos tongynaikon stin politiki* (The woman of resistance: Women's entrance into politics) (1994). She is currently researching questions of right-wing and left-wing women's history in the Greek civil war (1946–1949) and the postwar period.

Bronwyn Winter is a Senior Lecturer in the Department of French Studies at the University of Sydney. Recent publications include essays on women and human rights in Europe and feminist approaches to Islamism.

Index